EXPOSING SLAVERY

EXPOSING SLAVERY

Photography, Human Bondage, and the Birth of Modern Visual Politics in America

Matthew Fox-Amato

OXFORD
UNIVERSITY PRESS

OXFORD
UNIVERSITY PRESS

Oxford University Press is a department of the University of Oxford.
It furthers the University's objective of excellence in research, scholarship,
and education by publishing worldwide. Oxford is a registered trade mark of
Oxford University Press in the UK and certain other countries.

Published in the United States of America by Oxford University Press
198 Madison Avenue, New York, NY 10016, United States of America.

Library of Congress Cataloging-in-Publication Data

Names: Fox-Amato, Matthew, author.
Title: Exposing slavery : photography, human bondage, and the birth of
modern visual politics in America / Matthew Fox-Amato.
Description: New York, NY : Oxford University Press, [2019] |
Includes bibliographical references and index.
Identifiers: LCCN 2018024380 (print) | LCCN 2018042200 (ebook) |
ISBN 9780190663940 (Updf) | ISBN 9780190663957 (Epub) |
ISBN 9780190663933 (hardcover : alk. paper)
Subjects: LCSH: Slaves—United States—Social conditions—19th century. |
Slaves—United States—Portraits. | Portrait photography—United
States—History—19th century. | Photography—Social aspects—United
States—History—19th century.
Classification: LCC E449 (ebook) | LCC E449 .F768 2019 (print) |
DDC 306.3/6200222—dc23
LC record available at https://lccn.loc.gov/2018024380

1 3 5 7 9 8 6 4 2

Printed by Sheridan Books, Inc.,
United States of America

For my mom

CONTENTS

ACKNOWLEDGMENTS

This book has its roots in the generosity and support of so many people. I am thrilled to be able to thank them, beginning with my early mentors. To Mark Jerng, Tim McCarthy, and Werner Sollors: thank you for inspiring me as thinkers and teachers and setting me on a path to study the past.

In the Department of History at the University of Southern California, I wrote the dissertation that became this book, and I had the good fortune of an excellent committee. I am especially grateful to my advisor, Richard Fox. It was a joy to work with Richard, whose imaginative approach to history and unwavering support were instrumental in advancing this project. His passion for the vitality of ideas is a model for what a historian can be. For her intellectual generosity and persistently keen insights about this project, I am thankful to Karen Halttunen. Vanessa Schwartz's intellectual spark and creativity continue to astonish me, and I have benefitted greatly from conversations with her about visual culture and from her support. I also benefitted from Leo Braudy's expansive knowledge of American culture. The Visual Studies Graduate Certificate and Visual Studies Research Institute created a vibrant community to study all things visual and aided my work with a summer fellowship and the Anne Friedberg Memorial Grant. I thank Dornsife College for a graduate fellowship and the college doctoral fellowship. At USC, I owe a debt of gratitude to many more: Elinor Accampo, Sarah Banet-Weiser, Jen Black, Catherine Clark, Justin Clark,

Bill Deverell, Phil Ethington, Max Felker-Kantor, Sarah Keyes, Jason Glenn, Nick Glisserman, Jason Hill, David Levitus, Ryan Linkof, Peter Mancall, Richard Meyer, Steve Ross, George Sanchez, Carole Shammas, and Diana Williams. Lori Rogers, Laverne Hughes, Sandra Hopwood, and Joe Styles provided essential support. Friends in LA—especially Amy, Glenn, Matilda, Laura, Jer, Lauren, and Tony—made this a golden age. Mark Braude gave smart feedback on drafts of more things than I can count; I never thought I would leave graduate school having met such a close friend.

Much of my manuscript revisions took place at Washington University in St. Louis, where I spent two delightful years as a Mellon postdoc in the Modeling Interdisciplinary Inquiry program. I thank Joe Loewenstein for welcoming me into the fold, Amy Lehman for keeping things running smoothly, and Katy Hardy, Jess Paga, and Maggie Taft for their camaraderie on our hall in Umrath. Conversations with Michael Allen, Adrienne Davis, Andrea Friedman, Maggie Garb, Heidi Kolk, Dale Kretz, Long Le-Khac, and Rachel Lindsay pushed my ideas forward. My sincere thanks go to Rebecca Wanzo for discussing my project and inviting me to present material from it in one of her classes. I owe a special debt of gratitude to Iver Bernstein, for sharing his deep knowledge of the Civil War era and inviting me into the AMCS community, and to Peter Kastor, who became a go-to source for professional advice. I met Douglass Flowe in my first month at Wash U and have learned a lot from conversations with him ever since. My greatest thanks at Wash U go to Angela Miller, whose expertise, generosity, and verve made her the ideal mentor.

The University of Idaho has been a wonderful place to land. I am grateful to many colleagues within—and beyond—the history department, including Kathy Aiken, Ashley Kerr, Ellen Kittell, Dale Graden, Tara MacDonald, Aman McLeod, Sean Quinlan, Becca Scofield, Adam Sowards, Rick Spence, and Pingchao Zhu. I thank Debbie Husa, too, for her support.

Archivists and photograph collectors have been indispensable to my research. In particular, I would like to thank Anne Peterson at the Degolyer Library at Southern Methodist University; Randall K. Burkett and Kathy Shoemaker at Emory's Manuscript, Archives, and Rare Book Library; Mary Jo Fairchild at the South Carolina Historical Society; Gigi Barnhill, Paul Erickson, Lauren Hewes, Marie Lamoureux, Jackie

Penny, and Elizabeth Pope at the American Antiquarian Society; Jennifer McCormick and Jennifer Scheetz at the Charleston Museum; Sara C. Arnold at the Gibbes Museum; Lynette Stoudt at the Georgia Historical Society; Beth Bilderback at the South Caroliniana Library; Matthew Turi at the Wilson Library; Heather Beattie, Frances Pollard, and Katherine Wilkins at the Virginia Historical Society; Autumn Reinhardt Simpson at the Valentine; Clayton Lewis at the William L. Clements Library; Pamela Powell at the Chester County Historical Society; Lish Thompson at the Charleston County Public Library; Patricia Dockman Anderson at the Maryland Historical Society; Kate Viens and Conrad Wright at the Massachusetts Historical Society; Bob Zeller, president of the Center for Civil War Photography; Robin Stanford; and Lawrence Jones III.

Many organizations generously supported my work on this book. A Mellon Fellowship for Dissertation Research in Original Sources from the Council on Library and Information Resources as well as a Mellon/ACLS Dissertation Completion Fellowship were instrumental in assisting my research and writing. So, too, were various archive-specific grants, including the Jay and Deborah Last Fellowship at the American Antiquarian Society, Mellon fellowships from the Virginia Historical Society and the Massachusetts Historical Society, and research awards from the Frances S. Summersell Center for the Study of the South at the University of Alabama and the Clements Center-DeGolyer Library at Southern Methodist University. The Social Science Research Council's Dissertation Proposal Development Fellowship helped me to explore potential projects early on; years later, the Andrew W. Mellon Postdoctoral Fellowship in the Modeling Interdisciplinary Inquiry Program at Wash U offered incredible support.

This book has been shaped through conversations with, and suggestions from, many scholars beyond my home institutions: Margaret Abruzzo, Ed Ayers, Lisa Barbash, Robin Bernstein, Makeda Best, Richard Blackett, Josh Brown, Matt Clavin, Chris Dingwall, Carolyn Eastman, Matt Gallman, Lorri Glover, Aston Gonzalez, Ken Greenberg, Mazie Harris, Scott Heerman, Nathan Jeremie-Brink, Jessica Johnson, Cathy Kelly, Bonnie Martin, Tim McCarthy, Maurie McInnis, Yvette Piggush, Bradley Proctor, Martha Sandweiss, Manisha Sinha, Shawn Michelle Smith, John Stauffer, Zoe Trodd, Jennifer Tucker, Sarah Weicksel, A. B. Wilkinson, and Mike Zuckerman.

I am grateful to Francesca Ammon, Erica Ball, David Blight, Angela Miller, Mary Niall Mitchell, John Stauffer, Jennifer Tucker, and Deborah Willis for commenting on parts of this book at conferences and symposia. Ed Ayers, Mark Braude, and Manisha Sinha generously commented on portions of the manuscript, and Mike Zuckerman read an early iteration. I owe a special thanks to Iver Bernstein and Andrea Friedman for commenting on the whole thing, and to Ann Fabian and one anonymous scholar who reviewed the manuscript for Oxford University Press. At Oxford, I am especially grateful to Susan Ferber for her enthusiasm, sharp editorial pen, and guidance in bringing this book to fruition.

None of this would have been possible without the support of family. The Foxes welcomed me into theirs with joy, and their encouragement over the years has meant so much. I thank Dan and Joanna for their love and support. My dad made it a priority to take family trips to historical sites, and I am grateful for his unremitting encouragement. My mom enthusiastically read the first draft of the first chapter of what became this book. Though it has been bittersweet to complete it after she passed, her words continue to guide me and give me strength.

Above all else, I thank Kate. Her never-ending support and thoughtfulness have made this book better; her creative way of seeing the world makes my life rich. My best friend, she has been a loving partner every step of the way. I cannot wait for our next chapter together.

EXPOSING SLAVERY

INTRODUCTION

On august 24, 1839, the *Great Western* set sail from Bristol, England, carrying copies of the *London Globe* that described the much-anticipated technical details of the daguerreotype process, a French invention that many said would demolish old ways of picturing and seeing the world. One commentator typified the enthusiasm when he exclaimed, "What would you say to looking in a mirror and having the image fastened!!"[1] By the end of September, the *London Globe* had reached all corners of the United States, from Boston to New Orleans, and Americans had read about Louis Jacques Mandé Daguerre's image-making technique.[2] The invention that seemed to break so forcefully from the past gave rise to many visions of its future. Certain artists bristled at the increasingly common idea that daguerreotypy would render painting obsolete. "If you believe everything the newspapers say," artist Thomas Cole noted, "you would be led to suppose that the poor craft of painting was knocked in the head by this new machinery for making Nature take her own likeness, and we nothing to do but to give up the ghost."[3] Others were more optimistic. Inventor Samuel Morse saw the medium as a boon to science. "The naturalist is to have a new kingdom to explore," Morse proclaimed after viewing a daguerreotype of a spider.[4] In this still crude process, one man even imagined the makings of surveillance cameras: "What will become of the poor thieves, when they shall see handed in as evidence against them their own portraits, taken by the room in which they stole, and in the very act of stealing!"[5]

In 1839, however, no one foresaw that the daguerreotype would alter the institution of American slavery. But new technologies spark unintended consequences. By the mid-1840s, American slaveholders had already begun commissioning photographic portraits of their slaves. Ex-slaves-turned-abolitionists, such as Frederick Douglass, had come to see how sitting for a portrait could help them confirm and project humanity and dignity amidst northern racism. In the first decade of the medium, enslaved people had begun entering southern daguerreotype saloons of their own volition, posing for cameras, and leaving with visual treasures they could keep in their pockets. Years later, as the Civil War raged, Union soldiers would orchestrate pictures with fugitive slaves that envisioned racial hierarchy as slavery fell. In these ways and others, from the earliest days of the medium to the first moments of emancipation, photography powerfully influenced how bondage and freedom were documented, imagined, and contested. By 1865 it would be difficult for many Americans to look back upon slavery and its fall without thinking of a photograph.

The historical relationship between slavery and photography is the subject of this book. Despite enormous scholarly attention paid to the history of antebellum bondage over the past half century, its intertwined development with photography has gone largely unstudied. This oversight can be chalked up to the long-standing preference for written over visual sources in the discipline of history, to the limited consideration of the photographic business in the antebellum South, or to the scattered nature of the photographic archive. Perhaps the subject fell through the porous disciplinary cracks between history, the history of photography, and art history. Whatever the case may be, pressing questions remain unanswered about the historical collision between a particular social structure and a new visual technology that took the United States by storm. How did photography shape the culture and politics of American slavery? And how, in turn, did slavery shape the development of photography—as an aesthetic form and as a set of cultural practices?

It will not surprise scholars that antislavery activists sought out photography, for they had long drawn upon the media technologies at hand—from broadsides to illustrated magazines—to sway northern sentiment. But too often the slave South has been seen only as a place represented from afar, by artists in Boston and by northern and British travelers. Such a view has helped promote the notion that the Old South stood outside the historical transformations of the nineteenth century.[6] Recent work on the economy of nineteenth-century American bondage, however, has set the stage for a richer understanding of slavery's culture and cultural influence. Identifying slavery as a key engine of capitalism, historians have illuminated the dense financial and trade connections between the slave South, the North, and western Europe.[7] Their studies have underscored that antebellum slavery was not a closed system. To make good on that insight, however, means also grappling with the relation between slavery and the new types of market-driven consumer and communicative culture that spread across the nation and infiltrated the South, especially from the 1820s onward.

Part of a revolution in print and visual culture that included the rise of illustrated presses, popular prints, and cheap pamphlets, photography proves a particularly compelling site to grasp the ties between commercial media and slavery because of its geographical scope and production conditions. Although the illustrated journalism of *Frank Leslie's Illustrated Newspaper* and *Harper's Weekly* undoubtedly defined and deepened sectional animosity through coverage of such events as John Brown's trial, these publications were produced only in the North and did not arrive on the scene until the mid-1850s. Photography, in contrast, entered America more than a decade earlier and turned both North and South into producers of visual culture. In the 1850s Charleston could not boast of an illustrated newspaper to match *Leslie's*, nor was it home to a print shop to rival Nathaniel Currier's operation in New York.[8] But Charleston did have a nationally recognized photographer in George Smith Cook, and during the 1850s Charlestonians could stop by one of many daguerreotype galleries operating on King Street and Meeting Street to purchase personal portraits.[9] Photography quickly became a common cultural ground between North and South.

The intersection of photography and slavery also proves particularly rich because the first generation of photographers ushered in a new, immensely popular form of self-representation and self-definition.[10]

"'Tis certain that the Daguerreotype is the true Republican style of painting," Ralph Waldo Emerson declared in 1841. "The Artist stands aside & lets you paint yourself."[11] Emerson obviously exaggerated the power of the sitter, but he was hardly alone in marveling at this new form of mechanical image consumption. In the 1840s and 1850s, American photography broadened the market for portraiture, opening up an elite practice to the masses.[12] Portrait-taking quickly became an everyday pastime in cities and towns, and the community of photographers grew alongside this impulse to purchase likenesses—surging from 938 artists in 1850 to 3,154 in 1860.[13] An emergent discourse characterized the photograph as a document of the self. As Philadelphia artist Marcus Root declared, a portrait was "worse than worthless if the pictured face does not show the *soul* of the original,—that *individuality* or *selfhood*, which differences *him* from all beings, past, present, or future."[14] Photographers and photographic commentators fashioned the portrait as a vehicle for capturing the inner essence of the sitter in external form. They made a particular mode of visibility commonplace as a means of shaping and understanding identity.

Understanding photographic self-representation as a historical force demands moving beyond approaches that focus solely or even largely on the photographers. It means treating image-making as a serious human activity for non-artists—one with important social, cultural, and political effects. The new social history of the 1970s fundamentally altered who counted as a significant historical actor, opening up the study of the working class, women, and racial minorities, but neither that intellectual shift nor the subsequent "cultural turn" transformed basic assumptions about what counts as communication, documentation, and expression in everyday life. That historical actors are not simply speakers, writers, and gesturers but also picture-makers is confirmed by cave paintings made thirty-four thousand years ago and camera-phone photos taken today, but history books consistently ignore this dimension of experience.[15] One sliver of a millennia-long history of vernacular image-making, this study casts slaveholders, slaves, abolitionists, and Civil War soldiers not only as visual subjects but also as "photographic practitioners." While visual-culture scholars Shawn Michelle Smith and Maurice O. Wallace have coined this term to describe a select group of African American political leaders, this book applies the concept more broadly, describing how many historical actors, even though they did not operate the cameras, used personal and mass-produced photographs toward various ends.[16] Fusing the methods of history and visual-culture studies means, in this case, illuminating images and image-making as important aspects of lived experience and informal politics. It means reconceiving the past as a world of picture-makers.

Enslavers, enslaved people, abolitionists, and Civil War soldiers form the backbone of this study because of their deep investment in two vital social and political problems of the Civil War era—problems they addressed, to a striking degree, through photography. The first concerned the character and destiny of enslaved African Americans: who, precisely, were enslaved people, and who might they be? These questions were rendered increasingly pressing by the sectional crisis of the 1850s (over the potential spread of slavery) and the eventual demise of bondage during the Civil War. At the center of the debate was the commodification of human beings and the worldview that propelled it. As many ex-slaves would testify in their narratives and lectures, American slavery was defined by the paradoxical legal and cultural status of slaves as both people and property. For Frederick Douglass, the determining quality of bondage was not "the relation in which a great mass of the people are compelled to labour and toil almost beyond their endurance," though he surely stressed that slavery entailed a brutal labor regime. It was, instead, "that relation by which one man claims and enforces the right of property in the body and soul of another man."[17] Or as ex-slave James W. C. Pennington hauntingly put it, "The being of slavery, its soul and body, lives and moves in the chattel principle."[18]

This person/property contradiction has, of course, long been central to American historians' views of slavery, ever since David Brion Davis famously articulated it in *The Problem of Slavery in Western Culture*. For Davis, the "inherent contradiction of slavery lay not in its cruelty or economic exploitation, but in the underlying conception of man as a conveyable possession with no more autonomy of will and consciousness than a domestic animal."[19] Later scholars have shown how this contradiction played out on the ground, in the southern courtrooms where slaves were "human subjects and the objects of property relations," and inside the many bustling slave markets of the antebellum South, where slaves were turned into people with prices.[20] Historians have shown, in short, that a racial ideology positioning African Americans as people and commodities undergirded the particular legal and economic mechanisms of the "peculiar institution." The advent of photographic consumer culture raises new questions about how enslavers and bondspeople sustained and subverted this ideology within the South, how ex-slaves and abolitionists protested it beyond slavery's borders, and how Confederate and Union soldiers perpetuated it as slavery fell. What would happen in the 1840s as floating daguerreotype boats began pulling up at southern docks and urban galleries opened their doors to southern cities, selling cheap portraits widely cast as vehicles for conveying social identity and even, for some, the unique qualities that constituted the visual subject? How would a southern regime (that increasingly felt the heat of the abolitionist movement) employ a novel visual technology that seemed to capture the social world with sparkling visual detail? And how would slaves and ex-slaves engage photography? What would a popular new form widely known for depicting bodies mean to those who painfully experienced the policing and possession of their bodies?

Part of photography's uniquely powerful and unsettling role in the Civil War era was to open up a new cultural space—a new realm of visual symbols and symbol-rich social practices—through which Americans defined the boundaries of personhood and debated the social potential of enslaved African Americans.[21] Of course, black and white Americans often held very different stakes in the photographic claims they made. Castigated as inhumane by antislavery proponents, enslavers projected their treatment of slaves as people, not commodities, by picturing and displaying well-dressed bondspeople in studio portraits. In the process, owners made sure to conscript the possibilities of those portraits by limiting slaves to certain poses and postures, cordoning off the broader range of social identities enslaved sitters might achieve in visual form. Slaves and ex-slaves, too, wanted photographs, for they offered a powerful means of remembering loved ones sold away in the domestic slave trade and of highlighting, at least in their eyes, their status as full people. "Man is the only picture making animal in the world," Frederick Douglass asserted. "He alone of all the inhabitants of earth has the capacity and passion for pictures."[22] For Douglass and other black Americans, the very act of photographic image-making served as a crucial sign of their humanity, as it enabled the expression of that humanity. That African Americans and other social groups embraced photography so quickly is a testament to the commercial dominance and emergent cultural associations of the medium: its availability and affordability, its reputation as an unusually effective means of conveying character, and its seemingly unparalleled capacity to picture the body, head, and face—features central to defining racial identity and difference in the antebellum era. Ironically, photography brought opposing forces into the same cultural sphere precisely because it proved an especially useful tool to address the urgent political and social problem of who enslaved people were and who they could be.

This photographic clash over enslaved people's status and character was tangled up with a conflict over racial order. For slaveholders, slaves, abolitionists, and soldiers, photography proved a vital new tool to address an increasingly urgent predicament in the Civil War era: what was the ideal social relationship between blacks and whites? Although many Americans began taking group pictures with daguerreotypy, these four groups were distinctive in their use of photography to address this national dilemma by pictorially asserting the societies they sought to perpetuate or create. Abolitionists, for example, envisioned and enacted a miniature version of the national, interracial community they hoped to build. They did so by photographing interracial events and exchanging images amongst black and white activists. Likewise, northern soldiers responded to the flight of fugitives during the Civil War and the uncertainty of an interracial nation without slavery with images of white superiority and black servility, as seen in the many pictures of African Americans serving white army men in Union camps. Certain material qualities made photography an exceptionally good means for evoking interracial socialities. Even though the camera proved a poor instrument for distinguishing among gradations of skin color, the portability and eventual reproducibility of photographs enabled Americans to socially enact themselves as groups—to knit themselves together through practices of circulation, display, and preservation.[23] As photography proved a privileged vehicle to debate enslaved people's status and social potential, it simultaneously formed a contested terrain to portray and enact interracial futures.

To be sure, Americans had debated the social potential of African Americans, the nature of slavery, and the prospects of a nation without bondage well before 1839, and they would continue to do so in many non-photographic ways after photography arrived—through such forms as oratory, pamphlets, newspapers, and novels.[24] But reconceptualizing this era as a world of photo-makers unlocks new ways of thinking about who debated racial identity and order as it reframes how these debates unfolded. It divulges messier everyday struggles, fought by rich masters and poor slaves, prim southern mistresses and underground radicals, who waged ideological battles through social practices and pictures. The most common daguerreotype measured only 2¾" by 3¼", but the import of such images far outweighed their size. In these small images, enslaved and free Americans often felt they gripped the many consequential abstractions of the day— notions of superiority and subservience, benevolence and righteousness, cruelty and courage, and beauty and freedom—in the very palms of their hands. And these pictures in hands also sparked raw emotions. "It is evident," Frederick Douglass noted in a lecture on photography, "that the great cheapness, and universality of pictures, must exert a powerful though silent influence, upon the ideas and sentiment of present [and] future generations."[25] In photography, Douglass saw nothing less than a potent new marriage of the visual, visceral, and political.

Grasping this "silent influence" reveals the place of photography as a largely unrecognized catalyst in the coming of the Civil War. Historians of the causes of disunion have long taken interest in the question of modernization, and in recent decades many scholars have rejected an older view of the sectional crisis as a battle between a modernizing North and an anti-modern South. They have shown, instead, how antebellum slavery set itself on an uneven path toward modernization—one that included the construction of railroads in the Upper South, the use of steamboats along the Mississippi River, and the hybridization of cotton in many slave states.[26] Slavery was undeniably central to the eruption of war, and though scholars no longer explain disunion by stressing how the slave states failed to keep pace with or turned their backs to modernity, there is still much to learn about how modern elements shared by North and South—including modern visual culture—exacerbated sectional animosity.[27]

Initially a scientific curiosity, photography was quickly turned into a cultural weapon on both sides of the sectional divide, a phenomenon that helps explain why the 1850s proved such a contentious and emotional powder keg. Slaveholders launched the use of photography as a tool for maintaining a racialized social order in America, deploying studio images of nursemaids, butlers, and boatmen as well as outdoor pictures of the plantation household to project a benevolent form of white rule. Across the Mason-Dixon line, abolitionists initiated the use of photography for reform, though in surprising ways. Rather than embarking on a campaign of photographic moral suasion, one meant to convert moderate northerners to their cause, northern radicals primarily used the medium to build solidarity amongst committed activists, by making and exchanging images of abolitionists and fugitive slaves. What bound these antagonistic sides, though, was the "silent influence" of photography on political sentiment. When fugitive slaves passed along the Underground Railroad, for instance, they paused to take photographs that never circulated widely yet aroused intense feelings of admiration and outrage in the abolitionists who kept and exchanged them.[28] In these ways and others, photography injected the cultures of proslavery and abolitionism with a stronger sense of legitimacy, animosity, and urgency that heightened the sectional crisis and made compromise all the more unthinkable. Efforts to define racial identity and order were shaped by, and in turn hardened, the political divide over slavery.

———

IMAGE-MAKING PRODUCES CONFLICT, BUT conflict also elicits image-making. It stokes desires for public images to reveal political events and social conditions. It animates aspirations for personal images to stake claims to particular identities, often precisely because it renders those identities unstable.[29] Political struggles, especially wars, have played a crucial role in the development of photography as a central currency of modern communication. From Roger Fenton's pictures of the Crimean War (1855) to Joe Rosenthal's iconic *Old Glory Goes Up on Mount Suribachi, Iwo Jima* (1945) to images of America's twenty-first-century war in Afghanistan, artists and viewing audiences have engaged in a reciprocal exchange that has privileged the capacity of the photograph to serve as eyewitness evidence of distant strife. Though Fenton represents the first major wartime photographer, scholars all point to the Civil War as the first systematically documented conflict. An estimated three thousand photographers produced tens of thousands of photographs, including gruesome scenes of battle aftermaths at Antietam and Gettysburg as well as portraits of generals and views of military fortifications. Further, they turned the Civil War into the first "living room war," connecting the home front to the battlefront by selling mass-produced photographs and by turning photographs into engravings published in magazines.[30] But during the 1840s and 1850s, well before the first battle at Fort Sumter, photography shaped the proslavery defense, as the medium helped bolster and define the movement that fought against the "peculiar institution." Conflicts over slavery decisively shaped the cultural associations, social practices, and visual aesthetics of photography as it emerged in the United States. As photography sparked and shaped debates over racial identity and community, slavery generated a modern form of social struggle with photography at the center: it gave rise to a modern visual politics.

Modern visual politics describes a historically specific mode of informal political engagement with photographic images as its currency. While the history of American political imagery obviously predates photography, the rise of the daguerreotype rendered an entirely new political infrastructure because it democratized portraiture. It opened up the possibility that all invested parties could, in the context of commercial image-making, debate through the same visual language. Elites had, of course, long commissioned paintings (including regular and miniature portraits) to convey stature, solidify familial and romantic bonds, and memorialize loved ones, yet photography created the conditions for all non-artists to help produce and use commercial images.[31] Rather than the world of formal politics—the arena of policymaking, election cycles, and political institutions—modern visual politics took shape in the domain of informal politics, defined as the power struggles of daily life. Its emergence has only been glimpsed by recent studies of race and early American photography, which have broken new ground in their own right by illuminating instances of black self-representation, antislavery propaganda, and racial pseudo-scientific image-making.[32] Only by conceptualizing all historical actors as image-makers, by taking the millions of enslaved and free Americans most deeply invested in the potential futures of slavery as the object of inquiry, does the broad transformation in political culture that took place in the Civil War era come into view.

Abolitionists were at the center of this transformation. By recasting the first twenty-five years of American photography as a story of social and political conflict over bondage, this book reveals abolitionists' signal role in turning mechanically reproducible image-making into a vital means of waging social justice struggles. Scholars have shown how artists of the Progressive and New Deal eras—including Jacob Riis, Lewis Hine, Dorothea Lange, and Walker Evans—highlighted urban and rural poverty for distant audiences as they promoted the notion of the photographer as intrepid social documentarian in search of truthful views.[33] Other scholars have illuminated how photography was powerfully used by humanitarian organizations such as the British Congo Reform Association, which protested the violence committed by the regime of King Leopold II of Belgium in the Congo Free State, as well as by black activists in twentieth-century America, including the Student Nonviolent Coordinating Committee.[34] Yet antebellum abolitionists actually established photography as a key instrument of reform. In their display of photographs of slaves on the lecture podium, they anticipated the lantern slide shows of the late nineteenth century. By initiating the subgenre of "atrocity" photography, with pictures such as *Branded Hand* and *The Scourged Back*, abolitionists gave rise to the capacity of the photograph to publicize violations of the body and to serve as a social witness.[35] And in their circulation of private and mass-produced photographs, abolitionists launched a new means of forging an oppositional community; they pioneered the idea that the internal and external visibility of a social movement was essential to its effectiveness. Indeed, it was not inevitable that the twentieth century would witness the widespread use of photography as a means of documenting social conditions, of visualizing abstract claims about justice and exploitation, and of building politicized communities through images. The origins of this distinctly modern disposition lie in heated battles over late American slavery.

In the South, meanwhile, masters and slaves remade photography into a central means of bolstering and weathering racism and racial exploitation. Scholars' emphasis on photojournalism and viewer response has often overlooked the role of vernacular photography and self-representation within exploitative systems, much as the focus on the twentieth century has obscured the significant forms of image-making that emerged in the antebellum South.[36] In the Civil War era, slaveholders initiated a "quiet habit of power" that entailed the use of photographs of black bodies to self-justify exploitation, build white identity, and construct white supremacist networks. After 1865, this habit would continue to evolve in southern white communities, in the form of private family photography as well as lynching photography.[37] Ironically, this white supremacist photographic culture actually planted the seeds of its own unmaking. Since enslavers needed enslaved people to sit and pose for cameras, they helped introduce those bondspeople to a new medium for seeing themselves and society. Through their own photographic practices, moreover, some enslaved people nurtured a "quiet habit of endurance" by using private photographs to maintain social ties, memorialize loved ones, and withstand white supremacy. This habit would continue to influence African American life from Reconstruction to the present.[38]

Modern visual politics, then, signifies a new set of photographic habits born in the Civil War era for challenging, perpetuating, and enduring exploitation and debasement. Take the case of Robert Brown, an enslaved man from Virginia. In 1856, after his wife was sold away, Brown ran northward with a daguerreotype of her on his person.[39] He eventually made it to an Underground Railroad safe house, and soon after he arrived, he took the daguerreotype from his pocket to show the activists in the room and to gaze lovingly upon it. Public commentators in 1839 had envisaged a multitude of applications for the daguerreotype, yet no one had forecast that this invention would enable a fugitive slave to maintain a loving bond amidst the social disruptions of slavery. Robert Brown's story stands as just one example of how everyday actors in the Civil War era took a new form of technology and consumer culture and transformed its uses and associations. They made a series of photographic practices central to the informal political world.

The evolution of modern visual politics ultimately forces us to reimagine the persistently vexing historical relationship between American slavery and modernity. Recent studies of the economy of slavery have shifted the locus of inquiry from an older debate—was slavery precapitalist or not?—to a new framework that explores how slavery made capitalism. This sets the stage for similar questions about slavery's culture and cultural effects. The historical problem in this case is not whether the culture of slavery was or was not modern, but instead how slavery produced a key element of modern political culture.

━━

THE PROMISE THAT VISUAL STUDIES offers history is twofold: first, it provides wider contexts and new tools to pose fresh questions about the past; second, it opens up new ways of addressing old questions. To make good on such promises, this book analyzes images as historical evidence in their own right—as building blocks of identity, culture, and ideology rather than as illustrations of predetermined arguments rooted in the analysis of written texts. Amidst the landscape of visual sources—from illustrated books to monuments to Hollywood films—photographs have proven especially tempting as avenues of unmediated access into the past. As with diaries, letters, newspaper articles, and speeches, however, photographs are textual constructions. They stand as a record of choices made by people—about technical matters such as lighting and composition as well as about what to picture and what not to picture.[40] Scrutinizing photographs as historical sources and forces, this book joins works that have extended cultural history's emphasis on the power of language and social performance to actively shape politics and society through a focus on visual culture.[41]

This study treats photographs as discursive and material objects. Drawing on the methods of art history, it examines the production of images alongside the form and visual content within the images. In doing so, it pays particular attention to how the subjects and conventions of the photographs drew upon and broke from past and contemporaneous images. It also moves beyond the often artificial conceptual divide between "visual culture" and "material culture" by foregrounding the physical properties of images. Despite the ways in which photographs have severed viewers from the physicality of their subjects, such images each contain a history of mobility and tangibility: over the past two centuries, photographs have been shared and smashed, torn and worn; they have been placed in attics, books, and lockets.

As photo historians Elizabeth Edwards and Janice Hart write, "It is not merely the image *qua* image that is the site of meaning, but that its material and presentational forms and the uses to which they are put are central to the function of a photograph as a socially salient object."[42] It is precisely in this realm that historians stand to contribute to visual-culture studies, for the deep archival research that grounds the discipline of history is ideally situated to illuminate conditions of reception, circulation, display, and preservation. Combining an attention to visual discourse and social practice, this study moves beyond an exploration of depictions of slavery, abolition, and emancipation to illuminate how images forged a part of those worlds. The history of late American slavery, for instance, is the history of photographs viewed in parlors, displayed on desks, and hidden in cabins.

Whether private or public, unique or mass-produced, photographs mattered a great deal to nineteenth-century Americans. In certain cases, photographs were significant because of the functions they performed, as in the case of cartes de visite used to catch fugitive slaves in the South; here, the photograph as informational object was integral to the action at hand. In other cases, photographs were significant because they were mass-produced and mass-consumed. That thousands of Americans bought and gazed upon images of branded, whipped, and white-looking slaves in the 1860s reveals something about the culture in that moment. Many of the images that Americans made, contemplated, and held dear, however, were not public and mass-produced but instead private.[43] The significance of these private photographs lies in their social lives and the broad spectrum of emotions they sparked—from admiration, affection, and longing to pity, contempt, and indignation.[44] Studying private photographs, which demands a thoroughgoing history of use and response, broadens the meaning of informal political culture.

At the heart of this study is an original photographic archive, drawn from research in over thirty public institutions across the United States and from private collections. The archive includes daguerreotypes, ambrotypes, tintypes, and cartes de visite of slaves, ex-slaves, and abolitionists from the 1840s onward as well as Civil War stereographs and other albumen prints.[45] The source base from the 1840s and 1850s skews toward the private because an estimated 95 percent of daguerreotypes were portraits.[46] Since the historical study of such imagery is impossible without sources testifying to conditions of production, circulation, and response, this book also uses a range of written materials: manuscript collections of slaveholders and abolitionists, which include letters, diaries, wills, and family record books; mainstream newspapers from the North and South as well as antislavery publications; slave narratives; and the letters and memoirs of Civil War soldiers. It further utilizes the rare logbooks, letters, and memoirs of antebellum photographers, as well as the underutilized photographic trade journals that emerged as this first generation of image-makers began to professionalize in the 1850s.

This book traces a dominant photo culture that began with the photographic efforts of southern whites in the prewar era and, unexpectedly, was largely adopted by northern whites during the Civil War. Drawing upon dozens of unstudied and unpublished slave photographs, Chapter 1 explores how slaveholders translated the people they owned into images they could view, hold, and show. While photography spurred the widespread practice of self-representation, slaveholders reshaped private photography into a quiet habit of domination. Through gallery pictures of favored slaves and outdoor scenes of the plantation household, masters projected their own identities as humane and their institution as familial as they started building white social networks through the exchange of slave photographs. Yet a closer look at the visuality and responses to slave photographs reveals how owners took care to limit how slaves' humanity could be expressed. To make these images, slaveholders relied upon their slaves' humanity, but they only allowed certain postures, poses, and, thus, social identities. In effect, photography enabled owners to police the cultural and imaginative boundary that divided slaves—especially those most favored slaves—from the social recognition of their full humanity.

Bondspeople did not simply pose for their owners' images, though. They also had their own images taken. Chapter 2 explores what it meant for enslaved people to purchase and use photographs in the South. Historians of photography have shown how ex-slaves such as Frederick Douglass and Sojourner Truth used photography to craft public personas in the antebellum North, and how antebellum artists and racial scientists used photography to demonstrate supposed biological distinctions between blacks and whites.[47] Enslaved African

Americans in the South, however, have been seen for too long as passive victims of photographic representations and, thus, as subjects outside history, beyond the pale of technological change. Yet the scholarship on the "internal economy" of antebellum bondspeople produced over the past three decades makes it conceivable to explore slaves' active engagement with photography. Scholars have shown how some enslaved people secured small amounts of cash and took part in the consumer marketplace. Chapter 2 assesses how some of them obtained and exchanged visual commodities that could testify to their personhood.[48] It uses written materials such as slave narratives, newspapers, and photographers' records to reveal an enslaved people's culture of visual expression, communication, and memorialization that constituted a new, quiet habit of endurance. Whereas free antebellum Americans used photographs to record their families, images proved especially important to slaves seeking to assert the humanity that slavery undercut and constrained and the social ties that slavery persistently imperiled and disrupted.

To discern how photography altered debates over racial identity and community, to grasp how it stirred up political sentiment, and to assess how it was shaped into a political tool requires looking beyond slavery's borders. Thus, Chapter 3 moves to the antebellum North. Since the late eighteenth century, American and British antislavery proponents had used images to persuade a mass audience of the immorality of bondage. But the technical limitations of photography made the medium a poor tool for abolitionists to picture southern plantations and slave markets, as they did in lithographs and illustrated almanacs. Instead, as this chapter shows, white activists and ex-slaves used photography as a way to project alternative visions of black social identity, to envision and build their movement from within, and to pictorially enact the interracial society they sought to achieve. American abolitionists built their movement through photography as they remade the technology into a tool for movement-building.

Finally, Chapter 4 examines how the photography of slavery evolved during the Civil War. While it continues to trace the photographic practices of masters, slaves, and abolitionists, it focuses on a problem that became increasingly pressing within Union army camps: as slavery crumbled, what would the free racial order look like? The question of interracial relations became particularly acute because of the unanticipated confluence of three parties in these camps: hundreds of northern photographers, thousands of fugitive slaves, and thousands of Union soldiers. In a liminal geography between bondage and freedom, northern white soldiers and photographers created scenes of racial hierarchy, often posing African Americans sitting on the ground or serving Union personnel. Through a fleeting moment of interracialism, they tethered black freedom to racial subordination in the private and popular imagination. This northern vision of black inferiority would stand in tension with that of other public photographs and mass-periodical illustrations of black Union soldiers, which stressed courage and patriotism, as well as the portraits of many ex-slaves, who continued to craft a private counter-archive that staked claims to full humanity throughout the war. Photography continued to prove a vital, contested terrain to articulate racial status, interracial sociality, and national belonging as enslaved people entered freedom.

In the mid-nineteenth century, a startlingly new and exceedingly malleable visual technology entered the United States and, amidst great social and political conflict, became a stage to perform visions of the present and future. Through photography, slaveholders, slaves, abolitionists, and soldiers debated the pressing issues of racial identity and interracial life. Such photographic debates contributed to the political and ideological clash that led to war, and eventually they had a resettling effect, as they helped produce a dominant vision of racial hierarchy as slavery fell. But as photographic technology shaped the surrounding world, that world shaped the technology; as this book tells a story of ideological conflict and political causation, it also tells one of cultural transformation. Through the crucible of bondage, driven by the pleasures of domination and the instabilities of enslavement, by a national political crisis and the vast uncertainties of a racial order in a post-slavery nation, slaveholders, slaves, abolitionists, and Civil War soldiers fashioned a new way of seeing and being, at the heart of which were photographic images and image uses. The final decades and eventual death of slavery gave life to a new form of visual politics.

1

POLICING PERSONHOOD

DURING THE 1840s AND 1850s, the rise of photography unleashed a radically new way for American slaveholders to depict, possess, exchange, and preserve knowledge about the world of southern bondage. As itinerant and urban studio photographers spread throughout the South, masters and mistresses did not simply seek to represent themselves. From the older slave states of Virginia and South Carolina to the newer states of Alabama, Mississippi, and Louisiana, slave owners began photographing their slaves. Some of these images currently sit in the same archival boxes as slaveholders' written materials—the letters, diaries, and plantation logbooks upon which our knowledge of slavery is primarily based. They also are held in private hands, owned by descendants of slaveholders as well as by collectors of early photographs.

Slaveholders in cities and on farms and plantations made slave photographs—in the cosmopolitan centers of Richmond, Savannah, and Charleston as well as in rural areas such as northern Florida, central Virginia, and northwest Mississippi. The images themselves reveal individual slaves such as Moses (Figure 1.1) and the Minor family nurse (Figure 1.2) as well as slaves posing with whites, as in the case of Lydia and Charlotte Helen Middleton (Figure 1.3). The vast majority of enslaved people who sat for pictures—including boatmen,

Figure 1.1 *Moses*, c. February 1857, carte de visite. Manigault Family Record, vol. II, p. 320, courtesy of the South Carolina Historical Society.

butlers, coachmen, and nannies—were nonagricultural laborers who held higher social status in enslavers' eyes. Though female house slaves are pictured most often, the archive also includes enslaved men and children. The selection of female portraits, moreover, can hardly be reduced to the stereotype of the "mammy," nor the other

Figure 1.2 *Minor Family Nurse*, c. 1850, daguerreotype, 3¾ × 4¼ inches. Minor Family Papers, 1838–1944, Accession #6055, 6055-a, Albert and Shirley Small Special Collections Library, University of Virginia.

African American stereotypes prevalent in nineteenth-century popular culture.[1] The photographs show slaves who never fled their owners, slaves who ran away before they were pictured, and slaves who ran away after they were pictured. Despite the temptation to treat these images as unmediated access into the American past, they deserve to be explained for how they operated in their world rather than

Figure 1.3 *Charlotte Helen Middleton and Her Enslaved Nurse, Lydia,* ca. 1857, by George Smith Cook (American, 1819–1902), ambrotype, 3¾ × 2¾ inches (image), 4¾ × 4 inches (case). Gift of Alicia Hopton Middleton, 1937.005.0010, image courtesy of the Gibbes Museum of Art/Carolina Art Association.

ours. Diverse in geography, gender, age, and visual composition, these images offer a largely untapped source base for the study of late antebellum slavery.

Slave photographs stood at the center of a photographic culture that entailed a set of practices of production, display, exchange, and preservation. This photographic culture emerged as the violence undergirding antebellum bondage—and the foundational view and treatment of bondspeople as both people and property—increasingly came under attack in abolitionist propaganda.[2] In the contentious political climate of the late antebellum era, slave photographs gave slaveholders a powerful new evidentiary tool to envision and perform a benevolent and intimate regime. Through the circulation and display of images of well-dressed bondspeople and portraits of enslaved caretakers with white children, enslavers projected a comfortable, harmonious, and familial form of bondage, which purportedly treated its laborers as people, not commodities. In the late antebellum era, slave photographs and their attendant photographic practices emerged as a key means for enslavers to persuade themselves and others of the just and beneficial nature of slavery.

On the face of it, this photographic culture might seem little more than a visual, material, and social manifestation of paternalist rhetoric—a slaveholding posture that claimed enslavers prioritized the well-being of enslaved people over profit, and that enslaved people benefitted from their enslavement. In one sense, it did materialize such widespread rhetoric in a politically charged moment. But in making slave portraits, especially individual portraits, owners actually produced a problematic contradiction: slaves were categorically denied full personhood in southern law and culture, yet the conventions of photographic portraiture theoretically suggested the uniqueness of those bondspeople sitting before the cameras. Could it be that slaveholders spent time, energy, and money on images that actually asserted the full humanity of their property? Was it possible that photographic portraits of slaves revealed, as photographer Marcus Root put it, "that *individuality* or *selfhood*, which differences *him* from all beings, past, present, or future"?[3]

Though they never stated so explicitly, slaveholders evidently sensed the dangers of these implications. Visual evidence, private letters, and diaries reveal how owners walked a fine line between elevating and subordinating their slaves through photography. Enslaved people could pose, but they were limited to certain poses. Slaves' clothing and postures might suggest bourgeois respectability, but slaveholders consistently undercut that status as they discussed and displayed slave photographs. Limiting slaves from realizing the full spectrum of social identities and character traits available to whites was a subtle but vital means of maintaining the imaginative boundaries that divided enslaved from free.[4] After 1839, as this chapter shows, the very photographic practices that helped owners insist their slaves were not treated as commodities simultaneously amplified the cultural denial of full personhood.

THE EMERGENCE OF THE DAGUERREOTYPE—the first photographic process—dramatically altered the ways in which masters depicted their slaves. Since the beginnings of bondage in colonial America, few artists or masters had made common slaves the central subjects of visual representation.[5] Justus Englehardt Kühn's *Henry Darnall III* (c. 1710) marks the first known painting of an African American in colonial America (Figure 1.4). Drawing upon a tradition in European portraiture that dated back to the Renaissance, Kühn pictured a subordinate black figure to signify the main subject's status.[6] His employment of the collar to symbolize the enslavement of the boy reflected the more patriarchal rhetoric of mastery in the colonial era. Though the collar would fall out of favor in the iconography of American slavery, the use of a marginal black figure as the foundation of white identity—of mastery, racial power, freedom, and wealth—would prove remarkably persistent in eighteenth- and nineteenth-century portraits and domestic scenes. Numerous artists painted George Washington, for instance, with a slave on the margins of the canvas (Figures 1.5 and 1.6). Artists did paint famous slaves such as Revolutionary War hero James Armistead Lafayette in individual portraits.[7] But despite the aristocratic appetite for paintings and miniature paintings amongst the planter elite, owners took little interest in commissioning individual portraits of their slaves. Non-celebrity slaves largely existed in painted portraiture as racial props to signify the standing of their masters, not as visual subjects in their own right.[8]

Figure 1.4 *Henry Darnall III*, c. 1710, by Justus Englehardt Kühn, oil on canvas, 137.4 × 112.2 cm (image). Museum Department, courtesy of the Maryland Historical Society, 1912.1.3.

In a similar vein, nineteenth-century landscape paintings and house portraits conveyed the beauty and grandeur of southern plantations and estate homes while marginalizing or erasing the slave labor that made such vistas imaginable.[9] *Rose Hill* (c. 1820) was typical (Figure 1.7). A visitor to wealthy planter Nathaniel Heyward's estate

Figure 1.5 *The Washington Family*, 1789–1796, by Edward Savage, oil on canvas, 84⅛ × 111⅞ inches (image), 97½ × 124½ inches (framed). Courtesy Andrew W. Mellon Collection and the National Gallery of Art, Washington.

home, or perhaps to his Charleston townhouse, might have encountered *Rose Hill* hanging over the mantel; its size and placement were unmistakable reminders of the world Heyward governed. The perspective of the painting helped frame this plantation world as socially harmonious, allowing the visitor to move her or his eyes upward from the horses tranquilly grazing in the field to the voluminous stacks of rice to be threshed and stored in a nearby barn to the stately manor residing on the hilltop. What the visitor would not have seen was that by his death in 1851, Heyward owned 2,340 slaves—making him the largest slaveholder in American history.[10] This very same erasure could be found in house portraits, a far more popular genre than landscape paintings, exemplified by the many images of Monticello and Mount Vernon with no slaves in sight.[11] Yet even when slavery was the subject of the painting, as in artist Francis Guy's *Perry Hall, Slave*

Figure 1.6 *George Washington*, 1780, by John Trumbull, oil on canvas, 36 × 28 inches. The Metropolitan Museum of Art, New York, Bequest of Charles Allen Munn, 1924.

Quarters with Field Hands at Work (c. 1805), the land and livestock, rather than slaves' bodies, still predominated (Figure 1.8).

The arrival of the daguerreotype would alter these visions. Throughout the spring and summer of 1839, southern newspapers talked excitedly of a new invention by Frenchman Louis Jacques

Figure 1.7 *Rose Hill*, artist unknown, c. 1820, oil on canvas, 40 × 56 inches. Courtesy of The Charleston Museum, Charleston, South Carolina.

Figure 1.8 *Perry Hall, Slave Quarters with Field Hands at Work*, c. 1805, by Francis Guy, oil on canvas. Museum Department, courtesy of the Maryland Historical Society, 1986.33.

Mandé Daguerre. For the *Daily Picayune* of New Orleans, news of the daguerreotype was "exciting great sensation in the scientific world."[12] Meanwhile, as Baltimore's *Sun* declared, the daguerreotype "is expected to prove of as much value to the fine arts as the power loom and steam engine have to manufacturers."[13] While postbellum southern literature mythologized the Old South as an agrarian land opposed to modern industry and its fruits, southern elites and intellectuals awaited the daguerreotype with much enthusiasm.[14]

For many southerners, the daguerreotype broke with the past by offering a striking new way to preserve it. This first photographic process, which produced unique, non-reproducible images on silver-coated copper plates, appeared the ideal tool for capturing the seemingly accelerating present and the remnants of human history.[15] As a poem in the *Southern Literary Messenger* exclaimed, "Ye pupils of Daguerre! improve the hour— / Make haste to paint the fragments which are left us / Of what stern Time and Vandals have bereft us."[16] While southern poets lauded the memory-making possibilities of Daguerre's invention, wealthy southerners visited traveling exhibitions of Daguerre's work in 1841. In cities such as Baltimore and Charleston, large, genteel crowds gazed with "wonder and delight" and "universal admiration" at daguerreotypes of the city of Venice and the midnight mass at Saint-Étienne-du-Mont.[17] In dramatic fashion, the daguerreotype memorialized the monuments of Western civilization as it democratized their visual consumption.

The widespread perception of the objectivity of the photographic process, the notion that the photograph captured far more visual detail than other image types, and the general artistic quest for new subject matter helped launch a range of new visual practices in the 1840s and 1850s, including urban, news, and celebrity photography.[18] But the commercial portrait reigned supreme in the first two decades. Though exposure times varied due to the photographer's knowledge of the latest chemicals and the amount of sunlight in the studio (the more light, the quicker the picture), they dropped sharply in the early 1840s, from minutes in the fall of 1839 to as little as thirty seconds by the spring of 1840. By the end of 1840, one New York chemist noted that exposure times had dropped as low as ten seconds.[19] These faster exposures opened up the commercial potential of the medium. A business for portraits emerged—one that photographers tethered to antebellum sentimentalism. They linked likenesses to feeling, attachment, and the sense of loss.[20] As inventor, daguerreotype booster, and commercial operator Samuel Morse put it in 1840, to hold in "our possession the likeness of some one who has been loved by us is a delicious, even if sometimes a melancholy, pleasure."[21] Some daguerreans were not afraid to use fear to make this point. John Armstrong Bennet, a daguerrean in Mobile, Alabama, reminded customers that his images were especially important in times of widespread disease: "Call immediately," Bennet exclaimed, "if you want accurate and beautiful Miniatures of yourselves or friends—for soon the raging epidemic may hurry many into the grave! and the oh! how you will regret that you had not obtained a true copy of those loved features, when you find them fading from your memory."[22] The uncertainty of the future, Bennet suggested, made photographs of the past, as intimate mementos of a loved one, a pressing need.

The photograph made an especially good memento, antebellum artists and boosters proclaimed, because it revealed the inner essence of the sitter. Influenced by the ideas of Swiss physiognomist Johann Caspar Lavater, many artists placed special importance on the meaning of the face. As Marcus Root argued, the "face is to a man what the dial is to a clock, or a table of contents to a book, viz., the index of the soul."[23] Other artists such as E. K. Hough chided their colleagues to not lose sight of the body. "It is too generally considered that expressions in pictures are all confined to the face," Hough wrote, "whereas the position and carriage of the head, the hands, the body, have each a particular and necessary relation to the entire effect."[24] Whether they stressed the centrality of the face or body, however, the first generation of photographers found common ground in Hough's assertion that "outward expression is the revealment of inward feeling."[25] They cast photography as a privileged means of conveying the character of its subjects.

Driven by potential profits, imbued with visions of scientific and industrial progress, and inspired by notions of art and truth and beauty, Americans took up daguerreotypy in droves during the early 1840s. Many commercial daguerreans came from backgrounds in the visual arts, including engraving, lithography, and, especially, portrait, landscape, and miniature painting.[26] Others had worked as craftsmen—as blacksmiths, inventors, and cobblers—and brought to daguerreotypy

a familiarity with electricity, small tools, and metals.[27] As daguerreotypist James F. Ryder recalled, there was "but a step from the anvil or
the sawmill to the camera."[28] The transition was manageable because
start-up costs were low. While cameras initially ranged in price from
$25 to $50, they dropped to $15 by the early 1850s.[29] With cameras and
chemicals in tow, daguerreans founded commercial galleries in major
southern port cities such as Charleston, New Orleans, and St. Louis
by 1841, and in inland cities such as Columbia as well as smaller
coastal cities such as Mobile by 1843.[30] Yet many of the first southern
galleries were short-lived. In Charleston, at least fifteen daguerreotype galleries opened in the 1840s, but most only stayed in business
for a few weeks to a few years.[31] In Columbia, meanwhile, it was not
until 1846, when Joseph T. Zealy opened for business, that the city
could boast of an established gallery.[32]

Given the small number of established galleries in the early to mid-
1840s South, many masters and slaves may have first encountered
photography from northern itinerant daguerreans. These "humbugs"
and "country operators," as their more urbane gallery counterparts
disparagingly called them, helped extend the early-nineteenth-century
culture of northeastern peddlers and limners into the slave states.[33]
Dramatic transformations in communication and transportation technologies over the previous decades—including the rise of steamboats,
turnpikes, and railroads as well as the expansion of the postal system—
made this possible. Daguerreans moved by wagon, stagecoach, steamboat, and railroad, selling likenesses from their wagons, out of storefronts,
in hotel rooms, and on their vessels.[34] Capitalizing on the infrastructural
developments of the early nineteenth century, itinerant daguerreans
flourished nationally in the mid-nineteenth century.

These artist-entrepreneurs crisscrossed the South. The Atlantic
seaboard experienced a steady flow of northern itinerants during the
1840s, and South Carolina and Georgia, because of their wealth and
weather, proved particularly popular destinations. Some itinerants
came to Charleston, Savannah, and Columbia for the winter season,
while others stayed for months or even years. New Yorker Samuel
Broadbent, for instance, first traveled to Augusta in 1840 as a miniature painter. After adopting daguerreotypy, Broadbent came back to
Savannah in the winter of 1843–1844 and 1844–1845, to Charleston in
October 1845, and finally to Columbia in December 1845.[35]

The antebellum boomtown of New Orleans proved a prime spring-board for artists to popularize the process in the southwestern slave states, and George Smith Cook took on the principal role in doing so. A Connecticut-born transplant, Cook adopted daguerreotypy when it arrived in the city. From 1845 to 1849 he traversed the Deep South, hawking portraits and tutoring future daguerreans in various towns in Mississippi, Alabama, and Georgia.[36] Cook and others made notewor-thy arrivals in the small towns they entered. "We have a most excel-lent Daguerreotype artist in town now, whose name is Cook. I have not seen such pictures as he takes this side of Philadelphia," a resi-dent of Athens, Alabama, noted in his diary.[37] Such residents took pleasure in the way that talented itinerants seemed to demolish the cultural distance between large cities and small towns, the southwest-ern frontier and the cosmopolitan Northeast. Likewise, a slaveholder in South Carolina described the fun when "the Dauguerian car...arrived at Laurens."[38] As much as the daguerreotype itself was a bracing new form of visuality, the mobility of the photographer injected a sense of novelty in the largely pre-industrial South.

As itinerants such as Broadbent set up shop in southern cities, others traveled the rural pathways of the South. In *The Photographic Art-Journal*, an itinerant who went by the name Wanderer described his southern business in a series of articles, "Peregrinations of a Daguerrean." In one article, he related a recent image-making trip to a plantation home in Buncomb County, North Carolina, in the 1850s. "Taking an extra camera and other 'means and appliances to boot,'" Wander described, "I drove out last week into the country, about six miles from town, at the request of a gentleman who had expressed a desire to have a view of his residence, ('Wakefield,') and the like-nesses of several members of his family taken, in groups and single pictures."[39] Wanderer took his fellow artist-entrepreneurs on a tour of Wakefield: "Along the carriage road,—bordered with shrubbery and flowers,—we sped at a rapid rate, passing the negro quarters,—off the road a piece,—then the overseer's house, then the keeper's lodge."[40] At "the great hall door," the slaveholding family greeted Wanderer, while "Cato," likely a house slave, "had the 'bloods' by the heads in the wink of an eye."[41] After listening to music in the parlor, eating dinner, and flirting with the master's niece, Wanderer took pictures of the white family in various poses and perhaps a view of Wakefield as well.[42] His account of the itinerant in the southern parlor reflected the eagerness of the daguerrean community to cater to the planter elite.

The most mobile of these artists traveled along southern waterways. It is unclear who operated the first daguerreotype boat, but by the 1850s numerous artists traversed the Mississippi River (and many smaller rivers) hawking images. Samuel F. Simpson owned two floating galleries, and in *The Photographic and Fine Art Journal* he gave other artists a detailed tour of his facilities. The interiors of his boats included a waiting room and a sitting room, which, Simpson boasted, used "a large side and sky light that enables us to operate in from five to ten seconds in fair weather." Above all, the floating saloon increased efficiency, and Simpson urged others to follow in his wake. "I am almost induced to think that there cannot be a more convenient plan devised for traveling operators than a Floating Gallery," Simpson proclaimed. "As soon as the boat is landed we are ready for operations, without all that extra trouble that traveling artists usually experience in unpacking and setting up ready for operating." On one trip down the Mississippi—which took him as far as the "sugar coast" between Baton Rouge and New Orleans—Simpson made approximately fifty stops and took almost one thousand photographs.[43] Along major waterways, it would not have been unusual for masters and slaves (especially enslaved boatmen) to encounter photographers such as Simpson, pulling up unannounced at the docks.

By the 1850s urban galleries had grown increasingly numerous and visible in southern cities, coexisting with the early wave of itinerants. Charleston, Richmond, New Orleans, and St. Louis emerged as the centers of southern photography, and galleries (also known as saloons or studios) sprang up in concentrated pockets in these cities. At any given point in the 1850s, one would pass by numerous photograph galleries while walking down King Street and Meeting Street in Charleston, Canal Street in New Orleans, and Main Street in Richmond. Artists such as George Smith Cook (Charleston), Joseph T. Zealy (Columbia), William A. Pratt (Richmond), Jesse Whitehurst (Richmond), and John H. Fitzgibbon (St. Louis) rose to national prominence.[44] Many successful artists turned their studios into hubs of instruction and supplies, where photographers and aspirants could obtain tutoring and purchase the necessary cameras, plates, chemicals, and studio implements.[45] Urban daguerreans also put great effort into the look and feel of their galleries for customers seeking likenesses. One newspaper extolled the "great taste and elegance" of Joseph Zealy's Columbia gallery, which was outfitted with an "ante-room, for the proper adjustment of toilette, &c., by his visitors," as well as "an elegant piano, for the accommodation of his lady visitors."[46] Like many southern gallery operators, Zealy constructed photographic portraiture as a refined activity.

The men who ran these southern studios were not simply artist-entrepreneurs packaging gentility in a slave society. Many were themselves slaveholders. Daguerreotypist John Werge remembered that in Baltimore, "many of the Daguerreans owned slaves."[47] Numerous other photographers became masters, including William A. Pratt, John Freeman Hillyer, and photographic gallery magnate Thomas Jefferson Dobyns.[48] Joseph T. Zealy owned as many as six slaves by the late 1850s. For Zealy, like others, photography offered a route to mastery.[49] Later, artists including George Smith Cook would donate to the Confederacy.[50] That photography became an integral part of slavery's culture is not surprising given the importance of mastery to southern operators, many of whom invested in cameras, plates, and the racial regime of the slave South.

Whether slaveholding or non-slaveholding, lavish gallery owners or striving itinerants, southern photographers helped usher in the national phenomenon of photographic portrait-taking. By the early 1850s, the *New York Tribune* estimated that Americans were buying three million daguerreotypes per year.[51] The colossal popularity of the daguerreotype (and later photographic processes) was built upon price and perception. While a moderately priced miniature portrait painting cost about $15 in the late 1840s, the average price for a sixth-plate daguerreotype in 1845 was $5, and in the rural South one might find daguerreotypes for as low as $1.[52] By 1850 the average daguerreotype price had dropped to $2.50, and by the mid-1850s one could find such photographs in many places for as little as 25 cents, equivalent to the cost of publications such as the monthly *Harper's Magazine* and *Godey's Lady's Book*.[53] A drop in prices fueled the portrait craze, but so too did the formal qualities of the photograph. When one man wrote from San Francisco to his sisters in Lynchburg, Virginia, he delighted in how "truthful and life like" their photographs appeared. These portraits enchanted the man so much that, as he noted, "I almost fancy when

I gaze upon those beloved countenances that I am once more in your midst."[54] For all Americans, the perceived transparency of the photograph rendered it an extraordinary surrogate of the body and an entrancing virtual vehicle to visit distant places and loved ones.

The accessibility, affordability, and cultural associations of photography laid the groundwork for slaveholders to build up a new visual world. George Smith Cook's logbooks—a rare set of surviving archival records of a southern photographer—occasionally list enslaved sitters and many black sitters who might have been slaves. For instance, on April 18, 1848, Cook listed one quarter-plate daguerreotype for $5.50 in Columbus, Mississippi: "Col Girl of Mr. Moore."[55] On the following day, April 19, a "Mr. Moore" purchased a sixth-plate daguerreotype for $3.50 from Cook.[56] If, as is likely given the timing, this was the same Mr. Moore, then he not only would have daguerreotyped his slave first but also would have bought a larger and more expensive image of her ($5.50) than of himself ($3.50).[57] Little is known of the female slave whom Cook daguerreotyped on this day, nor is much known of the slaveholder, Mr. Moore. We do know, however, that Cook took photographs of other slaves. Only three days earlier, he made a daguerreotype of the same size and price (quarter-plate, $5.50) of a different slave woman.[58] The way in which Cook logged these portraits—simply jotting down the name, size, and price, as he did for all his images—suggests that by 1848 slave photography had become a normal, unremarkable part of his practice.

The purchase of southern slave photographs did not fall solely under the domain of slaveholding men. Slaveholding women such as Mary Pringle, an aristocratic Charlestonian, also had photographs taken of their chattel. Slaveholding children, too, took trips with their slaves to take pictures.[59] Owners may have even commissioned photographs of slaves holding white children as one of many portraits taken on a single trip to the gallery. For instance, the daughter of Benjamin Daniel Cogbill and Harriet Cogbill of Petersburg, Virginia—likely their child Lelia Courtney Cogbill—sat with her grandmother Matilda Burwell Boyd and a black woman who might have been one of the Cogbills' slaves (Figures 1.9 and 1.10).[60] Since the child's dress, haircut, age, and position appear identical, as do the brass frames around the images, it seems likely that she sat in back-to-back sessions (in strikingly similar poses) with her grandmother and her black caretaker.

Figure 1.9 *Matilda Burwell Boyd and Grandchild (Cogbill Child)*, ambrotype, sixth plate. 1994.180.1, Virginia Historical Society.

Every level of enslavers' families played a role in the creation of slave photography.

Mainly within the photograph saloon, enslavers transformed the visual depiction of slavery and enslaved people. On rare occasions, owners commissioned outdoor photographs of the slaveholding household, thereby extending the most popular form of plantation painting, the house portrait.[61] In the late 1840s, for example, an itinerant daguerreotyped Richard Thompson Archer's home at Anchuca, a plantation in Claiborne County, Mississippi, visualizing whites on the porch and slaves on the balcony.[62] But enslavers, like all Americans, commissioned studio portraits far more often, most likely because outdoor scenes required the photographer to travel to the plantation, which raised the price considerably. Rather than the camera coming to the slave, slaveholders brought the slave to the camera. Large paintings

Figure 1.10 *Cogbill Child with African American Nanny*, ambrotype, sixth plate. 1994.180.2, Virginia Historical Society.

showing the world the master governed gave way to small photographs showing the people his family owned (Figure 1.11). Southern slave photography moved slaves' bodies, faces, and emotions to the centers of frames. In doing so, it made claims about slavery, mastery, and the enslaved people posing before the camera.

But what sorts of claims were they? While such portraits departed from the long-standing visual formulas used in painting, they also stood in stark contrast to a set of photographs historians of photography have studied at length: the fifteen daguerreotypes of South Carolina slaves that Columbia artist Joseph T. Zealy made for Harvard scientist Louis Agassiz in 1850. Agassiz sought to use these images to prove the theory of polygenesis, which described how blacks and whites came from different biological origins.[63] Upon invitation from Dr. Robert Wilson Gibbes, Agassiz visited Columbia, where he toured a number

Figure 1.11 *Martha Ann "Patty" Atavis*, daguerreotype, 3.75 × 3.25 inches. Cased Photograph Collection, courtesy of the Maryland Historical Society, CSPH 545.

of plantations with the purpose of studying native-born Africans. Gibbes subsequently brought at least seven enslaved people to Zealy's studio, attached identifying labels (documenting the sitters' names, owners, and African origins, and for a few men their trades) to the resulting daguerreotypes, and sent the images back to Agassiz at Harvard, where the scientist would later exhibit them during a lecture in Cambridge.[64] In these images, Zealy forced the enslaved subjects to pose nude and captured them in straight, frontal poses that foregrounded anatomy. The Zealy-Agassiz daguerreotypes functioned through a process of racial classification: they stripped enslaved people of the portraiture conventions—the typical postures, props, and clothing—that signaled individuality.

The bulk of slave photographs left behind in the archive by masters differed greatly from the Agassiz images. These photographs did, in fact, share many mainstream photographic conventions, including formulas that linked certain poses and props to particular social identities. For instance, the ambrotype of Mammy Kitty, described as a "faithful servant" on an attached note and very likely a slave of the Ellis family in Richmond, and the likeness of Eliza Washburn had formulaic similarities (Figures 1.12 and 1.13).[65] Both women pose in three-quarter-length portraits, gazing to the side of the camera. Both women place one arm on a cloth-covered circular table (a common piece of early photographic furniture) and drape one hand off the side. The placement of hands—typically orchestrated by the photographer—was a small but significant detail in the gendered conventions of early photography. Famed Philadelphia artist Marcus Root prescribed that the "hands of a lady" "may rest easily upon the lap, and should be

Figure 1.12 *Mammy Kitty*, c. 1860, ambrotype, 3¼ × 3¹¹⁄₁₆ inches. Ellis Family Daguerreotypes, Accession #2516-c, Albert and Shirley Small Special Collections Library, University of Virginia.

Figure 1.13 *Eliza Washburn*, daguerreotype, quarter plate. Courtesy American Antiquarian Society.

presented edgewise, neither too high nor too low, which will give them a small, delicate appearance. Or one hand or arm may be laid upon a table, while the other hand may hold a book or some other object, if the sitter so choose."[66] Thus Kitty's pose suggests, at the very least, an effort on the part of the photographer to present her body delicately. An antebellum viewer might have seen the hands as a sign of feminine virtue, though such readings were more complicated for the slave portrait.

Portraits of enslaved and free people also shared the convention of employing simple props to signal something about the sitter. For instance, Rosetta, a slave of the Alston family of South Carolina, holds a white handkerchief in her right hand (Figure 1.14).[67] A slave of the Partridge family of Jefferson County, Florida, Mauma Mollie grasps a walking stick, leans back in her chair, and rests her arm on a decorated table (Figure 1.15). The Minor family nurse, likely the slave of Lancelot Minor of central Virginia, sits in a wooden chair, cradling a set of worn wool carders in her weathered hands (Figure 1.2).[68] The handkerchief, a common item in photographic portraiture, was generally seen as a sign of gentility.[69] For viewers, Mollie's walking stick (and her leaned-back posture) might have signaled her advanced age, and the

Figure 1.14 *Rosetta*, n.d., artist unknown, ambrotype, 2½ × 2 inches (image), 3¹¹⁄₁₆ × 3³⁄₁₆ inches (case). XX1978.002, image courtesy of the Gibbes Museum of Art/Carolina Art Association.

Minor nurse's carders could have suggested her status as a dutiful farm laborer. Understanding the many meanings of these photographs, of course, requires more than a cursory analysis of their contents. But the aesthetic choices embedded in these portraits clearly reveal how slave photography drew upon the paradoxical process by which generalizable formulas were employed to convey a certain measure of social status and individuality for enslaved sitters, at least at the level of visual symbolism.

The visual contours of individual slave photographs constructed human bondage as a humane form of bondage—one in which slaves were ostensibly treated as individual people rather than as categorized commodities. Interracial images went one step further: they projected slavery as a system of harmonious, intimate relations between blacks and whites. Interracial intimacy most commonly manifested itself in

Figure 1.15 *Portrait of Mauma Mollie—Monticello, Florida*, c. 1855, daguerreotype, 10 × 8 inches. Courtesy of the State Archives of Florida.

portraits of enslaved nurses with white children. Sometimes, of course, enslaved women only sat in such pictures to hold fidgety white children, a fact made evident by portraits in which the white child literally blocks the woman's face.[70] But many portraits clearly cast enslaved women as important figures in the overall composition (Figure 1.16). These portraits fused the sentimental trappings of early

Figure 1.16 *Martha Ann "Patty" Atavis with Anna Whitridge*, tintype, 3.25 × 4.25 inches. Cased Photographs Collection, courtesy of the Maryland Historical Society, CSPH 546.

American photography with a long-standing Christian iconography: the Madonna and child (Figure 1.17).[71] As historian Laura Wexler notes, the Madonna iconography "is a tribute to the highest achievement that womanhood can attain in Christian culture and a paean to the actual woman who occupies that mythical role."[72]

Surely many slaveholders would have seen this Christian relationship in these images, for, as historian Drew Faust notes, the vision of mastery as an "evangelical stewardship" had become a mainstay of proslavery arguments.[73] Take the example of Dolly Lunt Burge, mother to Sadai and mistress to Rachel. On the day Lincoln was re-elected, November 8, 1864, Burge described her own slaveholding practice in her diary: "The purest & holiest men have owned them & I can see nothing in the Scriptures which forbids it. I have never bought nor sold & I have tried to make life easy & pleasant to those

Figure 1.17 *Madonna and Child*, late 1480s, by Giovanni Bellini, oil on wood. The Metropolitan Museum of Art, New York, Rogers Fund, 1908.

that have been bequeathed me by the dead. I have never ceased to work, but many a Northern housekeeper has a much easier time than a Southern matron with her hundred negroes."[74] In a cruel inversion characteristic of self-proclaimed paternalists, Burge formulated bondage as a burden to the mistress and a gift to the slave. She justified this position through the Bible as well as by self-consciously distancing herself from the slave market. That she would commission a photograph of her young daughter with her enslaved nurse (Figure 1.18) suggests that Burge sought to memorialize a domesticated, Christian vision of bondage for the years ahead.

Still, in the present, such images actually amplified the tensions of bondage—tensions between enslaved women as commodified racial subordinates and as important workers within white families. On one hand, chattel mothers were still subject to the authority of the blood

Figure 1.18 *Sadai Burge and Rachel*, c. 1858. Burge Family Papers, Stuart A. Rose Manuscript, Archives, and Rare Book Library, Emory University.

mothers of the children they held and, for that matter, to the whims of those tiny children. Their visual presence as nurturers within the frames belied how easily and abruptly they could be sold thousands of miles away. Further, as historian Thavolia Glymph has shown, mistresses rarely hesitated to use violence to maintain authority in plantation households. The formerly enslaved Harriet Robinson, for instance, remembered how "Miss Julia whipped me every day in the mawning" and how she was even punished when her mistress's children did poorly in their spelling lessons: "At every word them chillun missed, she gave me a lick 'cross the head for it."[75] On the other hand, many slaves received the same visual tribute that white women received within the photographic frames (Figure 1.19).[76] The choreography of such tributes varied. Enslaved women sat next to standing white toddlers and held babies around the waist with one or two hands; they sometimes gazed down at the babies they held, but more frequently they gazed back at the camera. Assuming the role of nurturing surrogate mother, Martha Ann Patty Atavis held Anna Whitridge closely, with black and white hands touching, presenting her to the viewer (Figure 1.16). For masters, whom better to picture than enslaved women with white children? Many of these children, because of their ages, might have seen the black women who held them as extended members of their families. Anna Whitridge might not have known that her father had bought Atavis in 1839 for $200.[77] Subordinated and elevated, commodities and nurturers, chattel Madonnas served as the most conspicuous symbols of benevolent intimacy in the southern photographic landscape.

Figure 1.19 *Mary Louise May Pearson with Baby Mary Frances Pearson*, daguerreotype, sixth plate. Courtesy American Antiquarian Society.

The chattel Madonna formula became so important that slave-holder Alfred J. Boulware even made it the centerpiece of his house-hold portrait at Buena Vista, his plantation in Spotsylvania County, Virginia (Figure 1.20).[78] In front of the house, white family members and slaves posed for a carefully orchestrated shot that miniaturized the contradictions of slavery. At the center of the picture, at the door-way of the plantation household, stood a chattel Madonna. Though she and the black woman on the balcony faced the camera as typical antebellum subjects, the slaves on the ground served as little more than props. Two of the women framed the porch in side profile, each standing with one leg on a step. More objects than subjects, they served to enhance the symmetry of the portrait. Boulware's image bifurcated his slaves. It devalued certain people as property while it elevated the nursemaid as an important member of the household.[79]

Figure 1.20 *View of Buena Vista*, c. 1858, daguerreotype, half plate. 1969.28, Virginia Historical Society.

Of course, slave photographs erased as much as they made visible: the sexual coercion enslaved women faced, the slave trade they feared, the physical violence used by masters and mistresses to maintain control in the plantation household. Perhaps no image did so more clearly than a July 1860 portrait of Louis Manigault's son, Louis V, called "Petit Louis" by his parents, and Captain, Petit Louis's enslaved caretaker (Figure 1.21). As in many images of the period, Petit Louis and Captain place their hands delicately on a small circular table covered with a patterned cloth. Petit Louis's white dress was customary attire for young boys in the nineteenth century.[80] The artist gave Louis's arms, shoulders, and cheeks a flesh tone and reddened the chair cushion as well as Captain's lips. That the photographer colored the image for an extra price and enclosed it in an ornate frame underscores the nature of the portrait as a memento of black and white dependents. That this memento belied Captain's treatment outside the studio was made markedly clear during the Civil War, when Captain moved with mistress Fannie Manigault and Petit Louis from Gowrie, the Manigault plantation near Savannah, to a safer inland location at the Lanier House in Macon, Georgia. Here Captain was tasked with watching over Petit Louis and running many of Fannie's errands to the local store and post office. At night, Captain (like many house slaves) sometimes slept in Fannie's bedroom to wait on her.[81] As their stay in Macon lengthened, however, Fannie Manigault started to feel that Captain was testing her authority in the absence of master Louis Manigault. "Captain is *awfully* stubborn we will have a chat about him when you return," wrote Fannie to husband Louis in December 1861. He "talks *loudly* after me…if I did not find him useful with Louis I would not have him about me, when you are present he is very good, but when not, *Oh!* my."[82] Louis soon responded, suggesting two options. If Fannie wanted to send Captain back to Gowrie, Louis would have the overseer "lock him up in the plantation Dark Room for two weeks + feed him on homony + water." Alternatively, Fannie might keep Captain in Macon and "have him well flogged at the Macon jail." Whatever method of punishment Fannie chose, Louis Manigault assured her, "Captain will return to you a Changed Negro."[83]

In drawing upon many photographic conventions of the day, photographs such as the portrait of Louis V and Captain also contested abolitionists' visual, oral, and written depictions of slavery, particularly

Figure 1.21 *Louis Manigault and Captain*, 1860, ambrotype, 4 × 6¾ inches. 1999.57.15, courtesy of The Charleston Museum, Charleston, South Carolina.

scenes of slaves in pain.[84] Especially since the 1830s, abolitionists had circulated images of chained, lynched, tortured, and whipped slaves, as seen in the *American Anti-Slavery Almanac for 1838* (Figure 1.22). Despite little aversion to inflicting pain to maintain their regime, southern defenders took umbrage at abolitionist claims that the South was bereft of sympathy. In 1836, for instance, South Carolina politician

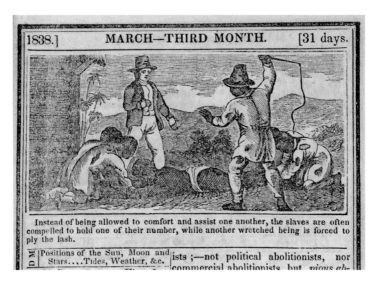

Instead of being allowed to comfort and assist one another, the slaves are often compelled to hold one of their number, while another wretched being is forced to ply the lash.

Positions of the Sun, Moon and Stars....Tides, Weather, &c.   ists ;—not political abolitionists, nor commercial abolitionists but *pious ab-*

Figure 1.22 *The American Anti-Slavery Almanac, for 1838.* Courtesy American Antiquarian Society.

and slaveholder James Henry Hammond came to Congress and urged the House not to accept an abolitionist petition as he made broader arguments against abolitionist print and visual culture. He protested illustrations of masters flogging enslaved people in the *Antislavery Record*, "pictures calculated to excite the feelings" of children in the *Slave's Friend*, and images "libeling the slave holders with their vile caricatures" in the *Anti-Slavery Almanac for 1836*. In turn, Hammond described slavery as "no evil" but instead "the greatest of all the great blessings which a kind Providence has bestowed upon our glorious region."[85] Such "positive good" arguments emerged hand in hand with the onslaught of abolitionist visual culture.

In the 1850s, debates over benevolence and cruelty were increasingly pitched within the categories solidified by *Uncle Tom's Cabin* (1852). Harriet Beecher Stowe's novel experienced astonishing success, selling three hundred thousand copies in the first year of its American publication alone, and was read by both northerners and southerners.[86] While Stowe's words depicting characters such as Tom, Eva, Eliza, Harry, and Simon Legree resonated with an international audience, the story's power was enhanced through engravings by Hammatt Billings of Boston. The head illustrator for *Gleason's Pictorial* as well as the artist who had recently reworked the masthead design of the *Liberator*,

Billings was steeped in the realms of mass illustration and antislavery imagery. The main element he had added to the masthead, an image of Christ standing over a kneeling slave, revealed an evangelical sensibility that made him the perfect fit for Stowe's novel. In the first edition Billings produced six full-page engravings. For the second American edition, published in December 1852, Billings crafted more than a hundred images, including Tom's brutal beating at the close of the story (Figure 1.23).[87] Billings framed Tom's martyrdom between Christ and Simon Legree, making the point clear to slaveholders: God stood on the side of abolition.

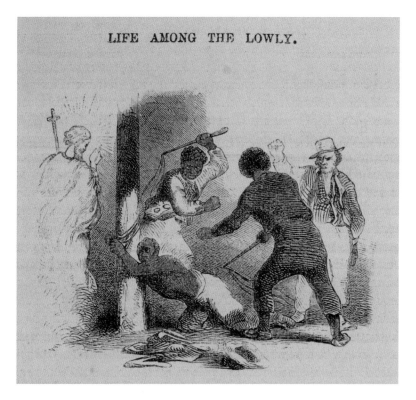

Figure 1.23 Illustration in *Uncle Tom's Cabin: or, Life Among the Lowly*, by Harriet Beecher Stowe, illustrated edition, complete in one volume, designs by Billings, engraved by Baker, Smith, and Andrew. Boston: John P. Jewett and Company; Cleveland, Ohio: Jewett, Proctor, and Worthington, 1853, p. 517. Courtesy American Antiquarian Society.

The private letters of one Charleston family suggest that some slaveholders likely viewed their slave photographs as responses to *Uncle Tom's Cabin*. On August 6, 1852, Annie Middleton confided to her husband, Nathaniel Russell Middleton, that Stowe had raised troubling questions for her as a slave owner:

> *I have been reading "Uncle Tom's cabin" this afternoon the second volume. What do you think of it? Do you think there is any place like that of the monster Legree? It seems too horrible to think of, but I do not see but our laws make it possible. I cannot express what a new view of the whole subject the consideration of these possibilities has opened to me. I do not know what you will think of me but I feel that, if those things are possible I am willing to give up all claim that I may have to any property for the sake of redeeming even those yet unborn from so fearful a doom.*[88]

After reading *Uncle Tom's Cabin*, the Middletons did not sell their slaves.[89] Nathaniel Russell Middleton was part of a group of South Carolina merchants and planters that donated hundreds of dollars to fund the *Southern Press*, a proslavery newspaper, in 1850.[90] But the Middletons did subsequently go to George Smith Cook's Charleston gallery to make a chattel Madonna image of their daughter Charlotte cradled by their slave Lydia (Figure 1.3).[91] Did this pristine image help Annie Middleton distance herself from the Simon Legrees of the South? Did looking at a chattel Madonna portrait help owners reaffirm the Christian benevolence Stowe had rattled while helping them to look away from the commonplace racial violence of the antebellum southern household? Personal photographic evidence must have gone a long way in persuading owners they were not Legrees. For slaveholding parents, well-dressed slaves and visual attachments within sentimental photographs must have offered a tangible response to the assertions of unchristian southerners in Stowe's text and Billings's images.

———

SELF-PERSUASION WAS ONE OF THE KEY functions that slave photographs performed for southern whites. To more fully understand the uses and meaning of these images requires looking at the ways in which slaveholders gave them social lives. These visual and material objects stood at the center of a set of practices of production, circulation, display, and preservation. While historians of photography have stressed how southern whites bolstered white supremacy by circulating lynching photographs in the late nineteenth and early twentieth centuries, this fusion of racial power and photo sharing actually began during slavery.[92] It involved images not of violence and raw power but of respect and condescension, affection and possession. By channeling their slaves' humanity down particular photographic pathways, enslavers presented themselves and their institution in new ways.

At the root of these social practices was the distinctive materiality of the photograph. The size and durability of early photographs enabled southern whites to touch, hold, and wield miniature versions of their chattel. Whereas the painting *Rose Hill* measured 40" by 56", daguerreotypes generally ranged from the tiny sixteenth plate (1⅜" by 1⅝") to the most common size, the sixth plate (2¾" by 3¼"), and the whole plate (6½" by 8½"), which was best suited for display on a parlor table or mantel.[93] Display and exchange were aided by the photographic frame. Daguerreotype plates were typically housed in wooden or Moroccan leather cases with faux-gold mats encircling the image. Opposite the image, the inside of the frame was lined with red, purple, or green silk or velvet (to which antebellum Americans often attached paper notes about the sitter). The ambrotype and tintype—photographic processes popularized in the mid-1850s—were equally suitable for exchange. Ambrotypes came in sizes and cases similar to those of the daguerreotype. Tintypes were produced in a broader sweep of sizes, ranging from miniatures on rings to the whole plate, housed in cases and paper frames, and made on iron, which rendered them lightweight and sturdy keepsakes.[94] The frames, sizes, and compositions of early photographs enhanced their durability and portability.

The emergence of portable photographs enabled slaveholding families to circulate their chattel in visual form as the nation expanded from Atlantic to Pacific. Postal reforms in the mid-1840s drastically reduced the costs of sending a daguerreotype in the mail. After this point, many Americans began tucking photographs into envelopes and sending them hundreds of miles away.[95] Slaveholding families such as the Pringles participated in this practice. During the mid-1850s, Edward J. Pringle moved to San Francisco to practice law. He kept in touch with his wealthy slaveholding family back in Charleston through letters and, on one occasion in the mid-1850s, wrote to his mother to thank her for sending photographs of familiar faces westward. Pringle felt his mother's portrait was "good enough to recall you to me exactly as you are" and that looking at the image was "almost like a visit to you." He reserved his deepest enthusiasm, however, for the photograph his mother had sent of Mack, an enslaved butler in the Pringle's Charleston home:

> *And old Mack! How Magnificent he is! I have laughed over him a dozen times. I keep him in the office that I may exhibit him as a specimen of the "Institution." How natural the old fellow looks! What a magnificence of white cravat and white Pants! gold studs, gold ring etc. Tell him I am delighted to see him looking so young and well. He does not look a day older than when I left him. Tell him his white cravat is a miracle, that there is nobody so well dressed in California. I wish you had sent some more of the servants Mauma, Cretia, + Ishmael.*[96]

Pringle's celebration of Mack as "a specimen of the 'Institution'" placed the image at the center of political debates over the expansion of bondage. This was not the first time Pringle had entered the fray. In 1852 he had penned *Slavery in the Southern States, by a Carolinian*, a proslavery pamphlet attacking the "wild and unreal picture of slavery" in *Uncle Tom's Cabin*.[97] Pringle lauded the humaneness of slave over wage labor and the Christian and reciprocal bonds of the master-slave relationship. He sharply rebuked the harsh world of northern and British liberalism, urbanism, and industrial capitalism. In the South, Pringle argued, the slave "depends upon a master, whose interest it is to raise him up," whereas in the free states the "poor man may be starving in his garret…because there is no visible claim upon him, and the evil is far out of his sphere of life."[98] Pringle likely saw Mack's photograph as visual evidence of these long-standing arguments and may well have urged others to see the image in the same way.

But Mack's image was more than a simple reflection of written arguments. The portrait emerged from and catalyzed new ways of asserting mastery in private and in public. Mary Pringle had engaged in a series of sentimental performances when she first commissioned the portrait of Mack in Charleston: bringing Mack to the studio, making sure he was dressed properly, sending the image in the mail.[99] That Edward could see Mack's gold jewelry indicates that Mary Pringle had even paid extra money to have those items colored (as early photographs could only be colored afterward by hand). Moreover, Mack's photograph gave Edward J. Pringle a material touchstone to engage all who walked into his San Francisco law office. It enabled a community of onlookers to see Pringle as the familial master and to encounter Mack through an image rather than through social interaction. Unlike paternalistic rhetoric found in the proslavery tract, sermon, and letter, Mack's body presented a seemingly truthful vision of comfort, loyalty, and respectability. Crucially, his image must not have shown him dissenting from his own enslavement. The likeness served as evidence of the comfort and obedience of a specific slave and an illustration of the broader system. Embedded in the image was the implication that a sentimental trip had been taken to the gallery. Embedded in its display were the suggested contours of Edward's slaveholding disposition. As the case of the Pringles illustrates, slave photography both lent visual proof of the benevolence of slavery (as channeled through the well-dressed body of an individual slave) and helped owners to express their humaneness in front of family, friends, and acquaintances by investing time, money, and energy into representing their bondspeople.

What went unspoken in Pringle's letter was how the miniaturization of Mack also enabled Pringle to actualize a long-standing metaphor of southern domination. As William Johnson remembered, his master "used to say, that if we didn't suit him, he would put us in his pocket quick—meaning he would sell us."[100] For enslavers, turning a slave into a photographic object meant the materialization of this fantasy of complete control. They could literally put the (surrogate) bodies of their slaves in their pockets. The cases of early daguerreotypes, ambrotypes, and tintypes further underscored their fusion of domination and intimacy in social settings, as slaveholders might need to undo the latch and open the cover so an acquaintance could see the slave's face and body, skin and clothing. In the case of Mack's image and others, the photographic object actualized possession even as the photographic image envisioned benevolence.

The history of Mack's image—and the broader patterns of production and display it illustrates—revises how we understand the justification of bondage in the late antebellum era. Historians have largely looked to the written and oral arguments of public spokesmen—of politicians, professors, Protestant clergy, and doctors—to understand this justification.[101] Slave photography demonstrates how proslavery proponents supported bondage by drawing upon a new form of market-driven visual culture. Though never mass-produced, enslavers' photographs of enslaved people proved a potent means of self-justification and justification in immediate social circles. This was a rationalization that manifested itself in seemingly mundane photographic acts, such as those of Mary and Edward Pringle, and in the photographs themselves, images that created isolated scenes that severed enslaved people from a social world of violence, as in the case of the ambrotype of Lydia and Charlotte Helen Middleton. As this photographic culture demonstrates, the defense of bondage in the late antebellum era pulsed through and animated everyday life across slaveholding households, as average owners countered abolitionist claims to the debasement of slaves and the degradation of white humanity. Enslavers found in photographs and photographic practices a dynamic new way to make claims about the social fabric of slavery. Increasingly in the late antebellum era, photography enabled them to socially perform and visually package bondage as benevolent.

OWNERS MADE THE ABSTRACTIONS of "slavery" and "mastery" concrete through miniature photographic depictions and social performances. They constructed and enacted a benevolent, intimate form of slavery for themselves and those in their social circles, one that implicitly and explicitly rejected the notion that slaves were viewed and treated as commodities. But slave photography actually constituted a precarious tool of power for southern slaveholders. A photographic portrait also made claims about the identity of the enslaved sitter. The very same portraiture conventions used to convey a humane form of bondage simultaneously implied the individuality and subjectivity of the enslaved sitter—at least in theory. This was the bargain slaveholders made, consciously or not, when commissioning slave portraits. Elevating favored slaves helped owners to rationalize bondage and to perform a benevolent form of mastery, but elevating the slave too much imperiled the ideological foundations of their world. How slaveholders dealt with the implications of slave portraits is partially revealed in written records. Rare diary entries, private letters, and paper notes attached to photograph cases reveal how southern whites articulated what slave photographs conveyed and confirmed. Time and time again, slaveholders sought to define, undercut, and limit slaves' expressions of humanity. Photography created a venue that cast enslavers as the arbiters of enslaved people's social identities.

To start, slaveholders framed these photographs as acts of intimate possession over their slaves, rather than as vessels for slaves' self-expression. This is illustrated by Louis Manigault and Hector. A boatman as well as a favored slave at Gowrie plantation outside Savannah, Hector often traveled to the city to deliver mail and obtain supplies for Manigault.[102] In 1861 Hector posed in the full-length portrait necessary to capture his oar (Figure 1.24). Hector's image was part of the broader genre of "work photography," one that emerged as the daguerreotype became less expensive. It permitted all types of workers to pose with their tools, as in the case of Isaac Jefferson, a free blacksmith and the former slave of Thomas Jefferson, whose apron, hammer, bare arms, and exposed chest signified his labor (Figure 1.25). Hector might have taken a pride in his image similar to that which Jefferson took: the oar that dominates the picture suggests the geographic mobility prized by enslaved boatmen; the newspaper suggests how Louis Manigault depended upon Hector to bring him news from the outside world. Yet Louis Manigault made sure to assert his control over Hector. As Manigault would later write, "In this picture I had him taken with his paddle in one hand, and a newspaper in the other, with the Gowrie plantation mail-bag over his shoulder."[103] Manigault enveloped Hector's possession within his own authority. Hector could claim "his paddle," but Manigault claimed ownership over Hector and mastery over the photographic process: he framed this photograph as an act of possession. Hector could strike a pose, but this was only a product of his master's bidding.

Manigault's statement outside the photograph gallery likely reflected the power dynamics inside it. In their trade journals, photographers theorized the primacy of the artist in positioning sitters, directing light,

Figure 1.24 *Hector*, 1861, ambrotype, 4 × 6¾ inches. 1999.57.16, courtesy of The Charleston Museum, Charleston, South Carolina.

and placing accessories, but they also related—often in exasperation—their actual attempts to please customers, who demanded certain poses and requested re-sittings when they disliked their pictures. As one daguerrean noted, "People are becoming critical, almost hyper-critical, not necessarily from pure taste, but because good pictures are the rule."[104] Artist-entrepreneurs went to great lengths to cater to this

Figure 1.25 *Isaac Jefferson*, 1847, daguerreotype, 3⅛ × 3⅝ inches. Isaac Jefferson, Memoirs and Daguerreotype, 1847, McGregor Library of American History, Albert and Shirley Small Special Collections Library, University of Virginia.

increasingly discerning and assertive clientele. In *The Photographic and Fine Art Journal*, the Louisville firm Webster & Brother recounted its attempts to please a mother who sought a picture of her small child, depicted standing alone. "Aint the child rather young for that?" Webster asked. The mother retorted, "Why, Willie is nearly fifteen months old, and stands alone *with somebody*, or by a chair, at home, and I am sure you ought to be able to make a likeness of him in that way." Despite his reluctance, Webster proceeded to take the picture as the mother requested; the resulting image was blurry, for the child moved during the taking, and the mother left without purchasing it.[105] Such incidents make clear how the production of the photographic portrait often stood as a negotiation between the artist and the customer. It stands to reason that inside photograph galleries, enslavers such as

Louis Manigault must have enjoyed the power to dictate how their slaves were being represented.

Within the frames, slaveholders placed further limits on slaves' expressive possibilities. Though southern slave photography emerged within the mainstream tradition of early photographic portraiture, it differed in a few crucial respects. In the available photographic archive, slave portraits rarely employed certain common formulas. Enslaved people did not pose with books, the ubiquitous signs of literacy in portraits of white women.[106] They did not touch a hand to the chin in a thinking pose—a posture commonly associated with a romantic and intellectual character. One also finds no pictures of enslaved people holding photographs of their loved ones. This denial of a pose employed often by free people to memorialize a loved one meant the denial of images highlighting the import of black familial ties. Free black men might convey their physical power, as Isaac Jefferson did through a portrait that emphasized his strong chest and brawny forearms, but enslaved men could not strike such a manly pose. Nor, for that matter, are slaves depicted standing on their own, much less standing in a commanding stance. As a commentator in the *American Journal of Photography* put it, a "proud man carries his head erect, a little thrown back, and with a stately air."[107] Low country planter Charles Manigault might gaze beyond the camera, with a hand assertively placed on his hip, in a full-length portrait—elements that worked to convey his elite social stature (Figure 1.26). But Manigault's enslaved gardener Moses sat close to the camera, hands in his lap, gazing to the side (Figure 1.1). In this case and others, artists and masters actively avoided picturing slaves with visual devices that connoted certain attributes, including culture, stature, literacy, interiority, and intellect. These subtle but meaningful decisions channeled slaves down certain expressive pathways while limiting them from the wider array of poses available in freedom. Slave photographs defined the limits of slaves' social identities.

Enslavers also limited enslaved people's self- and cultural expression through the selective hand-coloring of their photographic portraits. Many enslaved women, for instance, posed wearing headwraps, including Mammy Kitty, Rosetta, and Mauma Mollie. Though the origins of the headwrap remain unclear, by the nineteenth century these coverings—also known as bandannas, headscarves, headkerchiefs, or

Figure 1.26 *Charles Manigault*, 1856, ambrotype, 4 × 6¾ inches. 1999.57.14, courtesy of The Charleston Museum, Charleston, South Carolina.

tignons—served many purposes for enslaved women: they maintained clean hair, hid dirty hair, kept braids intact, offered sun protection, and, for fugitives, covered up scars.[108] Moreover, as historians Shane and Graham White suggest, "the often brilliantly colored bandanna or headkerchief offered an alternative means of self-adornment and aesthetic display."[109] Many observers were struck by this vibrancy. Northern journalist Frederick Law Olmsted described the "gay patterns, and becomingly arranged" nature of black women's headwraps in Georgia.[110] Painters such as Eyre Crowe took care to visualize the colorful fabrics of these adornments, as in the case of *Slaves Waiting for Sale, Richmond, Virginia*.[111] While many enslaved women likely posed for cameras in brightly colored bandannas, such articles were routinely left uncolored in the subsequent production process.[112]

After the photographs were finished, slaveholders' rare written commentaries often subtly undercut the respectability that Americans commonly associated with such visually dignified portraits. In 1859, the young Ella Grimball brought her slave Peggy to a Charleston photograph gallery, where Peggy had her portrait taken. As Ella's mother Meta Grimball wrote in her diary, "The old woman looked so much pleased and has really made a very nice one. It is a great gratification to Ella having a likeness of the old woman for she has always been particularly attached to her."[113] Meta Grimball celebrated this photographic outing for suturing the bonds of slavery across race and generation, but she also made sure to undermine Ella's pretensions. Grimball described how Peggy was "quite delighted with her Ambrotype: only time she says that I should like to have 'my picture drawed,' and after looking at it she said 'I is a very markable looking old woman.'"[114] There was a gentle racial humor in Meta's recording of this idiomatic remark; Peggy was at once the respectable adult sitter and the childlike aspirant, an imposter only pretending to acquire bourgeois status. For slaveholders such as Meta Grimball, Peggy could only mimic the air of respectability that taking one's portrait in a Charleston studio connoted.

Grimball was not alone in these perceptions. Narratives of African Americans as comically ignorant of photographic technology proved a continuous source of amusement in nineteenth-century America, perhaps most forcefully presented in the enormously popular theatrical *The Octoroon* (1859). At the beginning of the play, an enslaved character named Paul asks a photographer to "take me in dat telescope." Later on, in the absence of the photographer, a comical scene ensues in which Paul seeks to take the picture of a Native American character named Wahno; when Paul subsequently turns to take his own photograph, he exasperatingly exclaims, "I must operate and take my own likeness too—how debbel I do dat? Can't be ober dar an' here too—I ain't twins."[115] The notion that African Americans could equally partake in the culture of self-possession and respectability that surrounded photographic self-representation struck most antebellum whites as little more than a joke.

Not surprisingly, then, on more than one occasion owners reacted with a mix of affection and humorous condescension as they gazed upon their photographed slaves. Take the case of the Quitman family of Natchez, Mississippi. During the winter of 1846–1847, John Anthony Quitman served as a volunteer general in the Mexican War. A proslavery extremist, Quitman would eventually become the governor of Mississippi. When he traveled to Mexico, he—like many soldiering slaveholders—brought along a trusted house slave, Harry, to perform a variety of menial tasks.[116] Little is known about what Harry felt about the war in which he fought, a war that his master hoped would ensure the future expansion of slavery. We only know he earned his master's praise, as Quitman proclaimed that he could "not speak sufficiently well of this excellent servant. He is invaluable to me."[117]

One day during the war, Quitman sent a photograph of Harry home to Mississippi. He felt that Harry's image would "cause a loud laugh in the kitchen."[118] When she received the image, Quitman's daughter felt similarly, calling Harry's portrait "admirable" and mentioning how it met with "a *good* laugh both in the house + kitchen," perhaps because Harry looked "corpulent."[119] The photograph of Harry offered a touchstone for the Quitmans to perform the paternalist ideal by expressing their bonds with Harry. But equally significant are the ways in which this act was framed as amusing.[120] Quitman's initial letter stands as an exceedingly rare document, for it sheds at least partial light on slaveholding intent. It is not clear why Quitman thought the image would produce a laugh, nor is it clear why those back in Mississippi found it funny. That Harry's image was deemed "admirable" yet also caused "a *good* laugh" tells us, though, how quickly southerners could both elevate and humorously undercut the enslaved sitter. The Quitmans' remarks recall Edward Pringle's reaction to the portrait of his enslaved butler, Mack. While Pringle lauded the portrait, he also remarked that he had "laughed over him a dozen times." As Pringle further exclaimed, "How natural the old fellow looks!" To Pringle, Mack served as little more than an imposter who could never actually achieve the respectability, dignity, and full personhood that the portrait implied.[121] Mack could be so well dressed only because the Pringle family had dressed him that way, unlike the free laborers in California. In these subtle ways owners differentiated between themselves and their most favored slaves, lending weight to one of Hegel's key insights. As Hegel wrote, "The distinctive difference of anything is rather the boundary, the limit, of the subject; it is found at that point where the subject matter stops, or it is what this subject-matter is *not*."[122] Through letters that framed the production of slave photographs, visual restraints within the photographs, and comments and gestures as the photographs were displayed, slaveholders such as the Pringles and Quitmans defined and fortified the boundaries that divided slave from free.

Masters could never completely master the meanings of slave photographs, though. The very mechanical nature of photography that lent slaveholders such as Edward J. Pringle the veneer of evidentiary proof simultaneously required slaves to pose for cameras. Unlike letters and diaries, speeches and pamphlets, photography required the enslaved person to actually take part in the production. No evidence conveys the extent to which slaves had a say in the various aspects of the photographic process—from the clothing they wore to their postures and facial expressions. Enslaved people might have seen this as another moment of domination and drudgery, but some must have taken pleasure in their depictions, even if they could not control the resulting image. Recall how Meta Grimball described how Peggy was "quite delighted with her Ambrotype: only time she says that I should like to have 'my picture drawed,' and after looking at it she said 'I is a very markable looking old woman.'"[123] The description reveals Meta's condescending attitude toward Peggy, but embedded in Meta's recounting is Peggy's own deep pride and satisfaction in her looks. Or consider how Harry might have felt when his master John Quitman sent his portrait home to Mississippi. The week before, Quitman had told his wife that "Harry begs to be remembered to you and all the children + servants."[124] Insofar as this photograph reached those Harry did hope to connect with, he may have taken satisfaction in it. Though the evidence from slaves' perspectives is scant, it is possible that slave photographs promoted enslaved people's sense of self-possession and worth even as they solidified the imaginative divide in slaveholders' minds.

Every slave portrait, no matter how benevolent it seemed, could be used as a tool to police slaves' movement. This point is illustrated by the case of Dolly, a washer and a cook at the Manigaults' Silk Hope Plantation, just outside Charleston, and at Gowrie. When the Civil War came, Dolly labored for her mistress Fannie Manigault in safer inland terrain in Augusta, Georgia, but on April 7, 1863, she took flight.[125] Her master Louis quickly responded, circulating at least two fugitive advertisements in Charleston and Augusta (Figures 1.27 and 1.28). The advertisements laid bare only part of what Louis Manigault felt he knew about Dolly. They described Dolly's appearance in detail: "thirty years of age," "light complexion," "rather good looking, with a fine set of teeth." Manigault considered one personality trait worth mentioning: she "hesitates somewhat when spoken to." The ads also suggested Dolly had been "enticed off by some White Man." But in private, Manigault and the overseer at Gowrie, William Capers, discussed how they actually suspected Dolly had run off with an enslaved man named Lewis, a bellhop at the L. L. Hotel in Augusta.[126] It is entirely possible, particularly given the mention that Dolly was "rather good looking," that Manigault had enjoyed or sought sexual relations with Dolly. This could help to explain why he was willing to use various means to catch Dolly but was unwilling to reveal that she had left with an enslaved man.

These means included the use of Dolly's carte de visite, commonly made by the dozen. Manigault's innovation in policing tactics reflected an emergent understanding of the draconian possibilities of photography across the country. An 1860 *New York Times* article suggested that "daguerreotype likenesses of servant girls" could help employers find servants who had stolen from them and absconded.[127] In the South, Manigault had updated fugitive slave ad technology—which had long used generic, crude woodcuts of slaves, often holding a satchel of goods on a stick. His private correspondence, moreover, reveals that he felt the very qualities of portability, transparency, and individuality that made slave photographs windows onto seemingly consenting slaves also made them useful tools to identify fleeing slaves. "Will you be kind enough to show the following to my father who will stick it up at the Police Station + take all necessary

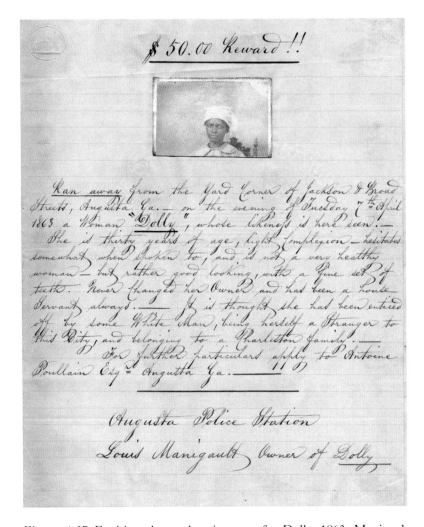

Figure 1.27 Fugitive slave advertisement for Dolly, 1863. Manigault Plantation Journal, p. 179, Manigault Family Papers #484, The Southern Historical Collection, Wilson Library, The University of North Carolina at Chapel Hill.

steps," Manigault asked a contact in Charleston. He highlighted how a "similar notice is at the Augusta Police Office, with likeness, which is very important in such cases. This woman left during my absence to the plantation and took with her an ample wardrobe of her own clothes."[128] Manigault knew that Dolly's "ample wardrobe" could

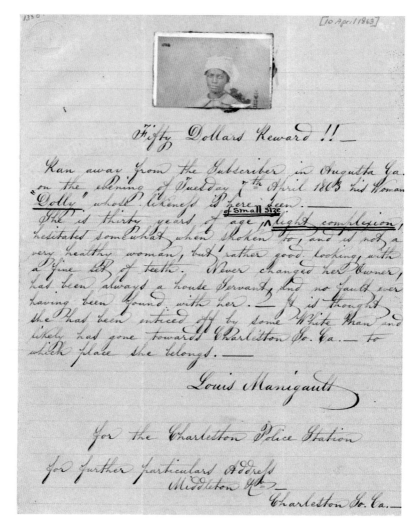

Figure 1.28 Fugitive slave advertisement for Dolly, 1863. From the Manigault Family Papers, South Caroliniana Library, University of South Carolina.

easily defeat the typical slave ads, which mentioned only what a runaway was wearing on departure. The photograph, however, captured Dolly's face.

Manigault's photographic want ads suggest that slave photographs could be both benevolent and possessive, intimate and draconian, at the same time. Clearly, a slaveholder such as Louis Manigault would have seen how the image could serve both purposes when he commissioned it. His small mention that the likeness "is very important in such cases" indicates that photographic identification had likely become a common practice in the South Carolina and Georgia low country, perhaps even across the South. The photograph would have helped illiterate whites to recognize the slave without needing to read a paragraph about the fugitive's markings, clothes, and character. Surely this double function grew increasingly desirable for Manigault and other owners during the tumultuous years of the Civil War, when slaves escaped by the thousands, and became increasingly manageable after the arrival of the carte de visite in 1859, which allowed customers to purchase multiple lightweight paper portraits in one sitting.[129] Further, the paper carte de visite, unlike contemporaneous metal and glass photographs, could be easily attached to a poster. All that is known about Dolly subsequently is that she was not captured, making her the only Manigault slave to ever escape Gowrie for good without being irreparably injured in the process.[130] Dolly's personal revolt elicited the latent, authoritative possibilities of the slave portrait, making evident how vital photography had become for slave owners to mark not only the imaginative divide between slaves and non-slaves but occasionally the very geographical boundaries as well.

PHOTOGRAPHY PROVED A FLEXIBLE TOOL of power for slaveholders. Within individual and interracial photographs, and through the exchange and display of such images, they cast their regime as a benevolent world of interracial intimacy and harmony, run by paternalist masters who treated their slaves as people, not property. At the core of this visual landscape was the chattel Madonna, an image that oriented the eye toward the religiosity, domesticity, and tenderness of bondage—and away from its violence and commodification. This sentimental intimacy was seen in miniaturized visions of the people that stood for the world slaveholding families sought to preserve. Slave photographs gave masters potent tools to materialize "slavery" and "mastery" in visual and social form.

But these images also represented a delicate and dangerous bargain. A photograph that enlisted the individuality of a slave came with threatening implications for what it said about that enslaved person's character and social potential. Owners ran the risk of casting their slaves, especially those most favored slaves, as whole people. Surely there was never any grand scheme by slaveholders across the South to use photography as a way of denying blacks full personhood. But visual and written evidence testifies to the subtle ways in which slaveholders solved the dilemma of the slave portrait by barring slaves from certain poses and the associations of those poses. In effect, slave photography placed full personhood beyond the grasp of enslaved people, at least in the eyes of southern masters. The double-edged sword of slave photography lies in how it gave slaveholders evidence of their humaneness while restricting slaves from expressing and confirming their whole humanity.

In the process, slaveholders altered the informal political landscape of the South. While many Americans were infatuated with getting their photographic portraits taken in the 1840s and 1850s, slaveholders put the studio portrait to new uses. Whether one looks to photographic self-justification (Annie Middleton), propaganda (Edward Pringle), or surveillance (Louis Manigault), it is abundantly clear that enslavers had transformed photography into a powerful—though largely private and semi-public—means of maintaining racial ideology and social order. As the cheapness and availability of photography enabled all enslavers to become photographic practitioners, they developed a quiet habit of domination: the routine use of personal photographs to defend exploitation and build white supremacist networks. They made vernacular, mechanical image-making central to southern white supremacist culture. Ironically, slaveholders' keen interest in photographing their slaves surely catalyzed enslaved people's desires to obtain their own views.

2

ENDURING IMAGES

"THE WALL OVER THE FIREPLACE was adorned with some very brilliant scriptural prints, and a portrait of General Washington, drawn and colored in a manner which would certainly have astonished that hero, if ever he had happened to meet with its like."[1] Although this passage could have easily described many white parlors in the mid-nineteenth century, it actually depicted the most famous slave home in antebellum America: Uncle Tom's cabin in Harriet Beecher Stowe's 1852 novel. Stowe offered a domestic image of bondage that would have been thoroughly familiar to her primarily northern, white, middle-class audience.[2] But her depiction only partially conveyed the realities of late antebellum slave life. Stowe could envision slaves using popular patriotic and decorative images that memorialized national leaders and enlivened their cabin walls. She was unable, however, to envision enslaved people buying, obtaining, and exchanging photographs—with their own money and of their own volition. In the hands of Stowe, as in those of American historians, this visual world has remained invisible.[3]

For some enslaved people, photography generated new ways to reject their status as commodities and to constitute family ties. Those who acquired photographs did so in a society governed by the chattel principle, which viewed slaves as people and property, and amidst a flourishing internal slave trade, which sold approximately two million

people between 1820 and 1860 and broke up roughly one-half of all enslaved families.[4] This trade expanded slavery from its origins along the
eastern seaboard to the Lower South states of Alabama, Mississippi,
Louisiana, and Texas. For enslaved people, the trade produced
persistent uncertainty—since a downturn in the market or a master's
death could abruptly lead to sale and removal—as it created isolation,
loneliness, and longing.[5] In this context, acts of photographic representation and contemplation allowed enslaved people to see themselves
through their own eyes and take pleasure in their bodies. And when a
family member was sold, slaves used photographs as a matter of course,
just as whites did when family members moved away. The stakes were
of course higher for enslaved African Americans, who could not look
forward to future reunions as whites could. Photographs were prized
possessions for many whites; for enslaved people they were an essential
means of building identity, keeping a loved one's memory from fading,
and even, at times, reconnecting with those loved ones.[6]

Through photography, some enslaved people nurtured a new, quiet
habit of endurance and resistance on the eve of the Civil War. While no
public archive holds a photograph that was clearly commissioned by an
enslaved person, written records reveal bondspeople as photographic
practitioners and illuminate the social functions and meanings of photographs. Slave narratives, newspapers, and photographers' records demonstrate that slaves received images from sold family members in the
mail, stowed images of sold family members in their cabins, and carried
those images on their person. Photography was in many ways uniquely
suited to the task of offsetting social and geographic instability. While its
portability offered the capacity for linking lives across distance and for
keeping and concealing unique mementos, its visuality made literacy
unnecessary for communication. As slaves lacked control over the mobility of their bodies and the categorical breakdown of these bodies into
marketplace values, photography constituted a new mechanism to project and confirm full personhood and to endure the threat and actuality
of constant separation. In photography, enslaved people harnessed the
South's image marketplace to endure the slave marketplace.

——

BEFORE SLAVEHOLDERS BEGAN MAKING PHOTOGRAPHS of their
slaves in the 1840s, slaves had actually spent decades observing their

owners' images. While masters' landscape and portrait paintings of the eighteenth and early nineteenth centuries rarely pictured bondspeople as central subjects, these images did not go unnoticed. When enslaved people entered the wealthiest masters' homes they stepped into virtual galleries; some remembered the pictures. An early account appears in Olaudah Equiano's remembrance of bondage in mid-eighteenth-century Virginia. Not long after being shipped from West Africa to Virginia by way of Barbados, Equiano found himself gazing at a portrait in his master's bedroom as he fanned the "unwell" man. The portrait "appeared constantly to look at me, I was still more affrighted, having never seen such things as these before," Equiano recounted. "At one time I thought it was something relative to magic; and not seeing it move I thought it might be some way the whites had to keep their great men when they died, and offer them libations as we used to do our friendly spirits." For Equiano, portraiture furthered a sense that Virginians were "all made up wonders."[7]

By the nineteenth century, however, the tradition of Western portraiture was no longer simply wondrous, strange, and animate in enslaved people's eyes. As Frederick Douglass recalled upon leaving Colonel Lloyd's plantation to return to Baltimore, "I had the strongest desire to see Baltimore. Cousin Tom…had inspired me with that desire by his eloquent description of the place. I could never point out any thing at the Great House, no matter how beautiful or powerful, but that he had seen something at Baltimore far exceeding, both in beauty and strength, the object which I pointed out to him. Even the Great House itself, with all its pictures, was far inferior to many buildings in Baltimore."[8] Disdain and admiration were not mutually exclusive for Douglass, whose perception of grandeur manifested itself in image consumption as well as urban spectatorship. Meanwhile, Daphne Williams, a slave in Florida, remarked that in her mistress's house, "they have they ownself painted in pictures on the wall, jus' as big as they is. They have them in big frames like gold. And they have big mirrors from the floor to the ceilin'. You could see your ownself walk in them."[9] Mirrors displayed in slaveholders' homes gave both whites and blacks the opportunity for self-scrutiny. Paintings, moreover, forged a common viewing experience. Yet the means for self-presentation within paintings—given their cost—divided slave from free in the nineteenth century.

Some masters believed paintings could serve as sentimental touchstones to bridge the cultural gulf that separated blacks and whites. In

1851 John Jones brought a painted portrait of his deceased father, slaveholding patriarch Joseph Jones, back to his plantation home in Liberty County, Georgia. While he displayed the image for white family members, he also beckoned for his slaves to come look. "I called in momma and old Pulaski," John related. Soon thereafter, John left the house, only to return to find Pulaski "bending over the picture in a most solemn attentive manner." According to John, a weeping Pulaski later remarked, "We are so thankful that you brought old master to see us." Pulaski was one of the many enslaved people who gazed at his deceased master's portrait that day, but the story, recounted by John, goes much further in revealing white perceptions of black understandings of portraiture than it does in illuminating slaves' actual perceptions. John related how the slaves "all evinced in a very quiet manner a remarkable degree of veneration and affection for their deceased master."[10] He cherished the loyalty and affection his slaves seemed to show his father. To John, the portrait extended a benevolent bond between master and slave well beyond the master's death.

Slaveholders also found ways to employ images as disciplinary devices. Two recollections of slaves describe how masters sought to use personal portraits to supervise bondspeople in the plantation household. Recalling his teenage years, Francis Fedric related how his "mistress was anxious to teach me to pick some wool. 'You must pick it very quickly,' she said. 'Your master's brother will watch you, and tell me if you don't.'" Fedric described how the mistress "placed me in a room where my master's brother's portrait hung on the wall. 'There he is,' she said, 'looking at you. Now, mind, you must pick away as fast as you can. Don't stop, or he will come and tell me.'" Fedric detailed how he approached the wall and touched the image, at which point his mistress returned and immediately flogged him as punishment. "She was no doubt annoyed that I had found out she was fooling me," Fedric noted. "When working within sight of the picture afterwards, I would say, 'I's not going to work. You don't know nothing. They don't give us nothing.'"[11]

Published in 1863, Fedric's story seems at first a fabrication invented to present the stifling power of a slaveholding mistress. But in the 1930s, former slave Julia Blanks remembered a similar incident from the antebellum era: "When my aunt would go to clean house, she (Mrs. Wilcox) would turn all the pictures in the house but one, the meanest looking one—you know how it always looks like a picture is watching you every where you go—and she would tell her if she touched a thing or left a bit of dirt or if she didn't do it good, this picture would tell."[12] As it seems unlikely that Blanks would concoct such a specific and unusual story, her recollection likely indicates the great lengths whites went to in order to extend their visual authority through the watchful eyes of portraits. Perhaps owners had grasped the wonder with which Africans such as Olaudah Equiano first experienced Western portraiture and sought to turn those perceptions against them. At the very least, these stories can be seen as slaves' and former slaves' revelations of surveillance as an unremitting practice in the plantation household.

Long spectators (and perhaps even targets of surveillance) in the master's gallery, antebellum slaves also constituted an audience for religious images. Christian iconography served as an important visual aid for the white missionaries who, especially after the 1830s, sought to convert and instruct slaves as part of a broader movement to preserve the "peculiar institution" by reforming it. At missionary gatherings, Charles Colcock Jones, an influential Presbyterian minister in Liberty County, Georgia, supplemented hymns and prayers with "scripture cards." Produced by the American Sunday School Union, these large posters showed scenes ranging from Adam and Eve to Noah's Ark to the Tower of Babel. Jones portrayed a common ocular-centric disposition when he declared the usefulness of these images: sight, he argued, "greatly assists the memory."[13] A tool of instruction within bondage, religious imagery also served as a means to represent missionary work to outsiders, as this stereograph (a form popular among middle-class consumers) illustrates (Figure 2.1). The Charlestonian photographic duo of Osborn and Durbec made the image at a slave chapel in the Sea Islands south of Charleston.[14] They constructed a scene that stressed the black subjects' attentiveness to the crucifixion.

Most didacticism went unpublicized. While slaveholding women such as Francis Fedric's mistress used personal images as visual scare tactics to deter misdeeds, they supplemented this practice with rituals of religious image consumption with an eye toward maintaining domestic control. As one former bondswoman recalled of her enslavement in Texas, "On Sunday mornings before breakfast our Mistress

Figure 2.1 *Plantation No. 7, Rockville Plantation Negro Church, Charleston,*
S.C., c. 1860, by Osborn and Durbec, stereograph. Civil War Collection,
Stereograph Cards Collection, Prints and Photographs Division, Library
of Congress, LC-DIG-stereo-1s03923.

would call us together, read de Bible and show us pictures of de Devil
in de Bible and tell us dat if we was not good and if we would steal and
tell lies dat old Satan would git us."[15] Such cautionary images on the
Sabbath made the abstract tangible. Drawing upon biblical pictures,
southern whites enlarged the world of watchful eyes, informing slaves
of the invisible forces, forces no less than the devil himself, that mon-
itored their behavior.

By the late 1830s, then, slaves had served as image viewers in at
least four ways: as casual observers of paintings, as audiences for masters' portraits, as consumers (and objects) of surveillance imagery, and
as subjects of religious instruction. It was in this visual milieu that the
daguerreotype would emerge and reorient enslaved people's relation
to visual culture. It allowed individual bondspeople to become practitioners (not just spectators) of commercial, personal images. Though
nineteenth-century enslaved people crafted visual representations
through such folk arts as quilting and doll-making, the cost of full-
length and miniature painted portraits was prohibitive.[16] Since photographs were far more affordable than paintings and slaves had
access to photo galleries across the South, slaves found ways of taking
part in this broader practice of commodified visual self-representation.
Their active participation reveals that the leveling effects of the

daguerreotype—often seen as opening up portraiture for the middle class and white working class—were far more pronounced than historians of photography have suspected. Some enslaved people adapted their expressive culture amidst this broader transformation in popular visual and consumer culture.

Enslaved people marveled at the first daguerreotypes they encountered. This was not an uncommon reaction to the daguerreotype when artist-entrepreneurs began selling likenesses in the early 1840s. All Americans were struck by the novelty of the image, not only because it seemed *"infinitely* more accurate" than paintings, as poet Edgar Allan Poe put it, but also because of its reflective qualities.[17] The actual image, on a silver-coated copper plate, is difficult to discern unless the light hits it at a forty-five-degree angle.[18] Otherwise, the daguerreotype operates more like a mirror than a portrait, allowing the viewer to see oneself in the image. Enslaved people must have experienced this sensation, and it is possible that a few bondspeople in New Orleans might have even gazed upon the first daguerreotype made in the city. At least slaveholder Eliza Ripley thought so. As Ripley recalled,

> *I think I can safely say I possess the first daguerreotype ever taken in New Orleans. An artist came there about 1840 and opened a studio (artist and studio sound rather grand when one views the work to-day). That studio was at the corner of Canal Street and Exchange Alley. The artist needed some pictures of well-known men for his showcase, so he applied to my father, who was of the "helping hand" variety. And dear Pa was rewarded with the gift of a picture of himself all done up in a velvet-lined case, which he brought home to the amazement and wonder of every member of the family, white and black.*[19]

The very novelty of this new technology put all on the same playing field, as both white and black, free and enslaved, looked together with "amazement and wonder" at this entrancing new type of portrait, bound in a velvet case. Such viewing experiences must have stoked enslaved people's desires to obtain their own pictures.

Urban slaves (and rural slaves hired out in cities) undoubtedly had the easiest access to photographs. The conditions of bondage in cities such as Baltimore, Richmond, and Charleston gave these slaves greater freedom of movement and more cash in their pockets. Likewise, photographic galleries were concentrated in cities. In fact, black abolitionist photographer James Presley Ball remembered selling photographic portraits to slaves in a gallery very close to the Virginia state capitol in Richmond in 1846. As Ball remarked, "Virginians rushed in crowds to [my] room; all classes, white and black, bond and free sought to have their lineaments, stamped, by the artist who painted with the Sun's rays."[20] Evidently these enslaved sitters required no clandestine means to purchase daguerreotypes in mid-1840s Richmond. They sat and posed for documents that captured their "lineaments," the distinctive visual qualities of the face. Capturing the specificity of one's external form, especially the face, was a process by which antebellum photographers such as J. P. Ball typically sought to reveal the interiority of the sitter. The images that resulted were undoubtedly a new type of consumer good for slaves.

Slaves may have also bought portraits from the most prominent white urban studio daguerreans in the South. The logbook of artist George Smith Cook offers a window into this image consumption in early 1850s Charleston. While Cook spent the mid- to late 1840s traveling through Mississippi, Alabama, and Georgia, he established a permanent gallery in Charleston in 1849 and worked there until after the Civil War. As he became a leading national artist, Cook continued to photograph slaves at the behest of their masters.[21] But, as his logbook shows, Cook occasionally made daguerreotypes of African Americans who came to his studio unaccompanied by whites, images that ranged in cost from $2.50 to $4.75. Cook's language may reveal clues to these sitters' identities. While in November 1849 Cook recorded images of "two colored ladies," in June 1851 he made a sixth-plate daguerreotype of a "negro girl."[22] Cook may have used the terms "lady" and "girl" simply to designate the relative ages of free black sitters, but he may also have used these terms (as well as "colored" and "negro") to designate free blacks and slaves, respectively.[23] At the very least, his logbook reveals the interracial nature of urban gallery consumption.

Itinerant daguerreans also diminished the divide between enslaved and free, black and white, by linking rural areas with broader patterns of image-taking. The bondspeople of Winchester, Virginia, in the northwestern part of the state, discovered white itinerant

John W. Bear to be a particularly welcoming traveling salesman. Born in Maryland to "poor but respectable parents," Bear spent the 1820s and 1830s as a blacksmith, learning the trade in Ohio. Since 1840 he had made a name for himself as the "Buckeye Blacksmith," a popular stump speaker for the Whig party.[24] Accustomed to the itinerant life-style, familiar with small tools, and seeking a new livelihood, Bear took up daguerreotypy in 1845. He spent the later part of the decade traveling throughout the Northeast and the Upper South, selling images from Boston, Massachusetts, to Alexandria, Virginia, from Wilmington, Delaware, to Chambersburg, Pennsylvania.[25] Bear ar-rived in Winchester, Virginia, in the fall of 1847. As he recalled, "I opened my business here with the fairest prospects that I had ever had. The people had never had a picture taken for less than three dol-lars, so when I hung out my sign at one dollar and a half everybody came to see me."[26] As Bear sold cheap pictures to whites, he adver-tised an especially low rate for the local slaves:

> *In this place I reserved every Friday afternoon for colored people, this seemed to please both white and colored; I also published that slaves would be taken for fifty cents less than others, this made me very popular with them, they came in droves to see me on their day, the white people all agreed that my plan was a good one, so much so that the owners of them willingly gave them time to get their pictures taken, and many of them came with them to see that they got good ones taken.*[27]

By catering to bond and free, Bear sold more than 1,500 photographs in Winchester from the fall of 1847 to the spring of 1848. It is unclear why local slave owners encouraged transactions between their slaves and Bear, though two scenarios seem likely. They might have seen this allowance as an extension of their own benevolence. They might also have seen it as a new way to control slaves' self-presentation and self-definition, explaining why they supervised the portrait sittings, much in the same way that they had long taken it upon themselves to name their slaves.[28] But this much is clear: the mechanization of photography had allowed a blacksmith to turn himself into an image-maker. That very same mechanization allowed him to make portraits cheaply enough to cater to enslaved people. The modernization of portraiture thereby opened up the opportunity for slaves to visually represent themselves, linking their means of expression to the southern marketplace.

Photographs may have proven particularly important for enslaved people in the Chesapeake region as it became a primary exporter of slaves. A main entry point for African slaves in the colonial era, the Chesapeake hit an economic downturn in the late eighteenth century, as decades of tobacco cultivation had sapped its soil of vitality. Masters and traders began selling slaves, or moving with them, to the expanding Upper South (Kentucky and Tennessee) as well as to the Carolinas. At the turn of the nineteenth century, various factors pointed slave coffles increasingly toward the southwest. The invention of the cotton gin (1793) along with the purchase of Louisiana (1803) created a boom in cotton and sugar production. Government wars eradicated the Indian population of these lands, opening up rich agricultural territory for white settlers, who migrated to the new states of Alabama, Mississippi, and Louisiana.[29] In Virginia, masters and slave traders brought enslaved people to Washington, Richmond, and Norfolk, where they then shipped them by land and sea to markets in New Orleans, Natchez, and Mobile. In all, historians estimate that one million slaves were shipped from the Upper to the Lower South between 1790 and 1860.[30]

This constant market of human commodification was a conspicuous element in John Quincy Adams's everyday experience as a slave in Winchester, Virginia. As Adams remembered, Winchester was "one of the handsomest little towns I ever saw," with "some very fine hotels, the best one was called Taylor's Hotel, where all the 'big bugs' stopped; and I will tell you who else stopped there—those great and unthinking gentlemen who called themselves Negro Traders. You could see them walking around with their bags of silver and gold that they had received from selling the poor slaves."[31] The constant sight of slave traders must have played a role in propelling the slaves of Winchester "in droves" to the mobile gallery of John W. Bear. They could obtain portraits to identify loved ones in case of separation.

These likenesses were part of a broader realm of property ownership for nineteenth-century enslaved people.[32] The goods enslaved people purchased ranged widely, from watches, clothing, and bonnets to shovels, fishing hooks, and saddles, from tobacco, coffee, and flour to shoes, handkerchiefs, and even umbrellas.[33] Scholars have found that slaves' consumption took place as "underground" interactions between slaves and non-elite whites as well as public interactions between slaves and white shopkeepers. Moreover, they have found that slaves' internal economy and property ownership transcended the particular labor roles and labor regimes of the South—from house slaves to field hands, from the task system in the South Carolina and Georgia low country to the gang system that thrived across much of the rest of the region.[34] As historian Dylan Penningroth notes, "Slaves buying and selling small items was probably a familiar sight for people in nearly every part of the South before the Civil War."[35]

Although enslaved people as a social class were defined by extreme poverty, they took part in the economy in various ways. At southern markets, it was primarily enslaved women who sold the handicrafts slaves made, and the fruits, vegetables, and staple crops (such as corn) that slaves grew in their own gardens.[36] The overwhelmingly male job of boatman could turn water travel into income. Some boatmen owned their vessels and used them to transport passengers over large and tiny southern tributaries alike.[37] Hiring out one's labor could also reap small rewards, and in 1860 as much as 31 percent of the urban enslaved population (and 6 percent of the rural population) did so.[38] In Upson County, Georgia, slaves could earn 50 cents per day by hiring themselves out to local businesses.[39] Skilled slaves such as carpenters and coopers stood to profit the most; historian Roderick McDonald has shown, for instance, how three enslaved coopers in Louisiana received sums of $19.50, $16, and $8 respectively for exceeding their quotas of barrel and hogshead production.[40] In short, enslaved people's practices of entrepreneurship made the purchase of photographs possible.

It is possible that Juddy Telfair Jackson, an enslaved cook and maid in Savannah, commissioned the daguerreotype she sat for with her granddaughter Lavinia (Figure 2.2). Both Juddy and Lavinia were owned by Mary Telfair, a prominent enslaver in the city, and around 1849 they posed for an image that revealed the striking diversity of enslaved people's clothing. Juddy's headwrap and her plain outfit contrast sharply with Lavinia's stylish hair and polka-dotted dress. The resulting image offers a curious fusion of African American and Euro-American styles that, along with the women's facial expressions

Figure 2.2 *Juddy Telfair Jackson and Granddaughter Lavinia*, photographic copy of c. 1849 daguerreotype. Georgia Historical Society, Archival Material on Deposit from the Telfair Museum of Art, Savannah, Georgia.

and poses, works to individualize these women from two generations of one enslaved family.[41] While no evidence illuminates the creation of the image, we do know that in 1841 Mary Telfair had offered to hire out Juddy as a cook. Telfair wrote that Juddy could be "trusted with your keys at 6 dollars a month pay her out of it one dollar every month for herself."[42] This arrangement would have given Juddy enough money to purchase a daguerreotype with her granddaughter, though it is not clear if Juddy was, in fact, hired out.

The avenues for photographic purchases—from gallery owners and traveling peddlers—fell in line with slaves' broader patterns of consumption. Ex-slave Charles Ball recalled how, in South Carolina and Georgia, "the store-keepers are always ready to accommodate the slaves, who are frequently better customers than any white people; because the former always pay cash, whilst the latter almost always require credit."[43] Sometimes the entrepreneurs came to the slaves. One Canadian traveler observed considerable economic activity between boat peddlers and blacks on a trip down the Mississippi from St. Louis to New Orleans: "The small vessels which, owned by pedlars, pass from plantation to plantation, trading with the negroes principally, taking in exchange the articles which they raise, or when the latter are sold to the boats, offering to their owners the only temptations on which their money can be spent." The traveler observed the sale of goods including "ribbons, tobacco, gaudy calicoes, and questionable whiskey."[44] These exchanges between peddler and slave also included transactions in visual prints. Martha Stuart, a slave on the Black Creek plantation in Louisiana, described how bondspeople "could have pictures on the wall." Stuart further noted how "we could have as many as you want." Slaves would "send off and buy 'em" or purchase such images from "picture men [who] come thru the country."[45] Such itinerants, who passed swiftly and quietly through the southern countryside and along the southern waterways, offered outlets that were more anonymous than shops for slaves to purchase goods of all kinds.

Enslaved people's material acquisitions represented a negotiation that often fit neatly into the material needs and everyday wants of slaves and the efficiency demands of owners. As Dylan Penningroth notes, "Slaveowners stood to save a lot of money because the average cotton plantation spent more than one-fifth of its total output on feeding and clothing the slaves."[46] By purchasing food and drink, housewares and livestock, dresses and shoes, slaves did little to unravel the southern power structure.[47] What deeply concerned southern whites, however, was that slaves would consume antislavery messages through written and visual materials—a concern that grew more pronounced in the late 1820s and 1830s because of the circulation of David Walker's *Appeal* and the abolitionists' postal campaign of 1835. Within this context, slaves' displays of antislavery images could quickly lead to fierce punishment. When Missouri master William Lewis searched the room of his slave Mrs. Jackson, he found "a picture of President Lincoln, cut from a newspaper, hanging in her room." Lewis demanded to know why she had displayed Lincoln's picture. When Jackson responded that "she liked" the portrait, he beat her and ordered a month-long punishment in the slave trader's yard.[48] Possessing decorative commercial prints was generally permissible, it seems, but proudly displaying the likeness of an antislavery politician put enslaved people in peril.

How did photography fit into this negotiation between masters and slaves? Southern whites do not seem to have universally condemned enslaved people's photographic consumption. But during the 1850s acquiring photographs became paradoxically both easier and harder for slaves. On one hand, they found it progressively easier to seek out and afford personal portraits, for the medium had grown from an unusual scientific curiosity in 1839 to a ubiquitous presence by the 1850s. The transition from painting to daguerreotypy had drastically reduced the duration of sitting for one's portrait to as low as an average of fifteen to twenty seconds in the 1850s.[49] Photograph prices dropped across the country, and the number of southern itinerant and gallery photographers increased dramatically. Most slaves would have struggled to purchase a daguerreotype in the mid-1840s, when the average portrait cost $5.00. (There is no evidence that other daguerreans followed John W. Bear in lowering prices to a dollar for slaves.) Even in the average price range, though, some slaves were willing and able to buy "luxury goods." In Louisiana, for example, a slave of Colonel Pugh's had his watch repaired for $3; meanwhile, Elias, a slave on the Gay plantation, paid $3 for a "fine Russian hat" in New Orleans, while another enslaved man paid $4 for two bonnets, perhaps for his daughter and wife.[50] By the mid-1850s, photographers advertised daguerreotypes for 25 cents; by the early 1860s, artists everywhere sold a dozen cartes de visite for a dollar.[51] This drop in prices indirectly legalized the sale of photographs to slaves in some states. In Georgia, for instance, an 1833 law required the master's written permission for a slave to purchase anything costing more than a dollar; by the 1850s, however, this law no longer applied to photographs.[52]

On the other hand, as the sectional crisis intensified in the 1850s, photographic transactions grew increasingly dangerous for bondspeople and the artists who catered to them. This was due, in no small part, to the fact that itinerants offered a key outlet for slaves to buy photographs, and southerners had grown increasingly antagonistic toward all sorts of "Yankee peddlers" traversing the slave states.[53] Suspicions of insurrectionary photographers in their midst might not have been totally unfounded, for in 1860 the *Montgomery Weekly Mail* reported the execution of a southern daguerreotypist who was charged with inciting slaves to revolt against their masters. A short notice in the paper, titled "Another Emissary," described how "a man by the name of Palmer, a daguerrean artist, has been detected at Opelika, Ala., tampering with the slaves of John Smith, (T.) and others, between Opelika and Auburn. He gave several negroes bowie knives, and otherwise attempted to instil into their minds seditious acts. He was detected, pursued, and apprehended, and the proof being positive, *he is to be hung at Auburn to-day!*" For the *Mail*, Palmer was but one of many outside agitators. "Let him swing high and long," the paper declared. "There are many others in the South that should be dealt with in a like manner."[54]

Other times it took little more than a commercial encounter between photographers and slaves to prompt white ire. In May 1859 a daguerreotypist named Robbins was flogged for taking pictures of black subjects in Alabama. As the *Alabama Whig* triumphantly reported,

> *Warning to Evil Doers—We learn from a friend that a Deguarrean Artist, Robbins by name, was found on Sunday last in his room in Warsaw, busily engaged taking pictures for negroes. He was waited on forthwith, summary punishment was dealt out to him with a rope's end, and he was then ordered to pack up his traps and leave instanter. Which request was readily complied with.*[55]

Warsaw was a small river landing on the Tombigbee River in Sumter County, the type of place a floating daguerreotype gallery might stop. Though Robbins might have been an abolitionist, he was probably one of the many southern whites who, despite state laws and local customs, catered to slaves to earn his living.[56] Several factors suggest that the "negroes" to whom Robbins catered on this Sunday by the river were probably slaves. First, in 1860 Sumter County had an enslaved population of 18,091 but only 25 free black people; the black population in the state of Alabama, likewise, was predominately enslaved.[57] Second, the fact that these black customers sought their likenesses on a Sunday was not insignificant. On Sunday, bondspeople, particularly field hands, received time off from work, and they used this time to sell their goods and spend their earnings in town.[58] Third, Robbins's punishment—presumably a whipping with the "rope's end"—reflected laws regarding economic exchanges between whites and slaves in many southern states. In 1857, for instance, the South Carolina legislature had passed a law detailing how a person convicted for a second time for trading with slaves should be given up to thirty-nine lashes for the offense.[59] In general these laws were only partially enforced in the South, suggesting how subversive this transaction must have seemed to the whites in Warsaw. It is not entirely clear whether they found something threatening about photography in particular or whether they would have reacted similarly to any secretive exchange of goods. Nor is it clear whether there were any consequences for the black portrait-seekers. But the violent reaction to Robbins amply demonstrates how photographic transactions between artists and southern blacks—at least in the Deep South states—had grown increasingly controversial and even dangerous by the eve of the Civil War.

Nonetheless, slaves acquired photographs. It is impossible to know how many enslaved people bought and used daguerreotypes, ambrotypes, tintypes, and cartes de visite. Photographic ownership may have grown common for bondspeople in the years prior to and during the Civil War, or at least prevalent enough that most slaves knew other slaves who owned portraits. Yet quantity alone does not signal historical significance. A photographic portrait—which an enslaved person could hold in the palm of her or his hand—offered a visually realistic and portable surrogate of the body amidst the oppressive violence of bondage. Studying the uses and meanings of these photographs reveals the creative ways in which some slaves integrated a new technology into their means of self- and communal definition and preservation.

To be sure, enslaved people invested a landscape of possessions with meaning. They might find pleasure, dignity, and means of self-expression through the hats and watches they purchased, the clothing they made, and the wooden dolls they created.[60] They might beautify their cabin walls with decorative prints, or link themselves to a liberationist social movement in the North with antislavery images.[61] Through the exchange of these and other objects, they might acknowledge and strengthen social bonds. The gifting and preservation of locks of hair could prove a means of remembrance, as in the case of a fugitive from Virginia who kept locks of hair of his wife and children, or in the case of Rose, a low country South Carolina woman who gave her nine-year-old daughter Ashley a lock of hair (along with a dress and three handfuls of pecans) in a cloth seed sack when Ashley was sold.[62] For the enslaved, possessions gave them a means to beautify their everyday lives, find moments of pleasure and dignity, identify with broader political trends, and maintain affective ties.[63]

But the photograph was no ordinary possession. Only photographs testified, as J. P. Ball noted as he pictured enslaved people in Richmond, to their "lineaments." In the antebellum era, picturing the specificity of one's external form was a central goal of photographic portraiture, which theoretically aimed to reveal the inner essence of the sitter, and the face took on particular importance in giving form to that interiority. "The human face is assuredly the most complete symbol of the infinite diversity which presides over the works of creation," one commentary in the *Photographic Art Journal* noted. "Since the world began, nature, who has given birth to hundreds of millions of human beings has never perhaps cast two faces in the same mould."[64] The face was seen as the primary sign of human individuality for many photographic portrait-makers. An ordinary photographic portrait, then, could be an extraordinary object in a slave society. It testified to an enslaved person's individuality in a society that denied her or his full personhood.

Perhaps the closest material possession to the photograph was the mirror. Quantifying slaves' mirror ownership has proven difficult, but archeological work has uncovered mirror glass at plantation sites associated with African Americans, and account books show that enslaved people in Virginia had been purchasing small mirrors from merchants since the late eighteenth century.[65] Like small mirrors, photographs offered the capacity to enjoy and scrutinize one's own body. But what separated the photographic image was its aesthetic permanence and material durability. The leather cases of daguerreotypes and ambrotypes, the resilient metal of the tintype, and the lightweight nature of the paper carte de visite made photographs ideal for exchange in the mail or for safekeeping in one's pocket. Photographs went beyond the practice of self-scrutiny that one might find in the mirror to offer lasting and transportable statements of selfhood.

Enslaved people left behind no evidence detailing the role they played in crafting these visual statements. We are left to wonder how they felt as they arrived at urban galleries or itinerant boats, encountered photographers, requested certain types of pictures, and arranged their bodies to assume certain poses. Itinerant photographer John W. Bear did leave behind an account of the production process in Winchester, Virginia. Though not from an enslaved person's perspective, the anecdote can be used to illuminate the process by which they sat for portraits. As Bear wrote,

> *I had lots of fun with them, no odds how black they were I made their pictures light, this would please them, they would say "bless de Lord it looks just like dis chile," and when a black man and a yellow girl would set together I would throw the largest amount of light on the man so as to make them both as light as possible, this took with them like hot pancakes, and pleased their owners also.*[66]

Did the slaves of northwestern Virginia really appreciate the whitening effects of Bear's daguerreotype portraits, as Bear later claimed? Or did these enslaved people simply acquiesce to what this white photographer (and many of their owners) thought would prove visually pleasing? Bear's recollections do not offer transparent access to enslaved people's perceptions of their photographs. But his words do suggest that by the late 1840s white photographers already perceived that slaves were aware that elements of the photographic process (such as light) could be manipulated to achieve various aesthetic outcomes.

It is unclear where enslaved people kept or hid their pictures after they left the gallery, though archeological excavations of cabins have revealed that they hid a range of other possessions—including coins, buttons, and mirrors—in their cabin walls, and that some constructed shelves to hold small objects, such as musical instruments.[67] Written evidence more readily reveals practices of exchange. Photography offered new ways, amidst the persistent social disruptions of bondage, for some slaves to maintain familial and communal ties. Evidence from slave narratives and abolitionist records illustrates how photography gave slaves a new form of cultural mobility—the ability to transcend one's bodily immobility through the transport of images—to communicate. In one sense, mailing photographs was an extremely common practice, by which all Americans sought to reduce the physical and emotional distance between loved ones. As the increased mobility that accompanied industrialization and urbanization in the North and national expansion to the West encouraged this practice, so too did the market conditions of slavery.[68] In a slave society sustained through forced mobility, which rendered all social ties permanently fragile, photographs produced networks of visual recognition amongst the enslaved.

Slave narratives and rare slave letters suggest that bondspeople sought the virtual gaze photography offered. *Louisa Picquet, the Octoroon: or Inside Views of Southern Domestic Life* (1861) published one such letter, written from Elizabeth Ramsey, still in slavery in Texas, to her free daughter Louisa Picquet in Cincinnati. As the letter concluded, "I want you to hav your ambrotipe taken also your children and send them to me I would giv this world to see you and my sweet little children."[69] It is unclear whether Ramsey actually wrote this request for an ambrotype portrait herself. The editor of the narrative quickly assumed "some white person" had written it. Other evidence, however, indicates this was a common sentiment for slaves. Separated by sale, one enslaved daughter told her mother in a letter, "I want to see you very bad and you to rite to me."[70] As with any person distant from loved ones in the antebellum era, slaves longed for the surrogate presence of portraits. But theirs must have been a particularly powerful desire, since they were ripped from friends and family and thrust into new communities of strangers.

Sending pictures inside letters was possible after 1845, but for slaves such exchanges involved the use of the mail, which in turn required the help of a master, mistress, or some other southern white.[71] An ex-slave-turned-Union-soldier from Kentucky, Aaron Oats, sent a letter back to his wife, Lucrethia, with a picture of himself during the war, but Lucrethia never received the image. Oats would later hear from the owner, who described Oats's correspondence as "insolent" and made clear to Oats that "Lucretia don't belong to you."[72] In such cases, it seems, an authoritative master stood in the way of black visual communication. On other occasions the breakdown was unclear. For example, a slave named Owen, a blacksmith and wheelwright living in Clear Springs, near Hagerstown, Maryland, was separated from his wife and son at a Baltimore slave market. Once she was sold, as black abolitionist William Still described, Owen "sent her his likeness and a dress; the latter was received, and she was greatly delighted with it, but he never heard of her having received his likeness."[73] Since a photograph sent was no guarantee of a photograph received, photographic mobility could sometimes only compound the sense of distance.

On occasion, however, slaves successfully used photographs to bridge the divide wrought by the auction block. Take the story of John Quincy Adams, mentioned earlier in this chapter, who detailed a photographic exchange on the eve of the Civil War. In 1857 Adams's twin brother, Aaron, and his sister Sallie were sold away from Winchester. Adams related how he was especially sad to have lost his twin: "If I could just die to get rid of my sorrow and distress, I would be satisfied. I could do no good, but suffered day and night for months and years." Adams would not hear from his sister again, but he did eventually regain contact with Aaron, who had been sold seven more times before finally ending up as a house slave in Memphis. Around 1859, Aaron wrote to his family, and Adams told of the surprise he, his oldest brother, and his father felt in receiving this letter. "What a rejoicing time we had that Sunday," he recalled. Since all were illiterate (Adams's father and oldest brother "could read print, but not writing"), they found a friend to read the letter and to reply to Aaron. Soon thereafter, Aaron sent Adams another letter as well as "his picture," which was almost certainly a photograph, given the popularity and affordability of the medium.[74] Though photographic consumption and slave sales occurred across the South, it stands to reason that the circulation of Aaron Adams's photograph was typical: the exchange of slaves' photographs mirrored the geographic thoroughfares of slave trafficking, reconstituting family ties over the same pathways that had broken them.

The exchange between Adams and his twin shows how photographic mobility initiated a new form of communication between distant slaves. Historian Phillip Troutman has documented the select population of literate slaves who, separated by sale, used letters to maintain connections and to commiserate over their fate.[75] Photographs emerged within this tradition but also broadened it, for they made reading and writing skills irrelevant. Though the South never enacted a comprehensive ban on slave reading, a volatile mix of internal and external threats, including Nat Turner's shocking Virginia rebellion in 1831 and the infiltration of northern literature such as David Walker's incendiary *Appeal to the Colored Citizens of the World* (1829), led to a series of restrictive measures initiated by southern states in the early 1830s; Virginia, North Carolina, South Carolina, and Georgia banned the instruction of slaves until 1865.[76] Historians estimate that less than 25 percent of the enslaved population acquired reading skills, and an even smaller percentage (5 percent or less) learned how to write.[77] Such measures deeply divided enslaved from free when it came to the means for acquiring knowledge and for communicating with each other through the written word. These barriers further tied literacy to a sense of pride for the slaves who could achieve it. The less obvious result of literacy curbs was that they made visual communication more important to slaves. Though John Quincy Adams and his family members could not read the letter written by Aaron, they required no special skills for viewing his image.

But why would southern whites allow bondspeople to send photographs in the first place? The novelty of photography may have contributed to a lack of consensus over how it might influence and potentially undermine the slaveholding regime. Judging by the photographic practices of owners, many whites clearly saw the studio photograph as a powerful means of documentation and expression. Some masters, though, must have seen photographs as harmless, allowing their slaves to exchange them in the same manner that they let slaves write letters to each other. Furthermore, slave owners might have actually seen these photographic exchanges as humane substitutes for releasing their slaves, as *Louisa Picquet, the Octoroon: or Inside Views of Southern Domestic Life* reveals. *Louisa Picquet* tells the story of how Elizabeth Ramsey, her daughter Louisa Picquet, and Louisa's brother John were separated at the slave auction in Mobile, Alabama, in the 1840s. Louisa was sold to a master in New Orleans, while Elizabeth and John were sold to a slaveholder south of Houston, Texas. When Louisa's master died, Louisa gained her freedom and moved to Cincinnati. After searching for her mother for over a decade, Louisa finally located Elizabeth in 1859 and wrote her a letter. She soon received a response. Elizabeth detailed how her master, Col. Horton, would sell her for $1,000 and would sell Louisa's brother John for $1,500.[78]

This letter initiated a string of letters and photographic exchanges between Louisa, Elizabeth, and Elizabeth's master. Louisa wrote back to Elizabeth, enclosing a daguerreotype of herself and asking her mother to send photographs northward. (Louisa might have commissioned her own portrait from James Presley Ball, who had relocated to Cincinnati by the 1850s.) Louisa also wrote to Horton, the owner, asking him to sell her mother, Elizabeth, for a lower price. Horton refused, declaring, "You know that she is as fine a washer, cook, and ironer as there is in the United States." Horton would not cut the cost for Elizabeth's freedom, and as he would later reveal, he would not sell Louisa's brother John for any price. Yet Horton did allow this family to "see" each other. In his letter to Louisa, Horton made sure to mention that "your mother received yours in a damaged condition." He also remarked, "I send you by this mail a Daguerreotype likeness of your mother and brother, which I hope you will receive.…Your mother and all your acquaintance are in fine health, and desire to be remembered, and would be pleased to see you."[79] It is not hard to grasp how these images, in Horton's mind, served as substitutes for actually releasing Elizabeth and John. He would allow surrogate bodies to travel northward, but the real enslaved bodies would remain in slavery.

Although slaves likely exchanged photographs through the accommodating hands of southern whites, they also took such exchanges into their own hands, sending and receiving portraits during dramatic moments of resistance. Not surprisingly, the desire to visually communicate by image did not stop at slavery's edge. In September 1849, for instance, the *Liberator* republished a report by the *Cincinnati Commercial* that detailed how "a runaway negro, who had made his way to an interior town in Indiana, went to a daguerreotypist to have his likeness taken to send to his lady love." This daguerrean had seen advertisements for the runaway slave and offered to help the fugitive travel safely to the Northeast. After the two men boarded a boat, the daguerrean promptly tricked the fugitive. While he had claimed they would travel to Pennsylvania, he actually ferried them both to Kentucky, where the daguerrean sold the fugitive back to his old master for a tidy profit.[80] Despite the tragic ending, this story reveals how by the end of the 1840s slaves had started to conceive of photography as a way to endure self-enacted social separations.

If the portability and visuality of the photograph made long-distance communication possible, then the possession of a familial portrait could prove crucial to establishing identity. This practice of photographic identification allowed former slave and pastor J. Sella Martin to redeem his sister and her two children from slave traders in Covington, Kentucky, in 1862:

> *I had written to T. J. Martin, Esq., who was one of my earliest and most faithful friends, asking him to act as my agent in buying my sister and her children, as he had promised to take them into his employ; and he very kindly consented to do so. I wrote to him, also, should he get to Cincinnati before me, to go over to Covington, a place opposite Cincinnati, on the Kentucky side of the river to where the traders brought my relatives, and get their ambrotypes, so that I should not be cheated in buying others than my sister and her children. He did so, and when I got them, finding by the likenesses that those were the ones I wanted, there was nothing left me to do but to count him out two thousand dollars in gold, and he went over to Covington and made the purchase.*[81]

In Martin's case, an ambrotype could prove the identity of a distant loved one. He could ensure he was purchasing the right people out of bondage without actually taking a risky trip back into the slave South. A photograph could also help to prove one's own identity in person, as revealed in the slave narrative *Running a Thousand Miles for Freedom; Or, The Escape of William and Ellen Craft from Slavery*. The narrative is well known for its striking escape story. In the late 1840s, Ellen Craft, a light-skinned bondswoman, posed as a southern master and, accompanied by her husband, William Craft, passing as her "slave," traveled from bondage in Macon, Georgia, to freedom in Philadelphia. Less well known is another incident in the narrative involving Ellen Craft's relatives that occurred before Ellen and William took flight. After their master died suddenly, Ellen Craft's aunt and her children were sold to different masters at a slave auction. Two of these children, Frank and Mary, eventually escaped their new master, found their way to Savannah, and located two other siblings, a little brother and sister, in Georgia. At first Frank tried to buy his siblings' freedom. When these efforts failed, he sought to maintain contact by visiting them in disguise "as a white man," cutting his hair, wearing a wig and glasses, and donning "large whiskers and moustachios."[82] When Frank arrived to meet his sister, however, he "had so completely disguised or changed his appearance that his little sister did not know him, and would not speak till he showed their mother's likeness; the sight of which melted her to tears,—for she knew the face."[83] In the shadowy borderland between slavery and freedom, where disguises proved crucial to escape and survival, the photographic portrait had a particularly powerful connotation of true identity.[84] Expressive pictures, for slaves and fugitives, doubled as tools of identification.

Photographs testified to a slave's identity and human ties; they also helped slaves preserve those connections. The flight of Stephen Jordon reveals how much care slaves took to keep portraits of sold loved ones, illuminating a transition in slave culture toward a more visual, material, and consumer-oriented form of remembrance. When Jordon's master (who was also his biological father) went broke, Jordon was sold to a nearby plantation, while his mother was sold to a New Orleans merchant. Jordon had a wife on a neighboring plantation, but his new master forced him to live with a new woman. This indignity led Jordon to run away. In his preparations for escape, Jordon forged a set of "free papers" (documents proving non-slave status) from a free black man who lived nearby. He would use these, if ever caught, to "get off all right."[85] Yet in the crucial hours before his planned departure, it was not simply the practical words on a page that Jordon hid away. As he recalled, "I took those papers and stowed them away in a secret place in my cabin, together with my mother's picture and my own picture, which was taken when we belonged to Mr. Jordon, my first old master, together with some old passes, books, and papers."[86]

Jordon did not elaborate further on the origins or later uses of these images. They may have served a practical function for him. He may have seen his mother's picture as a precious document that could help the dispersed family reconnect—which, in fact, the family did after the Civil War. But these images were surely more than just visual information to Jordon, based on the care he took to keep both his mother's and his own image in such a dramatic moment. They may have served as emboldening visions, images of dignity that Jordon sought to realize more fully by fleeing. Surely such visual mementos also shaped his own lived experience of time. He remembered how at least his picture "was taken when we belonged to Mr. Jordon, my first old master." These images gave Jordon many things, not least of which was a specific and material marker of a "before" and "after" amidst the uncertainties of past and future in bondage and in escape. Photographs marked particular points in enslaved people's lives as they simultaneously linked and memorialized family members severed by the slave trade. They testified to the timeline of one's own life as they helped one remember someone else.

Slaves such as Stephen Jordon, Owen, and the Adams twins did not describe the look of their photographic portraits in any detail. But one enslaver's letter makes clear that by the mid-1850s enslaved people were familiar with the convention of evaluating a photographic portrait to discern information about the sitter. In January 1856 mistress Ann B. Archer wrote a letter to her husband, Richard T. Archer, from Anchuca, their 1,200-acre plantation in Mississippi.[87] Ann took care to describe the daguerreotypes she had just received of her daughters Mary and Anna Maria, who were away at boarding school in Philadelphia, detailing the moment she received the images:

> *Marys was opened (unintentionaly) first. It is a very good*
> *likeness of her when distressed, and I thought tears stood in her*
> *eyes when it was taken. Most of the servants first remark was*
> *"Miss Mary does not look well." "She does not look satisfied."*
> *I listened to their remarks with interest to see how like my feelings*
> *(in regard to the expression of her face) theirs were. I took care*
> *they should not know what I thought before they made their*

> *remarks. Most said of Anna Maria "She does not look like herself she does not look pleased." They said "she looked cold besides looking disturbed." My opinion of hers was she looked distressed + confused and as if she felt cold.*[88]

Ann, who would later describe her "anxiety" about her daughter Mary's health, had allowed (and perhaps even invited) a few enslaved people to collectively analyze her daughters' portraits. There may have been self-interest in her recording of these reactions, as they only further underscored her own opinion of how Mary looked for the children's father, Richard, the recipient of the letter. But Ann surely would not have included these reactions if she had felt these enslaved people were unacquainted with photographic portraiture. Their comments—"Mary does not look well" and "She does not look satisfied"—demonstrated that they were evaluating the visual information in a portrait to discern the sitter's health, mood, and desires. Many enslaved people must have approached photographs of their own loved ones in similar fashion, especially when they were separated, studying the image to discern or imagine the physical and emotional state of the sitter.

For some enslaved people, as Allen Allensworth's slave narrative shows, photographs went beyond mere visual representation to embody a spiritual trace of the people they depicted. At the beginning of the Civil War, Allensworth's master, Fred Scruggs, departed Louisville to travel south for business. Scruggs left Allensworth to work on the nearby farm of James Ficklin in Jefferson County. By his own account, Allensworth quickly found solidarity with other slaves on the farm, bound as they were by a common thirst for education and a mutual enemy in Ficklin.[89] Significantly, they did not express their antagonism through the well-known means of everyday dissent—by, for instance, breaking tools or stealing. They did so with photographs:

> *Mr. Ficklin was what they called a "mean man." So much so, that the boys all hoped that he would take sick and die. They resorted to every known device to realize their hopes. They tried every remedy known to the superstitious among them. They had heard that if the face of the picture of a person were covered with ink, and the picture buried in the road where a great many people would walk or drive over it, the owner would dwindle to death.*

> *So some of the boys took from the house a daguerreotype picture of*
> *their common enemy, covered the face with ink, buried the picture,*
> *and waited for him to die,—but he didn't die. This superstition,*
> *firmly believed in by the slaves, never worked where white people*
> *were concerned.*[90]

Allensworth and his fellow bondsmen had made the daguerreotype of
Ficklin into a counter-charm. Historian of slave religion Albert J.
Raboteau details how slaves used materials such as hair, nail clippings,
clothing, dirt, powders, roots, and herbs for "fixing" someone—for
causing or curing illness.[91] Photographs, it appears, offered new tools
for "fixing" southern masters through material defacement. Oppositional
in its own right, such defacement is also important for what it divulges
about slaves' perceptions of the link between the photographic picture and its represented subject: some bondspeople clearly perceived
photographs not simply as aesthetic visions but also as material objects that contained the souls of sitters. This understanding surely
rendered photographic mementos, such as the portrait of Stephen
Jordon's mother, especially potent forms of private commemoration.

Photographs served many functions, but those functions had symbolic meanings in themselves. Memorialization and the other photographic practices with which slaves engaged—namely, representation,
communication, identification, and contemplation—acquired significance in the context of a slave society governed through practices of
bodily control. Central to the maintenance of southern plantation
labor and life was a system of passes, curfews, and slave patrols. Whites
enacted this system to limit slaves' physical mobility, and though it
was a distinctly local and uneven southern development, the system
grew tighter and the patrols more vigilant in the antebellum era.[92]
While planters relied on such measures to stop slaves from moving,
traders used bodily restraints to move slaves. In their narratives,
bondspeople vividly described the size, strength, and placement of
the ropes, chains, and collars that facilitated the transfer of human
property across land and sea. Charles Ball, for instance, reported with
considerable specificity the character of the coffle from Maryland to
Georgia: women were "tied together with a rope, about the size of a
bed-cord, which was tied like a halter round the neck of each," while
the men were handcuffed "with a short chain, about a foot long, uniting

the handcuffs and their wearers in pairs" and a "strong iron collar was closely fitted by means of a padlock round each of our necks."[93]

Within this context of geographic regulation and coerced movement, photographic mobility could have symbolized the reassertion of some measure of authority over one's body. For "those who encounter oppression through the body," historian Stephanie Camp theorized, "the body becomes an important site not only of suffering but also (and therefore) of enjoyment and resistance."[94] Perhaps Aaron Adams was especially gratified to send his portrait back to his twin, John Quincy Adams. Sold a total of eight times before he sent his photograph from Memphis to Winchester, likely enduring many of the degrading corporeal experiences of the slave trade, Aaron Adams might have understood this action as a way of declaring some degree of control, of ownership, over his body. The exchange of a photograph could have meaning in its own right.

In a similar fashion, photographic viewership and contemplation must have accrued additional power because of the surrounding visual regime of the South. Life in a slave society, for the enslaved, also meant life in a society of surveillance and inspection. In fields and in white homes, slaves worked under the watchful gazes of masters, mistresses, and overseers. Frederick Douglass, for instance, described how the slavebreaker Covey "had the faculty of making us feel that he was ever present with us...He appeared to us as being ever at hand. He was under every tree, behind every stump, in every bush, and at every window, on the plantation."[95] Solomon Northup, like Douglass, highlighted how such omnipresence bolstered white authority. Northup's master Epps, "whether actually in the field or not, had his eyes pretty generally upon us. From the piazza, from behind some adjacent tree, or other concealed point of observation, he was perpetually on the watch."[96] Enslaved people were acutely aware of such practices of looking, which played a vital role in plantation control.

The most degrading experience of being looked at undoubtedly occurred not in the fields but in the bustling slave markets of the antebellum South. When masters and traders purchased human property, they relied upon visual signs of a slave's past to imagine that individual's future. As Mississippi planter John Knight stated, "As to the character and disposition of all slaves sold by traders here, we know nothing whatever, the traders themselves being generally such liars. Buyers therefore can only judge by the *looks* of the negroes."[97] Buyers carried out physical examinations, routinely stripping slaves either down to the waist or fully naked.[98] They were looking for injuries, illnesses, and the scars from whippings that they read as signs of rebelliousness. They were also looking at skin color, seeking blacker slaves for fieldwork and lighter-skinned slaves for skilled and domestic work. At the market, bondspeople's bodies were often viewed closely and intently for their industriousness, reproductive potential, and sexual appeal.

One set of tintypes (Figure 2.3) suggests that by the eve of the Civil War, enslavers and traders had found in photography a means of facilitating such sales. In *Lens on the Texas Frontier*, photo historian Lawrence T. Jones identifies the subject as an enslaved boy in Texas, based upon information shared by descendants of the slaveholding family when the images were sold to an initial photography collector. The oral history described how the photographs were taken when the boy was for sale.[99] Similar to physical inspections performed at actual slave markets across the South, the tintypes were clearly composed to enable viewers to inspect the boy's entire body, both front and back.

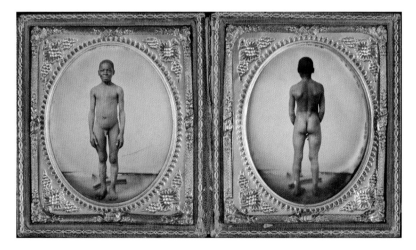

Figure 2.3 *Young Texas Male Slave*, c. 1858, tintypes, sixth plate, double-cased. DeGolyer Library, Southern Methodist University, Lawrence T. Jones III Texas Photographs.

The informational capacity of the tintypes may have served as a stand-in for actual physical inspections. Further, the boy's smile is an extremely unusual and jarring element of the left image, differentiating these tintypes from the Agassiz/Zealy daguerreotypes, in which none of the subjects feign happiness. Surely coerced, the smile suggests a conscious effort on the part of enslavers and the photographer to stage the boy's disposition, much in the same way that antebellum traders dressed slaves for the market and downplayed or explained away illnesses, despair, and opposition.[100] By the eve of the Civil War, enslavers and traders involved in human trafficking could very well have started to grasp photography as a tool for sharing information about enslaved bodies across distance—without risking the dramatic moments and small acts of resistance that could take place in person.

Enslaved people knew that the look and makeup of their bodies were tethered to monetary value. "When I was about 10 years old a man from Lexington...offered $800 for me," Peter Bruner recalled. His master declined, as he felt Bruner "was just growing into money" and "would soon be worth $1,000."[101] Likewise, John Brown recalled how, when he was a young boy, his mistress would "give us a dose of garlic and rue to keep us 'wholesome,' as she put it, and make us 'grow likely for market.'" Later in life, as Brown recalled, a trader "agreed to purchase me by the pound."[102] From an early age, slaves such as Peter Bruner and John Brown grasped how whites scrutinized their bodies and calculated how that would translate at the point of sale.

In one crucial respect, owners interrupted the incessant visual objectification of their slaves. Amidst the surveillance and inspection in slaves' daily lives, owners demanded with great regularity that bondspeople gaze upon spectacular cruelty. Coursing through the many descriptions of whippings, beatings, and tortures found in slave narratives is an emphasis on the deeply theatrical nature of masterly power: "horrible exhibition,"[103] "demoniac exhibition,"[104] "painful spectacle."[105] Charles Ball remembered the massive crowd—his enslaver estimated "at least fifteen thousand people"—that came to watch the punishment of three slaves (two to be hung, one to be whipped), "more than half of whom were blacks; all the masters, for a great distance round the country, having permitted, or compelled, their people to come to this hanging."[106] Perhaps Frederick Douglass most profoundly articulated the effect of spectacular violence when, recalling the savage beatings of an aunt during his childhood, he described how he "was doomed to be a witness and a participant."[107] Douglass made unmistakable the unavoidable reality of bondage, in which he lived his days as both the victim to and audience of the lash. As he and others painfully indicated, masterly authority enlisted slaves as spectators of their loved ones' suffering. Slavery meant watching and being watched.

For slaves, then, image viewing reversed the set of disciplinary visual practices that governed work, facilitated sale, and reinforced hierarchy. Ironically, both slaveholders and slaves likely valued how slave portraits visually removed slave bodies from the mechanisms of exploitation, racial power, and commodification. For enslaved people, photographic portraits could emphatically point toward the person, not the property, as the case of Virginian slave Robert Brown illustrates. After his wife was sold to a slave trader, Brown fled to the North with her daguerreotype on his person. When he made contact with abolitionists on the Underground Railroad, as William Still noted, Brown revealed the image, "speaking very touchingly while gazing upon it and showing it."[108] One might argue that such an image only furthered Brown's sense of loss over the separation from his wife, or his fury and despair about her continued enslavement. But it is highly unlikely that Brown and other impoverished people would invest their money in photographs, even risking violent punishment to do so, if they did not find great value in them. Brown's photographic practices demonstrate how the very same portability of photographs that gave slaves a means of communication also gave them a measure of control over how they were seen.

The great irony of photographic image-making and image practices for enslaved people was that they asserted their very personhood and social ties by turning themselves and their loved ones into things. In a sense, the very act of photographic self-representation entailed a process of self-objectification, by which a person achieved the dual status of aesthetic subject and material object through the picture itself.[109] It was precisely through the process of self-objectification that slaves took pleasure and found a measure of possession in their bodies. Recall how Peggy Grimball, the Charlestonian slave of Meta Grimball, remarked as she looked at her photograph, "I is a very

markable looking old woman."[110] It is not hard to imagine that enslaved people who actually owned, carried, and brandished their
images would have felt much the same. Such photographs constituted
a private familial archive. Through this alternative visual world, some
enslaved people displayed and pondered their bodies and those of
their kin on their own terms. Objectification went hand in hand with
the quest for de-commodification.

This quest was at the center of the quiet habit of endurance that
some enslaved people had begun nurturing in the decades prior to the
Civil War. In certain respects, they engaged in common practices, including buying, exchanging, contemplating, and preserving personal
portraits. It was the context of their enslavement—the internal slave
trade, their status as commodities, and the visual regime of the
South—that imbued such practices with different and more dramatic
meanings than for free people. In other respects, enslaved people
were the innovators: they took a nascent medium and cultivated new
uses out of necessity. In 1839, no artists or photographic boosters had
anticipated that photographs would help a fugitive to maintain ties
with his wife (Robert Brown), a father to identify distant loved ones
he sought to redeem (J. Sella Martin), or a sibling to prove he was, in
fact, a sibling (Frank in the Craft slave narrative). No one foresaw how
an exploited class would employ photography in such subversive
ways. By the late 1850s, though, some enslaved people found great
meaning in these practices. Out of a primarily oral and musical culture, some enslaved people had begun a new mode of informal political engagement, with the photograph at its core.

Enslaved people would draw upon this habit to keep and reforge
connections during the Civil War. Judging by the spike in the number
of black customers in George Smith Cook's Charleston logbook, the
social disruptions of the war likely expanded the opportunity for
slaves to purchase images.[111] Furthermore, when slaves fled during
the conflict, they brought images of their kin northward, as in the case
of Thomas Sims, his family, and a few other bondspeople who took off
from Vicksburg. The *Liberator*, which recorded the story of these fugitives, described how they "brought with them a few household treasures, keepsakes of friends, and daguerreotype pictures of dear relatives,
still in bondage, but whom they hope soon to greet as free."[112]
Photographs thereby offered practical tools to find old faces. Like

many soldiers during the war, one slave-turned-Union-soldier, Aaron Oats, sent a portrait back to his wife in Kentucky, as we have seen.[113] William B. Gould also maintained ties through photographs. Gould fled slavery by boat with seven other men in Wilmington, North Carolina, and was picked up by the USS *Cambridge* in September 1862. Joining the U.S. Navy, Gould sailed on the *Cambridge* and the *Niagara* during the conflict, traveling up and down the eastern seaboard and even to Europe. In Brooklyn, Gould "went ashore in afternoon" to have "some Pictures takeen."[114] He also received pictures on at least two occasions, including from nephew George L. Mabson.[115] And on one occasion he sent a photograph to his future wife, Cornelia Williams Read, whose freedom was purchased in 1858 through fundraising efforts by her influential uncle, Henry Highland Garnet, and the Reverend James E. Crawford of the African Baptist Church on Nantucket (where Read would settle).[116] Gould nonchalantly noted the exchange in his diary while at Gloucester: "Sent A Picture to C.W.R."[117]

After the war, photography continued to constitute a means of maintaining bonds of affection. John Quincy Adams kept in touch with his twin brother, Aaron, through letters and images. Receiving a portrait of Aaron around 1867, Adams described how "you could not tell it from mine."[118] In Aaron's portrait, Adams saw time pass: with two photographs of his brother, one from slavery and one from freedom, Adams could see his twin aging from afar. This and other instances of image-sharing reveal a new wrinkle in the trajectory from slavery to freedom, as enslaved people entered emancipation with dignified depictions in their pockets. Photographs clearly gave African Americans the capacity to assert individuality and to construct social bonds. Expressive and evidentiary documents helped slaves and ex-slaves express and verify their full personhood as they simultaneously constituted and actualized meaningful bonds.

━━

In the late antebellum era, some bondspeople drew upon a new form of popular visual culture to endure the practices of the slave trade and to actively assert their personhood in the face of the ideology undergirding that trade. The rise of photography allowed enslaved people to transition from viewing their masters' images to making their own unique visions, for its cheapness and availability opened up commercial access. The portability and materiality of these images, moreover, gave slaves new ways to communicate, identify, remember, and contemplate. It is difficult, given the paucity of sources left by slaves, to estimate the extent of this cultural transformation. For some bondspeople, however, photography clearly served as a means of maintaining familial attachments across distance; the brutalities of slavery must have given them an even greater need than free people for this practice. Treating enslaved people's active engagement with photography on its own terms reveals a new habit of endurance, as some enslaved people turned a new technology into a resource to survive the pains of bondage. Treating it in relation to the photographic efforts of southern slaveholders shows how enslaved people built up a meaningful, alternative visual world. Of course, this contest was uneven, as enslaved people surely did not commission as many images as their owners. Still, written evidence makes clear that some enslaved people contested the dominant photographic narrative put forth by their masters, which cast enslaved people as mimics and imposters, by actively asserting their sociality and full humanity through photographic self-representation.

3

REALIZING ABOLITION

IN THE SPRING OF 1846, sometime after radical abolitionist and feminist Abby Kelley Foster sat for a fairly conventional daguerreotype portrait (Figure 3.1) at the Philadelphia gallery of black abolitionist photographer Robert Douglass Jr., she received a warm, urgent letter from the artist himself. "Esteemed Friend," Douglass wrote,

> *Anxious to give the world a correct transcript of the features of one so entirely devoted to the interests of humanity as yourself, I have placed one of the Daguerreotype Pictures you so kindly allowed me to take in the hands of a skilful artist, for the purpose of being lithographed. I have to ask pardon for the liberty thus taken, which would be certainly inexcusable, were it not for the motive which has impelled me. I have imagined that others feel the same pleasure in contemplating an accurate representation of the features of the good and kindhearted, which I experience myself, and if in regarding your Portrait a single spirit is encouraged to enter upon the same glorious although arduous labor, or excited to action for the advancement of the great and Holy cause in which you are so indefatigably engaged I shall be amply rewarded.*
>
> *Please send me your autograph which I intend placing beneath the Portrait.*

Figure 3.1 *Abby Kelley Foster*, 1846, daguerreotype, sixth plate. Courtesy American Antiquarian Society.

> *With sincere prayers for your happiness + the speedy triumph of Liberty.*
>> *I remain yours,*
>>>> Robt Douglass[1]

In one sense, this letter confirms many aspects of abolitionist culture that scholars have illuminated in the past few decades: the interracial and cross-gender friendships distinctive to this radical wing of the broader antislavery movement; the religiously infused fiber of the movement ("the great and Holy cause"); and, of course, the actual use of letter-writing to build intimate bonds and political networks.[2] But Robert Douglass's words and actions also reveal how photography had catalyzed the abolitionist investment in the power of radical self-representation and political identification.[3] While Douglass could not mass-reproduce Foster's portrait with the daguerrean process, he found a way around this issue through lithography, a transfer that seemed to bother him little, perhaps because the paper print (17 ⁷⁄₁₀" × 12 ⅕") actually enlarged the size of Foster's sixth-plate daguerreotype (2 ¾" × 3 ¼") and turned her gaze upward and away from the viewer, offering a more displayable image and a more romantic persona (Figure 3.2). To build and energize the abolition movement, as

Figure 3.2 *Abby Kelley Foster*, 1846, by Alfred M. Hoffy from a daguerre-otype by R. Douglass Junr., printed by Wagner & McGuigan, litho-graph. Courtesy American Antiquarian Society.

Douglass suggested and enacted, he and others needed images of inspiring abolitionists as much as suffering slaves.

Studying such acts of photographic representation complicates the conventional view of antislavery visual media in the United States. Scholars have stressed how abolitionists applied a host of visual forms to spark sympathy toward slaves and venom toward slaveholders.[4] Pictures of southern plantations and slave markets trickled through America in the late eighteenth century and flooded through it from the 1830s onward. These scenes reached onlookers in almanacs, novels, broadsides, engravings, and lithographs, expanding their mental and moral horizons and creating new forms of voyeurism in the process.[5] Photography, however, could not give abolitionists their customary views of slavery, for early cameras lacked the physical mobility and quick exposures necessary to make eyewitness shots of floggings and auction sales. Abolitionists found their photographic subjects close at hand: rank-and-file activists and national leaders, white rebels and fugitive slaves who escaped under their aegis. These images raise a new set of issues about self-representation rather than southern representations.

Abolitionist photography helped forge intra-movement sympathy and political solidarity, a process historians have typically associated with the functions of print culture, public events, and social institutions, including churches, political organizations, and Masonic lodges.[6] Abolitionists never articulated any overarching strategy for their uses of photography, for it constituted the "new media" of the late antebellum era. As photography emerged, abolitionists learned about its technical capacities and shaped its uses as a political tool. They did so through three main image practices. First, they built social and political bonds by exchanging portraits among themselves. If Robert Douglass's letter is any indication, they were inviting themselves to admire one another's moral standing and heroism. Second, they photographed white rebels who suffered in attempts to rescue slaves and spark slave rebellion, circulating these images within the movement. Third, they documented fugitive slaves who traveled northward along the Underground Railroad, displaying these images at abolitionist gatherings and sharing them amongst friends. These practices, which produced a vast and varied visual landscape, were rooted in the need to define the unstable identities of ex-slaves and white radicals as well as the desire to capture and convey the latest political action as it happened. By the late 1850s, abolitionists had initiated the use of photography as a political tool for social movements in America and for conveying the suffering of others (though, surprisingly, by picturing the suffering of white northerners rather than slaves).[7] In doing so, abolitionists produced a largely internal visual culture that heightened their sense of social connection and political urgency, adding fuel to the broader sectional crisis.

———

IN THE DECADE PRIOR to the emergence of the daguerreotype, American abolitionism underwent a foundational shift in political aims and cultural tactics. Though abolitionist societies had emerged in the late eighteenth century, particularly in Pennsylvania, the early 1830s marked the first moment in which a sizable white population turned from gradual plans for emancipation and colonization to the notion that slavery could—and should—end immediately.[8] By the 1830s an estimated 140,000 activists had established around 1,300 societies, spread across the North and concentrated in the states of Massachusetts, New York, and Ohio.[9] A confluence of forces brought about this sea change, with the work of black activists increasingly considered the primary factor in bringing about this white conversion. Most notably, William Lloyd Garrison came to reject colonization through interracial social encounters during his work as a newspaper editor in Baltimore. Founding the *Liberator* in 1831, Garrison famously called for "immediate, unconditional, and uncompensated emancipation," but his quest for the "revolution in public sentiment" that black activists called for undoubtedly elicited the support of black subscribers, who soon made up the majority of the paper's readership.[10]

Whereas the first generation of abolitionists in the early republic had relied primarily on legal efforts to free slaves, 1830s immediatists launched a broad cultural assault against slavery and racism, a campaign of "moral suasion" they carried out through institutions and meetings as well as through oral culture (lectures and songs), print culture (newspapers, pamphlets, children's magazines), and visual culture (mastheads, broadsides, lithographs). The emergence of new media aided this campaign, especially the accessibility of lithographs, which Americans adopted from Europe in the late 1820s and 1830s.[11] Transformations in printing technologies further fueled such efforts in political persuasion. In 1833 the introduction of the steam-powered press gave abolitionists a way to print materials at a tenfold increase from older presses.[12] A cheaper and more diverse set of cultural tools equipped immediatists to link themselves across space and to achieve an influence that far outweighed their numbers.

As emergent print technologies helped abolitionists to create imagined communities in the North, they also helped them to infiltrate the South.[13] In the mid-1830s, William Lloyd Garrison and Elizur Wright set out to convert a group of approximately twenty thousand moderate southerners from colonization to immediatism through a cultural onslaught that came to be known as the "Postal Campaign." By the end of 1835, abolitionists had produced more than one million pieces of print material that they sent directly to southern moderates. Most southerners detested the "vile Pamphlets, Prints &c distributed by the Abolitionists and their agents," as one Georgian planter put it.[14] Supported by President Andrew Jackson, southerners responded by blocking the dispersal of mail to its intended recipients. As historian Daniel Walker Howe notes, this "refusal of the Post Office to deliver abolitionist mail to the South may well represent the largest peacetime violation of civil liberty in U.S. history."[15] Some states passed laws to block visual materials in particular. Not only did the state of Mississippi bar abolitionist print materials, but in 1840 it also punished any person who circulated "any pictorial representation calculated to produce disaffection among the slave population hereof."[16]

Abolitionists complemented their strategy of sheer numerical quantity with visual appeals that underscored southern barbarism. Drawing upon visual formulas that dated back to the late eighteenth century, engravers and illustrators offered up a world of cruel masters, violent overseers, and suffering slaves, typically inhabiting plantations and domestic slave markets. Flogging scenes in publications such as the *American Anti-Slavery Almanac*, for instance, were indebted to a decades-old British iconography of half-nude Africans receiving beatings as spectators looked on from the margins (Figures 3.3 and 3.4). Angelina Grimké felt these images altered the most basic perceptions of bondage from afar. "Until the pictures of the slave's sufferings were drawn and held up to the public gaze," she argued, "no Northerner had any idea of the cruelty of the system, it never entered their minds that such abominations could exist in Christian, Republican America."[17] Grimké undoubtedly exaggerated the power of images, perpetuating a disposition that privileged sight as the sensory vehicle for best sympathizing with distant pain.[18]

More than any other image, the kneeling slave performed this function in abolitionist culture. This icon gained influence in Britain in the 1780s before it arrived in America.[19] Angelina Grimké took pride in the role women had played in promoting the image. As she noted in the mid-1830s, female antislavery societies in America "are doing just what the English women did, telling the story of the colored man's wrongs, praying for his deliverance, and presenting his kneeling image constantly before the public eye."[20] In the 1830s, Americans continued to reproduce male and female versions of the

Figure 3.3 *The Abolition of the Slave Trade or the Inhumanity of Dealers in Human Flesh Exemplified in Captn. Kimber's Treatment of a Young Negro Girl of 15 for Her Virjen Modesty*, 1792, by Isaac Cruikshank, 1 print: etching, hand-colored. Cartoon Prints (British) Collection, Prints and Photographs Division, Library of Congress, LC-USZC4-6204.

image on numerous forms including broadsides and writing paper (Figures 3.5 and 3.6).

Visual elements made the kneeling slave a powerful tool not simply for illustrating a slave and concretizing the abstraction of slavery but also for helping abolitionists to imagine themselves and to express their commitments. Whether man or woman, the slave crouched with one knee on the ground, looking upward in side profile, wrists shackled, pleading for help and acknowledgment of his or her humanity. The typical caption, "Am I Not a Man and a Brother?," further strengthened the purpose of evoking the viewer's identification. These qualities resonated deeply with prominent immediatist minister Theodore Dwight Weld when he wrote to Angelina and Sarah Grimké in 1837, so much so that he could not help beginning his letter with exclamatory remarks about the bondsman kneeling at the top of the page: "Ah! Still kneeling, manacled, looking upward, pleading

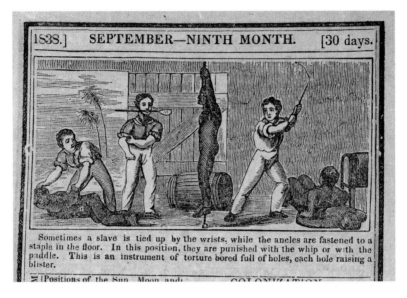

Figure 3.4 *The American Anti-Slavery Almanac, for 1838.* Courtesy American Antiquarian Society.

for help! As I caught a sheet at random from a large quantity on the desk at the office to write you a line my dear sisters, I had almost dashed my pen upon it before I saw *the kneeling slave*! The sudden sight drove home a deeper lesson than my heart has learned these many days! The prayer of the slave!"[21] The kneeling slave's performance of submission and its abstraction from the social world allowed distant abolitionists such as Weld to envision themselves as the Christian liberators who could answer slaves' prayers.

As the icon shaped the political identities of individuals, it came to serve broader purposes in the movement. It stood as an instant symbol of abolitionism as a collective, which explains why it was plastered across Weld's letterhead. A nascent form of political branding, the kneeling slave also mattered as a material commodity. In 1836, for instance, the Boston Female Anti-Slavery Society (BFASS) brought a case against Thomas Aves, the father of a Louisiana slaveholding mistress who was visiting Boston with her slave Med. In the ensuing case, *Commonwealth v. Aves*, Chief Justice Lemuel Shaw ruled that Med was free, for enslaved people were not recognized as property in Massachusetts.[22] Soon thereafter, the BFASS memorialized

Figure 3.5 *Am I Not a Man a Brother?*, 1837, 1 print: woodcut on wove paper. Cartoon Prints (American) Collection, Miscellaneous Items in High Demand Collection, Rare Book and Special Collections Division, Library of Congress, LC-USZC4-5321.

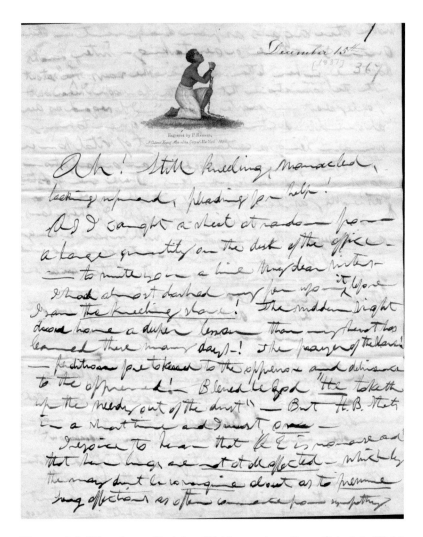

Figure 3.6 Theodore Dwight Weld to Angelina Grimké Weld, December 15, 1837. Box 4, Weld-Grimke Papers, Clements Library, University of Michigan.

this event—and raised money from it—by selling workbags with "the representation of a Slave kneeling before the figure of Justice," as the *Liberator* described.[23] Stamped, etched, and sewn onto political paraphernalia of all kinds, the kneeling slave gave thousands of northern activists visceral membership in a movement of the righteous.

In 1839 the daguerreotype arrived in the United States, and northern commercial photography soon blossomed at a rate that far ex-
ceeded the southern industry. Boston, Philadelphia, and New York
became centers of image-making, with an explosive growth in studios
from the mid-1840s to the 1850s. From 1845 to 1856, the number of
daguerreotypists working in Boston rose from six to thirty-nine. In
New York, the number of studios surged from sixteen in 1844 to fifty-
nine in 1850.[24] How would this transformation reshape abolitionist
political culture?

Like slaveholders, some abolitionists took up photography in the
1840s and 1850s. One of the earliest adopters was Boston minister
Edward Everett Hale, who started experimenting with the medium
soon after it arrived in the United States.[25] Hale made at least one
widely circulated image: the daguerreotype of fugitive slave Ellen
Craft, a portrait used for the frontispiece of her slave narrative.[26]
Fugitives such as Craft may well have felt safer sitting for the camera
of a committed activist. Various free African Americans also started
commercial businesses. Philadelphia artist Robert Douglass Jr. began
his career as a portrait painter and printmaker before claiming the
title of first black photographer in the city.[27] In York, Pennsylvania
(fifty-two miles north of Baltimore), three black brothers—Glenalvin,
Wallace, and William Goodridge—started a studio that was soon
noticed by Frederick Douglass's *North Star*, which posted ads for it
beginning in the late 1840s.[28] Black photographer Augustus Washington,
the son of a former slave, opened up a gallery in mid-1840s Hartford.[29]
Finally, in Cincinnati, black artist James Presley Ball established a
studio in 1849 that would gain national acclaim in the 1850s and be
covered in spreads by *Gleason's Pictorial* and *Frederick Douglass' Paper*.[30]
All these artists were first and foremost businessmen, representative
of the broader transformation in market-driven visual and consumer
culture that had swept the nation. By establishing studios, they
opened up sympathetic image-making spaces to northern radicals, reformers, and fugitives.

As abolitionists adopted photography, they adopted photographic
metaphors in their language. Wendell Phillips equated abolitionists'
rhetorical tactics to photographic artistry, relating that, like "a Grand
Jury for Christendom, we summon the slaveholder, and his apologists
and instruments, before us. If their character appears bad, it is not our

fault; the fault is in the character. We are daguerreotype painters, sir. Our pictures may, like them, be sad, but are always faithful and exact."[31] Harriet Beecher Stowe introduced the character Uncle Tom in *Uncle Tom's Cabin* with similar photographic language: "At this table was seated Uncle Tom, Mr. Shelby's best hand, who, as he is to be the hero of our story, we must daguerreotype for our readers."[32] Meanwhile, an author describing a slave auction in the *Liberator* exclaimed, "I would give something if you could see the daguerreotype of the family standing upon the platform, to be sold at auction. But, no—I recall the wish. Thank God that you cannot see that picture, because it would haunt you like a dreadful vision."[33] This use of "daguerreotype" was utterly common at the time, for photography became a popular "linguistic practice," as historian Alan Trachtenberg puts it.[34] Rooted in the apparent objectivity of the mechanism of the camera, rather than the subjective work of the paintbrush, "daguerreotyping" a scene involving enslaved persons connoted an unmediated vision of bondage, seemingly technological rather than political.

By the 1850s, abolitionists had even begun to notice photographic practices of intimate power in the South. In 1853, for instance, the *Liberator* republished a *New York Examiner* article describing how Virginian men "keeping an office, who are unable to own a slave, find no difficulty in hiring one from planters or farmers for purposes of prostitution." These "*gentlemen* of the first families," the story noted, "present their daguerreotype likenesses (a common thing it is said at the galleries, where, in some instances, we have witnessed it) to those Cyprian mistresses, and oftentimes upon the same plate with themselves, doubtless that the 'noble blood of the Old Dominion' may be thus contrasted with the 'inferior animal.'"[35] Such sarcastic pronouncements of slaveholding corruption might seem common fare in an abolitionist paper, yet the focus on photography was new. The very use of sentimental photo practices rendered the coercive sexual practices in the slave South all the more cruel because they amplified the contradictions of the system. Virginia men sought the affection symbolized by the daguerreotype exchange as they simultaneously reified a human-animal divide, the contrast between the "noble blood" and the "inferior animal," through group portraits. Perhaps what angered the author most was how southern whites seemed to use daguerreotypy to simultaneously recognize and deny enslaved women's personhood.

Despite the ease with which the daguerreotype seeped into the businesses, metaphorical language, and perceptual landscapes of abolitionists, the medium initially proved ineffective as a tool to extend many of the mass-persuasion strategies cultivated in the 1830s. For instance, in the 1840s abolitionists could not mass-reproduce photographs with the daguerreotype process. They found their way around this problem by transferring portrait photographs into mass-reproducible prints, as Robert Douglass did with Abby Kelley Foster's image.

The more significant issue abolitionists faced was that photography could not easily show the scenes of violence that had come to constitute slavery in the radical imaginary. On rare occasions abolitionists did talk of photographing the South. Commenting on a slaveholder and an overseer, the latter of whom had recently shot a resistant slave after a confrontation on a farm near Richmond, *Frederick Douglass' Paper* noted that "such monsters as this owner and overseer ought to be daguerreotyped and placed where the scorn of the whole world should be pointed at them."[36] Doing so was easier said than done, though. An engraver or illustrator could easily imagine a barbarous slaveholder with his whip in the air, poised to lash the back of a slave. A photographer, on the other hand, needed to be present. Moreover, bulky tripods and long exposure times made eyewitness photography nearly impossible in the 1840s and 1850s. Finally, getting a slaveholder to stop and pose for an abolitionist camera would have been no easy task. In the 1840s and 1850s eyewitness imagery would be left to travelers, who toured the South and returned to tell of what they saw; to fugitives, who described their experiences on the bustling abolitionist lecture circuit; and to sketch artists, who snuck into slave auctions and published their illustrations in the mass press, including the *Illustrated London News* and *Harper's Weekly*.[37]

To more fully understand the possibilities and limitations of photography as a tool of abolitionist propaganda requires looking beyond technical matters. As the case of Jonathan Walker and *Branded Hand* illustrates, the mechanical nature of photography enabled abolitionists to represent violence in new ways, but it also enabled ex-slaves to avoid making such images. A white shipwright and tradesman, Walker moved in the early 1840s from New England to Pensacola, Florida, where he soon agreed to help seven slaves escape to the Bahamas by boat.[38] Walker and the slaves set sail, but only fourteen days into their journey an American ship caught them and brought them back to land. A Florida judge subsequently sentenced Walker to an hour in the pillory, fifteen days in jail, and a lifetime with a particular brand on his right hand: "SS," for "slave stealer." Four of the slaves were also imprisoned and beaten. Scarred but free, Walker returned to Boston, where prominent Boston physician and abolitionist Henry Ingersol Bowditch suggested he daguerreotype his branded palm. Walker eagerly complied, placing his right hand on a table before the camera of Southworth and Hawes, two prominent photographers located on Tremont Row. The daguerreotype process, which captured a mirror image of its subject matter, reversed Walker's hand (making it look like a left hand) as well as the "SS" inscribed in his palm (Figure 3.7).

Tiny in size, measuring only 2 by 2.5 inches, *Branded Hand* did much to authenticate and dramatize Walker's recent suffering.[39] In its

Figure 3.7 *The Branded Hand of Captain Jonathan Walker*, 1845, by Southworth & Hawes, daguerreotype, 6.5 × 5.5 cm (visible image), 8 × 9.5 cm (half case). Photo 1.373, Collection of the Massachusetts Historical Society.

original form, the daguerreotype reached the Boston community, displayed, for instance, in 1845 at the Twelfth National Anti-Slavery Bazaar at Faneuil Hall, where it "elicited much attention," the *Liberator* noted.[40] Most abolitionists saw *Branded Hand* reproduced as an engraving in newspapers, pamphlets, and Walker's popular biography (Figure 3.8).[41] Rarely did abolitionists let the hand stand without the aid of written text. The photograph served as the pre-text to illustrations. One pamphlet followed the image with a poem by John G. Whittier, who paid tribute to Walker and his hand, "smote" by the "fiery shafts of pain!" The poem turned Walker's sacrifice into a symbol of ongoing Christian struggle: "Lift that manly right hand, bold ploughman of the wave! Its branded palm shall prophesy, 'Salvation to the Slave!'" The *Boston Chronicle* made the links between Christ and Walker even clearer as it admonished the southern branders: "Into His hands, still bearing the nail-marks of the cross, have ye burned the liberal signet of your malignity to man and human freedom."[42] Through a combination of print and daguerreotypy, Walker's hand became an icon of white Christlike suffering—a condition incurred to alleviate black suffering.

In the mid-1840s, *Branded Hand* revealed to abolitionists how they could use the daguerrean process for politics. They could draw upon the same photographic powers of mechanical representation that had astounded initial onlookers and photographic boosters. Many observers were struck by the capacity of the daguerreotype to visualize its subjects with exacting precision. As a former mayor of New York, Philip Hone, remarked, "Every object, however minute, is a perfect transcript of the thing itself; the hair of the human head, the gravel of the roadside, the texture of a silk curtain, or the shadow of the smaller leaf reflected upon the wall, are all imprinted as carefully as nature or art has created them in the objects transferred."[43] Other observers such as Samuel Morse envisioned that this capacity for detail would benefit science. As Morse proclaimed, "We are soon to see if the minute has discoverable limits. The naturalist is to have a new kingdom to explore, as much beyond the microscope as the microscope is beyond the naked eye."[44] *Branded Hand*—the first instance of "damage photography" in American history—applied Morse's vision to illuminate a body abused by southern whites with unprecedented visual specificity.

THE BRANDED HAND.

Walker resided in Florida with his family from 1836 until 1841. He then removed to Massachusetts because he would not bring up his children among the poisonous influences of slavery. While in Florida, the colored people whom he employed were treated as equals in his family, much to the chagrin of the slaveholders of that region. In 1844 he returned to Pensacola in his own vessel. When leaving, seven of the slaves who had in former years been in his employ, and were members of the church with which he communed, begged to go with him. He consented. When out fourteen days, a Southern sloop fell in with and seized them. Prostrated by sickness, he was confined in a dungeon, chained on a damp floor without table, bed or chair. He was in the pillory for an hour, pelted with rotten eggs, branded S. S.—slave stealer—in the palm of his right hand, by Ebenezer Dorr, United States Marshal, fined $150, and imprisoned eleven months.

THE BRANDED HAND.

BY JOHN G. WHITTIER.

Welcome home again, brave seaman! with thy thoughtful brow and gray,
And the old heroic spirit of our earlier, better day—
With that front of calm endurance, on whose steady nerve, in vain
Pressed the iron of the prison, smote the fiery shafts of pain!

Is the tyrant's brand upon thee? Did the brutal cravens aim
To make God's truth thy falsehood, His holiest work thy shame?
When, all blood-quenched, from the torture the iron was withdrawn,
How laughed their evil angel the baffled fools to scorn!

They change to wrong, the duty which God hath written out
On the great heart of humanity too legible for doubt!
They, the loathsome moral lepers, blotched from foot-sole up to crown,
Give to shame what God hath given unto honor and renown!

Why, that brand is highest honor!—than its traces never yet
Upon old armorial hatchments was a prouder blazon set;
And thy unborn generations, as they crowd our rocky strand,
Shall tell with pride the story of their father's BRANDED HAND!

Figure 3.8 Image in J. G. Whittier, *The Branded Hand* (Salem: Office of the Anti-Slavery Bugle, c. 1845). Courtesy American Antiquarian Society.

Yet it is striking, given the extensive publicity around *Branded Hand*, how rarely abolitionists employed the tactic of damage photography over the next two decades. One might have expected immediatists to have capitalized on Walker's success by picturing the scarred bodies of the many fugitive slaves who came northward in the 1840s and 1850s. Between 1850 and 1858, for instance, the vigilance committee in Boston helped 407 fugitive slaves find homes and livelihoods; surely some of these fugitives had scars.[45] Had they in fact made more aftermath images, such pictures would have partnered with the many scenes of whippings in abolitionist prints, magazines, and books. In 1863 abolitionists would pursue this path, widely distributing *The Scourged Back*, a carte de visite that displayed the flagellated back of a fugitive slave, called both Gordon and Peter at different points by newspapers, who entered Union army lines near Baton Rouge (Figure 3.9). But in the prewar era, abolitionists do not appear to have made any photographs that documented ex-slaves' scars or brands.

Why did *The Scourged Back* not happen sooner? Many white and black abolitionists encountered, or at least read about, ex-slaves with scars. In his *Narrative of William W. Brown, a Fugitive Slave* (1847), William Wells Brown recalled how a slaveholder from Natchez "struck me over the head with the cowhide, the end of which struck me over my right eye, sinking deep into the flesh." Brown received this bludgeon for merely conversing with another slave who was being punished, but the cowhide left "a scar which I carry to this day."[46] Georgian slave John Brown also acquired scars, though not from a master's whip. They came from a doctor's racial experiments. Brown's master Thomas Stevens had lent him to a local doctor named Hamilton for a series of crude studies. Hamilton sought a remedy for sunstroke by repeatedly placing Brown in a heated pit, with "only my head being above the ground," to see which medicines let Brown "withstand the greatest degree of heat." In another torturous trial, Hamilton wanted to see, as Brown put it, "how deep my black skin went." The doctor did so by creating blisters on Brown's legs, feet, and hands, which, as Brown lamented, "bear the scars to this day."[47]

The best-known scars might have been those on Frederick Douglass's back. Douglass sometimes called upon his own lacerated body as important evidence of his former enslavement, as in the case

Figure 3.9 *Gordon*, 1863, by Mathew Brady Studio, copy after William D. McPherson and Mr. Oliver, albumen silver print, 3⅜ × 2³⁄₁₆ inches (image), 4 × 2⅜ inches (mount). National Portrait Gallery, Smithsonian Institution.

of one mid-1840s lecture in Ireland: "I am the representative of three millions of bleeding slaves. I have felt the lash myself; my back is scarred with it."[48] Abolitionist leaders commented on these scars as well. After seeing Douglass lecture in 1842, William Lloyd Garrison noted in the *Liberator*, "He stood there a slave—a runaway from the southern house of bondage—not safe, for one hour, even on the soil of Massachusetts—with his back all horribly scarred by the lash—with the bitter remembrances of the life of slavery crowding upon his soul—with everything in his past history, his present condition, his future prospects, to make him a fierce outlaw, and a stern avenger of outraged humanity!"[49] As Douglass's intellect on the lecture podium often led audiences to question his bona fides as a former slave, Garrison's bodily reference worked to reinforce Douglass's authenticity for abolitionist readers.

Abolitionists could have taken a photograph of Douglass's back to display at their well-attended public functions. Indeed, the 1845 Faneuil Hall Bazaar exhibited a daguerreotype of Douglass alongside *Branded Hand*, yet newspaper accounts mention nothing unusual about Douglass's image, indicating it was a regular portrait.[50] Moreover, the notion of such a photograph might have crossed Douglass's mind, for he knew *Branded Hand* well. He would later recall "the sensation produced by the exhibition of the branded hand. It was one of the few atrocities of slavery that roused the justice and humanity of the North to a death-struggle with slavery."[51] Why, then, did abolitionists not photograph Douglass's back? Why did Douglass not do it himself, especially since he clearly recognized the capacity for such an image to intensify antislavery sentiment?

That there were barriers to mass-reproducing photographs in the 1840s and 1850s hardly answers the question. Lacking a negative, daguerreotypes were unique images. In this period, only a small number of American artists experimented with techniques of mass-reproducibility—including the collodion wet-plate process, introduced in 1851, which made paper images from glass negatives. Most artists did not initially take up the more complicated negative-positive processes, instead opting to continue to make daguerreotypes (as well as unique ambrotypes and tintypes) throughout the 1850s.[52] For abolitionists, the unique photograph remained important because it allowed for the personal exchange of visual information. Unique images could also be used to bolster the authenticity of mass-produced images on paper, and publishers of radical prints and slave narratives often made sure to indicate that likenesses originated in daguerreotypes—as Robert Douglass Jr. did with his print of Abby Kelley Foster.[53] While abolitionist photography was shaped by the changing nature of the technologies at hand, these technologies were not the only determining factors. For fugitives, the deep desire to de-commodify their selves and to combat the oppressive conditions of northern racism shaped what they made and did not make.

Even though Douglass never commented on why he avoided photographing his own scars, one can infer that he opposed doing so from his publicized ideas about visual representation and his personal image practices. In Douglass's 1849 review of Wilson Armistead's *A Tribute for the Negro* in the *North Star*, he argued that it was "next to impossible for white men to take likenesses of black men, without most grossly exaggerating their distinctive features. And the reason is obvious. Artists, like all other white persons have adopted a theory respecting the distinctive features of negro physiognomy," which led them to "associate with the negro face, high cheek bones, distended nostril, depressed nose, thick lips, and retreating foreheads."[54] These images found expression in the everyday perceptions of whites, as Douglass recalled hearing "many white persons say that 'negroes look all alike,' and that they could not distinguish between the old and the young."[55]

Douglass's comments highlight the double-edged transformation of written and visual consumer culture that began in the early nineteenth century. The very same media that gave abolitionists new weapons to reach a mass audience also helped spread anti-black racism in the North. Rising literacy rates and accelerating urbanization expanded the market for inexpensive magazines, almanacs, lithographs, and engravings, which generated a flood of derogatory, anti-black images.[56] Scholars have located the origins of such popular racist imagery in early national Boston and Philadelphia, two cities that, not coincidentally, were home to flourishing communities of white image-makers and free blacks. From at least the 1820s onward, Boston artists lampooned the local black community, particularly its banquets, parades, and meetings celebrating the 1808 ending of the transatlantic slave trade, through "Bobolition" broadsides. In Philadelphia, meanwhile, artists including Edward W. Clay, David Claypoole Johnston, and James Thakera crafted prints and etchings that mocked free black aspirations for middle-class life, as seen in the case of Edward Clay's *Life in Philadelphia* series, which circulated throughout the United States and Britain in multiple editions.[57]

From the 1840s onward, Douglass offered a massive body of photographic evidence countering widespread racial perceptions. In fact, new scholarship reveals that he posed for his portrait photograph more than 160 times in his lifetime—more than any other nineteenth-century American (including Abraham Lincoln and Walt Whitman).[58] His most aggressive visual counterattack came in a side portrait (Figure 3.10), an unusual image that posed a clear challenge to the scientific racism of George R. Gliddon and Josiah C. Nott, who placed blacks at the bottom of a racial hierarchy understood through the anatomy of the skull, and used image comparisons as their own evidence.[59] Prior to the Civil War, Douglass made at least seven other individual daguerreotypes (and at least two ambrotypes) that challenged northern popular imagery as well as southern slaveholders' more private photographic archive.[60] He may have gone to the gallery to concretize the vision of a fugitive slave, for in his review of Armistead's book he had

Figure 3.10 *Frederick Douglass*, c. 1850, daguerreotype, sixth plate. Courtesy of the Moorland-Spingarn Research Center, Manuscript Division, Howard University, Washington, DC.

faulted his own image, describing how it had "a much more kindly and amiable expression, than is generally thought to characterize the face of a fugitive slave."[61] Certain visual elements underscore this usage. Douglass frequently gazed directly at the camera in his portraits before 1865 (in seventeen out of the thirty-eight portraits). He mirrored this bold gaze, one challenging the viewer, with a late 1850s ambrotype in which he stood and defiantly crossed his arms.[62] Such poses, which were undoubtedly unavailable to the enslaved people who posed in their masters' portraits, marked Douglass as a defiant fugitive. Simultaneously, his images revealed how a slave could become a dignified citizen and bourgeois subject, in a suit, tie, and vest (Figure 3.11). The images of Gliddon and Nott made claims to blacks' subhuman status. Douglass's photography, in striking contrast, staked claims to his personhood, his stance as a fugitive dissenter, and the potential for African Americans as prosperous and productive participants in northern life.

Though Frederick Douglass made far more images than anyone else at the time, his search for visual dignity was hardly unique amongst fugitive slaves. Many former bondspeople found the practice of self-objectification to be a vital means for asserting their full personhood and defining their social identities. In her many cartes de visite of the 1860s, Sojourner Truth drew upon symbols of middle-class femininity—she often posed knitting in a white shawl—rather than markings of her former enslavement.[63] Likewise, John W. Jones portrayed pride and dignity rather than victimization in his portrait. After escaping from Loudon County, Virginia, in 1844, Jones eventually settled in Elmira, New York, where he soon became an operative of the Underground Railroad.[64] He posed in what was likely a "wide-awake" hat, a popular style of the time, along with a necktie, suit, and vest (Figure 3.12).[65] In grasping the gloves in his right hand, Jones underscored the assertive and lively expression in his eyes. His portrait was a vivid and enduring statement of self-possession, a vision unavailable to the slaves who posed for their masters. Likewise, ex-slave John Brown—the Georgian slave scarred by medical experiments—posed for a dignified photograph that was translated into the frontispiece for his 1854 narrative, *Slave Life in Georgia: A Narrative of the Life, Sufferings, and Escape of John Brown* (Figure 3.13). The frontispiece bolstered the expressed aims of Brown's book: "To advance the anti-slavery cause

Figure 3.11 *Frederick Douglass*, 1847/1852, by Samuel J. Miller, daguerreotype, 5½ × 4⅛ inches (plate). The Art Institute of Chicago/Art Resource, NY.

by the diffusion of information; and to promote the success of the project John Brown has formed, to advance himself by his own exertions, and to set an example to others of his 'race.'"[66] A portrait of his well-dressed respectability may not have sold as many books as a picture of his earlier victimization, but it may have proved essential to his

Figure 3.12 *John W. Jones*, photographic copy of c. 1850 image. Courtesy of the Ohio History Connection, AL03088.

ongoing quest to show how he had "as much will, and energy, and purpose in him as any white man."[67] With this visual opening, Brown visualized his present and his future, not his past.

The dearth of photographs depicting the scarred bodies of ex-slaves in the wake of *Branded Hand* reveals how photography had

FROM A COLODION BY J. DUDMAN.

Figure 3.13 Frontispiece of John Brown, in John Brown and Louis Alexis Chamerovzow, *Slave Life in Georgia: A Narrative of the Life, Sufferings, and Escape of John Brown, a Fugitive Slave, Now in England*, W. M. Watts, 1855. Documenting the American South, University Library, The University of North Carolina at Chapel Hill, http://docsouth.unc.edu/neh/jbrown/jbrown.html.

altered the power dynamics of abolitionist cultural production. In the decades since the creation of the kneeling slave trope, abolitionists had consistently drawn on the new media of the nineteenth century, including magazines and prints, to convert the unconverted. Jonathan Walker's *Branded Hand* was merely a continuation of this trend. For a white abolitionist like Walker, a photographed brand could spur sympathy and mobilize energy without downgrading his own humanity. Fugitive slaves, on the other hand, needed every tool they could find to convey their sense of personhood. They jeopardized this aim if they pictured victimization, which recalled a former condition of violence and commodification, particularly since they would lose control over a circulating image. Those who had escaped from a slave state after 1840 may even have reviled the whole idea of a "slave portrait," which was already common in their experiences as a testament to slaveholding benevolence. White abolitionists might have loved to circulate more images of victimized slaves; their putative black subjects appear to have resisted that opportunity to serve the cause. For African Americans, freedom meant they could shape the uses of photography positively and negatively: they could sit for images they considered liberating and refuse to sit for those that evoked past humiliations. In that way they compelled the abolitionist movement to revert to the older technologies of engravings and lithographs if they sought to show the suffering of bondage.[68]

RATHER THAN EXTENDING the abolitionist iconography of suffering slaves, photography enacted a transformation that reshaped the means through which abolitionists understood themselves and their relations to one another. From the 1840s onward, abolitionists largely used photography to stake claims to their political identities and bonds rather than to picture slavery.[69] They articulated and built community through pictures. On rare occasions they did so within group portraits. In 1850, for instance, the Executive Committee of the Pennsylvania Anti-Slavery Society daguerreotyped itself as the intergender and interracial community it sought to realize in American society.[70] In the same year, British abolitionist George Thompson posed for at least three group daguerreotypes with William Lloyd Garrison and Wendell

Phillips in Boston (Figures 3.14 and 3.15). All three men had made names for themselves through their prowess as orators. On Garrison's first encounter with Thompson, in 1833, Thompson's lecturing had filled his "mind with admiration."[71] The daguerreotypes brought them down from the podium, placing them casually around a parlor table in a simulated group conversation. Part group portrait and part action shot, these hybrid images of white radicals as parlor gentlemen visualized the transatlantic political bonds of abolitionist leadership.

To be sure, photography did not initiate abolitionist portraiture. The 1830s shift to immediatism walked hand in hand with the sale of commercial images of white leaders, including Robert Douglass Jr.'s 1833 lithograph of William Lloyd Garrison, which was meant for mass distribution and sale to a growing population of admiring activists.[72] Further, photographs of Frederick Douglass, John Jones, and others extended a tradition of black American portraiture that dated back to

Figure 3.14 *Wendell Phillips, William Lloyd Garrison, and George Thompson,* 1850, by Southworth & Hawes, daguerreotype, whole plate. Print Department, Boston Public Library.

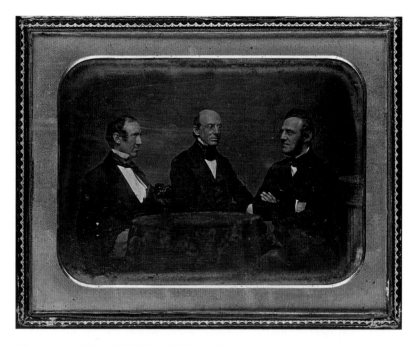

Figure 3.15 *Wendell Phillips, William Lloyd Garrison, and George Thompson,* 1850, by Southworth & Hawes, daguerreotype, whole plate. Print Department, Boston Public Library.

the late-eighteenth-century frontispiece portraits of Olaudah Equiano and Phyllis Wheatley.[73] Portraits of ex-slaves would continue to adorn slave narratives as a means of conveying the authenticity and authority of the author in the antebellum era, and these frontispieces complemented paintings and lithographs of notable black figures. Perhaps the most widely seen black portrait in the early 1840s was Nathaniel Jocelyn's painting of Cinque (c. 1840), the famed leader of the *Amistad* revolt. Though denied a place at the sixth annual Artists' Fund Society exhibition in Philadelphia due to the political turmoil sparked by the *Amistad* rebellion, the painting served as the foundation for a lithograph, made by John Sartain and distributed with the help of Lewis and Arthur Tappan. The painting would also be viewed by abolitionists and ex-slaves in the home of its commissioner, Robert Purvis. Soon after acquiring the portrait, in fact, Purvis sheltered fugitive slave Madison Washington. As Purvis later contended, the portrait of

Cinque helped inspire Madison Washington to eventually lead a revolt on the slave ship *Creole*.[74] Though impossible to verify, Purvis's recollection reveals, at the very least, how much he linked radical portraits with radical action.

Photography enlarged this aesthetic and political tradition by personalizing portraiture. The intimate exchange of likenesses amongst friends helped knit activist social circles together. Indeed, the more popular expression of political bonds was through the physical exchange of individual portrait photographs, rather than through pictures that depicted bonds between activists. One such visual-material connection that emerged was between George Thompson and American activists. While Thompson posed with Garrison and Phillips, he also found when he lectured throughout the Northeast in 1850 that many a rank-and-file abolitionist sought a visual souvenir of his visit. "Locks of my hair—autographs—& likenesses are in great demand," Thompson remarked about his visit to Rochester.[75] Reports revealed how Thompson kept images of American abolitionists in his home in England as well. As London reporter William Farmer noted in the *Liberator*, "Mr. Thompson's drawing-room table is graced with the daguerreotype portraits of a few of the choicest of what may be termed American Anti-Slavery Apostles," including Gerrit Smith's likeness.[76] Even if most abolitionists could not obtain their own daguerreotypes of Thompson—or Garrison or Phillips, for that matter—newspaper accounts helped them to imagine the reach of their movement across the Atlantic.

Image exchanges occurred across racial lines, a practice that distinguished abolitionists from the rest of American culture. Upstate New Yorker Gerrit Smith, a white abolitionist, owned a photo album with cartes de visite of many comrades, including his friend James McCune Smith, a black abolitionist.[77] Meanwhile, black abolitionist William Still would keep the image of the Executive Committee of the Pennsylvania Anti-Slavery Society, an almost all-white picture, well after the Civil War.[78] Frederick Douglass related how personal images were generally shown to you "in every house you enter."[79] Douglass returned the favor by circulating his own photographs, as in the case of one daguerreotype, made around 1847, which he gave to his Rochester friend and women's rights activist Susan B. Anthony. She in turn displayed the image of him on the mantel in her house.[80] The

prevalence of such private photo exchanges held the social movement together.

For ex-slaves such as Douglass, the urgency of projecting their humanity and social potential fueled desires for self-portraiture. For
radical whites, anti-abolitionist sentiment undoubtedly rendered pictures and picture exchanges a means of reinforcing their sense of belonging.[81] Take the example of Gerrit Smith. In response to Smith's
involvement in an anti–Fugitive Slave Law convention in Cazenovia,
New York, in 1850, one northern newspaper described how Smith
"has become insane" and called him a "madman or knave."[82] Pasting
a local newspaper article into his scrapbook, Smith wrote above it,
"Even in my own county I am regarded as crazy."[83] It should come as
no surprise, then, that Smith would keep an album full of photos of
his radical comrades as a tangible testament to a community of like-
minded activists.

External antagonism and photographic circulation come together
in the example of the Quaker Joseph Carpenter, who owned a farm
that doubled as an Underground Railroad safe house in New Rochelle,
New York. Though Carpenter's name is not well known today, he was
never short of admirers and enemies in his own day. Lydia Maria
Child, who visited Carpenter's farm, described in an 1858 private
letter how he "is called an infidel, but he is the *best* man I ever knew,
without any exception. For thirty years he has been an out and out
Garrison abolitionist, has spent money and time freely in the cause,
and endured great prosecution from his Quaker brethren. More fugitive slaves have been sheltered in his house than any other house in
the U. States."[84] Carpenter evidently saw photography as a personal
vehicle to convey anti-racist sentiment, and it is not hard to imagine
that he saw this behavior as a response to the moniker "infidel."
Former abolitionist Aaron Powell recalled how Carpenter had "a large
circle of warmly attached personal friends, and had many requests for
his photograph." As Powell further noted, Carpenter "had one photograph taken with a little colored boy, the child of a colored woman
whom they had befriended, standing by him, and these he would give
to friends from whom he had such requests, feeling that he was at the
same time conveying silently the lesson he so much desired to teach
concerning the cruel and unjust color prejudice."[85] In his memoir,
Powell published a photograph of Carpenter with a child that was

likely the one he described (Figure 3.16). The touching hands in the portrait symbolized the interracial bonds Carpenter wanted to build. But the choice to picture himself with a black child, and the positions of the two subjects (which resembled the formula for presenting father and son), revealed a vision of white patriarchy and black dependency. Whites such as Carpenter pictorially enacted the interracial society they sought to achieve, but white paternalism could still plague that imaginary.

Whether they made and circulated group portraits, individual likenesses, or interracial visions, abolitionists were reworking the new visual language of the moment to shape their self-conceptions and build their movement.[86] Scholars have often associated such exchanges of unique photographs with the sentimental practices that bolstered middle-class families in the antebellum North. But these practices could just as easily build political networks. Every one of the tens of thousands of abolitionists likely made at least one photograph, and many shared these images with other activists, not just family members. Of course, this practice was not distinctive to abolition. It would have helped the mid-nineteenth-century temperance and women's movements as well. Every social network—whether familial, reform, or radical—surely benefited from the introduction of photography and photo-sharing practices in the 1840s.[87] Abolitionists were merely at the vanguard of this broader cultural transformation. Within and through photographs, they pictorially enacted an alternative visual world—a world that contested northern popular culture and southern slave photography by asserting visions of white benevolence and, in the case of ex-slaves, black personhood, dignity, and potential.

―――

ABOLITIONIST PHOTOGRAPHY WAS SHAPED by two key forces, the first of which was a desire on the part of both white and black activists to stake claims to certain social identities. Aspirations for sturdier self-conceptions, stronger political communities, and new social formations catalyzed the production of white likenesses. For ex-slaves, meanwhile, photography offered a vehicle to demolish an older conception of them as people with prices and instead stress their humanity and

JOSEPH CARPENTER.

Figure 3.16   Joseph Carpenter, in Aaron M. Powell, *Personal Reminiscences of the Anti-Slavery and Other Reforms and Reformers*, 1899, print with text. Jean Blackwell Hutson Research and Reference Division, Schomburg Center for Research in Black Culture, The New York Public Library, Astor, Lenox and Tilden Foundations.

social potential. The second force driving abolitionist photography was direct action. While *Branded Hand* represents the first "direct action" photograph, this political practice grew increasingly prominent in abolitionist efforts of the 1850s, shaping the public and private events that injected the movement with urgency and lit broader fires of sectional animosity.

The impetus for this shift was the passage of the Fugitive Slave Law in 1850. Part of the Compromise of 1850, the law penalized northern citizens (with a fine up to $1,000 and six months in jail) for failing to aid in returning fugitive slaves, instituted federal commissioners (rather than state judges) as overseers, and barred fugitive slaves from testifying in court and from the right to a trial by jury.[88] Abolitionists responded quickly, organizing protest meetings across the North. In November 1850 Senator Charles Sumner spoke before a crowd at Faneuil Hall, urging the nonviolent approach that had long served as a touchstone of immediatism. "There is another power, stronger than any individual arm, which I invoke," Sumner charged. "I mean that irresistible public opinion inspired by love of God and man which, without violence or noise, gently as the operations of nature, makes and unmakes laws. Let this public opinion be felt in its might, and the Fugitive Slave bill will become everywhere among us a dead letter."[89] Others took a much more aggressive tone, as exemplified by Frederick Douglass's hostile comments in Pittsburgh. For him, the only way to limit the power of the law was "to make half a dozen or more dead kidnappers," which would "cool the ardor of Southern gentlemen, and keep their rapacity in check."[90] Though abolitionists such as Sumner and Douglass pitched different messages, the law bound them in a common antagonism against the slave power.

Abolitionists began to respond to the law with direct action, if rarely violence, during the 1850s. They formed organizations to aid fugitive slaves, including the Committee of Vigilance and Safety in Boston, the New York Vigilance Committee, and the new Philadelphia Vigilance Committee. More than eighty times in the 1850s, abolitionists sought to rescue fugitive slaves and free blacks before they were returned to slavery, including the famous cases of Shadrach Minkins (Boston, 1851), Thomas Sims (Boston, 1851), Jerry McHenry (Syracuse, New York, 1851), Anthony Burns (Boston, 1854), and Charles Nalle (Troy, New York, 1860). Many of these incidents attracted national attention, and, as historian Lois E. Horton notes, "each one infuriated slaveholders, garnered increasing Northern sympathy for antislavery, and intensified the determination of abolitionists to fight the Fugitive Slave Law."[91]

Within the movement, images of white rebels and escaping fugitives—what I term "rebel photography" and "underground photography"—shaped the meanings of this transition from moral suasion to direct action.[92] Changing in tandem with the increasingly confrontational culture of the 1850s, photography reoriented abolitionist visuality from the centrality of idealization and imagination to the growing importance of documentary evidence. Abolitionists had once envisioned ties amongst activists through the image of the kneeling slave, and slavery through illustrations. Now they gazed upon actual activists and fugitives. Direct action photography built solidarity amongst activists, symbolized resistance to the Slave Power, and advanced a narrative that prized the courage and humanity of white radicals and fugitive slaves.

On August 21, 1850, only two days after Congress had passed the Fugitive Slave Law, more than two thousand abolitionists gathered in Cazenovia, New York, where they enacted a social, written, and photographic protest.[93] A key purpose of the convention was to write "A Letter to the American Slaves from those who have fled from American Slavery," actually penned by Gerrit Smith and endorsed by the approximately fifty fugitives in attendance, which characterized slavery as a state of war and emphasized to slaves that "by all the rules of war, you have the fullest liberty to plunder, burn, and kill, as you may have occasion to do to promote your escape."[94] Many who authorized the letter also posed for the camera of Cazenovia daguerreotypist Ezra Greenleaf Weld, older brother of Theodore Dwight Weld, who had operated a studio in Cazenovia since 1845 (Figure 3.17).

At first glance, the image appears to be an early attempt to record a political event, one reflecting the interracial and intergender composition of abolitionism. For those at the convention, however, the image held more specific purposes and meanings, which surrounded one particular white abolitionist: William L. Chaplin. The general agent of the New York State Antislavery Society and a member of the social orbit surrounding Gerrit Smith, Chaplin had initially planned to make a dramatic appearance at the convention with fugitives whom he had

Figure 3.17 *Fugitive Slave Law Convention, Cazenovia, New York*, August 22, 1850, by Ezra Greenleaf Weld, daguerreotype, 2⅝ × 2⅛ inches. Digital image courtesy of the Getty's Open Content Program.

ferried from the South. Chaplin's plan failed spectacularly, though. Only a few days before the convention, he was imprisoned for seeking to help the slaves of Georgia congressmen Alexander Stephens and Robert Toombs escape in Washington, D.C.[95] Given these events, Chaplin played an unusually prominent role in the activities of the Cazenovia gathering. The incendiary "Letter to American Slaves" advised bondspeople of how "the precious name of William L. Chaplin has been added to the list of those, who, in helping you gain your liberty, have lost their own. Here is a man, whose wisdom, cultivation, moral worth, bring him into the highest and best class of men: and, yet, he becomes a willing martyr for the poor, despised, forgotten slave's sake."[96] At Cazenovia, abolitionists agreed to raise $20,000 to aid this "willing martyr."[97] As the *Liberator* reveals, they also sought to aid Chaplin with a group photograph:

> *Novel Idea. —At the meeting of fugitives and sympathizers held at Cazenovia, much sympathy was expressed for* W. L. CHAPLIN, *Esq., who, in his efforts to let the oppressed go free, has fallen into the hands of the "Philistines." But in order to give him an idea of the meeting, at which he was prevented by "circumstances" from*

attending, a daguerreotype picture of the Convention, with some
of the most prominent members on the stand, was taken, to be sent
to him. This must be highly gratifying to him, as affording the
sensible proof that the Convention are not unmindful to
"remember them that are in bonds."[98]

The notice in the *Liberator* illuminates how the daguerreotype operated on multiple levels. On one level, it served as a means of communication between the group and Chaplin held "in bonds," a material
token of solidarity, a shared image of symbolic protest and together-
ness. One can clearly view the personal and political connections
between Chaplin and the subjects in the portrait. His fiancée, the
bonneted Theodosia Gilbert, literally took center stage, seated next
to Frederick Douglass. The Edmonson sisters, ex-slaves who had
gained their freedom with Chaplin's help, stood behind the desk;
white abolitionist Gerrit Smith stood between them.[99] Those at the
convention would have taken pride in the fact that this portrait revealed the blurry outlines of tree branches: the first day of the convention took place at the Free Congregational Church, but since too
many people had attended, the second day's proceedings moved to a
nearby apple orchard on the property of a local activist, and so the trees
signified the measure of abolitionist resourcefulness and the strength
of abolitionist resolve.[100] It is not clear if Chaplin ever received the
daguerreotype and saw his loved ones and friends under those apple
trees, though someone might have brought it to him on a visit to the
jail, as those at the convention planned to do with other material objects, including a silver pitcher and goblets.[101] On another level, the
image achieved its influence through its written description in the
Liberator. Terming the image a "novel idea," the *Liberator* revealed
these abolitionists' self-conscious efforts to engage in a new practice
of photographic solidarity with an imprisoned martyr, in doing so
highlighting Chaplin's very inability to see the convention firsthand.

In ensuing years, abolitionist photography would continue to testify to white rebels who suffered for the cause. In the summer of 1855,
abolitionist Passmore Williamson—secretary of the Acting Committee
of the Pennsylvania Society for Promoting the Abolition of Slavery—
took the lead alongside William Still in helping the enslaved Jane
Johnson escape when she stopped in Philadelphia with her master,

John H. Wheeler, the U.S. minister to Nicaragua, on their way to South America. Jailed for four months, Williamson became a national sensation, his story covered extensively by mainstream papers such as the *National Tribune* as well as the antislavery press. Williamson received no shortage of visitors and letters of condolence and praise. Black luminaries such as Frederick Douglass and Harriet Tubman called upon Williamson in his cell, while others wrote to him with admiration. Senator Charles Sumner told Williamson that it was a "privilege to suffer for truth."[102] For abolitionist Mary Grew, Williamson was an inspiration, and she related how "we, your fellow laborers, are growing strong by your courage, patient by your endurance, and earnest by your self-sacrifice."[103] Williamson was also visited by a photographer, Philadelphia artist John Steck, who stopped in on the same day as lithographer August Kollner and bookseller Thomas Curtis. Perhaps Steck took the daguerreotype as a model for the print that Curtis eventually published.[104] Sitting in Philadelphia's Moyamensing Prison, Williamson posed respectably yet defiantly—cravat tied, arms crossed, gazing boldly at the camera in front of a cell door that signified his captivity (Figure 3.18).

Likewise, in 1858, an interracial crowd of men from Oberlin, Wellington, and Pittsfield, Ohio, helped free an arrested Kentucky fugitive named John Price, who had been living in the black community of Oberlin, and immediately hastened him to Canada. Subsequently, at least twenty of these "Oberlin-Wellington" rescuers were jailed for more than a year, becoming yet another case of abolitionist martyrdom in the presses. In April 1859, Cleveland photographer J. M. Green captured the captured activists in at least two images as they stood in the courtyard of the Cuyahoga County jail (Figure 3.19).[105] Though primarily envisioning white men, this news picture also included black rescuers, including Orindatus S. B. Wall, John Scott, John Watson, and Charles Langston, who stood in the center of the line holding his wide-brimmed hat high. In 1855 Williamson posed as the lone white defiant; in 1859 the Oberlin rebels exhibited an interracial martyrdom emblematic of the grassroots radicalism of the many slave rescues of the decade. It showed black and white rebels in solidarity.

Later in 1859, Dr. John Doy posed for two photographic portraits after his own direct actions landed him in jail. Doy had sought to help

Figure 3.18 *Passmore Williamson in Moyamensing Prison, Philadelphia*, 1855, attributed to John Steck, daguerreotype, quarter plate. DG300, Chester County Historical Society, West Chester, PA.

thirteen blacks—who feared they would be kidnapped and sold into slavery in Missouri—by transporting them in wagons from Lawrence, Kansas Territory, to Iowa. Only twelve miles outside Lawrence, Doy and the African Americans were accosted by a group of ruffians, who kidnapped Doy and those blacks seeking refuge and brought them to

Figure 3.19 *The Oberlin Rescuers at the Cuyahoga County Jail*, April 1859. Oberlin College Archives.

Weston, Missouri. Wilson George Hays and Charles Smith, two black men, were soon sold into bondage in Independence, Missouri. Doy's narrative made only vague mention of the tragic fate of the others, who were "taken away forcibly or prevailed on to choose their masters." Doy was eventually convicted of abducting slaves and sentenced to five years in prison.[106] But Doy would not need to wait five years, since a group of rescuers helped him escape in the summer of 1859. As the *National Era* detailed, the rescuers presented themselves to the jail guard as men who sought to throw a horse thief in jail. Once inside, the men pulled their guns, obtained the keys, set Doy free, and ferried him back across the river to Lawrence. There they posed for at least two emancipation images, taken by a local photographer, Amon

Gilbert DaLee (Figures 3.20 and 3.21).[107] The proudly brandished guns and knives of the rescuers and the lack of such weaponry on Doy's person pulled differing strands of abolitionism into one frame: the nonviolent rebel and the militant dissidents unafraid to use force in the service of freedom.

Figure 3.20 *John Doy and Rescue Party*, 1859, by Amon Gilbert DaLee, ambrotype, 4½ × 3¼ inches (image), 6 × 4¾ inches (case). Kansas State Historical Society.

Figure 3.21 *John Doy and Rescue Party*, 1859, by Amon Gilbert DaLee, ambrotype, 4½ × 3¼ inches (image), 6 × 4 ¾ inches (case). Kansas State Historical Society.

    Direct, voluntary action tied these men together, but so too did their experience as prisoners. Ironically, the Fugitive Slave Law proved a boon to abolitionist photography, for jails—as physical sites and places of national and religious significance—were tailor-made for documentary pictures. First, long prison stays—like downtime during the Civil

War—gave photographers the necessary time to make images that seemed part of the event. Second, prison escapes created easy before-and-after moments, in which abolitionists such as John Doy became emancipated figures. Third, the prison experience helped abolitionists make imaginative connections between white martyrs and black slaves, for they often called slavery a "prison house."[108] *Frederick Douglass' Paper* urged abolitionist support to "give liberty to every slave" and to "open the prison door of every Passmore Williamson."[109] Finally, these events would have easily recalled to many abolitionists biblical stories of those imprisoned for their beliefs, including Paul and Silas.[110] Abolitionists' prison photography resonated throughout the 1850s precisely because it testified to the drama and specificity of direct action as it simultaneously recalled a multiplicity of narratives to northern radicals.

In the fall of 1859 the greatest output of rebel photographs surrounded the violence, suffering, and martyrdom of John Brown. On October 16, 1859, Brown had led a group of black and white radicals into Harpers Ferry, Virginia, a town at the split of the Shenandoah and Potomac Rivers. Brown and his men sought to seize the arsenal and armory, which would give them the foothold to spark a broader slave rebellion. They immediately captured prisoners, shot the night guard for the Potomac River bridge, and sent sentries to alert local slaves to the rebellion. Brown had thought his actions would inspire an army of revolutionary slaves, but all he attracted was a horde of southern militiamen, who arrived to crush his efforts. By the morning of October 18, Marines had captured Brown as he made his last stand at the engine house. News of Brown's failed raid at Harpers Ferry and his subsequent trial touched off a ferocious national debate over a looming sectional conflict; within abolitionist ranks, Brown's raid sparked a photographic explosion. By mid-November 1859, after Brown's death sentence but before his execution, abolitionists had begun circulating photographs of Brown en masse.

Photographs of Brown and others amplified the suffering of white male abolitionists, humanizing men who were cast as maniacal monsters in the mainstream presses. While *Branded Hand* served as the basis for engravings, Williamson's actual daguerreotype was exchanged amongst friends. "Mr. Pierce was so kind as to send me your daguerreotype," Lewis Tappan wrote Williamson in November of

1855. "I pinned to it your letter of Sept 29th to a gentleman in this city & have gratified many in this city & vicinity and in Boston during my late visit there, who have seen it."[111] Never mass-produced as a photograph, the Williamson daguerreotype still steeled abolitionist resolve through private circulation. It also might have served as the visual foundation for a lithograph, published by Thomas Curtis of Philadelphia, depicting Williamson gazing out at viewers from his cell.[112] Meanwhile, *Frank Leslie's Illustrated Newspaper* made the photograph of the Oberlin rebels its front-page illustration on May 7, 1859, a venture that surely set the stage for its extensive visual coverage of John Brown's trial and execution. "Everybody," *Leslie's* described in an accompanying article, "wanted to see the criminals, and Mr. J. M. Green, a successful and favorite artist of the city (Cleveland), gratified the desire of such as could not gain admittance to the prison, by taking the excellent photographic view accompanying this article."[113] Finally, John Doy's *The Narrative of John Doy, of Lawrence, Kansas* (1860) soon sold "a fine likeness of Dr. Doy"—as well as "the grouped picture of the heroic Kansas men who rescued him"—likely based upon one of his emancipation ambrotypes.[114] If photographs gave abolitionists internal views of their movement, then such images also occasionally shaped mainstream views of direct action.

Naturally, not all of these artists and outlets could be categorized as "abolitionist." Little is known of the politics of photographers John Steck, Amon Gilbert DaLee, and J. M. Green and the lithographic firm of Thomas Curtis in Philadelphia. *Frank Leslie's Illustrated Newspaper* was a strong Union supporter during the Civil War, but before Fort Sumter, it walked a fine line between covering political events that bred sectional animosity and maintaining its southern readership.[115] Thus, rebel photography emerged as the product of different groups with various political and commercial agendas: abolitionist photographic subjects who engaged in direct action, committed abolitionist photographers and commercial networks, sympathetic artists, and commercial news outlets. In concert, they crafted and magnified a narrative of the abolitionist, particularly the white activist, as the sympathetic, suffering rebel.

More than anyone, it was John Brown who catalyzed this narrative through his photographs, which abolitionists sold widely in their newspapers. William Cooper Nell quickly launched the sale of Brown's portraits after Harpers Ferry, collaborating in December 1859 with artist Thomas M. Johnson and photographer T. H. Webb for a photo-lithograph.[116] Many others joined Nell, and perhaps no abolitionist took greater interest in this enterprise than Thaddeus Hyatt. A manufacturer from New York, Hyatt had helped fund the National Kansas Committee to support free state battles in Bleeding Kansas.[117] "I have a photograph of the old man presented to me by his own [h]ands, an admirable likeness," Hyatt advertised. "Let all who sympathize in the purpose send each a dollar, and I will forward for each such sum an exact copy of the original, and with it, if possible, John Brown's autograph."[118] In November 1859, Hyatt felt he could easily sell ten thousand pictures. He made sure to mention in his advertisements that the images would "all be photographs, and not engravings."[119] Hyatt capitalized on the public perception of the photograph as an unmediated relation to Brown.

Brown's portraits gave abolitionists the best of both worlds: recognition of his courage and sacrifice, and a closer material connection to these qualities, without visual evidence of the actual violence at Harpers Ferry. Unlike *Frank Leslie's Illustrated Newspaper*, which offered engravings of the fighting (including an interior sketch of Brown holding hostages as he made his final stand) as well as full-page spreads of Brown's trial and execution, there were no aftermath photographs from Brown's raid, nor were there any photographs of the courtroom, as southerners barred photographers from taking pictures of the proceedings.[120] Abolitionists circulated images of John Brown in photographic portraiture, and it was J. B. Heywood who produced one of the most widely circulated likenesses (Figure 3.22). Many of Brown's previous portraits had cast him as a fierce and sharp man, with a gaunt face and a piercing gaze, as in the now-famous daguerreotype Augustus Washington made in 1847 or the portrait taken in the late 1850s by John A. Whipple and J. W. Black.[121] The Heywood image, on the other hand, offered a mellower Brown. Boasting a long gray beard, hands in his pockets, Brown was both a Moses-like figure who sought a mass exodus of enslaved people and an elder statesmen of the radical community, more ready to converse and advise than instigate violent rebellion.

In public and in private, photographs marking Brown's death actually gave him new cultural life. At a memorial in Cleveland, for

Figure 3.22 *John Brown*, 1859, by J. B. Heywood, albumen print, 18.7 × 13.5 cm (oval image), 25.1 × 20.2 cm (mount). Boston Athenæum.

example, viewers saw a "fine photograph of the Hero of Harpers Ferry, in gilt frame encircled with a wreath," on the stage of Melodeon Hall. The display surrounded Brown's portrait with lofty phrases such as "Remember them that are in bonds as bound with them" and "His noble spirit makes despots quail, and Freedom triumphs."[122] These images soon decorated abolitionists' homes. Lydia Maria Child told Thaddeus Hyatt his fundraising plan with photographs was "excellent," and she sought "to have every form of his likeness that can be devised, and have no corner of my dwelling without a memorial of him. The brave, self-sacrificing noble old man."[123] Child alluded to the broader visualization of Brown that contributed to his martyrdom, which included engravings in *Frank Leslie's* of Brown's coffin, of Brown "ascending the scaffold" to be hung, and of the Heywood photograph.[124] Part of this visual landscape, abolitionists were simultaneously reworking the tradition of postmortem photography, a popular practice through which Americans pictured the dead bodies of loved ones in order to preserve them in memory. The admiration and awe that Brown's image elicited is unmistakable. Whether a signal of his continuing presence or a sign of his absence, Brown's portraits filled up abolitionists' private visual shrines, and Brown lived on as the most famous of photographic rebel-martyrs for decades.

This direct action photography revises the traditional narrative of abolitionist visual culture. While abolitionist images of suffering slaves have received much attention, rebel photography largely generated sympathy for suffering whites. In a strange reversal, the fugitive slaves at the Cazenovia convention sent a photograph to show white abolitionist William L. Chaplin that they were "not unmindful to 'remember them that are in bonds.'" These photographs deepened a narrative of the white activist who suffered for the cause that had actually preceded the medium. In 1837, newspaper editor Elijah P. Lovejoy became an immediatist martyr when anti-abolitionists burned down his house in Alton, Illinois, and shot him as he attempted to escape.[125] Lovejoy's death was not accompanied by a flowering of portraits—only a print that depicted the riot.[126] Rebel photography, in contrast, allowed abolitionist spectators to contemplate the bodies and faces—and, further, the characters—of those who risked their lives to fight the slave power. Building a radical community meant seeing and connecting to its participants, especially the most courageous ones.[127]

Through this tradition of rebel photography, abolitionists helped to initiate the practice of photographing and consuming "the pain of others." Though scholars have discussed photographs of dead soldiers and impoverished prisoners of the Civil War, they have largely overlooked the role that suffering photographs have played in shaping political and moral sentiment in nineteenth-century America, beginning with abolitionists' efforts to connect to the suffering of activist rebels.[128] In place of a visual landscape stressing the inhumane nature of slavery, abolitionist photography emphasized the humaneness of the movement.

━━━

ALONG THE UNDERGROUND RAILROAD, abolitionists began developing a quieter photo culture that also bolstered movement solidarity and made claims to black identity, through images that documented and expressed fugitive action. A decentralized web of fugitive escape routes supported by interracial activist networks, the Underground Railroad played an important role in hastening the arrival of the Civil War. As historian David Blight writes, the "traffic in escaped slaves exerted pressure on slavery itself, caused significant political tensions between North and South, and prompted a small but important group of abolitionists to resist the law by aiding fugitives to freedom."[129] Yet the social and cultural experience of the Underground Railroad, and the relation between this experience and the politics of slavery, has proven notoriously difficult for historians to access, given the lack of sources.[130] This dearth of evidence is due in large part to the secretive nature of the work, which led some abolitionists to destroy their records, as Robert Purvis did with his logbook of fugitives who passed through Philadelphia.[131] Others took care to never document their actions in the first place. J. H. Tibbets, an Underground Railroad activist from Madison, Indiana, recalled, "I have often wished I had kept a journal, but it was not safe at that time to put such thing[s] on paper for we did not know how soon our enemies would mob us and burn our houses, of course any such paper would be a good witness and caus[e] us to be perhaps put to death or whiped."[132] These reasons help explain why very few photographs have survived in archives. But newspaper accounts, slave narratives, and the written records of operatives such as William Still offer a tantalizing glimpse into the making and social uses of underground photographs.[133]

Take the story of Richard Easler and Abram Galloway, two enslaved friends from Wilmington, North Carolina. After Easler broke North Carolina law by marrying a free woman, he faced a whipping and imprisonment. He decided to flee to the North, and Galloway joined him. They sought freedom by ship, but knew any vessel leaving a North Carolina harbor would be smoked, a method used to root out hideaway slaves stowed below deck. Easler and Galloway prepared by dressing for the voyage in shrouds of silk oilcloth to be drawn over their heads so that they would be able to breathe more easily. They arrived safely in Philadelphia, where they connected with members of the Philadelphia Vigilance Committee. Before helping Easler and Galloway onward to Canada, though, the conductors sought visual mementos of the fugitives. "Desiring to retain some memorial of them," William Still noted, "a member of the Committee begged one of their silk shrouds, and likewise procured an artist to take the photograph of one of them."[134]

Philadelphia Vigilance Committee members complemented their memorializing portraits of Easler and Galloway with an image of Lear Green, an enslaved woman from Baltimore. Green had also fled north by ship, but her escape took an even more sensational course: she escaped inside a chest, with only food, water, a blanket, and a pillow to sustain her. She eventually arrived in Philadelphia with the rest of the cargo. Before she continued onward, Green and members of the Vigilance Committee reenacted her escape north through photography. When Green departed for Elmira, New York, she left behind a photograph that pictured her inside the getaway chest.[135] These stories of Easler, Galloway, and Green reveal how photomaking had become part of the very transition from slavery to freedom in Philadelphia, one of the primary underground hubs.[136] That the Vigilance Committee never publicized these photographs in the antebellum era suggests that Underground Railroad operatives offset the public invisibility of their work through acts of private photographic documentation.

Written and visual evidence reveals the reach of underground image-making. In Rochester, where almost four hundred fugitives found shelter with Frederick Douglass before continuing on to Canada, it seemed commonplace by 1860 for a fugitive to leave his photograph in passing.[137] Describing the story of Ben, a fugitive from Georgia, *Douglass' Monthly* humorously jabbed at Ben's master, "Be assured that your lost BEN for whom you mourn by this time 'as those that have no hope,' shall be 'arrested' if he comes this way, and detained long enough to get a good night's sleep and a warm breakfast, and if he should leave us his daguerreotype, you shall see it when you come this way, for it would give us pleasure to let you view the 'shadow' of Ben, now his 'substance has fled.'"[138] Douglass's taunt reveals yet another way in which abolitionists drew upon mainstream photographic practices and turned them into social movement tactics: operatives were keeping mementos of travelers, in this case fugitives, like any antebellum American would—to preserve a moment and a personal connection. In this case, that practice carried added symbolic value. These very social exchanges, amplified by Douglass's newspaper, were in themselves recognition of enslaved personhood. An ex-slave such as Ben did not simply sit for someone else's daguerreotype but instead gave the abolitionists his daguerreotype. With subtle brilliance, Douglass's paper constructed a welcoming yet subversive abolitionist community as it identified Ben as the self-possessed master of his own image.

In Cincinnati, abolitionists possessed the two essential elements for underground image-making during the 1850s: a movement photographer in J. P. Ball and a renowned "stationmaster" in Levi Coffin. In 1862, with the Fugitive Slave Law still in force, Ball and Coffin collaborated to make a fugitive carte de visite, described by Coffin in his *Reminiscences of Levi Coffin, the Reputed President of the Underground Railroad*.[139] The history of this image began when an eighteen-year-old slave woman found herself sold to a new master who "designed placing her in a house of ill-fame at Lexington, Kentucky." Anticipating her future in a brothel, the woman fled to a Union army camp in Nicholasville, Kentucky, where she made contact with the 22nd Wisconsin Volunteers, a group known by many as the "Abolition Regiment" due to the politics of its leader, Colonel Utley. Two members of the regiment, Jesse L. Berch and Frank M. Rockwell, aided her on her journey to Cincinnati and made contact with Coffin. They rested for a few days at Coffin's house as the soldiers arranged for the fugitive to travel to their hometown of Racine, Wisconsin. Before the fugitive boarded a train, however, she and the soldiers stopped by J. P. Ball's gallery on West Fourth Street and posed for a picture (Figure 3.23). The fugitive sat in a dress, shawl, and hat, while Berch and Rockwell stood behind her, brandishing their guns in a common gesture for soldiers at the time. The image offered the same composition as the pictures of John Doy and his rescuers in Kansas territory, revealing a broader abolitionist rescue iconography. In this case Ball's portrait captured the fugitive's dress in full, thereby stressing her femininity. The soldiers were saving her virtue as much as they were aiding her liberation. Coffin underscored this claim of the photograph, commenting on how the men revealed "their readiness thus to protect her, even at the cost of their own lives."[140]

The speed of photography enabled such fugitive portraits. Abolitionists and fugitives likely never thought much about making fugitive paintings when they met on the Underground Railroad, as

Figure 3.23 *Jesse Berch, Quartermaster Sergeant, 22, Wisconsin Regiment of Racine, Wis. [and] Frank M. Rockwell, Postmaster 22 Wisconsin of Geneva, Wis.*, 1862, by James Presley Ball, carte de visite, albumen print, 10 × 6 cm. Civil War Collection, Gladstone Collection of African American Photographs, Prints and Photographs Division, Library of Congress, LC-DIG-ppmsca-10940.

paintings cost more money and took far more time to complete. By the 1850s, however, activists and escapees could take a daguerreotype in only fifteen to twenty seconds (sitting time) and an ambrotype or tintype in only six to ten seconds.[141] Getting in and out of the galleries likely posed the greater challenge. At that moment American photographers were experimenting with the use of artificial light for portraits, but they largely relied on skylights for natural light, which they directed into different spaces in the studio with screens and mirrors.[142] In the middle-class spaces of photograph galleries, fugitive slaves posed quickly enough to avoid detection.[143] Indeed, visual evidence suggests that Ball may have rushed his portrait of the Kentucky slave with the Wisconsin soldiers, for the unknown cylindrical object in the foreground reveals a sloppy composition, perhaps put together too hastily.

Occasionally abolitionists used fugitive photographs as visual evidence in mass-produced media and in public settings. J. P. Ball's carte de visite of the Kentucky fugitive and soldiers reached a wider audience when it was republished in James B. Rogers's *War Pictures* (1863).[144] Other times the photographic form itself constituted an important part of the testimony. For example, at an 1859 commemoration of West Indian emancipation in Abington, a town south of Boston, former slave Lewis Clark displayed ambrotypes of fugitives for the crowd, which had just heard such speakers as William Lloyd Garrison, Charles Lenox Remond, and Samuel May Jr. Clark sought to show, as the *Liberator* noted, "that slavery is not at all particular as to the color of its victim."[145] As the paper further detailed, "Some of the faces exhibited were as white as the fairest Anglo-Saxon of the tribe, and as beautiful, too. Mr. Clark said he did not care how man[y] Fugitive Slave Bills were passed, some slaves would still find their way to Canada, for Congress could not black their faces, or make their eyes other than blue."[146] Clark's delivery method fused the old and new, the podium lecture with the photograph—thereby prefiguring the lantern slide lectures that gained popularity in the late nineteenth century. Drawing on a prominent 1850s narrative of white slaves, which any audience member would have immediately linked to masters raping slave women, Clark revealed the unintentionally self-destructive nature of this behavior, which whitened the slave community and thus rendered it more difficult to police. Photography proved the perfect visual aid, for it was widely perceived as the premier medium for offering a transparent window onto the world, in this case the whiteness that never failed to rile northerners.[147]

Abolitionists also used fugitive images to reveal individual slave resistance in private settings, as the case of black abolitionist Charlotte Forten illustrates. In July 1857 Forten visited the gallery of Samuel Broadbent in Philadelphia. She recorded in her diary that she went at the request of a friend to have her likeness taken. While Forten was at the studio, as she recalled, "Miss J.[ames] was there and showed me a daguerreotype of a young slave girl who escaped in a box"—probably Lear Green. As Forten detailed: "My heart was full as I gazed at it; full of admiration for the heroic girl, who risked *all* for freedom; full of indignation that in this boasted land of liberty such a thing *could* occur. Were she of any other nation her heroism would receive all due honor from these Americans, but *as it is* there is not even a single spot in this broad land, where her rights can be protected,—not one. Only in the dominions of a *queen* is she free. How long, Oh! how long will this continue!"[148] Forten's reaction reveals the potency of private image exchanges to abolitionists. Miss James's daguerreotype was never circulated widely, unlike the famous print of Henry "Box" Brown, who also had escaped slavery by crate. But inside the photograph studio, Forten quietly gazed upon an image that activated fierce emotions. She might have been shocked to see a picture of any female slave, since male slaves escaped far more often. This female slave offered special resonance, for her courage struck Forten as unsurpassed. Undoubtedly, this sense of admiration was born out of the very "eye-witness" nature of the picture, which captured a specific moment of action by way of a reenactment. Though the daguerreotype never made it into the public realm, within Underground Railroad circles it symbolized a national tragedy while simultaneously informing abolitionists that resistance was ongoing. In no small way, unique images exchanged in person activated great political sentiment along the Underground Railroad.[149]

These visual and material objects gave abolitionists new ways to view, share, and admire the actions of fugitives. But it was not only the abolitionists, black and white, who did the photographic work of the Underground Railroad; runaway slaves brought photographs northward when they fled. Sometimes they were caught in the act of absconding with images, as in the case of William Lewis, a Louisville man charged with helping a mother and child flee. Lewis was found with "divers suspicious things" in his room, "including the wearing apparel of the negroes, and the daguerreotype of one of them, that of a small child, all nicely packed in a new chest."[150] When slaves succeeded in escaping, however, they became the figures that introduced photographs of actual slaves, still toiling in bondage, to the abolitionist ranks. In January 1856 William Still wrote a letter, published in the *Provincial Freeman* and republished in the *New York Daily Times*, that described a fugitive man who fled bondage after his master sold his wife and four children to a trader in Richmond. At the moment of flight, as Still narrated, "the severed and bleeding heart of the husband resolved to escape at all hazards, taking with him a daguerreotype likeness of his wife, which he happened to have on hand, and a lock of hair from her head, and from each of the children's, as mementoes of his unbounded (though sundered) affection for them." Arriving in the North, the fugitive made contact with Still's Vigilance Committee, and as soon as he entered a safe house he "took from his pocket his wife's likeness, and while gazing upon it made touching remarks, and showed it, &c." As Still described, "His wife, as represented by the likeness, was of fair complexion, prepossessing and good-looking—perhaps not over 33 years of age." Still did not mention any specific details about the man's identity in this 1850s article, certainly to ensure his safety, but in a post-slavery account Still identified him as Robert Brown, a slave from Martinsburg, Virginia.[151]

The case of Robert Brown reveals the spatial and symbolic contours of slave photography as it headed northward. Abolitionist and southern photography were linked not by aesthetic reappropriations enacted by famous activists and wealthy slaveholders but by fugitive slaves, who swam across rivers, traipsed through the woods, and hid themselves away in safe houses—all with photographs in their pockets. On the ground, these fugitives extended their own culture of southern photographs into the North. They joined the many other American travelers who kept images to preserve bonds across space. By the 1850s, fugitive slaves had helped create a largely secretive visual exchange between their communities and abolitionists' communities, between the slave cabins of Virginia and the parlors of the North, tied together by a new technology. In doing so, these ex-slaves humanized themselves in the eyes of those they encountered, by showing likenesses of their kin and demonstrating their participation in common sentimental practices of the day. As Robert Brown entered the abolitionist safe house, he performed his personhood and character as a loving husband through the symbol-rich gesture of sharing his wife's likeness.

For fugitives, photographic practices mattered as statements of personhood; as informational and expressive objects, photographs also helped ex-slaves maintain ties with the loved ones they left behind. Most fugitives escaped as individuals, but they still expended considerable energy in communicating with enslaved family members. Historians have excavated fugitives' letters that worked to such effect, including one James Masey wrote to his wife from Canada: "I take this opertunity to inform you that I have Arive in St. Catherines this Eving. After Jorney of too weeks, and no find myself on free ground and wish that you was here with me."[152] While no evidence suggests that Masey and his wife communicated through photographs, William Still documented one such exchange between Richard Eden—the fugitive who had escaped with Abram Galloway by boat—and his wife. After arriving in Kingston, Canada, Eden contacted William Still:

> *Dear Friend:—I take the opertunity of wrighting a few lines to let you no that we air all in good health hoping thos few lines may find you and your family engoying the same blessing. We arived in King all saft Canada West Abram Galway gos to work this morning at $1.75 per day and John pediford is at work for mr george mink and i will opne a shop for my self in a few days My wif will send a daugretipe to your cair whitch you will pleas to send on to me Richard Edons to the cair of George Mink Kingston C W*
> *Yours with Respect,*
> *Richard Edons*[153]

The daguerreotype allowed Eden's wife, a free woman in North Carolina, to communicate with her husband after he reached Canada, with the help of William Still and George Mink. The son of former slaves who fled to Canada during the American Revolution as well as an important contact for William Still, Mink had built up a substantial business portfolio that included a stagecoach line between Kingston and Toronto, a tavern, and a motel. These businesses meant that he could provide lodging for fugitives once they arrived in Canada, transportation throughout Canada West, and access to the mail to reach back to the South.[154] Mink and Still worked to facilitate the exchange of visual substitutes that linked families across the great divide between slavery and freedom.

It is not hard to imagine that fugitives used photographs for an additional purpose upon arrival in the North. They could give photographs of their family members to Underground Railroad operatives returning southward for rescue operations. Harriet Tubman, for instance, often helped to rescue the kin of escapees. Using Tubman's biblical nickname, William Wells Brown described how men "from Canada, who had made their escape years before, and whose families were still in the prison-house of slavery, would seek out Moses, and get her to go and bring their dear ones away."[155] Newspaper reports further support the idea that photography could have aided in this regard. In 1860, two men, A. H. Scott and John Henry, were arrested in Louisville, Kentucky, on suspicion of helping other slaves to escape. Though Scott initially claimed to be a painter from Covington, Kentucky, and looked white, both he and Henry were fugitive slaves from Georgia. As the *Louisville Daily Journal* reported, officers found in Scott's possession "several daguerreotypes of negro men and women, which have led to the supposition that he is an agent of the Underground railroad."[156] It is unclear whether Scott and Henry had these photographs made in the North or in the South. But it seems highly likely that they were using such images as identification tools, given the assumptions of the Louisville press. Underground Railroad agents and fugitives had adopted photography as "guerrilla tactic," by which they sought to identify slaves and bring them to freedom along the Ohio River.[157]

There was another facet of the Underground Railroad in which photography more clearly enabled action. For Harriet Tubman, the portability and precision of photographs served as a safety mechanism. Tubman lived an extremely mobile life after she escaped slavery in 1849 and began working in abolitionist hotspots in upstate New York (from Troy and Auburn to Petersboro and Rochester) and fugitive hotspots in Canada West (including St. Catherines and Chatham, in present-day Ontario). Her rescue attempts required dramatic trips into Maryland and Virginia, where she retrieved slaves and ferried them northward, through Wilmington, Philadelphia, and New York City.[158] In 1856 a $12,000 reward was issued for her in Maryland.[159] How could she know whom to trust among the many strangers she encountered on her journeys?

Tubman tested the identity of strangers by asking them to name the subjects in her collection of private photographs. As a biographical story in the *Commonwealth* described, "It was curious to see the caution with which she received her visitor until she felt assured that there was no mistake. One of her means of security was to carry with her the daguerreotypes of her friends, and show them to each new person. If they recognized the likeness, then it was all right."[160] Though photographic boosters had long envisioned portrait photography as a means of remembering loved ones, Tubman had quietly broadened the function of the genre, turning it into an insurance mechanism for subversive action.[161] Photographs served a profoundly practical function that actually permitted her movement. For Tubman, handheld photographs offered the visual proof to maintain the private social networks that were absolutely essential for carrying out her distinctly mobile work.

———

LIKE MOST SOCIAL MOVEMENTS in United States history, abolitionists did not invent new media technologies so much as they adapted them to new moral and political objectives. During the 1840s and 1850s, abolitionists harnessed photography as a way of picturing members of the movement, strengthening political networks, and conveying the often dramatic work of fellow radicals and fugitive slaves. Such image-making originated in abolitionists' own acts of self-representation as well as in enslaved people's culture of private images. Rather than a photographic culture of moral suasion that largely sought to transform the external culture, abolitionists and fugitives established a public and private culture of self-representation that bolstered the movement from within.

Memories of a life in slavery, anti-black racism in the North, an acute sense of political isolation, the search for political belonging, and the looming crisis of slavery's potential expansion: these forces all shaped abolitionist photo-making. A key strain of abolitionist photography crafted the social identities of ex-slaves, who prized the mechanical nature of the medium for offering cheaper and more accurate likenesses. From the moment ex-slaves entered Underground Railroad safe houses with images in their pockets to the moments in which they sat for their first portraits in the North, fugitives used photography as a vehicle to express and stake claims to their personhood and social potential.

4

DOMESTICATING FREEDOM

"I GOT MY 'PICTURE TOOK' Sat. + send it along in this. Don't take me for a contraband though I am such a black looking individual. You know of course that I am not so black looking. It was the fault of the taking."[1] So wrote Sgt. Henry Grimes Marshall of the 15th Connecticut Infantry Regiment as he sent his photographic portrait home from Suffolk, Virginia, in April 1863. Marshall's photographic act was, in one sense, unremarkable. For the past two decades many Americans had taken time to describe, in their letters to each other, how faithfully or unfaithfully a photographer had captured their likenesses. During the Civil War it had grown common for soldiers to keep ties with loved ones through the postal exchange of pictures. Instead, it is Marshall's racial anxiety that is notable. He surely never wanted to look black, as whiteness had carried with it particular privileges in America for centuries. But the social and racial disruptions of the war had vastly magnified the significance of his racial status. And photography would prove an indispensable way for northern whites to police the divide between white and black, superior and inferior, in the uncertain years of the conflict.

The Civil War marked a new episode in the cultural clash over the status and social identities of slaves and ex-slaves. While this chapter takes a broad view of the competing strands of Civil War photography, continuing to follow image-making amongst slaveholders, enslaved people, and abolitionists, it argues that the core photographic debate over the character and future of African Americans took place in Union army camps. In these liminal spaces—places between bondage and freedom—thousands of fugitives encountered thousands of northern soldiers. In these haphazard, biracial communities, white northerners produced photographs as a means of answering fundamental questions. Were slaves people or property? How did they relate to white men in the social hierarchy? And, especially after the Emancipation Proclamation, what role might African Americans play in freedom? What would the racial order look like in a nation without slavery? To answer these questions, northern whites turned to the medium that was widely understood as an easy yet powerful way of asserting identity and envisioning social order.

———

BY THE END OF THE WAR, the northern photographic imagination of African Americans and interracial relations had overwhelmed all other visions. At the beginning of the conflict, however, it was not clear that northern photography would dominate. During the buildup to the battle at Fort Sumter, and in its aftermath, southern artists actually took the lead. They began by making photographs of military leaders and ruins, not slaves. In January 1861 Charleston photographer George Smith Cook received requests from various photographic firms in the North to picture Maj. Robert Anderson, commander of Fort Sumter. "As major Anderson is quite popular [in the] North, I think that we might make considerable money if we had his picture," Walter Dinmore of Philadelphia wrote to Cook. "Answer soon, delays are dangerous; the furor may wear off."[2] In late December Anderson had stirred sectional controversy when he sought to inconspicuously move his approximately eighty soldiers from Fort Moultrie to Fort Sumter, a federally occupied garrison at the mouth of Charleston Harbor that South Carolina had unsuccessfully sought to wrench from President Buchanan when it seceded.[3] Though Anderson might have made this move to avoid war—he worried Fort Moultrie was vulnerable to a southern assault—he only heightened sectional animosity, becoming a hero to the North and a villain to the South in the process.[4] It is not surprising northerners wanted his portrait.

George Smith Cook's photography amplified the importance of Fort Sumter as the artist himself became part of the news. On February 8 Cook packed up his camera and chemicals and took the ferry to the fort, where he made portraits of Major Anderson and a number of other federal officers. While Cook subsequently sold these images at his Charleston studio, he also sent the negatives to artists in cities including New York and Louisville; other northern artists wrote to him, clamoring for their own copies.[5] Many northerners would also have seen the woodcut engraving of Cook's photograph in *Harper's Weekly* on March 23, 1861.[6] For the photographic community in these early months, profits, artistic innovation, and admiration far outweighed sectional animosity. Influential New York photographic manufacturer Edward T. Anthony extolled Cook's role. Anthony advertised Cook's 25-cent photographs by describing not the subject of the photograph but instead the photographer, casting the Yankee-turned-slaveholder as the intrepid wartime photojournalist: "Under cover of a bright sun, Col. George S. Cook, of the Charleston Photographic Light Artillery, with a strong force, made his way to Fort Sumter," where he "penetrated to the presence of Maj. Anderson, and leveling a double barreled Camera, demanded his unconditional surrender in the name of E. Anthony and the Photographic community."[7] Anthony celebrated the daring artistry of this southern photographer amidst escalating sectional tension.

Soon a cadre of Charlestonian photographers produced the first images of wartime destruction. No one captured action shots of the actual battle at Fort Sumter (April 12–14, 1861). Shortly after the battle ended and Major Anderson relinquished the fort to Confederate general P. G. T. Beauregard, however, local artist-entrepreneurs were on the scene. Within a week, operators from at least two well-known Charleston firms arrived: James M. Osborn, who ran a gallery with Frederick E. Durbec, and Alma A. Pelot, assistant for Jesse H. Bolles, owner of the "Temple of Art." Eschewing the grandeur of history paintings, these photographers captured the Confederate victory from multiple perspectives that highlighted the destroyed landscape. Pelot and Osborn canvassed the terrain of the fort, taking more than forty photographs from various heights and angles to show the extent of the damage in a fragmented panorama (Figures 4.1 and 4.2).[8] The artists were clearly drawn to the crumbling walls, busted turrets, and piles of

Figure 4.1 *The Evacuation of Fort Sumter, April 1861*, April 1861, by Alma A. Pelot, albumen silver print, 1¹⁵⁄₁₆ × 3⅛ inches (image), 3⅜ × 4¾ inches (mount). Accession 2005.100.1174.13, The Metropolitan Museum of Art, New York, Gilman Collection, Museum Purchase, 2005.

Figure 4.2 *The Evacuation of Fort Sumter, April 1861*, April 1861, by Alma A. Pelot, albumen silver print, 1¹⁵⁄₁₆ × 3⅛ inches (image), 3⅜ × 4¾ inches (mount). 100.1174.8, The Metropolitan Museum of Art, New York, Gilman Collection, Museum Purchase, 2005.

rubble on the ground. Newspapers and advertisements stressed the extensive coverage of these views. The *Charleston Mercury* pointed out that Pelot made images from "five different points of view."[9] Osborn and Durbec lauded how their "views of Fort Sumter comprise the whole interior in twenty sections for the Stereoscope, and six large Photographs for framing."[10] The artists and their publicists emphasized the value of the images by stressing the variety of perspectives pictured.

It is unclear how widely these images circulated in the South during the spring of 1861 and beyond. We can only speculate as to whether they offered proof that states such as Virginia, Arkansas, North Carolina, and Tennessee needed to secede.[11] At least in Charleston, these images steeled Confederate resolve in the first months of the war. The *Charleston Daily Courier* felt Pelot's images would assuage concerns of southern supporters, and it prescribed their material uses: "These pictures for the time will afford appropriate ornaments for our Drawing Rooms, Scrap Books and Albums, and a most acceptable present to distant and anxious friends." As the paper added, "Will our citizens call and see them, and especially our patriotic ladies, who may now have a hand in taking Fort Sumter?"[12] In the South, the first photographic representations of wartime ruins served not as symbols of a shameful past but as prideful reminders for southerners to keep in their homes.[13] Photography, early on, appeared as a powerful weapon in the Confederate arsenal.

In one sense, these images of Confederate firepower at Fort Sumter did constitute a new part of southern slave photography—at least to the extent that they immediately propped up an explicitly proslavery nation. As Confederate vice president Alexander Stephens had argued in March 1861, the "cornerstone" of the new nation rested "upon the great truth that the negro is not equal to the white man; that slavery, subordination to the superior race, is his natural and moral condition. This, our new government, is the first, in the history of the world, based upon this great physical, philosophical, and moral truth." Racialized slavery, for Stephens, served as the foundation of "one of the greatest revolutions in the annals of the world."[14] But how did Confederates picture enslaved people during wartime? After Fort Sumter, how did they more explicitly extend their prewar culture of photography to envision the master-slave relationship?

Even though black people did not play a prominent role in images at Sumter, they were frequently present in the military images of ordinary southern soldiers. Trips to the gallery for portraits forged a constitutive element of southern military preparations, as studio photographers explicitly catered to Confederate troops ready to depart for duty. For instance, in May 1861 Pugh & Brothers Gallery of Art in Macon, Georgia, sold portraits to soldiers for half price, and it announced to the 5th Regiment Georgia Volunteers that it had placed a photographer within their camp so that those "who wish their pictures with their guns, knap-sacks, and every thing on to start for the seat of war" would not need to travel to the uptown studio.[15]

In turn, Confederate militarization masculinized slave photography. Alongside chattel Madonna portraits, masters increasingly made military manservant portraits, which presented pairings of black and white men, a rare composition in the prewar era. The typical visual conventions of this subgenre—exemplified by Burrell and John Wallace Comer of Barbour County, Alabama (Figure 4.3)—inverted social power and height, a formula that drew upon contemporary depictions of husbands and wives.[16] Other choices underscored the differential: Comer wore his hat and displayed a sword across his body, perhaps the "very nice Sword" he received as a gift and had a "Scabbard made for."[17] Burrell, on the other hand, posed with no weapon and his hat at his side. The image surely reflected Comer's view of Burrell as an enslaved subordinate rather than a soldier, despite the Confederate private's uniform Burrell wore. In his private letters, Comer described how Burrell carried out such tasks as washing his clothes and ferrying his personal effects.[18] For Comer, Burrell's labor only enhanced his monetary value. "If Burrell holds out fast full to the end + stick to me as well as he has done" and "I come out safe," Comer felt, "a mint of money could not buy him."[19] The image for Comer was undoubtedly a master-slave image rather than a portrait of two soldiers. This image and other Confederate manservant portraits held the same implication of consent as prewar proslavery photographs. While antebellum images had pictured enslaved complicity in the "peculiar institution," wartime images constructed enslaved complicity in the fight to preserve that institution.

Enslavers' desires for such images surely increased over the course of the war as owners increasingly felt the brunt of open dissent from

Figure 4.3 *John Wallace Comer in Civil War Uniform with His Slave, Burrell*, photographic copy. Comer Family Papers # 167-z, The Southern Historical Collection, Wilson Library, The University of North Carolina at Chapel Hill.

their bondspeople, who refused to labor obediently, aided Union men in ransacking planter homes, and escaped to enemy lines by the thousands. In her diary, mistress Kate Stone recorded the self-emancipation of slaves on nearby plantations, mentioning striking moments of dissent, such as an instance in which "Negro women marched off in their mistresses' dresses."[20] Eventually abandoning her Louisiana plantation for safer Texas terrain in the spring of 1863, Stone wrote with disdain about one of her own slaves: "Webster, our most trusted servant, claims the plantation as his own and is renowned as the greatest villain in the country."[21] But one year later, in May 1864, Stone would write glowingly of two enslaved manservants, Pompey and Dan, whose enthusiastic military service rendered them fit to be photographed:

> *Pompey and Dan should certainly have their pictures taken. They*
> *are the most independent and consequential personages in Tyler.*
> *They speak very learnedly of their furloughs and have wordy*
> *debates on the subject of rank. Pompey maintains that he and*
> *Marse Joe outrank Dan and Marse Willy by reason of their*
> *longer service and doing more duty in the field, a fact that Dan is*
> *loth to admit. Pompey is quite contemptuous in speaking of Marse*
> *Willy and Dan as holiday soldiers and speaks with great respect*
> *of the pleasures of a campaign across the river where they have*
> *"so much more fun fighting and shooting."*[22]

Stone clearly found reassurance in the behavior of these two slaves, who—at least on the face of it—vigorously played the role of courageous southern defender. She might have meant to give them photographs as gifts for their seeming obedience, or she might have sought these images for herself. It is not clear whether Pompey and Dan did, in fact, have their pictures taken. But Stone's words provide a glimpse into the meanings of Confederate slave photography, which must have bolstered enslavers' self-deceptive sense that slaves were loyal participants in furthering the southern cause (and, of course, the slaves' own exploitation).

Still, a broader culture of slave photography never took hold in the Confederacy due to the economic disruptions of the war. On April 15, the day after Major Anderson surrendered at Fort Sumter, Lincoln called seventy-five thousand men into service to put down the southern rebellion.[23] On April 19 he issued a proclamation to blockade all ports in the Confederacy.[24] The blockade posed an immediate problem for southern photographers, since they relied on northern supplies. George Smith Cook—a major middleman for supplies between North and South—purchased alcohol, silver, and acid from Garrigues & Magee in Philadelphia,[25] plates, cases, tubes, boxes, and holders from Scovill Manufacturers in New England, and cases and glass from Edward T. Anthony in New York.[26] Immediately after Lincoln issued the blockade, artists began asking Cook to begin manufacturing the material himself. On April 20, photographer Joseph T. Zealy of Columbia, South Carolina, proposed, "I will take the liberty of suggesting to you to start a factory in this section, what do you think of it."[27] Early on, southern artists such as Zealy foresaw the collapse of their livelihoods at the hands of the blockade.

From this point onward, southern artists struggled to keep their businesses afloat. In South Carolina thirty firms operated on the eve of the war, yet by 1862 very few were placing advertisements in major newspapers, and by 1864 only George Smith Cook and Richard Wearn of Columbia remained open.[28] In Vicksburg, Mississippi, John H. Fitzgibbons operated until just before the city fell. The *American Journal of Photography* reported that Fitzgibbons had struggled due to the lack of some goods and the exorbitant costs of others ("alcohol at twenty-four dollars per gallon"). Further, there was "no money among the people to pay for pictures if he could produce them." Fitzgibbons eventually tried to break through the blockade but was caught.[29] Though the rates at which their businesses survived differed, southern photographers slowly succumbed to supply limitations and decreased regional purchasing power.

By 1862 major trade publications (all published in the North) were openly lamenting how the war had severed ties to the southern profession. "In the Southern states of the Union, photography like most other artistic and industrial pursuits, for lack of materials wherewith to work, and for lack of patrons, is well nigh a lost art," the *American Journal of Photography* wrote in October 1861. "The people of the South, eminent for boasting and perhaps for fighting, are yet not progressed far enough to have the cunning for manufacturing daguerreotype cases, glass, paper, or photographic chemicals."[30] In February 1862 *Humphrey's Journal* expressed hope for a united photographic community: "In a few months more we expect to see peace established, and our Southern Photographic friends will then be 'let out of jail,' as it were. They must be all out of stock and materials, and our dealers here will then have their hands full of business."[31] The dismay from northern photographic journals was partially genuine—the *American Journal of Photography* reported that it lost one-third of its subscribers after Sumter—but the circumstances also gave northerners the opportunity to celebrate their superior industrial progress.[32]

Southern photography did not entirely vanish after the blockade, as select artists in Charleston and Richmond bucked the broader trend. George Smith Cook continued to operate until March 1864, and the *American Journal of Photography* suspected that the British were keeping him in operation: "By favor of our British cousins who run the blockade with powder and guns, our friend Cook of Charleston, has still a precarious stock of photographic materials and still makes a business in the shadows of the people."[33] Meanwhile, galleries in Richmond also stayed open well into the war. In May 1864 a northern correspondent for the *American Journal of Photography* described how he "visited two of the principal galleries and found them busy. There seemed to be more done in ambrotypes than in photographs. The pictures are taken on plain glass, and put up in a common case for twenty dollars each; photographs, for a single copy, fifteen dollars, or four for twenty-five dollars. I was under guard, I was not permitted to ask any questions, but came to the conclusion that they were short of stock."[34] The artist's emphasis on ambrotypes implicitly suggested to the broader photographic community that the South lacked the paper necessary to make the mass-reproducible photographs—cartes de visite and stereographs in particular—that had grown immensely popular for northern artists.

If they had had the industrial connections, southerners might have transformed their photographic production and circulation from unique to mass-reproducible slave images, which might have left behind a large archive of stereographs framing slavery as a benevolent institution during the war. This was not an unimaginable cultural proposition, for Osborn and Durbec had begun doing so in the summer and fall of 1860. As the *Charleston Mercury* had reported in October 1860, the artists were "steadily engaged in obtaining the most accurate stereoscopic views of places in and around Charleston. Among these we may mention the Charleston Hotel, Mills House, Pavilion Hotel, Sullivan's Island, and a number of plantation scenes, including the negro quarters, cotton picking, etc."[35] At least ten of Osborn and Durbec's Charleston-area plantation views are extant. These scenes

Figure 4.4 *Planter's Summer Residence, No. 10*, c. 1860, by Osborn and Durbec, stereograph. Civil War Collection, Stereograph Cards Collection, Prints and Photographs Division, Library of Congress, LC-DIG-stereo-1s03920.

of black and white subjects offered an idealized visual tour of the plantation, stopping at notable sites including the master's house (Figure 4.4), plantation dock, and slave quarters. Osborn and Durbec sold their views until at least May 1861, advertising them alongside images of Fort Sumter in the newspaper: "THE VIEWS OF FORT SUMTER COMPRISE THE whole interior in twenty sections for the Stereoscope, and six large Photographs for framing. Also on hand, one hundred different STEREOSCOPIC VIEWS IN CHARLESTON, AND VICINITY, VIEWS OF PLANTATIONS IN THE STATE, etc."[36] Many southerners must have made the immediate connection between images of slavery and images of the first battle to preserve the institution. But Osborn and Durbec, like many southern firms, would fail to thrive as the war continued. By 1862 they appear to have ended their partnership, and with it the sale and circulation of plantation stereographs.[37] Though Osborn, Durbec, and other Charleston artists began the war with a flourish, they ultimately made a minor contribution to the proslavery Confederacy. Due in large part to the economic structures of American photography and the economic downturn of the Confederate South, northern anti-slavery photography would dominate the war. Southern photography dwindled and was dwarfed by northern photographic output.

AT THE START OF THE WAR, however, antislavery proponents did not convey any clear strategy for how they might use the medium to turn the conflict into a moral battle over the peculiar institution, rather than a military campaign to destroy the rebels. In a sense this is not surprising: abolitionists had never attempted to photograph the South in the 1840s and 1850s. They were far more concerned with using photographs to build their identities and build up their movement in the North. If anyone had envisioned a wartime photographic campaign, it would have been Frederick Douglass, who wrote four lectures on photography during the Civil War, including one he gave at Tremont Temple in Boston in December 1861, "Lecture on Pictures."[38] In a wide-ranging oration, Douglass hailed the invention of photography, signaling out Daguerre for praise: "Daguerre, by the simple but all abounding sunlight, has converted the planet into a picture gallery." In keeping with abolitionists' pre-war conception, Douglass articulated a vision of photographic representation as evidence of personhood, not of suffering. "I have said that man is a picture-making and a picture-appreciating animal and have pointed out that fact as an important line of distinction between man and all other animals," Douglass asserted.[39] Photography was a vital way for slaves to stake claims to their individuality, differentiating themselves from vicious associations with primates and dogs. If anything, Douglass wanted slaves to show their humanity by picturing themselves, just as he had done over the past two decades.

Not until the spring of 1863 did abolitionists begin circulating their first major propaganda photograph, an image obtained by appropriating the work of wartime photographers. It took two contingencies of the war to produce it: the massive flight of fugitive slaves, and the push to enlist black soldiers (including slaves) in the Union army, a strategy promoted by the Emancipation Proclamation. In Louisiana, the enlistment process—which included physical inspections of enslaved people's bodies—allowed officers and surgeons to see firsthand the physical aftermath of the persistent abuse of slaves. One officer told the *National Antislavery Standard* that surgeons often described how "not one in fifteen is free from marks of severe lashing. More than one-half are rejected because of disability arising from lashing of whips and the biting of dogs on their calves and thighs. It is frightful. Hundreds of them have welts on their backs as large as one of your largest fingers."[40] In the spring of 1863, one such fugitive entered Union lines near Baton Rouge. A story in *Harper's Weekly* called him Gordon and described how he escaped from a plantation in Mississippi.[41] A less prominent narrative told of how he came from central Louisiana and identified him instead as Peter.[42] Either way, that April he sat sideways in a chair and presented his back to the camera (Figure 4.5).[43]

Figure 4.5 *Gordon*, 1863, by Mathew Brady Studio, copy after William D. McPherson and Mr. Oliver, albumen silver print, 3⅜ × 2³⁄₁₆ inches (image), 4 × 2⅜ inches (mount). National Portrait Gallery, Smithsonian Institution.

Multiple Union surgeons sent images of the fugitive northward from Baton Rouge, and the idea that he had experienced typical treatment suffused their correspondence.[44] A black surgeon with the 1st Louisiana Regiment wrote to his brother, "I send you the picture of a slave as he appears after a whipping. I have seen, during the period I have been inspecting men for my own and other regiments, *hundreds of such sights*—so they are not new to me; but it may be new to you. If you know of any one who talks about the *humane manner* in which the slaves are treated, please show them this picture. It is a lecture in itself."[45] This vision of a former slave entered northern culture as a sensational medical photograph.[46]

The Scourged Back resonated so broadly not because it told viewers something new about slavery but because it reinforced so many long-standing antislavery narratives about bondage, which had fixated on the subjugated bodies of slaves. Not surprisingly, commentaries focused on the man's pain, finding multiple ways to convey the look of his scars for their readers. For the *New York Independent* the "back looks like a plate of iron, eaten by acids and corroded by rust; or like a walnut-table honey-combed by worms." It further reported how, "from the shoulders to the waist, great welts and furrows and ridges, raised or gouged by the lash, run crosswise and lengthwise, mingling in the middle in one awful mass of scab. Bits as big as the hand seem to have been cut out of the flesh."[47] Meanwhile, the *Liberator* cried out, "Upon that back, horrible to contemplate! is a testimony against slavery more eloquent than any words. Scarred, gouged, gathered in great ridges, knotted, arrowed, the poor tortured flesh stands out a hideous record of the slave-driver's lash."[48] Even as the image of the ex-slave had replaced the oral testimony of the fugitive on the lecture circuit, the intricate and graphic nature of his scars gave abolitionists a new stage to reiterate their long-standing argument about the cruelties of slavery. In doing so, they countered the growing proslavery insistence that it was emancipation that was inhumane.[49]

Since the image focused on the horrific scars, abstracted the scourged fugitive from his individual biography and from a world of social relations, presented the viewer with a side profile susceptible to phrenological readings, and—perhaps most important—refused to let the subject gaze back at the viewer, the photograph opened up a variety of other interpretations beyond the basic notion of physical abuse. The scars on his back, which suggested to mid-nineteenth-century viewers the suffering of Christ, led to his identification as an enslaved martyr—a figure Harriet Beecher Stowe had made famous a decade earlier with Uncle Tom.[50] From the ex-slave's physiognomy, commentators also inferred his manliness: "The head is well placed, and the profile—not a profile of the extreme African type—is full of manly energy. A strong short whisker and beard give power to the jaw which needs no such evidence to show its manliness, for resolution and force are stamped on the whole formation of the face."[51] For the *New York Independent*, the fugitive was also the noble agricultural worker: "This humble man, this poor man, this untaught man, this down-trodden man, this *working* man, this negro, represents the laboring class." He was so valuable because he was one "who eats little and toils much; a man who is nine-tenths production, and only one-tenth consumption."[52] In short, the image became an icon—the first photographic icon in United States history—that stood for a social world of four million slaves.[53] The image thrived because it could evidence and elicit so many perceptions of bondage and blackness at once. Because it could do so, it could be sold with a simple tagline: "THE 'PECULIAR INSTITUTION' ILLUSTRATED."[54]

The Scourged Back packed such a potent cultural punch because it fused this capacity to condense and amplify narratives about bondage and bondspeople with great visceral force. The *Liberator* described the image as "horrible to contemplate!"[55] The *New York Independent*, too, expressed its lack of an adequate vocabulary to describe the power of the image: "We look on the picture with amazement that cannot find words for utterance."[56] These papers did, of course, find many words to describe the image. But they also hinted at the forces beyond mere intellect—the emotions the image had stirred. For the *New York Independent*, these emotions were many: "pity" for "the agony of the poor victim"; "horror" over the violence he had experienced; and "bitterness" over "the senseless folly that can thus waste the resources of the working-man."[57] In bringing distant pain near and combining narratives about the cruelty of slavery with the visual precision of photography, the image generated a range of intense emotional reactions.

The image was equally bracing for what it conveyed about the potential of photography as a medium, which commentators were quick to locate within a broader narrative of industrial progress. As the *New*

York Independent proclaimed, "The poor slave shows his wounds in New York, and 'the instrument can't lie.' Deny the evidence of the sun, who can?"[58] *The Scourged Back* "tells the story in a way that even Mrs. Stowe cannot approach; because it tells the story to the eye. If seeing is believing—and it is in the immense majority of cases— seeing this card would be equivalent to believing things of the slave states which Northern men and women would move heaven and earth to abolish!"[59] This seeming visual objectivity sparked reflection on photography's newfound role as an instrument of political mass persuasion. The *New York Daily Tribune* reached back to the French inventors who had given birth to the first photographic process, pre- senting this moment as the culmination of Western technological in- novation: "Through the mysterious agencies of the camera obscura the most wonderful as well as beautiful results have been obtained, and it is to the genius and perseverance of Daguerre and M. Niepce that we of the nineteenth century today behold the outside view of the moon and the inside view of Slavery."[60] The image confirmed to its supporters the seemingly inevitable connection between material and moral progress. But this was a position they could easily adopt in 1863, because the military blockade had undermined the competing force of southern proslavery photography.

In the North and in Britain, abolitionists quickly harnessed the image to prove why the Emancipation Proclamation had not gone far enough.[61] While they initially cheered the proclamation, abolitionists criticized it for leaving almost 800,000 slaves (out of the 3.9 million held in bondage) untouched, including all bondspeople in the border states of Missouri, Kentucky, Delaware, and Maryland.[62] On June 13, 1863, the New England Anti-Slavery Convention in Boston passed a series of resolutions calling for slavery's "immediate abolition in such portions of the country as were exempted from the operation of the proclamation of January 1st, 1863." They demanded that there be "no possibility provided for future slaveholding concession and compro- mise." At some point in the convention, William Lloyd Garrison stood before the crowd at Tremont Temple and applauded "a representa- tion of the frightful scars caused by whipping on the back of a Louisiana slave."[63] Susan B. Anthony, too, used the image, which she held up alongside a photograph of Sojourner Truth to raise money in support of abolition at a meeting of the Women's Loyal League.[64] For the most part, the image seems to have been displayed as a small carte de visite, except in the case of British abolitionist George Thompson, who turned *The Scourged Back* into a massive placard and displayed it during wartime lectures in America in the winter of 1864.[65] Abolitionists now located the evils of slavery along the ridges of the ex-slave's scourged back rather than in the descriptions of slave narratives. Increasingly, they made photography a vital component of their political-truth apparatus.

In the wake of *The Scourged Back*, antislavery proponents turned to mass-marketed cartes de visite for propaganda and fundraising. They produced before-and-after images of impoverished slave children, including *As We Found Them* and *As They Are Now* (Figures 4.6 and 4.7), which the Quakers sold to promote the education of freedpeople at an orphanage in Philadelphia. Meanwhile, in the winter of 1863–1864,

Figure 4.6 *Virginia Slave Children Rescued by Colored Troops*, c. 1864, carte de visite. 2001.10.1, Virginia Historical Society.

AS THEY ARE NOW

The Mother of these children was beaten, branded and sold at auction because she was kind to Union Soldiers. As she left for Richmond, Va., Feb. 13th, 1864, bound down in a cart, she prayed "O! God send the Yankees to take my children away."

Profits from sale, for the benefit of the children.

Figure 4.7 *Virginia Slave Children Rescued by Colored Troops*, c. 1864, carte de visite. 2001.10.2, Virginia Historical Society.

military personnel, along with the American Missionary Association and the National Freedman's Relief Association, marketed a wide variety of portraits showing white-looking slave children including Rebecca (Figure 4.8), and several of Wilson Chinn, who posed multiple times with the torture implements from his past (Figure 4.9). These images were meant to raise funds for freedpeople's schools in Louisiana.[66] In various ways, antislavery cartes de visite drew upon and broadened a key element of *The Scourged Back*: they evoked the cruelty of slavery through bodily markers—scars, tattered clothing, whiteness, torture implements, or brands—on the bodies of specific individuals.

These images combined older abolitionist attacks against slavery with a heightened sense of an individual's experience of pain. On one hand, such suffering photographs conveyed nothing abolitionists had not already harped upon for decades: the institution impoverished

REBECCA, an Emancipated Slave, from New Orleans.
Photographed by KIMBALL, 477 Broadway. N.Y.
Entered according to Act of Congress, in the year 1863 by GEO. H. HANKS, in the Clerk's Office of the U. S. for the Sou. Dist. of N.Y.

Figure 4.8 M. H. Kimball, *Rebecca, an Emancipated Slave, from New Orleans*, c. 1863, carte de visite, albumen print, 10 × 6 cm. Gladstone Collection of African American Photographs, Prints and Photographs Division, Library of Congress, LC-DIG-ppmsca-11102.

and abused slaves; it separated them from their mothers (as in the case of the children with tattered clothing); it entailed the rape of black women that produced white offspring (such as Rebecca), whom masters gladly sold whenever necessary. In slavery, slaveholders branded their slaves like cattle to mark them as property; they used various devices—from plantation patrols to dogs to iron collars (like the one Chinn wore)—to curb slaves' mobility.

On the other hand, these photographs transformed the long-standing antislavery practice of oral witnessing into one of visual witnessing. Notably, commentaries about *The Scourged Back* mentioned that his image constituted "a lecture in itself."[67] Fugitive testimony now came as a marketable photographic commodity. Drawing upon strategies developed during the sale of John Brown's images, abolitionists advertised

WILSON CHINN, a Branded Slave from Louisiana.
Also exhibiting Instruments of Torture
used to punish Slaves.
Photographed by KIMBALL, 477 Broadway, N.Y.
Entered according to Act of Congress, in the year 1863, by
Geo. H. HANKS, in the Clerk's Office of the United States for
the Southern District of New-York.

Figure 4.9 *Wilson Chinn, a Branded Slave from Louisiana*, 1863, carte de visite. Hancock Papers, Manuscripts Division. Clements Library, University of Michigan.

The Scourged Back in newspapers and sent copies to consumers through the mail. Beginning in June 1863, subscribers to the *Liberator* and the *National Antislavery Standard* could purchase one copy for 15 cents, seven copies for $1.00, and one dozen copies for $1.50.[68] *The Scourged Back* reached the English market by August 1863.[69] Sales were so brisk that at one point in July the *National Anti-Slavery Standard* related how its "supply of this photograph is exhausted, with several orders unsupplied. We expect more in a few days, when the orders shall be attended to."[70] Commercial photographers such as Mathew Brady and McAllister & Brothers of Philadelphia also sold the image. To buy images of Wilson Chinn and the white slave children for 25 cents, northerners might go to the National Freedman's Relief Association office in New York or purchase them through the mail.[71]

The commodification of slave photographs set the stage for new modes of political identification. As much as such images made claims to the nature of slavery, they were as significant for their claims about the character of the abolitionist. Proponents of abolition began expressing their benevolence through these commodified visions of ex-slaves. For instance, in an August 1863 article in the *National Antislavery Standard*, a commentator asked, "Have you ever seen the card photograph of a slave's back? Scarred, wilted with marks of the lash, it makes every nerve in one's body shrink to look at the thing, taken from life, and in a civilized land. The patient expression of the slave's face makes his condition seem more pitiful. Spite of friendly remonstrance, I keep it in my photograph book among saints and Madonnas, and force myself to look at it."[72] The materiality of the carte de visite and the popularity of the carte de visite album enabled such consumers to turn the image into a sacred object by positioning it amongst saints and Madonnas in a narrative of enslaved Christian suffering.[73] Appealing to the Christian views of many northern antislavery advocates and fitting easily into the commodity culture of the 1860s, the image of the scourged fugitive heightened pity toward slaves as it forged a new vehicle for northerners to convey their own sympathetic disposition and public commitment to abolition. Something new had come to stand at the center of the humanitarian disposition: the affective photographic ritual.

While it produced new views and new modes of political expression, abolitionist photography also created a new mode of political authority. Cartes de visite positioned activists as informal "news outlets," offering evidence of the world they sought to demolish. In mid-November 1863, for example, abolitionist Cornelia Hancock described in a private letter how she had met a slave from Louisiana while working at a hospital for refugees of bondage in Washington, D.C. She told of how he "had his master's name branded on his forehead, and with him he brought all the instruments of torture that he wore," which included "an iron collar with 3 prongs standing up so he could not lay down his head" and "a contrivance to render one leg entirely stiff and a chain clanking behind him with a bar weighing 50 lbs." As Hancock promised, "I will try to send you a Photograph of him."[74] This was likely Wilson Chinn's image, but it is not clear whether Hancock actually met Chinn. Regardless, her words testify to the rumbling of cultural change. Hancock and others had created a mode of visual proof that was as much evidence of abolition as it was of slavery: while the proof of slavery lay in the visual depictions, the proof of abolitionist authority, benevolence, and humaneness lay in the display, exchange, and viewing of the images. In the process, photographic images and image practices deepened antislavery resolve across the North and solidified the belief that slavery had passed into history as a relic of barbarism.

———

DESPITE THEIR POWER, antislavery photographs ultimately did more to articulate what constituted "slavery" and "antislavery" than they did to define what the nation might look like without slavery. It was, instead, in Union army camps where photography was put to the service of addressing the uncertain future of the American racial order. In these camps, black subjects posed with northern soldiers and officers for numerous commercial photographers, including little-known artists as well as luminaries such as Alexander Gardner and Timothy O'Sullivan. Dozens of interracial images currently sit in the collections of the Library of Congress, as well as in various other photograph archives. Yet these have never been seriously studied, perhaps because the image titles in photographers' catalogs rarely mention the presence of black subjects, or because it is much harder to make sense of images that depict fugitives in a limbo state between slavery and freedom.[75] In addition, identifying the status of the black subjects in many images proves challenging. Soldiers' letters make clear that fugitives in particular were photographed, and titles and handwritten notes on the backs of images suggest much the same thing, as in the case of *Contraband Foreground* (Figure 4.10). While the vast majority of these images likely show ex-slaves, it is possible that certain interracial images show free blacks, particularly those from the North who traveled south to work with the Union army as laborers or enlisted in the later years of the war.[76] But this possibility does little to diminish the evidence at hand: whether specific images depict fugitive slaves or free blacks, all images made claims about race. Studying them helps us to grasp how northern whites drew upon photography to address an emergent and deeply pressing dilemma

Figure 4.10 *Contraband Foreground*, c. 1861–1865, stereograph, albumen print, 8 × 18 cm. Civil War Photograph Collection, Stereograph Cards Collection, Prints and Photographs Division, Library of Congress, LC-DIG-stereo-1s02759.

during the war: in a nation without slavery, what might the racial order look like?

These images were born out of a complicated interplay between white soldiers, African Americans, and white photographers. Assessing this interplay means reconceptualizing the relation between artists and non-artists during the war. In scale and subject matter, northern photographers turned the Civil War into a historic cultural moment alongside its political and social import.[77] By the war's end, an estimated three thousand artists, most of them northerners, had taken pictures related to the war; around three hundred photographers attached themselves to the Army of the Potomac alone.[78] These cameramen made an estimated tens of thousands of images.[79] They visualized the faces and happenings of political and military leaders, circulating now-famous images such as Alexander Gardner's view of Lincoln towering over McClellan at Antietam. Publishing the actions of the living, they also made major contributions in their pictures of the dead, especially Gardner and James Gibson, who photographed the first corpses on a wartime battlefield in United States history.[80] All told, the northern artists who documented the many facets of the war made it impossible for their contemporaries and later generations to think of the war without thinking of images of the war.

Yet as they made documentary images that would shape future views of the past, they also created a performative culture that shaped the everyday experience of the conflict. When photographers arrived in camps, soldiers often noted their presence in diaries and letters. Soon army men tracked these artists down to buy portraits so that distant family members could see them in their finest military garb.[81] Soldiers also enjoyed a strikingly new experience: they found that they were valuable as representable subjects in their own right. For instance, John P. Reynolds of the Massachusetts Volunteer Militia described how one embedded photographer "came up to us and invited us to 'sit' by way of experiment." Reynolds and the rest of his "pony squad" agreed and "adjourned to his establishment where after one or two trials" the artist "succeeded in getting a fine picture of us in the position of *ready*, in load and fire kneeling." The image was "so life-like that we agreed to take a copy each."[82] From 1861 onward, northern artists made Union army camps probably the most visually mediated place ever experienced by the Americans who served in combat.[83]

Many soldiers welcomed this visual stage. When artist Henry P. Moore arrived in Port Royal, South Carolina, in February 1862, one member of the 3rd New Hampshire Volunteer Regiment wrote, "He comes with the intention of taking views of the camps and plantations.... He is just the man we want, for it has been impossible to obtain pictures of any kind worth having."[84] Some officers and soldiers even helped artists build temporary studios. Henry Rogers Smith, a little-known photographic assistant, wrote that he and artist Charles Marcellus Pierce could not find a decently priced room in Poolesville, Maryland. Accordingly, they built their own eight-by-sixteen-foot "shanty" with the manpower of three soldiers, whom the local colonel designated to help.[85] A month later, the same colonel stopped by Pierce and Smith's saloon—unannounced—to see the image the artists had taken of camp headquarters.[86]

The nature of photographic technology in the 1860s must have underscored the soldiers' sense that they were important participants in the artistic process. During the war, photographers increasingly used the wet-plate process to make multiple paper prints from a negative. Though this spike in mass-produced photography broke sharply from the unique daguerreotypes, ambrotypes, and tintypes made in the 1850s, the wet-plate method still required that the photographer sensitize a negative immediately before exposure and necessitated several seconds to allow for exposure. Not until the rise of the Kodak in the 1880s could a photographer take several images without the awareness of the subject.[87] Throughout the Civil War, then, the still-lengthy setup and exposure times surely gave soldiers (and all other photographic subjects) a heightened recognition of the photographic process taking place and likely a greater say in the outcome as well. As in the case of customers requesting studio portraits in the 1840s and 1850s, northern soldiers were collaborators in the production of inter-racial camp scenes.

Illustrated presses further reinforced the soldierly self-image as visual documentarian. Lacking enough full-time sketch artists to cover the war, *Frank Leslie's, Harper's Weekly*, and the *New York Illustrated News* actively solicited (and promised to pay for) sketches from northern officers and soldiers. *Leslie's* asked soldiers to come visit its New York office and even extended a year-long subscription to anyone who submitted sample sketches. By July 1861, only a few months into the war, both *Leslie's* and *Harper's* professed to have a stable of more than fifty such vernacular artists.[88] In turn, soldiers saw the mass publication of their pictures as a real and exciting possibility. John P. Reynolds detailed his own attempt to sketch his surroundings on Harrison Island, which he felt stood a reasonable chance for wide circulation. "I drew a sketch of the island," Reynolds noted, "designating the positions and movement of the troops so far as they came within my own experience, and sent it in a letter to my father, authorizing him if he so desired to have it published in Harper's Weekly, as it was quite common to do at that time."[89] Soldiers such as Reynolds started to recognize that they mattered as vernacular artists who could play important roles in crafting wartime imagery.

As cameramen followed Union troops in search of profits, art, and adventure, and those troops took up the mantle of visual documentarians, fugitive slaves entered Union lines in search of freedom. While Lincoln's election helped slaves to imagine the president's support, thousands did not wait for him to secure emancipation.[90] As in the Revolutionary War and in the War of 1812, slaves seized the chance, amidst great social disruption and danger, to break for freedom.[91] Historian James Oakes cogently describes how "it did not take long before slaves realized that Union military installations in the

Confederate states represented a kind of counter-state within the southern states, an alternative government inside the South but beyond the reach of the police powers of southern slave society."[92] Fugitive slaves often made dramatic arrivals into Union camps, movements even witnessed by photographers. In Poolesville, Maryland, photographic assistant Henry Rogers Smith described in his private correspondence how, in February 1862, "four contrabands came across the river the other day, from Leesburg, they stole two horses of the Rebels and swam them across, two riding each horse."[93] By horse, wagon, and foot, an estimated 400,000 to 500,000 slaves had escaped by 1864 and effectively turned federal forts into the new maroon colonies.[94]

The massive flood of fugitives immediately raised questions about their status—especially whether the Union army could put ex-slaves into service or needed to give them back to their owners. In May 1861 three fugitives fled to Fort Monroe, in the Hampton Roads area of Virginia, and offered their services to the Union. Commanding Union general Benjamin F. Butler saw these men as additional labor; calling them "contraband of war," he put them to work. Only two months later, 850 "contrabands" had arrived at Fort Monroe. While the ex-slaves called Fort Monroe the "freedom fort," their legal and social position was unclear, in no small part because their status as people was undecided for many northern whites. As Butler asked in a letter to Secretary of War Simon Cameron, "Are these men, women, and children slaves? Are they free? Is their condition that of men, women, and children, or of property, or is it a mixed relation?"[95]

Butler's ambivalence over the slave's personhood status would permeate Union army camps in no time. From the spring of 1861 until the late summer of 1862, the status of "contrabands" in terms of federal policy remained contested and uncertain. Secretary Cameron told General Butler the ex-slaves could work, but he did little to decide their fate. In August 1861 Congress issued the First Confiscation Act, stipulating that the Union could take all property that helped the Confederacy, including its slaves. Yet, as historian Eric Foner notes, the law resolved little: "They no longer owed labor to their owners, but the act did not explicitly emancipate them."[96] Not until the Second Confiscation Act, in July 1862, did the government declare fugitives who made it to Union lines "forever free of their servitude."[97]

Still, emancipation was a process that took place on the ground. Along with the passage and application of federal law, emancipation meant a messy social phenomenon of face-to-face encounters and changing racial perceptions. Interracial camp photographs emerged from this messy world. On wartime soil, the incoming stream of fugitives into Union lines helped turn many moderate northerners into antislavery advocates. They saw fugitives entering Union-controlled territory and witnessed the masters and slave-catchers who came afterward, looking for their human property. Soldiers were disgusted when they saw how slavery tore black families apart, separating mothers from their children and sentencing teenage girls to the "fancy market."[98] When one soldier learned of an enslaved woman who had children with her master, a man who continued to keep the children in bondage, the soldier responded, "By G-d I'll fight till hell freezes over and then I'll cut the ice and fight on."[99] That antislavery images, magazines, and novels (especially *Uncle Tom's Cabin*) had made such behavior familiar to northerners by the time of the war did little to diminish the effects of seeing slavery in person. The weights, chains, and instruments that immobilized, imprisoned, and tortured slaves proved equally chilling, and for one northerner, these scenes were "enough of the horrors of slavery to make me an Abolitionist forever."[100] Of course, such antislavery sentiment was hardly universal. Yet in October 1861, as one soldier told the *Wisconsin State Journal*, "the rebellion is abolitionizing the whole army."[101]

As social interaction with slaves and fugitives altered the politics of slavery, it also brought about a social transformation within the army. It haphazardly created biracial communities at the geographical boundaries of the Union and the Confederacy. By the summer of 1862, the list of jobs that fugitives performed for the Union ranged widely. They supported the cause as guides, spies, laborers, laundresses, cooks, servants, hospital attendants, teamsters, carpenters, stevedores, blacksmiths, bridge builders, and coopers.[102] Union leadership recognized that ex-slaves served as valuable resources for information about Confederate terrain, strategy, and positioning; soon military personnel and newspapers began referring to the "intelligent contraband" and "reliable contraband" who provided knowledge of the enemy.[103] Other soldiers acknowledged this newfound support while disparaging the actual fugitives who provided it. As one Union soldier put it, the "army would be like a one-handed man, without niggers."[104] This interracial workforce was accompanied by unequal pay and racially segregated living arrangements in the form of hastily constructed contraband camps. Confronted with a swelling ex-slave population and seeking to calm northern fears about slaves heading northward, the U.S government began constructing camps, by the fall of 1862, in states including Florida, South Carolina, Virginia, and Arkansas. By the end of the war, thousands of former slaves would inhabit camps dotting Union-controlled territory. In these transitory, government-regulated way stations, ex-slaves managed to establish churches, civic associations, and schools, yet they also endured overcrowded living spaces, disease, often-callous northern soldiers, and the threat of reenslavement.[105] "By the ordinary privates of the army," one camp supervisor noted, the ex-slaves "are treated as savages and brutes. This treatment operates most discouragingly upon them."[106] There was nothing romantic about life in Union-controlled areas, but highlighting the interracial dynamics brings to the fore how many white northern soldiers were regularly interacting with African Americans on a daily basis for the first time in their lives.

These social interactions—as well as the passage of the Emancipation Proclamation on January 1, 1863—brought into sharp relief an even more controversial issue for many soldiers than the question of slavery's morality: racial equality. Most Union soldiers saw no contradiction in supporting slave emancipation while also harboring deepseated white supremacist beliefs. For example, David Nichol lauded the Emancipation Proclamation for getting "at the root of the Evil," but he still reassured his parents he was "no nigger worshiper."[107] Likewise, Leigh Webber, a longtime proponent of abolition, still asserted that "this talk about 'putting ourselves *on an equality with niggers*,' is to me, the *boldest nonsense* or rather an *insult* to me as one of the Saxon race." For Webber, the "natural superiority" of the white race made a level playing field between blacks and whites an "absurdity."[108] Nichol and Webber expressed intense anxiety over the nature of white freedom in a world without black slavery.

As the constant presence of photographers in Union army camps enabled soldiers to express pride and camaraderie, and to send visual reminders of themselves to their loved ones back North, it also helped white northerners to stake claims to black and white social identities and interracial relations. Most white soldiers did not produce articulate written visions about the place of African Americans in the social hierarchy, about how they might live and work with black people after slavery, or about questions of black education, labor, and rights. Nor, for that matter, did they find much instruction from their superiors. As historian Jim Downs points out, "The questions about where ex-bondspeople were to live, what they were to eat, and how they would find suitable work had not been asked, nor did they form a central piece of Congress's or the president's deliberations on the pending collapse of the institution of slavery."[109] Treating northern white soldiers as photographic practitioners reveals, however, that these men took active roles in enacting a visual transformation.[110] Through photography, they constructed concrete and lasting visions of black social identity. The images reveal a deep investment on the part of northern whites in asserting the status of ex-slaves and in envisioning the proper social relations between blacks and whites. Amidst social instability, northerners called upon the medium to resettle the racial order.

Northern white soldiers adopted photography as a quiet habit of domination, by which they communicated anti-black racism and asserted racial hierarchy. When Sergeant Joseph Emery Fiske wrote to his parents from Beaufort, South Carolina, in January 1863, he noted how he would send a picture of the ex-slaves in the area. "I think I'll send you a daguerreotype of myself as I appear in Beaufort, by one of our company, and perhaps one of our negroes who is the picture of laziness," Fiske remarked. For Fiske, "the negroes are pretty much all lazy and shiftless. They do not seem to appreciate the pleasures of liberty. You know all the slaves in Virginia, North Carolina, etc. are free now and we treat them all as free men."[111] Union soldiers valued personal photographs for their capacity to convey to family and friends on the home front what they perceived as the character traits of black people.

While Fiske aimed to picture ex-slaves on their own, the more common practice for white soldiers was evidently the production of interracial scenes. The letters of Charles F. Tew of the 25th Massachusetts Volunteer Infantry offer a window into this history of Union image-making.[112] Tew spent much of the war in North Carolina and Virginia, and in letters to his wife and children he often discussed fugitive slaves in the camp. "I make them wash my cloath and wait on me you can believe," Tew wrote. In the spring of 1862 Tew described how the fugitives "think we are going to set them all free," a sentiment that he felt was "nonsense," for "they are better off here for they don't know any thing."[113] Instead of emancipation, Tew opined for mastery on more than one occasion: "A southern home for me is just the thing give me a plantation and lots of nigs and my family and I will stop South as my home."[114] Tew expressed an envy not uncommon amongst northern soldiers and officers regarding the luxuries, racial power, and prestige of cotton mastery—sentiments that many would make real by trying their hand at southern planting after the war.[115]

Like many southern masters, Tew, at least by the later years of the war, expressed the sense that African Americans were loyal to him. He wrote of one African American named George, describing how "that same boy of mine goes into every Fight with me just as far as I will let him go." Tew equated George's loyalty to that of a dog: "He is the Laziest Nig you ever saw at other times but should I ever get hurt I know he would take care of me and save my things for you at home or fight for me as long as he lived for I have tried him many times he is like a big dog that you might have for a pet." And, like many southern masters, Tew could not entirely understand where this devotion originated: "He is no fool he is with me every step I take and I know he will fight for I have seen him do so when I came here and he will fight for one to the death I don't know what makes him like me but he does."[116]

Only a few days after comparing George to "a big dog that you might have for a pet," Tew posed with George for a portrait photograph. Though the image does not survive, Tew described its production to his family: "Right in our camp is a picture saloon and to prove that I am all right, I send you my miniature and my boy, George, on the same plate. I went out of the tent in my shirt sleeves, called George, did not tell him what I wanted of him, but told him to set down at my feet. How his eyes stuck out to see what was going on. It pleased him very much to think he was take[n] with lieutenant."[117] Tew's letters reveal how photography served as a quiet but important habit of domination in Union army camps. Tew framed the image— for his wife and in his own mind—as an act of authority. He stressed how he never told George what was happening, only to sit at his feet. Highlighting George's delight at posing for this degrading picture, Tew reinforced his own self-conception as the "good master." For Tew to order George to sit at his feet suggests how clearly the broader photographic culture influenced how he conceived of his relation to fugitive slaves—or at least how he wanted others to see this relationship.

Tew's letters hint at a primary reason the sitting pose proved such a popular formula in Union photography: it recalled the supplicant depiction of prayer and liberation from abolitionist culture (the kneeling slave) as it also resembled the conventions for picturing dogs in contemporary photographic culture (Figures 4.11–4.13). Written evidence suggests the visual equation of African Americans and dogs actually reflected the widespread racial perceptions that northern whites held. Indeed, Charles F. Tew was hardly alone in comparing the ex-slave George to "a big dog that you might have for a pet." In Louisiana, for instance, a Union soldier commented that "a negroes

Figure 4.11 *Portrait of Brig. Gen. Napoleon B. McLaughlin, Officer of the Federal Army, and Staff, Vicinity of Washington, D.C.*, August 1865, collodion negative. Civil War Glass Negatives and Related Prints Collection, Civil War Collection, Prints and Photographs Division, Library of Congress, LC-DIG-cwpb-03734.

Figure 4.12 *Am I Not a Man a Brother?*, 1837, 1 print: woodcut on wove paper. Cartoon Prints (American) Collection, Miscellaneous Items in High Demand Collection, Rare Book and Special Collections Division, Library of Congress, LC-USZC4-5321.

life is little more regarded than that of a dog" after another soldier guarding a plantation "got into difficulty with and shot a negro on the plantation."[118] Other Union soldiers were heard saying "they would as quickly shoot a negro as a dog."[119] Ironically, this reduction of African Americans to animality could sometimes give some soldiers the intellectual framework to argue for black rights. Frank Pettit described how "nine tenths of the army" felt that "a negro has rights as a dog has rights and they think his rights should be respected."[120] Such letters suggest that sitting images could be seen as both liberation and submission by soldiers. Through sitting portraits, soldiers acted out the role of emancipator even as they subordinated African Americans to the status of pet-like inferior.

Figure 4.13 *The Peninsula, Va. Lt. George A. Custer with Dog*, 1862, collo-
dion negative. Civil War Glass Negatives and Related Prints Collection,
Civil War Collection, Prints and Photographs Division, Library of
Congress, LC-DIG-cwpb-01553.

Photographs of black people sitting beneath white soldiers were
especially potent because the popularity of the term "contraband" in
wartime continued to amplify the uncertain legal and social status of
ex-slaves. Though his improvised declaration held little legal force,
Benjamin Butler's categorization of those first fugitives who entered
Fort Monroe resonated deeply across northern culture. In military
correspondence, newspapers, minstrel shows, cartoons, paintings, and
even the words of northern missionaries, free blacks, and abolitionists,
ex-slaves were described neither as "fugitives" nor as "refugees"
but as "contrabands." As army officer and New York lawyer Charles
Cooper Nott noted in 1862, "Never was a word so speedily adopted
by so many people in so short a time."[121] In its stranglehold on the
categorization of ex-slaves, "contraband" not only marked them as other
and inferior but also perpetuated their paradoxical status as people

and things. Many black activists contested the term with vigor. As a correspondent in the *Christian Recorder* contended, "This word is objectionable, because it is properly applicable to *things*, and not to *persons*." The author suggested the word "refugee," which signaled "a PERSON seeking shelter or protection from oppression or wrong, and not a thing prohibited from injurious use in time of war."[122] Frederick Douglass, too, protested the term, arguing in a speech calling for black military participation that the "Washington Government wants men for its army, but thus far, it has not had the boldness to recognise the manhood of the race to which I belong. It only sees in the slave an article of commerce, a contraband."[123] Black activists attacked the general thrust of the ubiquitous term "contraband," which amplified the instability of slaves' personhood status and accented slaves' uncertain future in American society. Though no evidence exists revealing how they responded to interracial sitting portraits, they must have reacted similarly, for such photographs symbolized an animalizing process, one which recognized yet restrained black humanity on the cusp of freedom.

Scenes of animalization walked hand in hand with views of black male feminization. In Union camps, images of homosocial domestic settings fused racial hierarchy with a sense of place, white privilege, and black subservience. Artists such as Alexander Gardner, Timothy O'Sullivan, William Morris Smith, and George Barnard often showed blacks with pitchers and glasses in their hands, ready to serve, standing behind lounging soldiers or crouching beneath them (Figures 4.14 and 4.15). These images could have served as responses to the debate about (and eventual introduction of) black soldiers in the Union army. That the vast majority of subordinating camp scenes in the archive show African American men (there are relatively few extant photographs of black women with white soldiers) further suggests a concerted effort by white soldiers and artists to undercut black manhood as black men were enlisting. These images must also have reflected the perceptions of many northern whites who commented in public and private about the seemingly unexpected—and welcome—experience of black servitude at mealtime. A story in *Harper's Weekly*, for example, described the "reliable contrabands" who cleaned up after soldiers had eaten.[124] Other northerners encountered black servitude in southern towns that neighbored army camps. Photographic assistant Henry Rogers Smith described to his family how, in Maryland, he had

Figure 4.14 *Brandy Station, Va. Dinner Party Outside Tent, Army of the Potomac Headquarters*, April 1864, by Timothy H. O'Sullivan, collodion negative. Civil War Glass Negatives and Related Prints Collection, Civil War Collection, Prints and Photographs Division, Library of Congress, LC-DIG-cwpb-00725.

"succeeded last Tuesday night in getting a place to board and lodge. It is one of the best places in town though they are Rebels at heart. We use silver forks and have a black servant to wait on the table."[125] Meanwhile, Sergeant Joseph Emery Fiske described how his quarters in Beaufort offered all the "conveniences of civilized life," which for him included "a dog, a cat, a nigger to wait on us, a horse to ride, oysters plenty, hoe-cake, sweet potatoes, and other luxuries fresh and cheap."[126] The novelty of a black servant seemed a symbol of civilization and refinement to many northern whites—one they visually concretized during the fleeting moments of war. Union interracial photography undoubtedly reflected the romantic views of many northern military

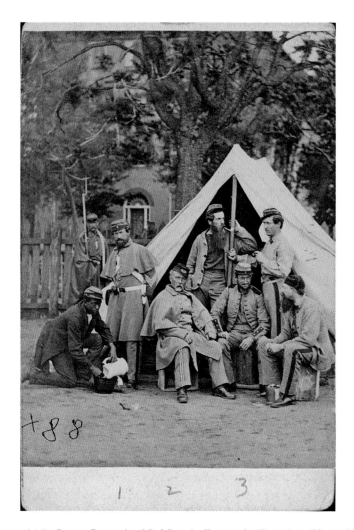

Figure 4.15 *Group Portrait of Soldiers in Front of a Tent, Possibly at Camp Cameron, Washington, D.C.*, c. 1861–1865, by George Barnard, albumen print, 10 × 6 cm. Civil War Collection, Gladstone Collection of African American Photographs, Prints and Photographs Division, Library of Congress, LC-DIG-ppmsca-11200.

personnel regarding the prestige of the planter lifestyle as it simultaneously undermined black masculinity.[127]

Perhaps it should not surprise us that soldiers and northern photographers would turn to domestic categories—namely, the master-dog relationship and the feminized black servant—to enact and imagine racial power relations. Soldiers spent a great deal of time and energy in constructing wooden cabins, building furniture to keep in those shelters, and even planting trees and flowers to beautify these temporary homes away from home.[128] Turning a cabin or tent into a home transcended the quest for material comforts; it also entailed a search for familiar power dynamics. Charles F. Tew, for instance, continuously described how fugitive slaves made his bed, unpacked his trunk, and cooked for him. As he wrote to his wife, "A nig is a good thing oute here as you have no wife to look after youre things."[129] Henry Warren Howe of Lowell, Massachusetts, felt much the same way, noting in his diary, "Have a negro wench for a cook; turkey, biscuits, and apple pie. Bully!"[130] Soldiers such as Howe and Tew turned the gendered power they left in the North into racial (and sometimes intertwined racist and sexist) power when they came south.

When Union soldiers traveled south, they also brought anti-black sentiments nurtured by racist amusements in the North. For decades before the war, popular prints (such as Edward W. Clay's *Life in Philadelphia* series) and minstrel shows had occupied a major place in northern culture and were influential in shaping white racial identity.[131] Many northerners' impressions of slaves drew upon black caricatures put forth in popular culture. Remarking upon an "irresistibly comical" quality to the look of slaves, one soldier described how "they are so black, and their teeth are of such dazzling whiteness, their eyes so laughing and rolling, their clothes so fantastic, and their whole appearance so peculiar."[132] Such racial perceptions underwrote whites' many acts of cruelty, as racist insults and jokes mingled with a coerced culture of black performance in Union camps, where soldiers forced fugitives to dance and sing for the gratification of white audiences. One soldier from New England happily described how there were "five negroes in our mess room last night, we got them to sing and dance!" As the soldier proclaimed, "Negro concerts [are] free of expense here" in Virginia.[133] For many slaves, however, such interactions with northern soldiers would have recalled the very same degradations they had experienced in slavery. Former-slave-turned-abolitionist Henry Bibb, for instance, described how, when slaveholders seek amusement, "they go among the slaves and give them whiskey, to see them dance, 'pat juber,' sing and play on the banjo."[134] In Union camps, slaves found that the white impulse to mix cruelty and merrymaking was a national phenomenon.

It would be a mistake, though, to view such scenes simply as an extension of northern life. Instead, these photographs can be seen as the products of a curious fusion of northern and southern culture at the crossroads of slavery and freedom: by constructing white superiority and black inferiority in personalized pictures, northerners gladly adopted the white supremacist photographic habits that slaveholders initiated across the South in the 1840s and 1850s. This shared impulse to concretize power relations through photographs was mirrored by the many visual conventions that Union domestic scenes shared with proslavery paintings and photographs. O'Sullivan's *Beaufort, South Carolina, "Our Mess"* (Figure 4.16) and Smith's *Maj. H. H. Humphrey and Others* (Figure 4.17) presented blacks as both subjects and objects—as people ready to serve and as racial markers of white privilege.[135] Such

Figure 4.16 *Beaufort, South Carolina, "Our Mess,"* April 1862, by Timothy H. O'Sullivan, collodion negative. Civil War Glass Negatives and Related Prints Collection, Civil War Collection, Prints and Photographs Division, Library of Congress, LC-DIG-cwpb-00800.

Figure 4.17 *Maj. H. H. Humphrey and Others,* June 1865, by William Morris Smith, photographic print. Civil War Glass Negatives and Related Prints Collection, Civil War Collection, Prints and Photographs Division, Library of Congress, LC-USZ62-131080.

images drew upon a formula that went back to the immensely popular painting and later lithograph of George Washington and his family (Figure 4.18). Much like the bulwark of proslavery photography—which presented well-dressed slaves such as Moses (Figure 1.1)—Union photographs often envisioned well-dressed fugitives despite the tattered nature of many fugitives' actual garments. Sympathetic northerners were often shocked when they saw the extreme disrepair of this clothing. As John Eaton wrote in 1864, "You saw them, of both sexes, of all ages, in every stage of health, disease, and decrepitude, often nearly naked, their flesh torn in escaping."[136] For fugitives, the *Freedmen's Record* reported, "clothing is their most pressing need, especially for women and children, who cannot wear the cast-off garments of soldiers."[137] Union interracial photography operated through, in part, the logic of erasure to convey a sense of white domestic luxury.

Figure 4.18 *Washington Family*, c. 1833, by M. E. D. Brown, lithograph. Popular Graphic Arts Collection, Prints and Photographs Division, Library of Congress, LC-DIG-pga-05454.

Domesticating photographs, then, performed two cultural tasks at once. They channeled black humanity into certain limited, degrading poses—thereby continuing to use the medium to maintain the imaginative divide between blacks and whites. In doing so, these images simultaneously reflected and fueled northern dreams of racial superiority. On occasion such images eschewed black figures as props, rendering them instead as subjects in more personal relationships of power with white superiors—most famously so in Alexander Gardner's *What Do I Want, John Henry?* (Figure 4.19). Gardner circulated this image from at least the fall of 1863 onward as a 7-by-9-inch paper print, a stereograph, and a carte de visite.[138] In 1866 Gardner labeled the sitting man "John's master" and described John, the black subject, as an "affectionate creature," a more subtle form of the animalizing processes within the camps.[139] Viewers during the war would not yet have seen Gardner's extended caption, but the image alone might

Figure 4.19 *What Do I Want, John Henry?*, by Alexander Gardner, illustration in *Gardner's Photographic Sketch Book of the Civil War*, 1866, 1 photographic print: albumen. Civil War Collection, Miscellaneous Items in High Demand Collection, Prints and Photographs Division, Library of Congress, LC-DIG-ppmsca-12548.

have recalled the print of George Washington, his family, and the slave on the margins of the dining scene. Further, Gardner's scene of servility came with a twist because of its interrogatory title. As literary critic Elizabeth Young notes, the effect of the title "dramatizes the authority of the white man through hyperbole; not only must John Henry serve the white man, but he must also magically anticipate the man's desires."[140] In *What Do I Want, John Henry?* white racial authority went hand in hand with a seemingly preternatural black obedience.

Domestic servitude proved so powerful a lens for concretizing the abstraction of an interracial and hierarchical society that military personnel and photographers even used domestic props in industrial settings. Perhaps no image did so more clearly than Alexander Gardner's *Aquia Creek Landing, VA. Clerks of the Commissary Depot by Railroad Car and Packing Cases*, taken in February 1863, a month after the passage of the Emancipation Proclamation, and circulated during the war as a stereograph and carte de visite (Figure 4.20).[141] Even in the rail yard, a black man kneels with a teacup and saucer, presenting a drink to a white subject. Though it is difficult to tell for certain, embedded in the center of the image could be a self-portrait of Alexander Gardner, the bearded man receiving the drink. His potential presence raises questions about the role photographers played in such assertions of white masculinity. But this much is clear: by importing a pose of domestic servility into a decidedly undomestic setting of transportation technology and war preparation, the clerks made evident how

Figure 4.20 *Aquia Creek Landing, Va. Clerks of the Commissary Depot by Railroad Car and Packing Cases*, February 1863, by Alexander Gardner, collodion negative. Civil War Glass Negatives and Related Prints Collection, Civil War Collection, Prints and Photographs Division, Library of Congress, LC-DIG-cwpb-03974.

they and others had turned image-making into a game of racial domination. The conspicuous artificiality of the scene projected a callous indifference to recognizing the fullness of black humanity.

How, one wonders, did the African American subjects understand these images? While no written sources tell us their perceptions, at least two meanings seem plausible. Ex-slaves likely understood such photographic practices as one part of the humiliation—the verbal and physical abuse—rendered at the hands of an army they had once seen as a liberatory force. A change in geography had done little to alter their social power, as one Norfolk slave encapsulated when she commented, "I reckon I'm Massa Lincoln's slave now."[142] It is equally possible that many fugitives who posed for pictures detected an advantage in catering to white men's fantasies of control. Take, for instance, an ex-slave named Henry, who had traveled with Charles Tew from New Bern, North Carolina, to Newport News, Virginia. In one letter to his wife and children, Tew noted, "While I am writing this letter my Nig comes in, takes off his hat. [H]e is watching me now. I wish you could see him grin how his eyes glisten and his teeth shines. [H]e wants something of me." Tew transcribed a subsequent conversation initiated by Henry:

> *Ise got a brother down Souf and I wants youse to gives me a writing to him. well tomorrow come in Henry. Tankey Lieut Charles has yous got a postage thing. yes I will see to it.*[143]

If Tew's dialogue expressed his own benevolence, it also indicated Henry's use of Tew to serve his own ends, which entailed maintaining contact with distant family by mail. It appears that Henry, like many fugitives, was using Union territory as the staging ground to reunite with loved ones lost during flight.[144] Although it is unclear whether Henry ever posed with Tew for a portrait, it is easy to see how he and other slaves might have accommodated the photographic desires of Union whites to achieve their own objectives.

Of course, Union soldiers and northern photographers were not alone in visualizing African Americans during wartime. From the first months of the conflict, in lithographs and engravings, sheet music and decorative envelopes, paintings and illustrated magazines, northerners had taken a keen interest in documenting and defining the character, actions, and prospects of ex-slaves in particular. Early on, the bulk of such images cast fugitives as submissive, pathetic, cowering, exotic, uncivilized, ignorant, and inferior. Fugitives entered Union lines in tattered clothing and crouching poses, obsequiously requesting aid and shelter from steadfast, armed white soldiers (Figure 4.21).

On occasion, white paternalism was added in the transfer from photograph to engraving. In *Arrival of the First Negro Family Within the Lines, on 1st January, 1863*, David B. Woodbury highlighted the social ties of fugitives in their own domestic scene (Figure 4.22). During the war, Gardner sold this image in his *Catalogue of Photographic Incidents of the War* as a stereograph and carte de visite.[145] But when the photograph was translated onto the pages of *Harper's Weekly* and the *New York Illustrated*, the mass presses removed the background soldiers

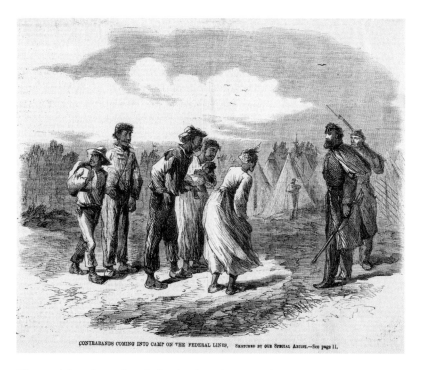

CONTRABANDS COMING INTO CAMP ON THE FEDERAL LINES.   Sketched by our Special Artist.—See page 11.

Figure 4.21 *Contrabands Coming into Camp on the Federal Lines, New-York Illustrated News*, May 10, 1862. Courtesy American Antiquarian Society.

Figure 4.22 *Arrival of the First Negro Family Within the Lines, on 1st January, 1863,* by David B. Woodbury, collodion negative. Civil War Glass Negatives and Related Prints Collection, Civil War Collection, Prints and Photographs Division, Library of Congress, LC-DIG-cwpb-01161.

and added one far more pronounced white soldier, closer to the action (Figure 4.23). In doing so, they injected a stronger sense of white authority into this scene of black domesticity. The transition also turned a scene of emancipation into one of white pity. In the article that accompanied his drawing in *Harper's Weekly,* A. R. Waud noted how, for him, there was "something very touching in seeing these poor people coming into camp—giving up all the little ties that cluster about home, such as it is in slavery, and trustfully throwing themselves on the mercy of the Yankees, in the hope of getting permission to own themselves and keep their children from the auction-block."[146] Waud linked Woodbury's news picture of emancipation to a sense of black dependency and desperation.

Slaves and former slaves were to be pitied, helped, and contained, but they were also available as a resource to aid white soldiers, a notion

Figure 4.23 *Contrabands Coming into Camp in Consequence of the Proclamation*, by Alfred R. Waud, *Harper's Weekly*, January 31, 1863, 1 print: wood engraving. Civil War Collection, Miscellaneous Items in High Demand Collection, Library of Congress, LC-USZ62-88812.

made clear by images such as *Dark Artillery, or, How to Make the Contrabands Useful* (Figure 4.24). In the foreground, a white soldier prepares a cannon strapped to the back of a fugitive, who is depicted with grossly exaggerated facial features—enlarged eyes, an outsized grin, and an empty, robotic gaze. Despite the absurdity of his role in the battle, this fugitive smiles gleefully and dutifully. Signaling racial difference, reinforcing the sense that only whites possessed the necessary intellect and self-government needed to fight a war, the image also highlighted the contradictions of the term "contraband." The fugitives were simultaneously exuberant subjects and, as the bases of cannons, oddly animated objects. By kneeling on all fours, the fugitive in the middle ground underscored this sentiment, as he would likely have recalled a beast of burden, a chattel, to many northern viewers. Though an obviously comical take on the question of the status of ex-slaves in the early years of the war, a serious kernel lay at the core of the image: ex-slaves might help the war effort as brutes, but they lacked the capacity to do much more.

Figure 4.24 *Dark Artillery, or, How to Make the Contrabands Useful*, by Frank Bellew, *Frank Leslie's Illustrated Newspaper*, October 26, 1861, 1 print: wood engraving. Civil War Collection. Miscellaneous Items in High Demand, Library of Congress, LC-USZ62-98516.

As the war proceeded, prints and illustrated periodicals haltingly transitioned from portraying African Americans as passive, racial inferiors to depicting them as assertive and heroic wartime figures. Coverage of the dramatic seizure of the Confederate steamer *Planter*, in the summer of 1862, marked a turning point. The vessel was taken by a group of African Americans (led by Robert Smalls), who piloted it out of Charleston to Union-controlled waters. *Frank Leslie's* published *Heroes in Ebony*, an engraving (based upon a photograph) of the black crew members, while *Harper's Weekly* published an individual portrait of Robert Smalls (also based upon a photograph). Instead of cartoon-like images with exaggerated facial features, the men appeared in dignified fashion, wearing suits, vests, and bow ties; in *Frank Leslie's*, the crew members even posed with hands on their hips, accenting their pride and heroic stature.[147] Illustrated periodicals accompanied these more dignified engravings of black men with before-and-after images charting the transition from slave to soldier. Most notably, *Harper's Weekly* used *The Scourged Back* and two other images as the

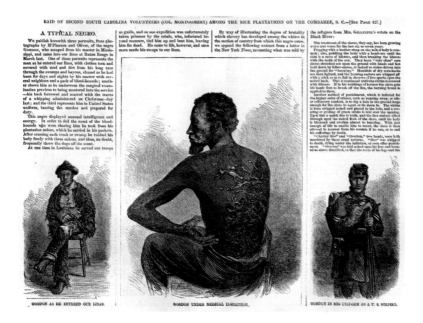

Figure 4.25 *A Typical Negro, Harper's Weekly,* July 4, 1863, 429. Courtesy of University of Idaho Library.

basis for a triptych, *A Typical Negro* (Figure 4.25), on July 4, 1863, a publication date that surely was interpreted by audiences as a testament to black patriotism as well as a jab at the contradictory development of slavery and freedom in the United States. *A Typical Negro* fell into a longer line of lithographic and mass-periodical depictions of black bravery that promoted African Americans' entry into the Union army from the summer of 1862 onward and continued to promote black heroism and manhood after blacks could join the army.[148] Such images collectively refashioned the popular portrayal of African Americans as the conflict proceeded—from racial inferiors to, broadly speaking, resourceful and courageous figures, men who had even made important contributions to the nation in wartime.[149]

Union photographs that circulated as photographs also contributed to this vision. Scholars Barbara Krauthamer and Deborah Willis have shown the diverse ways in which African Americans were photographed during the conflict. These scenes included groups of "contraband," ex-slaves working on plantations in South Carolina, and the many individual and group portraits of black soldiers.[150] Black soldiers lined up for dignified group pictures, including *Colored Army Teamsters, Cobb Hill, Va.*, as well as the widely reproduced group portrait of Company E of the 4th U.S. Colored Infantry, revealing a line of men posing with their rifles at Fort Lincoln.[151] They also occasionally posed alongside white soldiers and officers, as in the case of *Gen. Edward Ferrero and Staff*, an image that might have staked a claim to racial liberalism.[152] Though photographers pictured ex-slaves passively sitting in front of cabins gazing into the camera, as in James Gibson's *Contrabands*, others showed enslaved people as political actors on the move. Perhaps the most dramatic action shots were taken by Timothy O'Sullivan, who pictured fugitives crossing the Rappahannock River while he was photographing General John Pope's campaign in Virginia in the summer of 1862.[153] O'Sullivan's *Fugitive Negroes Fording Rappahannock* actually erased the watchful gazes of white soldiers, who appear on the left side in one negative but are cropped in the finalized color stereograph (Figures 4.26 and 4.27). By cropping the image, O'Sullivan and his boss, Alexander Gardner, created a tighter frame, and thus a more dramatic shot. Perhaps unintentionally, this alteration also worked to foreground the fugitives' mobility and made their collective action the main subject of the frame.

Figure 4.26 Rappahannock River, Va. *Fugitive Negroes Fording Rappahannock*, August 1862, by Timothy H. O'Sullivan, collodion negative. Civil War Glass Negatives and Related Prints Collection, Civil War Collection, Prints and Photographs Division, Library of Congress, LC-DIG-cwpb-00218.

Entered according to act of Congress, in the year 1862, by Alexander Gardner, in the Clerk's Office of the District Court of the District of Columbia.

Figure 4.27 *Fugitive Negroes Fording Rappahannock*, c. 1862, stereograph, albumen print, 8 × 17 cm. Civil War Collection, Stereograph Cards Collection, Prints and Photographs Division, Library of Congress, LC-DIG-stereo-1s02891.

Ex-slaves also contested subordinating imagery of "contrabands" as well as Union domesticating photographs, though in quieter ways. The commercial photographers who established themselves in Union camps created a cultural middle ground, through which northern whites and southern slaves fought over the very definition of African Americans' character and social potential. Though they had no means of influencing popular depictions crafted by sketch artists, ex-slaves could and did commission their own portrait photographs, thereby extending the photographic practices they had initiated during slavery. In his study of portraits of black soldiers, historian Ronald Coddington has shown how common it was for ex-slaves-turned-soldiers to pose for the camera. They posed in diverse ways: Silas L. Johnson (Mississippi) sat, legs crossed, with an American flag on a pole steadied between his arm and body; Albert E. Jackson (Alabama) stood and held a rifle with both of his gloved hands; John Hines (Kentucky) sat with hands together in his lap; Taylor B. Aldrich (Maryland) also sat, though he brandished a scabbarded sword for the camera; Jeremiah Saunders (Kentucky), too, held a sword, though he held his upright as he posed with his wife, likely after the conflict had ended.[154] William Henry Scott, originally a slave from Virginia, posed for his portrait before what appears to be a painted backdrop with a fort and American flag (Figure 4.28). The generic backdrop and rigid body posture belied the wartime drama Scott had experienced. After escaping slavery to join the 12th Massachusetts Regiment in April 1862, Scott spent the duration of the war as an aide to Major Loring W. Muzzey, including at battles in Fredericksburg and Gettysburg.[155] The setting and composition of Scott's image were unexceptional, but for Scott—as for many other former slaves in the U.S. Colored Troops—the photographic portrait testified to political participation and self-liberation that must have been anything but common. Photographic portraits, for slaves-turned-soldiers, were assertions of patriotism and self-possession.

Photographs also proved a vital means for black soldiers and sailors to maintain ties with loved ones. Lieutenant Henry Crydenwise of the 73rd U.S. Colored Troops, for instance, wrote home to his parents from Louisiana with gratitude for sending along their photographs. "You can better imagine than I can tell the great pleasure they gave me," Crydenwise related, alluding to his lack of words to describe the emotional impact of the images. "Yours and Fathers are very good

Figure 4.28 *William Henry Scott*, c. 1862–1865, tintype, 1 × 1.5 inches (image), 2.5 × 4 inches (frame). William H. Scott Family Papers, Stuart A. Rose Manuscript, Archives, and Rare Book Library, Emory University.

indeed and look just as when I saw you last but while Mary's is good it made me sad to see her looking so poor. I am very sorry to hear that she has been so very ill."[156] Photographic exchanges could stir feelings of closeness and distance: they could make a soldier feel as if he had never left ("look just as when I saw you") as they simultaneously underscored the time that had transpired ("sorry to hear that she has been so very ill"). Even Confederate soldiers noticed how much black soldiers valued such private portraits. Bartlett Yancey Malone, imprisoned at Point Lookout (a large prison camp in Maryland), recorded in his diary how Confederate prisoners often stole the knapsacks of the African American soldiers standing guard, and he noted how one soldier in particular reacted to this theft: "They have stold mine too but I want caring for the knapsack all I hate about it is loosing Sophys Garotipe."[157] Though Malone's diary entry should hardly be taken as a verbatim account, it still suggests how black soldiers privileged the photograph, as a possession, because of its sentimental associations.

Still, the visual narrative of black personhood, manhood, and dignity exemplified by the *Planter* engravings, Rappahannock River stereographs, and private ex-slaves' portraits competed with the many popular images of "contraband" as well as the onslaught of Union interracial camp photographs envisioning black inferiority. What made Union interracial views significant was not simply their content but also the fact that northern photography had industrialized during the war. Photographers such as Alexander Gardner and Timothy O'Sullivan were first and foremost entrepreneurs producing visual commodities for sale through networks of production and distribution in the northern marketplace, connected through manufacturing and distribution magnate Edward T. Anthony, the industrial hub of northern photography. Anthony's photographic output was unsurpassed in the 1860s. While he sold a modest 175 stereographs from his 1859 catalog, by 1864 he listed more than 5,000 pictures.[158] Anthony's carte de visite production was equally massive, and wartime reports indicate that he was producing an astounding 3,600 of these small paper images per day.[159] In this way, many domestic-subordinate images entered northern homes as stereograph amusements, which had only recently risen to popularity after the introduction of Oliver Wendell Holmes Sr.'s cheap stereoscope, the viewing mechanism for the images, in 1859.[160] When one looked at the two-dimensional images of the stereograph through the binocular lenses of a stereoscope, one saw a three-dimensional image. As Holmes wrote in the *Atlantic*, the "effect is so heightened as to produce an appearance of reality which cheats the senses with its seeming truth." He called the stereograph "the card of introduction to make all mankind acquaintances."[161] During the Civil War, many northerners began to encounter domesticated visions of black freedom through such a device. Civil War photographers brought such visions of emancipation and hierarchy, liberators and liberated, into northern parlors in three-dimensional form.

Domesticating images also entered the North through private channels. It is difficult to know how many other soldiers besides Charles F. Tew mailed photographs of African Americans home to their families, but the photographic landscape as well as soldiers' letters suggests this practice likely became commonplace. John White Geary, for instance, mailed at least four photographs to his wife, Mary, during the war, including one he described as a "'type' with Co."—which may have been the image Geary posed for, with a black man sitting at his feet, at Harpers Ferry (Figure 4.29).[162] This much is clear: in sending a photograph of himself and an escaped slave to his wife and children in Massachusetts, Charles F. Tew actually drew upon and extended the antebellum practices of slaveholders. In the letter home, he even told his children they could kiss the portrait if they wanted.[163] Tew found in photography a personalized way of defining the social identities of African Americans and cementing the seemingly unstable state of racialized power relations. Like southern masters, northern whites had harnessed photography to assert racial authority and superiority. Strikingly, though, northern and southern photographic visions of the war would ultimately differ greatly. Images of Confederate body servants stood to maintain an old order, whereas northern images stood to assert racial domination within a world of social tumult. The aesthetics differed, as one can see by comparing the image of Burrell and John Wallace Comer to many of the Union subordinating images, but the

Figure 4.29 *Gen'l. John W. Geary and Staff—Taken at Harper's Ferry*, c. 1861, carte de visite, albumen print. Civil War Collection, Miscellaneous Items in High Demand Collection, Prints and Photographs Division, Library of Congress, LC-USZ62-65083.

habit was shared. Ironically, enslaved resistance (i.e., fugitive escapes) actually helped expand the culture of white supremacist photography to the North. As whites across the nation entered Reconstruction, they did so with personalized and mass-produced images that policed the boundary of personhood—images that constrained blacks' full humanity in the moment of emancipation.

——

DURING THE WAR, northern soldiers and artists expanded a photographic disposition that began in the slave South. For northern photographers and white soldiers, photography proved a way of resettling the social and racial disruptions of the Civil War. The logic of domestication underwrote whites' photographic attempts to navigate this moment, shaping scenes of black people sitting, kneeling, and serving. Such images emerged at the intersection of long-standing iconographies of African Americans and on-the-ground experiences. Of course, these images were only one strand of the broader wartime visualization of African Americans. They existed alongside prints, mass-press illustrations, and public and private photographs (including those portraits made by formerly enslaved men) that stressed black manhood and patriotism. More fully recognizing the place of Union interracial photography within this contested visual field helps us explain the ongoing challenges to black personhood, in no small part, because soldiers adopted the very same disposition of racial power that many northerners believed was only possible or permitted in the South. Adopting this disposition included engaging in a set of photographic practices that refashioned southern slave photography. On the cusp of black freedom, photography enabled northern whites to present themselves as liberators even as it helped them to shape personalized visions of racial hierarchy through the categories of domesticity— visions that would live on long after the war and slavery had ended.

EPILOGUE

The Photographic Legacy of American Slavery

IN APRIL 1865, AS THE Civil War came to a close, Alexander Gardner stood on the banks of a canal in the industrial section of Richmond. The Confederacy had fallen, and in Richmond, as in Charleston and Columbia, actual buildings had crumbled to the ground as well. The image Gardner took, *View on Canal, Near Crenshaw's Mill, Richmond, Virginia* (Figure 5.1), pictured one such urban casualty in Haxall's Mill. Here, in the capital of the ruined Confederacy, this once-productive flour mill appeared as little more than a crumbling piece of honeycomb in the background of the image. Its looming presence marked the end of an old world.[1]

Only steps away from where he took this image, Gardner had made a very different picture, perhaps on the same day, that marked the transition to a new world: *Group of Negroes ("Freedmen") by Canal* (Figure 5.2). Ten African Americans—adults, teenagers, even two impatient (and, thus, blurry) young children—posed close together at the top of the embankment. A few men looked on from behind, some perched on fence posts. Behind them, Haxall's Mill crumbled, but, judging from the way the central man proudly posed with his corncob pipe, this image likely meant something closer to liberation than

Figure 5.1 *View on Canal, Near Crenshaw's Mill, Richmond, Virginia*, by Alexander Gardner, illustration in *Gardner's Photographic Sketch Book of the Civil War*, 1866. Civil War Collection, Miscellaneous Items in High Demand Collection, Prints and Photographs Division, Library of Congress, LC-DIG-ppmsca-12613.

destruction to him. There is no evidence for how Gardner circulated their image, nor did he include it in *Gardner's Photographic Sketch Book of the Civil War* (1866). For whatever reason, Gardner only published the canal view, which became Plate 92. The text that accompanied the photograph described the prowess and demise of Haxall's Mill, which "had a floor surface of eight acres and a water-power that never failed" and "was kept busy by the rebel government" during the war—yet eventually "fell prey to the fire." The resulting sketch mourned southern ruination rather than celebrating slave emancipation. Scholars have long seen Gardner's *Sketch Book* as a formal landmark in the visual depiction of war, but in choosing the mill over the freedpeople, Gardner actually followed the well-worn path of many

Figure 5.2 *Richmond, Virginia. Group of Negroes ("Freedmen") by Canal*, April 1865, by Alexander Gardner, collodion negative. Civil War Glass Negatives and Related Prints Collection, Civil War Collection, Prints and Photographs Division, Library of Congress, LC-DIG-cwpb-00468.

soldiers, artists, and slaveholders who had mobilized photography over the past quarter century to craft and re-craft visions of racial hierarchy. He extended this central photographic vision of the Civil War era—one that persistently undercut the full humanity and demarcated the social potential of African Americans—by actively neglecting the image of the freedpeople.

During the final decades of bondage and earliest moments of emancipation, as this book has argued, photography played a privileged role in animating debates over the boundaries of personhood, the social identities of African American slaves, and the ideal racial order of the nation. This powerful intersection of visual technology and racial conflict reveals how much Civil War–era notions of status, identity, and community were embedded in visual discourse and social practice. Spurred by the sectional crisis and the impending death of bondage, the photographic efforts of southern slaveholders and northern soldiers intentionally and effectively cast black Americans outside the bounds of full personhood as they generated concrete, miniature formulations of a world rooted in white supremacy. In turn, enslaved people, former bondspeople, and occasionally white abolitionists put forth an alternative future—a vision of slaves and ex-slaves as equal people, not property, and a vision of interracial community that could offer striking glimpses of a racially egalitarian world, even if it also periodically trafficked in the white paternalism of its day. These contentious, on-the-ground debates took place within and through photographs precisely because the medium was widely available, largely affordable, and generally perceived as an especially potent way to convey and confirm identity, status, and social relations. With this new technology, claims to racial identity and sociality were pitched in the Civil War era. Through camera lenses, the millions of Americans most deeply invested in the future of slavery actively stoked political sentiment and racial consciousness as they quietly built and strengthened networks in previously unrecognized ways.

Photography shaped the culture and politics of late slavery; in turn, conflicts over slavery produced modern visual politics. A new system of visual symbols and symbol-rich cultural practices oriented around social exploitation and cultural debasement, modern visual politics was and continues to be constituted by the use of photography to bolster and express domination, to develop alternative ways of seeing, and to build discernible and covert political communities. This distinctive means of waging ideological and political battles would have been entirely foreign to colonial and early-nineteenth-century Americans. Trained artists had long made political images, but ordinary Americans had never taken up the same visual medium as a political language. By the 1850s it seemed altogether commonplace to all Americans—from Boston to Charleston, from the big house to the slave cabin—to assert claims about fundamental questions of the day through the very same visual form. Photography enabled many to become practitioners, not just consumers, of commercial images. And these practitioners nurtured new photographic habits that were unforeseen when the medium arrived in the United States in 1839. There was nothing inevitable about the emergence of modern visual politics. It was forged through many large and small struggles over identity, status, family, and community. Whether one looks to Edward Pringle brandishing his portrait of Mack in a San Francisco law office, or to the northern abolitionists gazing upon photographs of fellow activists who suffered for the cause, or to the many enslaved people spending their cash to acquire private pictures, one glimpses this cultural transformation in action. They took a new and neutral technology and made a series of informal visual-political practices common sense. Their legacy was, in no small part, this new mode of informal political engagement, which would continue to shape battles over rights, equality, and dignity in the United States—in bold continuities and faint echoes—from Reconstruction to the present day.

In the wake of slavery, abolitionists' visual practices would continue to resonate in efforts to combat injustice and build social movements. One of the key legacies of abolitionist photography was the tradition of "damage photography," which radicals initiated through images such as *Branded Hand* and *The Scourged Back* to reveal social conditions through violations of the body. Drawing on those visual precedents, reformers documented how, well past legal emancipation, white-on-black violence persisted in the southern household. In July 1866 Wendell Phillips received such a picture in the mail, sent with a letter from John Oliver, a black reformer who had met Phillips at Oberlin College and spent the immediate postwar years serving as an official of the Freedmen's Bureau in Richmond.[2] The picture focused on the backside of a sixteen-year-old black girl who, as Oliver noted, had been burned as punishment by a former slaveholding mistress (Figure 5.3). Oliver hoped that the photograph would help Phillips "to see quite well the barbarism of Slavery as it now exists in King William Co, Virginia in 1866."[3] Oliver likely also sent the photograph to *Harper's Weekly*, which published it as an engraving, *Marks of Punishment Inflicted upon a Colored Servant in Richmond Virginia* (Figure 5.4), along with a letter from a "gentle-man in Richmond, Virginia." The letter described the girl's wicked punishment at length and noted that the Freedmen's Bureau was currently investigating it, despite the public opinion in Richmond. As *Harper's* related, Richmond newspapers "all with one accord sang out against the Bureau for its interference, and Mrs. A—— instead of the fiend that she is, was a martyred and chivalrous Southern lady. She was required to give bail in $5000. All the counsel of the city

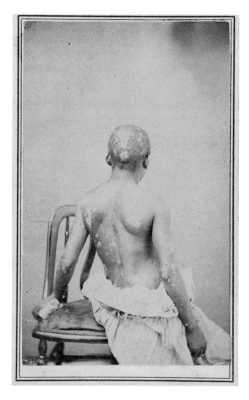

Figure 5.3 *Unidentified Woman*, 1866, by Vannerson & Jones, carte de visite. Wendell Phillips Papers, 1555–1882 (MS Am 1953), Houghton Library, Harvard University.

MARKS OF PUNISHMENT INFLICTED UPON A COLORED SERVANT IN RICHMOND, VIRGINIA.

Figure 5.4 *Marks of Punishment Inflicted upon a Colored Servant in Richmond Virginia, Harper's Weekly*, July 28, 1866, 477. Courtesy of University of Idaho Library.

tendered her their services." Undoubtedly, the photograph shaped *Harper's* opinion of the matter, as the girl's scars and pose, with her back turned toward the camera, would have immediately recalled the barbarous treatment of Gordon/Peter to American viewers. "The case stands on unquestionable authority," noted the paper, "and the time is now gone by when things of this nature are to be hidden from the public."[4] Through private and public circulation of the photo, Oliver highlighted southern practices of domination that the Thirteenth Amendment had done little to halt.

Still, northern reformers never engaged in any large-scale campaigns to photograph white-on-black violence during Reconstruction. In a sense, this is no surprise, for abolitionists had never built an apparatus for such a venture. After slavery, former activists' main engagement with photography was to archive their own movement. At the Massachusetts Historical Society, no abolitionist collection made photography more central to its mission than "A Catalogue of Portraits of American Abolitionists and of Their Allies and Opponents in the United States and in Great Britain and Ireland, 1831–1865," put together by Francis Jackson Garrison to "accompany his extended copy of The Life of William Lloyd Garrison 1805–1878." As Francis Jackson Garrison noted,

> *This collection of portraits includes not only a large number of the active participants in the struggle for the abolition of slavery in the United States who appears in the pages of the four-volume Life of William Lloyd Garrison, but a multitude of others not named therein who were no less zealous and devoted laborers in the cause. Their opponents, northern and southern, are also well represented. As the portraits, with a few exceptions, are arranged alphabetically in their boxes, and not bound together, it will be easy, if desired, to assemble those constituting any of the classified groups.*[5]

Toward these ends, Garrison broke the collection down into more than thirty social groups, including "Founders of the N.E.A.S. Society," "Women Pioneers," "Liberty Party," "British + Foreign Abolitionists," "Southern Converts," "Fugitive Slaves," "Southern Proslavery Men," and abolitionists by state (Massachusetts, New York, New Hampshire, Vermont, Maine, Connecticut, Rhode Island, Pennsylvania).[6] Oriented toward future views of the past, the catalogue revealed the centrality

of images in Garrison's own vision of how the history of the movement would be told. His archival work symbolizes the broader shift
American abolitionists had pioneered in making internal and external visibility integral to the function and meaning of modern social
movements.

Later movements would follow in their footsteps. In the early
twentieth century, the labor movement as well as African American
organizations harnessed the new technology of cinema to forge
sympathetic portrayals of labor and black culture, respectively.[7] In
the civil rights era, organizations such as the Student Nonviolent
Coordinating Committee took up photography as an important means
of community-building, while leaders including Martin Luther King
Jr. conceived of political rallies as visual performances before photo-
journalists and television news—showing an acute sensitivity to the
theatrical and visual nature of protest.[8] In recent years, Occupy Wall
Street and the Black Lives Matter movement have drawn upon new
social media platforms to make themselves visible and knowable to
themselves and the world, and photography has been an essential tool
in their efforts. New media will continue to shape disparate quests for
civil and human rights as well as equality, but whatever the issue at
hand, these quests will be indebted to the initial efforts of American
abolitionists and ex-slaves, who played a signal role in the making of
modern visual politics. By refashioning photography into a tool of
community formation and radical identification, they reconfigured the
informal political world.

As abolitionists were archiving their pictures in public, various
slaveholders moved visions of their bondspeople squarely into the
realm of private memory, where photographs of well-dressed slaves
would greet future generations descended from former slaveholders.
These images have been overlooked for nostalgic, plantation ro-
mances in postbellum literature and visual culture. But it is not hard
to imagine how personal photographs, for whites, could serve as powerful evidence of the contours of their slaveholding past.[9] Even for a
family as ferociously brutal as the Manigaults, whose Gowrie plantation witnessed an appalling child mortality rate of 90 percent, benevolent photographs offered visual evidence to support a story about
how "their family" treated its slaves well.[10] In this vein, the Manigaults
put their carte de visite of Moses in a family record book. As the accompanying caption detailed, "'*Moses*': the last African belonging to

our family. This likeness was taken February 1857. He died of an apoplectic fit in Charleston So.Ca. 16th July 1863. He worked to the last, his occupation being to keep the yard clean, and garden free from weeds" (Figure 5.5).[11] This 1850s image had once envisioned Moses's role as both decorative object and laboring subject for Charles Manigault in his aristocratic low country domain. The preservation of the image,

Figure 5.5 *Moses*, c. February 1857, carte de visite. Manigault Family Record, vol. II, p. 320, courtesy of the South Carolina Historical Society.

in concert with written text, allowed the Manigaults to narrate a particular story about their family's slaveholding history. The emphasis on
"the last African"—a phrase likely indicating his status as the final
Manigault slave to endure the Middle Passage—revealed Moses's long
life within one slaveholding family. Here, the record book claimed,
was a laborer with a deep history in one household, not a commodity
bought, sold, and shipped across the South. That Moses "worked to
the last" suggested, in turn, Moses's loyalty even during the tumultuous years of the Civil War, which was no doubt important for the
Manigaults to document, given the violent resistance of many enslaved
people across their properties.[12] Through word and image, Moses was
frozen in this individualized performance of racial deference—one
that would endure into the late nineteenth century and beyond.

As image preservation produced a romantic sense of enslaved loyalty, it also gave whites a way to continue to forge bonds between each
other through the bodies of their slaves. After the war, an ex-slaveholder
from Nashville had a photograph taken of Joe, a former slave, "that
each child and grandchild should have one of our faithful old friend."[13]
Or take the case of two slave girls of Rebecca Harriet Pindar of Ringgold,
Georgia (Figure 5.6). The differing dresses, hairstyles, and jewelry of

Figure 5.6 *Slave Girls of the Pindar Family*, c. 1860, tintype, 4 × 5 inches
(image). Pindar Family Papers, Stuart A. Rose Manuscript, Archives,
and Rare Book Library, Emory University.

the tintype articulated the girls' individuality. Their contrasting poses, moreover, differentiated them as sisters. But a handwritten note on the back of the portrait undercut this subjectivity: "Two slave girls given Aunt Harriet by her mother when she married" (Figure 5.7).[14] The very visual conventions that marked these girls' individuality also enhanced their status as giftable property. Moreover, the inscribable backside of the tintype cover enabled the Pindar family to pass on knowledge of the girls as subjects and objects, people and property,

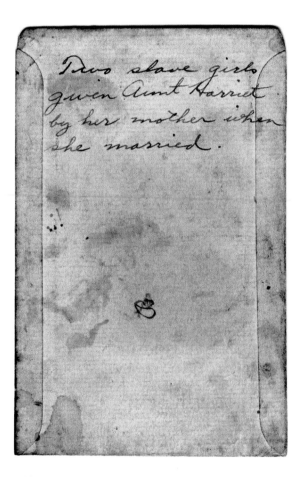

Figure 5.7 *Slave Girls of the Pindar Family*, c. 1860, tintype case. Pindar Family Papers, Stuart A. Rose Manuscript, Archives, and Rare Book Library, Emory University.

with handwritten text that revealed a personal touch in its own right. In this way, slaveholders materialized—and personalized—the long-standing practice through which they linked white generations with human commodities.[15] Even though they could no longer express white familial connections through the actual bodies of slaves, by passing them down in their wills or giving them as gifts, the Pindars continued to do so with photographs of those slaves.[16] After emancipation, the Pindar family passed the photograph, as they had once the slaves, from one generation to the next.

This private photo culture accompanied the commercialization of southern slave photography. While southern whites continued to produce personal portraits of black servants and nursemaids with white children and with former slaveholding families well into the twentieth century, postbellum memoirs also trotted out antebellum photographs.[17] *Life of Maumer Juno of Charleston, S.C.: A Sketch of Juno (Waller) Seymour* (1892), for instance, told the story of Juno, the enslaved nursemaid for generations of white families, who "made the descendants of her first mistress the object of her care and solicitude, and faithfully did she serve their interests with christian patience for eighty years."[18] Part of the evidence for this devotion came in the form of a chattel Madonna photograph on the cover, captioned *Juno (Waller) Seymour, Minding the Great Grand-daughter of Her First Owner (1853).*

The major change in southern photography, though, was the emergence of a popular commercial industry that crafted the South as a distinctive region and blacks as a distinctively uncivilized people within this region. Southern artists started mass-producing stereographs and other paper photographs of freedpeople working (typically in cotton fields) (Figure 5.8), in their leisure time (usually sitting or standing in front of dilapidated cabins) (Figure 5.9), and as racial and regional clichés (such as mammies and street vendors). While Charleston photographers Osborn and Durbec had begun this venture in 1860 with their plantation imagery in the Sea Islands outside Charleston, their influence would take hold after the war. South Carolina and Georgia emerged as the centers of this postwar trade, and photographers who specialized in the business included northern transplant George Barnard (Charleston), J. A. Palmer (Aiken, South Carolina), J. N. Wilson (Savannah), and O. Pierre Havens (Savannah). Palmer even developed a special line of African American scenes,

Figure 5.8 *Cotton Field,* stereograph no. 171 in *Characteristic Scenes,* by J. A. Palmer, Aiken, S.C. Photographs 15241.334, courtesy of the South Caroliniana Library, University of South Carolina, Columbia, SC.

Figure 5.9 *Whitaker Family in the Vicinity of Aiken*, 1874, by J. A. Palmer, albumen print mounted to a stereo card, 4 × 7 inches. MK 9034, courtesy of The Charleston Museum, Charleston, South Carolina.

labeled as "Characteristic Southern Scenes…A large Stock of Views of Negro Groups, Cabins, Teams, Cotton Fields and Plants, etc., kept constantly on hand." The southern artist-entrepreneurs who sold mass-reproducible paper photographs were in the business of visual and virtual tourism, offering distant onlookers a chance to glimpse black life after slavery; they were also in the business of presenting African Americans as passive subjects, who looked up from the cotton plants they laboriously picked and stared blankly at the camera (and viewer) from run-down shacks.

Naturalizing blacks as the laboring class, emphasizing their impoverished domestic conditions and seemingly unhappy demeanors, these popular images surely pleased former proponents of slavery, who had vociferously argued that blacks could not fend for themselves in a world of free labor without the guidance of their white masters. By doing so, they also revealed the curious cultural conditions wrought by photography: even after emancipation and the social separation that came with it, whites still evidently felt the need to maintain visual contact with African Americans. The photographic depiction, possession, and viewership of black people continued to undergird the production of whiteness in freedom.

The Janus-faced southern photograph industry manufactured images that decried emancipation and those that wistfully longed for slavery, particularly through the emergent genre of "character pictures." This is revealed in an anecdote in *Life of Maumer Juno*:

> *Some years after the war, the wife of one of her young masters went to have the photograph taken of one of the younger children. Maumer was of course with the little one. As they were about leaving, the photographer told the mother if there was no objection he would like very much to take Maumer's photograph, remarking that he had long desired to get the likeness of the characteristic old "Maumer" of ante-bellum times, and that she came nearer to it than any he had seen since the war. Of course there was no objection, if Maumer was willing. She consented with the condition that he would give her one for each of her children as she called us. He agreed to this and the photographs were taken and put among his character pictures for sale. Shortly after, a Northern military company visited the city, and many of them*

*carried to their Northern home this memento of Southern life in
ante-bellum times.*[19]

That the artist wanted the likeness of the "characteristic old 'Maumer'
of ante-bellum times" underscores that he and other whites sought
souvenirs of African Americans from a time in which they were still
considered commodities. In the 1850s photographs of enslaved
women circulated amongst southern white families; in the 1860s
photographs of formerly enslaved women circulated en masse, in
southern and northern hands. The particular cultural and military
conditions of the Civil War—which ramped up the photography
industry and brought photographers and soldiers south—catalyzed the
national consumption of white supremacist photographs in the guise
of nostalgia. Antebellum slave photography was the necessary precur-
sor to the conspicuously racist and quietly vicious photographic stereotypes of freedom.

It was undoubtedly the grotesque emergence of lynching photography in the late nineteenth century that marked the most significant
extension of slaveholders' image-making habits. A foundational form
of terror geared toward maintaining racial hierarchy in a post-slavery
world, lynching advanced a narrative of black savagery and white
female innocence as it helped build an intergenerational white
supremacist community. Notably, professional and amateur image-
makers produced photographs at lynchings. Documenting a 1915
lynching in Fayette County, Tennessee, the *Crisis* reported that "hundreds of kodaks clicked all morning at the scene of the lynching.
People in automobiles and carriages came from miles around to view
the corpse dangling from the end of a rope." These Kodak-wielding
southern whites were accompanied by "picture card photographers,"
who "installed a portable printing plant at the bridge and reaped a har-
vest in selling postcards showing a photograph of the lynched Negro."[20]
Such lynching photographs did more than document the spectacular
violence of the events. Photo historian Shawn Michelle Smith notes
how postcards "spread the news of lynching far and wide, claiming an
ever larger crowd of witnesses—terrorizing and symbolically empow-
ering ever greater numbers."[21] As Smith further argues, lynching photographs "always represent mastery, never resistance. They depict a
(usually) black (usually) male body violently separated from an African

American community, torn from ties of family and love and respect."[22] The circulation of lynching photographs injected the white South with visual evidence that actualized fantasies of complete domination. By foregrounding white control, linking whites through violence, denying black resistance, and dismantling black sociality, lynching photography marked a new iteration of modern visual politics and more specifically photography as a habit of domination. White supremacist photography stretched from the daguerreotype studios of the antebellum era to the handheld Kodaks of the Jim Crow era.

These photographs, however, were not the sort of images that a white sociologist and his students from Trinity College (now Duke University) found as they were conducting research in African American homes across Durham, North Carolina, in 1900. Studying African Americans' general engagement with art, the sociologist noted the presence of twelve portraits in this study of twenty-five homes, including "three of Fred Douglass; two of Abraham Lincoln; and one each of Wm McKinley, Booker Washington and George Washington." He was particularly struck, however, by the prevalence of personal photographs: "Quite numberless photographs were seen in albums and on tables, mantels and bureaus."[23] Although the researcher might not have anticipated the black affinity for vernacular photography, the significance of private photographs for African Americans in Durham was surely nothing new. Since the 1840s photography had served as an important mechanism—along with religion, literacy, and music—for African Americans in the South to find pride, pleasure, belonging, and dignity.[24]

Ex-slaves continued to patronize photography studios in freedom. While a small number of former slaves entered commercial photography during Reconstruction—including John Roy Lynch in Natchez, Mississippi, and James C. Farley in Richmond—most southern blacks likely continued to commission images from white artists.[25] The photographic archive is populated with black portraits taken in the late nineteenth and early twentieth centuries, from cabinet cards (the successor to the carte de visite) that African Americans posed for in Raleigh, North Carolina, to the many studio portraits African Americans sat for in eastern Kansas.[26] Most of these subjects remain anonymous, but scholars have identified ex-slaves-turned-soldiers who posed during and after the war in studios. On occasion these men posed in their Union uniforms with family members, as in the case of Corporal Jeremiah Saunders, a former slave from Scott County, Kentucky, who joined the 124th U.S. Colored Troops after his master died in February 1865 and, sometime after that, posed with his wife, Emily Spotts Saunders, in a full-length portrait.[27] After the fall of slavery African Americans gained greater freedom to envision familial bonds, particularly bonds of marriage.

Former slaves—even amidst financial hardship—continued to connect with loved ones through photographic exchanges, as in the case of Cyrus Branch's family. In the mid-1830s Branch was sold away from his wife and children (owned by a master in Petersburg, Virginia) and forbidden to see them. He fled, first to a swamp along the James River in Charles City County, where he lived for four years before eventually making it to the North in 1840 and settling in Manchester, Vermont. It took decades before Branch reconnected with his family. After the Civil War, Branch learned of a local acquaintance who was traveling to Petersburg, and he asked the man if he could locate the wife and four children he had left behind. In Petersburg, the traveler notified the pastor of Branch's former church, and the pastor in turn located one daughter: Elizabeth Smith. Branch had fled bondage when Smith was only five years old; she was now thirty-seven. Obtaining her father's address, the long-lost daughter wrote to him, and they began exchanging letters. Smith happily described how Branch's church "is in a prosperous condition." She told of those who had passed away (his wife, his sister Maria) and of those still living in Virginia ("your sister Lucy is well"). She told him, too, of the heartbreaking unknowns—the family members removed against their will by the slave trade. "You wished to know about Martha and Lucinda," Smith wrote. "They have been sold away for over twenty years." And she told him of her daughters. "The times are very hard here, as rent is very high," Smith noted. "Enclosed you will find the photographs of my two daughters; the eldest is named Lucinda, and the youngest Mary Ann, after my mother."[28] Branch had not seen his daughter in more than three decades, nor had he even known of his granddaughters' existence. At seventy-five years of age, he lacked the means to immediately travel to Virginia to reconnect. The hope was that the sale of his slave narrative, as announced in the preface, would help him fund the trip. For the time being, though, he had their photographs.

Freedpeople also expressed social ties and broader imaginative affinities through the production and consumption of photographs of black political and religious leaders. For instance, when former Charlestonian slave Juno Waller Seymour attended a lecture by a Methodist bishop, the bishop "gave her his photograph, which she ever afterwards kept among her choice treasures."[29] Moreover, limited evidence reveals that freedpeople combined personal and public images to forge a visible community of black kin, leadership, and celebrity, as in the case of ex-slave Benjamin Thornton Montgomery. In the aftermath of slavery, Montgomery purchased two plantations at Davis Bend, Mississippi; he also left behind a remarkable album, full of family portraits, images of unknown white people, and even famous figures such as Frederick Douglass.[30] The album reflected broader image-preserving practices of the nineteenth century in its mix of the ordinary and the extraordinary, but it also symbolized a point of continuity between the cultures of slavery and emancipation. Through photographs and photo albums, ex-slaves such as Benjamin Thornton Montgomery found durable ways to express and substantiate personhood and sociality, rendering black people and the black community a dignified and visible presence in private settings. They continued to find value in this quiet photographic habit of endurance.

Major black leaders of the late nineteenth and early twentieth century took a keen interest in photography for expressive, evidentiary, and community-building purposes. Ida B. Wells, for instance, would reappropriate lynching photographs to display white supremacist brutality in her anti-lynching pamphlet *A Red Record*.[31] Likewise, Booker T. Washington made photography a central element of his substantial publicity machine at the Tuskegee Institute. At the turn of the century, the institute employed multiple black and white photographers, as well as an in-house artist, to document activities on campus and to picture Washington himself. Through stereographs, albumen prints, lithographic posters, buttons, frontispieces, and other print publications, Washington and his photographers raised funds while they crafted an industrious and respectable persona for Washington (and Tuskegee more broadly). At the Paris Exposition of 1900, Washington exhibited photographs of Tuskegee to the world.[32] W. E. B. Du Bois also took part in the Paris Exposition, where, in the American Negro Exhibit, he displayed pictures of middle-class

African American life. Exhibiting 363 photographs, many of which were studio portraits, Du Bois contested the persistent stereotyping of black figures in popular visual culture as he rendered African Americans a visible, dignified presence for an international audience.[33]

Whereas Du Bois's photographs were shown at an international exposition attended by millions of people, the photographic portraits made and held dearly by antebellum slaves such as Robert Brown and Stephen Jordan were seen by only a few people. Nonetheless, the principle behind these acts of image-making was similar. Under slavery, everyday black people had nurtured a powerful tool of endurance and opposition, pleasure and pride. They charged this tool with expressing and affirming their personhood, social potential, and sociality, and it left them with a meaningful visual tradition taken up by Du Bois and many others. This photographic habit of endurance, born in part out of the efforts of slaves and ex-slaves, would—in the decades to come—exert what Frederick Douglass called a "powerful, though silent, influence" upon future generations. After slavery, African Americans would continue to use photography to craft self-images in the face of a seemingly relentless attack on their dignity and aspirations that has continued unabated.

NOTES

INTRODUCTION

1. [Nathaniel P. Willis], "The Pencil of Nature: A New Discovery," *The Corsair*, April 13, 1839, 71, Microfilm, American Periodicals Series 1800–1850, Microforms Dept., Knight Library, University of Oregon.

2. Floyd Rinhart and Marion Rinhart, *The American Daguerreotype* (Athens: University of Georgia Press, 1981), 24–25.

3. Thomas Cole to Mr. Adams, February 26, 1840, in Louis Legrand Noble, *The Life and Works of Thomas Cole*, ed. Elliot S. Vesell (Cambridge, MA: Belknap Press of Harvard University Press, 1964), 210.

4. Samuel Morse, "The Daguerrotipe," *New York Observer*, April 20, 1839, 62.

5. [Willis], "The Pencil of Nature," 70–72.

6. L. Diane Barnes, Brian Schoen, and Frank Towers, eds., *The Old South's Modern Worlds: Slavery, Region, and Nation in the Age of Progress* (New York: Oxford University Press, 2011), 6.

7. The new generation of slavery and capitalism studies includes Edward E. Baptist, *The Half Has Never Been Told: Slavery and the Making of American Capitalism* (New York: Basic Books, 2014); Walter Johnson, *River of Dark Dreams: Slavery and Empire in the Cotton Kingdom* (Cambridge, MA: Belknap Press of Harvard University Press, 2013); Calvin Schermerhorn, *The Business of Slavery and the Rise of American Capitalism, 1815–1860* (New Haven, CT: Yale University Press, 2015); Sven Beckert, *Empire of Cotton: A Global History* (New York: Knopf, 2014); Sven Beckert and Seth Rockman, eds., *Slavery's Capitalism: A New History of American Economic Development* (Philadelphia: University of Pennsylvania Press, 2016); Seth Rockman, "Slavery and Capitalism," *Journal of the Civil War Era* 2, no. 1 (March 2012); Anthony E. Kaye, "The Second Slavery: Modernity in the Nineteenth-Century South and the Atlantic World," *Journal of Southern History* 75, no. 3 (August 2009): 627–650.

8. Jay T. Last, *The Color Explosion: Nineteenth-Century American Lithography* (Santa Ana, CA: Hillcrest Press, 2005), 66–67.

9. Harvey S. Teal, *Partners with the Sun: South Carolina Photographers, 1840–1940* (Columbia: University of South Carolina Press, 2001).

10. Helpful introductions to nineteenth-century American photography include Martha A. Sandweiss, ed., *Photography in Nineteenth-Century America* (Fort Worth, TX: Amon Carter Museum, 1991); Alan Trachtenberg, *Reading American Photographs: Images as History, Mathew Brady to Walker Evans* (New York: Hill and Wang, 1989); and Keith Davis, *The Origins of*

American Photography: From Daguerreotype to Dry-Plate, 1839–1865 (Kansas City, MO: Hall Family Foundation and Nelson-Atkins Museum of Art, 2007). Other important works on early photography include Martha A. Sandweiss, *Print the Legend: Photography and the American West* (New Haven, CT: Yale University Press, 2002); Peter B. Hales, *Silver Cities: The Photography of American Urbanization, 1839–1915* (Philadelphia: Temple University Press, 1984); Michael L. Carlebach, *The Origins of Photojournalism in America* (Washington, DC: Smithsonian Institution Press, 1992); Allen Sekula, "The Body and the Archive," in *The Contest of Meaning: Critical Histories of Photography*, ed. Richard Bolton (Cambridge: MIT Press, 1989); Shawn Michelle Smith, *American Archives: Gender, Race, and Class in Visual Culture* (Princeton, NJ: Princeton University Press, 1999); and Mazie M. Harris, *Paper Promises: Early American Photography* (Los Angeles: J. Paul Getty Museum, 2018). The field of the history of American photography is indebted to two broad overviews first published in the 1930s: Beaumont Newhall, *The History of Photography from 1839 to the Present*, rev. ed. (New York: Museum of Modern Art, 1982); and Robert Taft, *Photography and the American Scene: A Social History, 1839–1889* (New York: Dover, 1938).

11. Ralph Waldo Emerson, *Emerson in His Journals*, ed. Joel Porte (Cambridge, MA: Belknap Press of Harvard University Press, 1982), 271.

12. Robin Kelsey, "Photography's Promise of Self-Representation," paper presented at *Photography's Past Futures* conference, Getty Research Institute, Los Angeles, May 8, 2013.

13. Taft, *Photography and the American Scene*, 61.

14. Marcus A. Root, *The Camera and the Pencil* (Philadelphia: J. B. Lippincott, 1864), 143.

15. On cave paintings, see Margaret W. Conkey, "Images Without Words: The Construction of Prehistoric Imaginaries for Definitions of 'Us,'" *Journal of Visual Culture* 9, no. 3 (December 2010): 272–283.

16. Maurice O. Wallace and Shawn Michelle Smith, eds., *Pictures and Progress: Early Photography and the Making of African American Identity* (Durham, NC: Duke University Press, 2012). Geoffrey Batchen has argued for study of vernacular photography in his "Vernacular Photographies," *History of Photography* 24, no. 3 (Autumn 2000): 262–271, and "Snapshots: Art History and the Ethnographic Turn," *Photographies* 1, no. 2 (September 2008): 121–142.

17. Frederick Douglass, "Slavery, the Free Church, and British Agitation Against Bondage," *The Frederick Douglass Papers*, series one, *Speeches, Debates, and Interviews*, vol. 1, *1841–1846*, ed. John W. Blassingame (New Haven, CT: Yale University Press, 1979), 317–318.

18. James W. C. Pennington, *The Fugitive Blacksmith; or, Events in the History of James W.C. Pennington, Pastor of a Presbyterian Church, New York, Formerly a Slave in the State of Maryland, United States* (1848), Documenting the American South. University Library, University of North Carolina at Chapel Hill, http://docsouth.unc.edu/neh/penning49/penning49.html.

19. David Brion Davis, *The Problem of Slavery in Western Culture* (Ithaca, NY: Cornell University Press, 1966), 62.

20. Ariela J. Gross, *Double Character: Slavery and Mastery in the Antebellum Southern Courtroom* (Princeton, NJ: Princeton University Press, 2000), 3. Scholarship on the internal slave trade includes Michael Tadman, *Speculators and Slaves: Masters, Traders, and Slaves in the Old South* (Madison: University of Wisconsin Press, 1989); Walter Johnson, *Soul by Soul: Life Inside the Antebellum Slave Market* (Cambridge, MA: Harvard University Press, 1999); Robert H. Gudmestad, *A Troublesome Commerce: The Transformation of the Interstate Slave Trade* (Baton Rouge: Louisiana State University Press, 2003); Walter Johnson, ed., *The Chattel Principle: Internal Slave Trades in the Americas* (New Haven, CT: Yale University Press, 2004); Steven Deyle, *Carry Me Back: The Domestic Slave Trade in American Life* (New York: Oxford University Press, 2005); Schermerhorn, *The Business of Slavery and the Rise of American Capitalism*; Daina Ramey Berry, *The Price for Their Pound of Flesh: The Value of the Enslaved, from Womb to Grave, in the Building of a Nation* (Boston: Beacon Press, 2017).

21. Personhood—the status of full humanity—was defined negatively and positively in the antebellum era. Many former slaves including Frederick Douglass defined personhood negatively when they posed it in sharp distinction to other animals. In effect, they argued that slaves were wrongly denied the status of legal personhood, which endowed humans with the right to self-ownership, by treating them like beasts of burden that could be bought and sold. To be a person meant one was not an animal and not property. But antebellum Americans also defined personhood positively, and photography served as a vital new venue to do so. Slaves and ex-slaves, for instance, used photography and photographic image-making as evidence of their full humanity—and to stake claims to certain social identities (such as bourgeois respectability) and certain individual traits (such as industry). Scholars from fields including philosophy, legal theory, history, and literary history have explored the concept of personhood. They have focused more on theorizing than historicizing it, and many have emphasized self-consciousness, verbal communication, and self-ownership in their conceptions. This book introduces image-making and visual thinking as a crucial cultural system that shaped the history of personhood in America. Arthur Riss has urged scholars to historicize personhood in his provocative literary history, *Race, Slavery, and Liberalism in Nineteenth-Century American Literature* (Cambridge: Cambridge University Press, 2006). Amy Dru Stanley has illuminated how antislavery proponents, amidst debates over slave breeding, envisioned free love as a condition of personhood. See Amy Dru Stanley, "Slave Breeding and Free Love: An Antebellum Argument over Slavery, Capitalism, and Personhood," in *Capitalism Takes Command: The Social Transformation of Nineteenth-Century America*, ed. Michael Zakim and Gary J. Kornblith (Chicago: University of Chicago Press, 2012), 119–144. On the history of legal personhood, see, for starters, Barbara Young Welke,

Law and the Borders of Belonging in the Long Nineteenth Century (New York: Cambridge University Press, 2010). The concept of "personhood" has also been the subject of much debate for philosophers, including Daniel Dennett, "Conditions of Personhood," in *The Identities of Persons*, ed. Amelie Oksenberg Rorty (Berkeley: University of California Press, 1976).

22. Frederick Douglass, "Pictures and Progress," Manuscript/Mixed Material, Library of Congress, http://www.loc.gov/item/mfd.28009 (accessed April 5, 2017).

23. Darcy Grimaldo Grigsby, *Enduring Truths: Sojourner's Shadows and Substance* (Chicago: University of Chicago Press, 2015), ch. 5.

24. On the history of racial thought in nineteenth-century America, see George M. Frederickson, *The Black Image in the White Mind: The Debate on Afro-American Character and Destiny, 1817–1914* (New York: Harper and Row, 1971); Mia Bay, *The White Image in the Black Mind: African-American Ideas about White People, 1830–1925* (New York: Oxford University Press, 2000); Bruce Dain, *A Hideous Monster of the Mind: American Race Theory in the Early Republic* (Cambridge, MA: Harvard University Press, 2002); and Winthrop D. Jordan, *White over Black: American Attitudes Toward the Negro, 1550–1812* (Chapel Hill: University of North Carolina Press, 1968). For the intellectual defense of slavery, see Drew Gilpin Faust, ed., *The Ideology of Slavery: Proslavery Thought in the Antebellum South, 1830–1860* (Baton Rouge: Louisiana State University Press, 1981); Larry E. Tise, *Proslavery: A History of the Defense of Slavery in America, 1701–1840* (Athens: University of Georgia Press, 1987); Eugene D. Genovese, *The Slaveholders' Dilemma: Freedom and Progress in Southern Conservative Thought, 1820–1860* (Columbia: University of South Carolina Press, 1992); Lacy K. Ford, *Deliver Us from Evil: The Slavery Question in the Old South* (Oxford: Oxford University Press, 2009); Jeffrey Robert Young, *Domesticating Slavery: The Master Class in Georgia and South Carolina, 1670–1837* (Chapel Hill: University of North Carolina Press, 1999); and Willie Lee Rose, "The Domestication of Slavery," in *Slavery and Freedom*, ed. William W. Freehling (New York: Oxford University Press, 1982). On debates over slavery and cruelty in particular, see Margaret Abruzzo, *Polemical Pain: Slavery, Cruelty, and the Rise of Humanitarianism* (Baltimore: Johns Hopkins University Press, 2011).

25. Frederick Douglass, "Lecture on Pictures," 8, Frederick Douglass Papers, Library of Congress.

26. For a helpful overview of Civil War causation that charts the shift from arguments about uneven modernization to the work that has moved beyond a stark dichotomy between northern modernization and southern anti-modernization, see Frank Towers, "Partisans, New History, and Modernization: The Historiography of the Civil War's Causes, 1861–2011," *Journal of the Civil War Era* 1, no. 2 (June 2011): 237–264. On the push to understand modernization in the Old South, the best starting point is Barnes, Schoen, and Towers, eds., *The Old South's Modern Worlds*. On the

steamboat, see Robert H. Gudmestad, *Steamboats and the Rise of the Cotton Kingdom* (Baton Rouge: Louisiana State University Press, 2011). For hybridization, see Johnson, *River of Dark Dreams*, 151–152. On railroads, see Aaron W. Marrs, *Railroads in the Old South: Pursuing Progress in a Slave Society* (Baltimore: Johns Hopkins University Press, 2009), and Calvin Schermerhorn, *Money over Mastery, Family over Freedom: Slavery in the Antebellum Upper South* (Baltimore: Johns Hopkins University Press, 2011).

27. Edward L. Ayers, *What Caused the Civil War? Reflections on the South and Southern History* (New York: W. W. Norton, 2005); Elizabeth R. Varon, *Disunion! The Coming of the American Civil War, 1789–1859* (Chapel Hill: University of North Carolina Press, 2008).

28. On the sectional crisis and emotions, see Michael E. Woods, *Emotional and Sectional Conflict in the Antebellum Era* (New York: Cambridge University Press, 2014).

29. On this point, I am indebted to John Stauffer's discussion of abolitionist images in his *The Black Hearts of Men: Radical Abolitionists and the Transformation of Race* (Cambridge, MA: Harvard University Press, 2001), 50.

30. On the estimate of the number of photographers, see Davis, *The Origins of American Photography*, 173. Starting points on Civil War photography include Trachtenberg, *Reading American Photographs*, ch. 2; Keith F. Davis, "'A Terrible Distinctness': Photography of the Civil War Era," in *Photography in Nineteenth-Century America*, ed. Martha A. Sandweiss (Fort Worth, TX: Amon Carter Museum, 1991); William A. Frassanito, *Antietam: The Photographic Legacy of America's Bloodiest Day* (New York: Charles Scribner's Sons, 1978); Jeff L. Rosenheim, *Photography and the American Civil War* (New York: Metropolitan Museum of Art, 2013); John Stauffer, "The 'Terrible Reality' of the First Living-Room Wars," in *War/Photography: Images of Armed Conflict and Its Aftermath*, ed. Anne Wilkes Tucker, Will Michels, and Natalie Zelt (New Haven, CT: Yale University Press, 2012); and Bob Zeller, *The Blue and Gray in Black and White: A History of Civil War Photography* (London: Praeger, 2005). On war photography more broadly, see Tucker, Michels, and Zelt, eds., *War/Photography*, and Mary Panzer, *Things as They Are: Photojournalism in Context Since 1965* (New York: Aperture Foundation, 2005).

31. On portraiture in early America, see Zara Anishanslin, *Portrait of a Woman in Silk: Hidden Histories of the British Atlantic World* (New Haven, CT: Yale University Press, 2016), and Robin Jaffee Frank, *Love and Loss: American Portrait and Mourning Miniatures* (New Haven, CT: Yale University Press, 2000).

32. Wallace and Smith, eds., *Pictures and Progress*; Nell Irvin Painter, *Sojourner Truth: A Life, a Symbol* (New York: W. W. Norton, 1996), ch. 20; Augusta Rohrbach, "Profits of Protest: The Market Strategies of Sojourner Truth and Louisa May Alcott" and John Stauffer, "Creating an Image in Black: The Power of Abolition Pictures," in *Prophets of Protest: Reconsidering the*

History of American Abolitionism, ed. Timothy McCarthy and John Stauffer (New York: New Press, 2006); John Stauffer, Zoe Trodd, and Celeste-Marie Bernier, eds., *Picturing Frederick Douglass: An Illustrated Biography of the Nineteenth Century's Most Photographed American* (New York: W. W. Norton, 2015); Stauffer, *The Black Hearts of Men*; Teresa Zackodnik, "The 'Green-Backs of Civilization': Sojourner Truth and Portrait Photography," *American Studies* 46, no. 2 (Summer 2005): 117–143; Grigsby, *Enduring Truths*; Darcy Grimaldo Grigsby, "Negative-Positive Truths," *Representations* 113, no. 1 (Winter 2011): 16–38; and Deborah Willis and Barbara Krauthamer, *Envisioning Emancipation: Black Americans and the End of Slavery* (Philadelphia: Temple University Press, 2013). On the history of black photographers, see Deborah Willis, *Reflections in Black: A History of Black Photographers 1840 to the Present* (New York: W. W. Norton, 2000). On racial pseudo-scientific photography, see Molly Rogers, *Delia's Tears: Race, Science, and Photography in Nineteenth-Century America* (New Haven, CT: Yale University Press, 2010); Brian Wallis, "Black Bodies, White Science: Louis Agassiz's Slave Daguerreotypes," *American Art* 9, no. 2 (Summer 1995): 38–61; and Trachtenberg, *Reading American Photographs*, 53–56. On race and photography in America more broadly, see Shawn Michelle Smith, *Photography on the Color Line: W. E. B. Du Bois, Race, and Visual Culture* (Durham, NC: Duke University Press, 2004); and Coco Fusco and Brian Wallis, eds., *Only Skin Deep: Changing Visions of the American Self* (New York: Harry N. Abrams, 2003).

33. William Stott, *Documentary Expression and Thirties America* (Chicago: University of Chicago Press, 1973); John Raeburn, *A Staggering Revolution: A Cultural History of Thirties Photography* (Urbana: University of Illinois Press, 2006).

34. Sharon Sliwinski, *Human Rights in Camera* (Chicago: University of Chicago Press, 2011); Heide Fehrenbach and Davide Rodogno, eds., *Humanitarian Photography: A History* (Cambridge: Cambridge University Press, 2015); Leigh Raiford, *Imprisoned in a Luminous Glare: Photography and the African American Freedom Struggle* (Chapel Hill: University of North Carolina Press, 2011). Though not focusing specifically on photography, Lisa Tickner illuminates how the British women's suffrage campaign used political images. See Lisa Tickner, *The Spectacle of Women: Imagery of the Suffrage Campaign, 1907–14* (Chicago: University of Chicago Press, 1988).

35. While photo historians have long noted photographs of death on the Civil War battlefield, studies of "atrocity photographs" have largely focused on the twentieth century. Whereas an older narrative positioned photographs of the Spanish Civil War in the 1930s as the first mass-circulated atrocity images, scholars have recently pushed the chronology back to the turn of the twentieth century, illuminating, for instance, photographs of the dead at the Battle of Wounded Knee (1890). See Jay Prosser, Geoffrey Batchen, Mick Gidley, and Nancy K. Miller, eds., *Picturing Atrocity: Photography in Crisis* (London: Reaktion Books, 2012).

36. Issues of exploitation have, of course, long been of interest to historians of photography. Focusing intently on spectatorship in the twentieth century, Susan Sontag and others have wanted to know whether public images of violence and pain spur empathy (that leads to political activism), or whether they simply produce desensitization. Susan Sontag, *On Photography* (New York: Farrar, Straus and Giroux, 1973); Susan Sontag, *Regarding the Pain of Others* (New York: Picador, 2003); Sliwinski, *Human Rights in Camera*; John Berger, *About Looking* (New York: Pantheon Books, 1980); Susan Moeller, *Compassion Fatigue: How the Media Sell Disease, Famine, War, and Death* (New York: Routledge, 1999); Susie Linfield, *The Cruel Radiance: Photography and Political Violence* (Chicago: University of Chicago Press, 2010).

37. On lynching photography, see Dora Apel and Shawn Michelle Smith, *Lynching Photographs* (Berkeley: University of California Press, 2007); Jacqueline Goldsby, *A Spectacular Secret: Lynching in American Life and Literature* (Chicago: University of Chicago Press, 2006); and James Allen, Hilton Als, John Lewis, and Leon F. Litwack, *Without Sanctuary: Lynching Photography in America* (Santa Fe, NM: Twin Palms, 2000). For photography and imperialism, see Laura Wexler, *Tender Violence: Domestic Visions in an Age of U.S. Imperialism* (Chapel Hill: University of North Carolina Press, 2000).

38. On the notion of a counter-archive, see Smith, *Photography on the Color Line*.

39. "The Underground Railroad," *New York Daily Times*, January 28, 1856, 6.

40. Wexler, *Tender Violence*, 133.

41. For introductions to the use of visual culture within history, see Michael L. Wilson, "Visual Culture: A Useful Category of Historical Analysis?" in *The Nineteenth-Century Visual Culture Reader*, ed. Vanessa R. Schwartz and Jeannene M. Przyblyski (New York: Routledge, 2004) and Peter Burke, *Eyewitnessing: The Use of Images as Historical Evidence* (Ithaca: Cornell University Press, 2001). For ways of linking American history with the history of photography, see Joshua Brown, "Historians and Photography," *American Art* 21, no. 3 (Fall 2007): 9–13. Model monographs that focus on photography include Sandweiss, *Print the Legend*; Jennifer Tucker, *Nature Exposed: Photography as Eyewitness in Victorian Science* (Baltimore: Johns Hopkins University Press, 2005); and Wexler, *Tender Violence*. More broadly, important works regarding visual culture in nineteenth-century America include David Morgan, *Protestants and Pictures: Religion, Visual Culture, and the Age of Mass Production* (New York: Oxford University Press, 1999); Joshua Brown, *Beyond the Lines: Pictorial Reporting, Everyday Life, and the Crisis of Gilded Age America* (Berkeley: University of California Press, 2002); and David Henkin, *City Reading: Written Words and Public Spaces in Antebellum New York* (New York: Columbia University Press, 1998). On the "cultural turn," see Lynn Hunt, ed., *The New Cultural History* (Berkeley: University of California Press, 1989).

42. Elizabeth Edwards and Janice Hart, "Introduction: Photographs as Objects," in *Photographs Objects Histories: On the Materiality of Images*, ed. Elizabeth Edwards and Janice Hart (London: Routledge, 2004), 2; see also Elizabeth Edwards, "Thinking Photography Beyond the Visual?" in *Photography: Theoretical Snapshots*, ed. J. J. Long, Andrea Noble, and Edward Welch (London: Routledge, 2009).

43. On private images, see Tina M. Campt, *Image Matters: Archive, Photography, and the African Diaspora in Europe* (Durham, NC: Duke University Press, 2012).

44. My thoughts on photography and emotion are indebted to the "affective turn" that has taken place in history and the history of photography. See Nicole Eustace, Eugenia Lean, Julie Livingston, Jan Plamper, William M. Reddy, and Barbara H. Rosenwein, "*AHR* Conversation: The Historical Study of Emotions," *American Historical Review* 117, no. 5 (December 2012): 1487–1531; Edwards, "Thinking Photography Beyond the Visual?"; Jennifer V. Evans, "Seeing Subjectivity: Erotic Photography and the Optics of Desire," *American Historical Review* 118, no. 2 (April 2013): 430–462; Elspeth H. Brown and Thy Phu, eds., *Feeling Photography* (Durham, NC: Duke University Press, 2014).

45. Invented in France, the daguerreotype was the first commercially successful photographic process in the United States, popular throughout the 1840s and 1850s. This process created a "direct positive": a unique, non-reproducible image without a negative, in this case consisting of a silver-coated copper plate with a silver image. Boasting a reflective, mirror-like quality, the daguerreotype was typically placed beneath a decorative mat and glass cover, all housed in a hinged case. In the 1850s, daguerreotypes began to compete with three new photographic formats—ambrotypes, tintypes, and cartes de visite—in the portrait marketplace. Ambrotypes were invented by British sculptor Frederick Scott Archer in the early 1850s, and in 1854 Bostonian James A. Cutting received three patents for the process. In December 1854, the *Photographic Art Journal* first mentioned the process, which the public grew familiar with in 1855. Made on glass plates, ambrotypes were often housed like daguerreotypes, with a brass mat and glass cover inside a hinged case; they remained popular through the Civil War. Tintypes—patented in 1856 by natural science professor Hamilton L. Smith of Kenyon College—were made on iron sheets and were thus more durable than glass ambrotypes. Like the daguerreotype, the ambrotype and tintype came in a range of sizes and lacked the capacity for mass reproduction. The ambrotype was created by darkening the backside of a collodion glass negative with cloth, paper, or black lacquer. (Collodion was a mix of alcohol, ether, and pyroxylin that artists began primarily coating on glass to create negatives in the 1850s.) The tintype image consists of a negative—formed out of collodion, potassium iodide, and bromide—with a dark background of coated iron that made the image look like a positive one. The carte de visite was the

first major format in American portraiture to use a negative to produce multiple paper images. Patented in France in 1854 and introduced in the United States in 1859, cartes de visite were paper images—usually albumen prints—mounted on cardboard and measuring about 4 by 2.5 inches. Produced with a special camera that made multiple images on the same collodion glass negative, the resulting print could be cut into many photographs. The collodion glass negative was invented in 1851 by Frederick Scott Archer and was the most popular type of negative in the United States until the 1870s. The wet-plate process, which used collodion glass negatives, created albumen prints (also called albumen silver prints) in formats including the carte de visite and stereograph. On photographic processes in mid-nineteenth-century America, see Sarah Kennel, Diane Waggoner, and Alice Carver-Kubik, *In the Darkroom: An Illustrated Guide to Photographic Processes Before the Digital Age* (New York: Thames and Hudson, 2009); Jeff L. Rosenheim, *Photography and the American Civil War* (New York: Metropolitan Museum of Art, 2013); Taft, *Photography and the American Scene*; and Amy K. DeFalco Lippert, *Consuming Identities: Visual Culture in Nineteenth-Century San Francisco* (New York: Oxford University Press), 383–385.

46. Stauffer, *The Black Hearts of Men*, 51.
47. On Frederick Douglass and photography, see Stauffer, Trodd, and Bernier, eds., *Picturing Frederick Douglass*; Stauffer, *The Black Hearts of Men*; and Wallace and Smith, eds., *Pictures and Progress*. For studies of Sojourner Truth's photographic image, see Painter, *Sojourner Truth*; Rohrbach, "Profits of Protest"; Zackodnik, "The 'Green-Backs of Civilization'"; Grigsby, *Enduring Truths*; and Grigsby, "Negative-Positive Truths." On racial science and photography, see Rogers, *Delia's Tears*; Wallis, "Black Bodies, White Science"; Trachtenberg, *Reading American Photographs*, 53–56.
48. Roderick A. McDonald, *The Economy and Material Culture of Slaves: Goods and Chattels on the Sugar Plantations of Jamaica and Louisiana* (Baton Rouge: Louisiana State University Press, 1993); Dylan C. Penningroth, *The Claims of Kinfolk: African American Property and Community in the Nineteenth-Century South* (Chapel Hill: University of North Carolina Press, 2003).

CHAPTER 1: POLICING PERSONHOOD
 1. On stereotyping, see John W. Blassingame, *The Slave Community: Plantation Life in the Antebellum South*, rev. ed. (New York: Oxford University Press, 1979), ch. 6; Deborah Gray White, *Ar'n't I a Woman? Female Slaves in the Plantation South* (New York: W. W. Norton, 1985).
 2. This work follows Walter Johnson's articulation of the chattel principle as central to the ideology and practice of antebellum slavery. See Walter Johnson, *Soul by Soul: Life Inside the Antebellum Slave Market* (Cambridge, MA: Harvard University Press, 1999). Other studies of antebellum slavery and the master-slave relationship that stress the importance of the slave

market include Michael Tadman, *Speculators and Slaves: Masters, Traders, and Slaves in the Old South* (Madison: University of Wisconsin Press, 1989); Walter Johnson, ed., *The Chattel Principle: Internal Slave Trades in the Americas* (New Haven, CT: Yale University Press, 2004); Edward E. Baptist, *The Half Has Never Been Told: Slavery and the Making of American Capitalism* (New York: Basic Books, 2014); and Walter Johnson, *River of Dark Dreams: Slavery and Empire in the Cotton Kingdom* (Cambridge, MA: Belknap Press of Harvard University Press, 2013). Other works on the master-slave relationship include Mark M. Smith, *Debating Slavery: Economy and Society in the Antebellum American South* (Cambridge: Cambridge University Press, 1998); Christopher Morris, "The Articulation of Two Worlds: The Master-Slave Relationship Reconsidered," *Journal of American History* 85, no. 3 (December 1998): 982–1007; Walter Johnson, "On Agency," *Journal of Social History* 37, no. 1 (Fall 2003): 113–124; Eugene D. Genovese, *Roll, Jordan, Roll: The World the Slaves Made* (New York: Vintage Books, 1972); Stephanie McCurry, *Masters of Small Worlds: Yeoman Households, Gender Relations, and the Political Culture of the Antebellum South Carolina Low Country* (New York: Oxford University Press, 1995); Kenneth Greenberg, *Honor and Slavery* (Princeton, NJ: Princeton University Press, 1996); Peter Kolchin, *American Slavery, 1619–1877*, rev. ed. (New York: Hill and Wang, 2003); Edward E. Baptist and Stephanie M. H. Camp, eds., *New Studies in the History of American Slavery* (Athens: University of Georgia Press, 2006); Kenneth Stampp, *The Peculiar Institution: Slavery in the Ante-Bellum South* (New York: Vintage Books, 1956). Studies of particular slaveholding families and their slaves include Drew Gilpin Faust, *James Henry Hammond and the Old South: A Design for Mastery* (Baton Rouge: Louisiana State University Press, 1982); William Dusinberre, *Them Dark Days: Slavery in the American Rice Swamps* (New York: Oxford University Press, 1996); Erskine Clarke, *Dwelling Place: A Plantation Epic* (New Haven, CT: Yale University Press, 2005); and Annette Gordon-Reed, *The Hemingses of Monticello: An American Family* (New York: W. W. Norton, 2008).

3. Marcus A. Root, *The Camera and the Pencil* (Philadelphia: M. A. Root, J. B. Lippincott, and D. Appleton, 1864), 143.

4. My thinking on the process of individualization and policing is indebted to Walter Johnson, who has suggested that scholars must move beyond an analysis of how slaveholders "dehumanized" their slaves to study how owners sought to limit their slaves' humanity. "Slaveholders were fully cognizant of slaves' humanity—indeed they were completely dependent upon it," Johnson writes. Instead, masters persistently aimed to "conscript…the forms that humanity could take in slavery." Johnson, *River of Dark Dreams*, 207–208. On the history of the self and slavery, see also Saidiya V. Hartman, *Scenes of Subjection: Terror, Slavery, and Self-Making in Nineteenth-Century America* (New York: Oxford University Press, 1997).

5. Gwendolyn DuBois Shaw, *Portraits of a People: Picturing African Americans in the Nineteenth Century* (Andover, MA: Addison Gallery of American Art, 2006); John Michael Vlach, "Perpetuating the Past: Plantation Landscape Paintings Then and Now," in *Landscape of Slavery: The Plantation in American Art*, ed. Angela D. Mack and Stephen G. Hoffius (Columbia: University of South Carolina Press, 2008); John Michael Vlach, *The Planter's Prospect: Privilege and Slavery in Plantation Paintings* (Chapel Hill: University of North Carolina Press, 2002). Other important scholarship regarding visual depictions of slavery and African Americans includes Albert Boime, *The Art of Exclusion: Representing Blacks in the Nineteenth Century* (Washington, DC: Smithsonian Institution Press, 1990); Michael D. Harris, *Colored Pictures: Race and Visual Representation* (Chapel Hill: University of North Carolina Press, 2003); Kirk Savage, *Standing Soldiers, Kneeling Slaves: Race, War, and Monument in Nineteenth-Century America* (Princeton, NJ: Princeton University Press, 1997); Peter H. Wood, *Near Andersonville: Winslow Homer's Civil War* (Cambridge, MA: Harvard University Press, 2010); Jackie Napolean Wilson, *Hidden Witness: African American Images from the Dawn of Photography to the Civil War* (New York: St. Martin's Press, 1999); Marcus Wood, *Blind Memory: Visual Representations of Slavery in England and America, 1780–1865* (New York: Routledge, 2000); Marcus Wood, *The Horrible Gift of Freedom: Atlantic Slavery and the Representation of Emancipation* (Athens: University of Georgia Press, 2010); Marcus Wood, *Black Milk: Imagining Slavery in the Visual Cultures of Brazil and America* (Oxford: Oxford University Press, 2013); Elizabeth Kuebler-Wolf, "The Perfect Shadow of His Master: Proslavery Ideology in American Visual Culture, 1700–1920," PhD dissertation, Indiana University, 2005; and *The Image of the Black in Western Art*, vol. IV, parts 1–2 (Cambridge: Belknap Press of Harvard University Press, 2012). On slave portraiture, see Agnes Lugo-Ortiz and Angela Rosenthal, eds., *Slave Portraiture in the Atlantic World* (New York: Cambridge University Press, 2013). On the visual culture of slavery in the Atlantic world, see also Kay Dian Kriz and Geoff Quilley, eds., *An Economy of Colour: Visual Culture and the Atlantic World, 1660–1830* (Manchester: Manchester University Press, 2003); Catherine Molineux, *Faces of Perfect Ebony: Encountering Atlantic Slavery in Imperial Britain* (Cambridge, MA: Harvard University Press, 2012); Huey Copeland, Krista Thompson, and Darcy Grimaldo Grigsby, eds., "New World Slavery and the Matter of the Visual," *Representations* 113, no. 1 (Winter 2011): 1–163; and Celeste-Marie Bernier and Zoe Trodd, eds., "Slavery and Memory in Black Visual Culture," *Slavery and Abolition* 34, no. 2 (May 2013).
6. Joaneath Spicer, *Revealing the African Presence in Renaissance Europe* (Baltimore: Walters Art Museum, 2012), 17–19.
7. For Lafayette, see the collections of The Valentine.
8. The Manigault family, for instance, held an extensive painting collection (which Charles Manigault would describe after the war) and commissioned

at least four slave photographs. But there is no evidence that they commissioned individual painted portraits of slaves. For the painting descriptions, see Charles Manigault, "Description of Paintings," and Charles Izard Manigault, "Souvenirs, of Our Ancestor's & of My Immediate Family," both in Charles Izard Manigault Papers, South Caroliniana Library, University of South Carolina.

9. Vlach, "Perpetuating the Past," 16; Vlach, *The Planter's Prospect*.
10. For more on this painting, see Angela D. Mack, "Introduction," in *Landscape of Slavery: The Plantation in American Art*, ed. Angela D. Mack and Stephen G. Hoffius (Columbia: University of South Carolina Press, 2008), 6. For the figures on Nathaniel Heyward, see Dusinberre, *Them Dark Days*, 4.
11. Vlach, *The Planter's Prospect*, 11–14.
12. "Late from Europe," *Daily Picayune*, June 5, 1839, 2.
13. *Sun*, March 18, 1839, 1.
14. On the history of the daguerreotype in America, see the following: Alan Trachtenberg, *Reading American Photographs: Images as History, Mathew Brady to Walker Evans* (New York: Hill and Wang, 1989); Merry A. Foresta and John Wood, *Secrets of the Dark Chamber: The Art of the American Daguerreotype* (Washington, DC: Smithsonian Institution Press, 1995); Martha A. Sandweiss, ed., *Photography in Nineteenth-Century America* (Fort Worth, TX: Amon Carter Museum, 1991); Floyd Rinhart and Marion Rinhart, *The American Daguerreotype* (Athens: University of Georgia Press, 1981); Grant B. Romer and Brian Wallis, eds., *Young America: The Daguerreotypes of Southworth and Hawes* (New York: Steidl, George Eastman House, and International Center of Photography, 2005); Beaumont Newhall, *The History of Photography from 1839 to the Present*, rev. ed. (New York: Museum of Modern Art, 1982); Keith Davis, *The Origins of American Photography: From Daguerreotype to Dry-Plate, 1839–1865* (Kansas City, MO: Hall Family Foundation and Nelson-Atkins Museum of Art, 2007); Richard Rudisill, *Mirror Image: The Influence of the Daguerreotype on American Society* (Albuquerque: University of New Mexico Press, 1971); Robert Taft, *Photography and the American Scene: A Social History, 1839–1889* (New York: Dover Publications, 1938); Tanya Sheehan and Andres Mario Zervigon, eds., *Photography and Its Origins* (New York: Routledge, 2015); and Sarah Kate Gillespie, *The Early American Daguerreotype: Cross-Currents in Art and Technology* (Washington, DC: Smithsonian Institution, 2016).
15. The ambrotype and tintype, processes that emerged in the mid-1850s, also could not be reproduced. On the ambrotype, see Taft, *Photography and the American Scene*, ch. VII. On the tintype, see Steven Kasher, *America and the Tintype* (New York: International Center of Photography, 2008).
16. St. Leger Landon Carter, "Pictures by the Sun," *Southern Literary Messenger*, March 1840, 193.
17. "Daguerre's Pictures," *Sun*, October 1, 1841, 2; "Daguerre.—The Fine Arts," *Charleston Mercury*, December 11, 1841, 2.

18. Peter B. Hales, *Silver Cities: The Photography of American Urbanization, 1839–1915* (Philadelphia: Temple University Press, 1984); Michael L. Carlebach, *The Origins of Photojournalism in America* (Washington, DC: Smithsonian Institution Press, 1992); Barbara McCandless, "The Portrait Studio and the Celebrity: Promoting the Art," in *Photography in Nineteenth-Century America*, ed. Martha A. Sandweiss (Fort Worth, TX: Amon Carter Museum, 1991); Trachtenberg, *Reading American Photographs*; Allen Sekula, "The Body and the Archive," in *The Contest of Meaning: Critical Histories of Photography*, ed. Richard Bolton (Cambridge: MIT Press, 1989); Shawn Michelle Smith, *American Archives: Gender, Race, and Class in Visual Culture* (Princeton, NJ: Princeton University Press, 1999).

19. Rinhart and Rinhart, *The American Daguerreotype*, 48–51.

20. On the discourses that promoted a sentimental attachment to commodities, see Lori Merish, *Sentimental Materialism: Gender, Commodity Culture, and Nineteenth-Century American Literature* (Durham, NC: Duke University Press, 2000).

21. Quoted in Rudisill, *Mirror Image*, 215.

22. Quoted in Frances Robb, "Shot in Alabama: Daguerreotypy in a Deep South State," in *The Daguerreian Annual: Official Yearbook of the Daguerreian Society*, ed. Mark S. Johnson (Pittsburgh: Daguerreian Society, 2004), 204.

23. Root, *The Camera and the Pencil*, 85. On Lavater's relation to the history of portraiture, see Joan K. Stemmler, "The Physiognomical Portraits of Johann Caspar Lavater," *Art Bulletin* 75, no. 1 (March 1993): 151–168.

24. E. K. Hough, "Expressing Character in Photographic Pictures," *American Journal of Photography*, November 1, 1858.

25. Hough, "Expressing Character in Photographic Pictures."

26. In the South, visual artists who transitioned to daguerreotypy included Jules Lion, John Houston Mifflin, George S. Cook, Solomon Numes Carvalho, and Edward Samuel Dodge. See Rinhart and Rinhart, *The American Daguerreotype*, 227.

27. Trachtenberg, *Reading American Photographs*, 21–22.

28. James F. Ryder, *Voigtländer and I: In Pursuit of Shadow Catching* (Cleveland: Cleveland Printing and Publishing Company, 1902; reprint, New York: Arno Press, 1973), 14.

29. David Jaffee, *A New Nation of Goods: The Material Culture of Early America* (Philadelphia: University of Pennsylvania Press, 2010), 284–289; *New-York Daily Tribune*, April 29, 1853.

30. Charleston (1840), St. Louis (1841), Tuscaloosa (1841), Columbia (1842), Mobile (1843), Houston (1843), Galveston (1844). For Charleston and Columbia, see Harvey Teal, *Partners with the Sun: South Carolina Photographers, 1840–1940* (Columbia: University of South Carolina Press, 2001), 13–15, 27–32. For St. Louis, see Peter E. Palmquist and Thomas R. Kailbourn, *Pioneer Photographers from the Mississippi to the Continental Divide: A Biographical Dictionary, 1839 to 1865* (Stanford,

CA: Stanford University Press, 2005), 3. For Tuscaloosa and Mobile, see Robb, "Shot in Alabama," 202, 204. For Houston and Galveston, see David Haynes, *Catching Shadows: A Directory of Nineteenth-Century Texas Photographers* (Austin: Texas State Historical Association, 1993), viii.

31. Teal, *Partners with the Sun*, 13–26.

32. Teal, *Partners with the Sun*, 27–28.

33. This group of entrepreneurs emerged largely in the rural Northeast after the Revolution and grew steadily during the early nineteenth century. Itinerant painters made up one segment of this peddler culture: traversing the back roads, these transient painters sold portraits to manufacturers, innkeepers, and middle-class farmers, helping to spread the taste for the consumption of individual likenesses. On peddlers, see David Jaffee, "Peddlers of Progress and the Transformation of the Rural North, 1760–1860," *Journal of American History* 78, no. 2 (September 1991): 511–535; David Jaffee, "One of the Primitive Sort: Portrait Makers of the Rural North, 1760–1860," in *The Countryside in the Age of Capitalist Transformation: Essays in the Social History of Rural America*, ed. Steven Hahn and Jonathan Prude (Chapel Hill: University of North Carolina Press, 1985); and Jaffee, *A New Nation of Goods*. On portraiture in New England, see Caroline F. Sloat, ed., *Meet Your Neighbors: New England Portraits, Painters, and Society, 1790–1850* (Amherst: University of Massachusetts Press, 1992). On northern peddlers in the South, see Joseph Thomas Rainer, "The Honorable Fraternity of Moving Merchants: Yankee Peddlers in the Old South, 1800–1860," PhD dissertation, College of William and Mary, 2000. On the revolution in communication and transportation technologies, see Daniel Walker Howe, *What Hath God Wrought: The Transformation of America, 1815–1848* (New York: Oxford University Press, 2007). On the history of miniature paintings, see Robin Jaffee Frank, *Love and Loss: American Portrait and Mourning Miniatures* (New Haven, CT: Yale University Press, 2000) and Catherine E. Kelly, *Republic of Taste: Art, Politics, and Everyday Life in Early America* (Philadelphia: University of Pennsylvania Press, 2016), ch. 3.

34. Rinhart and Rinhart, *The American Daguerreotype*, 351. On "humbugging," see Neil Harris, *Humbug: The Art of P. T. Barnum* (Chicago: University of Chicago Press, 1973).

35. A number of operators for the famous Boston-based photographer John Plumbe—including Reuben F. Lovering and William A. Perry—also spent winters in Savannah, Columbus, and Macon, Georgia between 1845 and 1847. See Rinhart and Rinhart, *The American Daguerreotype*, 70–71.

36. Jack C. Ramsay Jr., *Photographer—Under Fire: The Story of George S. Cook (1819–1902)* (Green Bay, WI: Historical Resources Press, 1994), 16–33.

37. November 5, 1847, Thomas Hubbard Hobbs Diaries, Collection Number 0683, Box 188, Folder 4, W. S. Hoole Special Collections Library, University of Alabama.

38. Zelotus Lee Holmes to Aunt, July 8, 1852, Zelotus Lee Holmes Papers, South Caroliniana Library, University of South Carolina.

39. Wanderer, "Peregrinations of a Daguerrean, Number Three," *Photographic Art Journal*, December 1851, 359.

40. Wanderer, "Peregrinations of a Daguerrean, Number Three," 359.

41. Wanderer, "Peregrinations of a Daguerrean, Number Three," 359.

42. Wanderer, "Peregrinations of a Daguerrean, Number Three," 358–361. Wander mentioned twice that he was going to take a view of the residence, Wakefield, yet he did not actually describe the making of this view of Wakefield in the article.

43. Samuel F. Simpson, "Daguerreotyping on the Mississippi," *Photographic and Fine Art Journal*, August 1855, 252–253. For more on floating daguerrean galleries, see Palmquist and Kailbourn, *Pioneer Photographers from the Mississippi to the Continental Divide*, 6–7.

44. For Charleston locations, see Teal, *Partners with the Sun*, 43–66. For New Orleans locations, see R.A.C., "New Orleans Photographic Galleries," *Photographic and Fine Art Journal*, August 1858, 244–245. For Richmond, see An Amateur, "The Photographic Galleries of America—No. III: The Richmond Galleries," *Photographic and Fine Art Journal*, July 1856, 217.

45. At Fitzgibbon's Daguerreotype Establishment in St. Louis, for instance, one might learn to take pictures, purchase the necessary "apparatus, plates, cases, frames, chemicals," and shop for "a great variety of gold lockets, watch keys, finger rings, and breast pins, suitable for daguerreotypes." Fitzgibbons to Scovill Manufacturing Company, April 21, 1854, Series II, Volume 4, Scovill Manufacturing Company Records, Baker Library, Harvard Business School. Fitzgibbons served as one of the middlemen between southern artists and northeastern manufacturers and supply houses. Other middlemen included George Smith Cook and Thomas Jefferson Dobyns. Dobyns was a western daguerreotype magnate and a vice president of the American Daguerre Association. He opened galleries in Memphis, Louisville, Cincinnati, Nashville, Vicksburg, New Orleans, St. Louis, and New York City between 1845 and 1853—and was a major photographic supplier of western daguerreans. See Palmquist and Kailbourn, *Pioneer Photographers from the Mississippi to the Continental Divide*, 209–210. On early photographic manufacturers and supply houses, see Reese V. Jenkins, *Images and Enterprise: Technology and the American Photographic Industry, 1839–1925* (Baltimore: Johns Hopkins University Press, 1975), 12, 27–28.

46. *Photographic Art Journal*, December 1851, 376. On early photograph studios, see Katherine C. Grier, *Culture and Comfort: Parlor Making and Middle-Class Identity, 1850–1930* (Washington, DC: Smithsonian Institution Press, 1988), ch. 1.

47. John Werge, *The Evolution of Photography* (London: Piper & Carter, 1890), 49.

48. William A. Pratt of Henrico County, Virginia, is listed as owning one male slave, thirty years old, in the 1850 Census's Slave Schedules. Hillyer was a

Baptist minister, physician, and college professor who began a daguerreotype business in Athens, Georgia, in 1847 and soon thereafter moved with his eleven slaves and his family to Galveston, Texas (in late 1847), and eventually Goliad, Texas, where Hillyer established a Baptist church. The family then moved to Gonzales, where Hillyer became president of Gonzales College. For John Freeman Hillyer, see Palmquist and Kailbourn, *Pioneer Photographers from the Mississippi to the Continental Divide*, 325; and William Russell Young III, "H. B. Hillyer: Life and Career of a Nineteenth Century Texas Photographer," MA thesis, University of Texas at Austin, 1985. Meanwhile, the R. G. Dun credit report on Thomas Jefferson Dobyns stated the following in May 1854: "He is wealthy, owns a lar. amt. of R.E. + slaves. He is Consid^d w 200^m\$." See Louisiana, vol. 10, p. 509, R. G. Dun & Co. Credit Report Volumes, Baker Library, Harvard Business School. Dobyns's partner, William C. Harrington, was also likely a slaveholder. As the R. G. Dun credit report noted in November 1856, Harrington "was once a wealthy Planter in Ala. lose^t [lost] all by endorsing." See Louisiana, vol. 10, p. 509, R. G. Dun & Co. Credit Report Volumes, Baker Library, Harvard Business School.

49. J. T. Zealy, South Carolina, vol. 12, p. 80, R. G. Dun & Co. Credit Report Volumes, Baker Library, Harvard Business School.

50. George Smith Cook purchased a substitute (for \$25) and also donated \$200 to the Confederacy. Entries for February 25 and March 1, 1862, George Cook Account Book, July 1859–August 1861, George S. and Huestis P. Cook Papers, The Valentine.

51. "Photography in the United States," *New York Daily Tribune*, April 30, 1853, 6. In his photographic survey, Robert Taft offers a reasonable explanation for the reliability of this estimate: "If we assume that there were two thousand daguerreotypists at work in 1853 and that each produced on the average 1500 daguerreotypes a year (an average of five a working day) the figure of 3,000,000 daguerreotypes annually would represent a reasonable figure. The large establishments and especially the daguerreotype factories mentioned later in the text must have turned out hundreds of these daguerreotypes daily." See Taft, *Photography and the American Scene*, 467.

52. William P. Abrams paid \$1.00 for a likeness at a gallery in Livingston, Alabama, in 1847. See May 24, 1847, William P. Abrams Diaries, Diary 2, Box 1, Folder 4, W. S. Hoole Special Collections Library, University of Alabama.

53. On *Harper's Magazine*, see, for instance, advertisements in Richmond's *Daily Dispatch* on October 30, 1855, 2; December 18, 1857, 2; April 30, 1859, 2. See also Lancaster, South Carolina's *Lancaster Ledger*, November 25, 1857, 4. On *Godey's Lady's Book*, see Richmond's *Daily Dispatch* on April 22, 1852, 1; October 23, 1856, 2. See also *Alexandria Gazette*, May 21, 1858, 4. Twenty-five cents in the mid-1850s is equivalent to around \$7 in 2015. On this relative cost, I have used the "real price" calculator for

commodities through the platform at MeasuringWorth.com. For
daguerreotype prices, see Wendy Wick Reaves and Sally Pierce,
"Translations from the Plate: The Marketplace of Public Portraiture," in
Young America: The Daguerreotypes of Southworth and Hawes (New York:
Steidl, George Eastman House, and International Center of Photography,
2005), 90. The *New York Daily Tribune* noted an establishment selling
daguerreotypes in New York City for 25 cents; "Photography in the
United States," *New York Daily Tribune*, April 30, 1853, 6. For miniature
portrait prices, see McCandless, "The Portrait Studio and the Celebrity," 52.
David Jaffee reveals greater variation in prices for provincial miniature
portraits—variation based on style and duration of completion. For
instance, Jaffee writes of William Matthew Prior, a New England artist
who in the 1830s offered cheaper portraits for around $3 and a more
academic style for $10 to $25. See Jaffee, *A New Nation of Goods*, 251.

54. Henry Dudley to Sisters Deb and Rose, March 15, 1854, Papers of Various
Lynchburg, Va. Families, Mss. 6188, Box 1, Albert and Shirley Small
Special Collections Library, University of Virginia.

55. Entry for April 18, 1848, Account Book 1845–1861, George Smith Cook
Collection, Manuscript Division, Library of Congress, Washington, DC.

56. Entry for April 19, 1848, Account Book 1845–1861, George Smith Cook
Collection.

57. Cook worked in Columbus, Mississippi, in the spring of 1848 and then
moved to Columbus, Georgia, by late May. In his entries for April of 1848,
labeled only "Pictures at Columbus," Cook listed a number of sitters who
appear in the 1850 census in Columbus, Mississippi—for instance, James
Benoit, resident of Columbus Ward I, Lowndes County, Mississippi.
Likewise, in his list of expenses, he noted "Expenses at Columbus *Miss*"
and listed stock sold on April 12 and money paid to the "Editor of Whig"
on May 4. Yet Cook moved to Columbus, Georgia, by May 31, 1848: he
stayed there through the summer, and then returned in the summer of
1849. See Account Book 1845–1861, George Smith Cook Collection, and
1850 United States Federal Census records, Lowndes County, Mississippi.

58. This entry lists a "Mr" and then a surname, followed by "Col Girl." The
surname looks like "Nasss," as in "Mr. Nass's Col Girl." In the 1850 Slave
Schedule, no man named Nass appears for Columbus, Mississippi, which
suggests that this slaveholder may have come from a different county to
have his slave photographed. See entry for April 1848, Account Books
1845–1861, George Smith Cook Collection.

59. Edward J. Pringle to Mary Pringle, August 18, 1856, Box 28/630, Folder
28/630/08: Correspondence, 1855–1856, Alston-Pringle-Frost Papers,
Manuscripts, South Carolina Historical Society; June 10, 1859, Diary of
Margaret Ann Morris (Meta) Grimball, Margaret Ann Morris Grimball
Family Papers, South Carolina Historical Society.

60. The subject has been labeled "Anne Courtney Cogbill" but there are no
records of an Anne Courtney in the Cogbill Family Bible, which lists

births and deaths. Lelia Courtney is listed as being born on June 15, 1858. See Cogbill Family Bible Records, 1812–1977, Virginia Historical Society, Richmond, Virginia (photocopies of originals privately owned). In 1860, the Cogbill family owned seven slaves, including a fifteen-year-old female who was listed as "black" in the census records. See U.S. Census, 1860, Slave Schedules, Petersburg, VA, 47. Harriet Cogbill might have brought Lelia Courtney with both her grandmother and her enslaved nurse to the photography gallery in the summer of 1859 to memorialize her in light of a recent illness, or after that illness. On July 20, 1859, Benjamin Daniel Cogbill (Lelia Courtney's father) wrote a letter to Harriett Cogbill (Lelia Courtney's mother) noting that he was "glad to hear that you were getting on so well without me and happy to learn that dear little Courtney was improving so fast." Benjamin Daniel Cogbill to Harriett Cogbill, July 20, 1859, Cogbill Family Papers, 1852–1889, Virginia Historical Society, Richmond, Virginia.

61. Vlach, *The Planter's Prospect*, 11.

62. Museum Collections, Virginia Historical Society.

63. Molly Rogers, *Delia's Tears: Race, Science, and Photography in Nineteenth-Century America* (New Haven, CT: Yale University Press, 2010); Brian Wallis, "Black Bodies, White Science: Louis Agassiz's Slave Daguerreotypes," *American Art* 9, no. 2 (Summer 1995): 38–61; Trachtenberg, *Reading American Photographs*, 53–56.

64. Rogers, *Delia's Tears*, 215–240.

65. We can be reasonably sure that Mammy Kitty was enslaved and that she was the slave of Margaret Keeling Ellis for at least some of her life. A note accompanying the photograph of Mammy Kitty reads, "The faithful servant / Charles + M. K. Ellis / Died in Richmond at the old family home in 1864 / our Mother's Mammy." Margaret Keeling Ellis was married to Charles Ellis, who died in 1840. Further, the 1850 U.S. Census Slave Schedules show Margaret K. Ellis of Richmond owning five slaves, including women who were 55 and 75 years old. For the note, see Ellis Family Daguerreotypes, n.d., Accession #2516-c, Albert and Shirley Small Special Collections Library, University of Virginia; see also 1850 Federal Census Slave Schedules, City of Richmond, Henrico County, Virginia. "Eliza Washburn" is likely Eliza Ann Washburn (1826–1853), daughter of Ichabod Washburn of Worcester, MA, as her daguerreotype came from the Washburn Family Papers at the American Antiquarian Society. Lauren Hewes, email to author, December 12, 2017; Washburn Family Papers Finding Aid, American Antiquarian Society, https://catalog.mwa.org/vwebv/holdingsInfo?searchId=1876&recCount=10&recPointer=4&bibId=272216 (accessed December 12, 2017).

66. Root, *The Camera and the Pencil*, 106.

67. Museum records include a note attached to the case detailing how Rosetta was enslaved at one point by Mrs. J. Motte Alston. Rosetta may wear the white and blue Welsh plaid common for the Alston slaves of low country

South Carolina. See caption to *Rosetta*, Unknown Artist, n.d.; Ambrotype; 2½ × 2 inches (image), 3¹¹⁄₁₆ × 3³⁄₁₆ inches (case); XX1978.002; Image courtesy of the Gibbes Museum of Art/Carolina Art Association; and J. Motte Alston, *Rice Planter and Sportsman: The Recollections of J. Motte Alston, 1821–1909* (Columbia: University of South Carolina Press, 1953), 10, 46.

68. Minor was a farmer, blacksmith, lay minister, and midlevel slaveholder in central Virginia. He operated farms in Louisa County, Virginia, during the 1840s and Amherst County, Virginia, in the 1850s and 1860s, primarily planting tobacco, corn, and wheat. The Minor family nurse daguerreotype presently sits in the Minor Family Papers at the University of Virginia. The original frame had the following note inscribed on it: "Old family nurse in Minor Family / Her name is found in the farm ledger of Lancelot Minor." The farm ledger of Lancelot Minor does not list any slave specifically as a nurse. Yet, given her age, the woman may have been called "Old Sukey." In January 1845, 1847, and 1848, Minor paid modest sums of cash to an "Old Sukey," ranging from $2.00 in 1845 to $4.25 in 1847. We cannot be sure that this woman is, in fact, "Old Sukey," nor can we be sure she was a slave, but both seem likely for three reasons. First, in the 1850 census's Slave Schedules, Lancelot Minor of Louisa County is listed as having fifteen slaves, including a sixty-two-year-old female slave. Second, Sukey was a distinctly African name that was popular amongst slaves. Third, given the fact that Lancelot Minor used slave labor on both his farms (Thompson Cron Roads in Louisa County and Briery Knowe in Amherst County), it seems unlikely that he would have obtained an occupational image of a free black woman. See entries for January 1845, January 1847, and January 1848 in Lancelot Minor Logbook, Minor Family Papers, 1838–1944, Accession #6055, 6055-a, Albert and Shirley Small Special Collections Library, University of Virginia Library; and 1850 Census Slave Schedules, Lancelot Minor, Louisa County, Virginia. On the prevalence of the name "Sukey," see Paul Finkleman, ed., *Macmillan Encyclopedia of World Slavery* (New York: Macmillan, 1998), 2:626. The Minor nurse might have sat for her daguerreotype when she accompanied Lancelot Minor on one of Minor's trips to Fredericksburg, Charlottesville, Washington, or Richmond, or when an itinerant passed through the Virginia countryside. Minor purchased various items—such as clothing, tumblers, candlesticks, and spoons—from these cities. See entries for February 1843, January 1844, and September 1847. For purchases from a peddler, see entry for April 1843. Minor also recorded a purchase of a photograph in August 1846: "By cash in exchange for likeness $3.00." Lancelot Minor Logbook, Minor Family Papers, 1838–1944.

69. Hannah Carlson, "Vulgar Things," *Common-Place* 7, no. 2 (January 2007), http://common-place.org/book/vulgar-things.

70. See, for instance, "African American Woman Holding a White Child," one photograph: ruby ambrotype, sixth plate, hand-colored, ca. 1855, from the

Library of Congress Prints and Photographs Online Catalog, www.loc.gov/
pictures/item/99404291. Visual culture scholars Deborah Willis and Carla
Williams have commented on this practical reason for images of nannies
with white children. See Deborah Willis and Carla Williams, *The Black
Female Body: A Photographic History* (Philadelphia: Temple University
Press, 2002), 129. On the figure of the "mammy," see Kimberly Wallace-
Sanders, *Mammy: A Century of Race, Gender, and Southern Memory*
(Ann Arbor: University of Michigan Press, 2008).

71. Laura Wexler offers a discussion of caretaker images post-1865. See Laura
Wexler, *Tender Violence: Domestic Visions in an Age of U.S. Imperialism*
(Chapel Hill: University of North Carolina Press, 2000), ch. 2. Other
examples of the many chattel Madonna photographs include *Juno (Waller)
Seymour, Minding the Great Grand-daughter of Her First Owner (1853)*, an
image published in *Life of Maumer Juno of Charleston, S.C.* (Atlanta: Foote
& Davies, 1892), and *Egbert Gilliss Handy in the Arms of Sarah, a Slave Given
to Mary Jones Purnell as a Wedding Gift by Her Father*, ambrotype, c. 1859,
Handy Family Papers, Clements Library, University of Michigan.

72. Wexler, *Tender Violence*, 61.

73. Faust, *The Ideology of Slavery*, 13.

74. Dolly Lunt Burge, *The Diary of Dolly Lunt Burge, 1848–1879*, ed. Christine
Jacobson Carter (Athens: University of Georgia Press, 1997), 156. As Sadai
was born in December of 1855, the image was likely taken in late 1857 or
1858. Sadai's parents, Dolly and Thomas Burge, lived on the Burge
Plantation, nine miles east of Covington, Georgia, where they owned
approximately one hundred slaves. See Finding Aid, Burge Family Papers,
MARBL, Emory University, http://findingaids.library.emory.edu/
documents/burge266.

75. Harriett Robinson, WPA Slave Narrative Project, Oklahoma Narratives,
vol. 13, Oklahoma, Adams-Young, 1936, Library of Congress, Manuscript
Division (accessed January 8, 2017). On relations between mistresses and
enslaved women, see Thavolia Glymph, *Out of the House of Bondage: The
Transformation of the Plantation Household* (Cambridge: Cambridge University
Press, 2008); Elizabeth Fox-Genovese, *Within the Plantation Household:
Black and White Women of the Old South* (Chapel Hill: University of North
Carolina Press, 1988); and Catherine Clinton, *The Plantation Mistress:
Woman's World in the Old South* (New York: Pantheon Books, 1982), ch. 10.

76. Little is known about Mary Pearson, but her daguerreotype did enter the
collections of the American Antiquarian Society with papers of a family
from Sterling, MA (Pearson Family Papers). Lauren Hewes, email to
author, December 12, 2017.

77. Bill of Sale for Martha Ann "Patty" Atavis, Douglass Hamilton Thomas
Manuscript Collection, MS 3090, Maryland Historical Society. Little is
known of Atavis's life before or after emancipation, though an obituary
does indicate that she continued to work as a domestic in Dr. John
Whitridge's Baltimore home after 1865; *Baltimore American*, October 28,

1874, 1. For more on Whitridge's biography, see "Dr. J. Whitridge (b. 1793–d.1878)," *Archives of Maryland Bibliography Series*, Maryland State Archives, http://msa.maryland.gov/megafile/msa/speccol/sc5400/sc5496/024200/024297/html/024297bio.html (accessed December 13, 2017). My thanks to Patricia Dockman Anderson for sharing her ongoing research about Atavis.

78. A note related to the image states that the following is written on the reverse side of the image: "Buena Vista—The residence of A. J. Boulware—sent to me by AJB Oct. 29th / 58." This note suggests that the image was not simply meant as a memento but also used as a means of communication. Heather Dawn Beattie, email to author, September 2011.

79. For more on Boulware, see the history prepared for the National Register of Historical Places Registration form for La Vista at www.dhr.virginia.gov/registers/Counties/Spotsylvania/088-0143_La_Vista_1997_Final_Nomination.pdf (accessed December 6, 2017). The 1860 Slave Schedules show that Alfred J. Boulware of Spotsylvania County, VA, owned thirty-nine slaves.

80. Jo B. Paoletti, *Pink and Blue: Telling the Boys from the Girls in America* (Bloomington: Indiana University Press, 2012).

81. Fannie Manigault to "Mon Cher Mari," November 26, 1861; Fannie Manigault to "Mon Cher Mari," November 27, 1861; Fannie Manigault to Louis Manigault, January 1, 1862; and Fannie Manigault to Louis Manigault, January 8, 1862; Box 4, Louis Manigault Papers, David M. Rubenstein Rare Book and Manuscript Library, Duke University.

82. Fannie Manigault to "Mon Cher Louis" [Louis Manigault], December 11, 1861, Folder: 1861, Box 4, Louis Manigault Papers.

83. Louis Manigault [Ton Mari/L.M.] to "Ma Chere femme" [Fannie Manigault], December 14, 1861, Folder: 1861, Box 4, Louis Manigault Papers. It appears that Fannie never sent Captain back to solitary confinement. She later noted that Captain became less resistant, due perhaps to threats imposed by Mr. Logan: "I expect your writing to Mr Logan gave Captain a fright, as he is doing very well now." Fannie Manigault to Louis Manigault ["My dear Louis"], December 16, 1861, Folder: 1861, Box 4, Louis Manigault Papers; and Fannie Manigault to Louis Manigault ["Mon Cher Mari"], December 18, 1861, Folder: 1861, Box 4, Louis Manigault Papers.

84. Margaret Abruzzo, *Polemical Pain: Slavery, Cruelty, and the Rise of Humanitarianism* (Baltimore: Johns Hopkins University Press, 2011), 146.

85. James Henry Hammond, *Remarks of Mr. Hammond, of South Carolina, on the Question of Receiving Petitions for the Abolition of Slavery in the District of Columbia, Delivered in the House of Representatives, February 1, 1836* (Washington, DC: Duff Green, 1836), 6–7, 11–12.

86. Claire Parfait, *The Publishing History of* Uncle Tom's Cabin, *1852–2002* (Padstow: Ashgate, 2007), 13–17; James Brewer Stewart, *Holy Warriors:*

The Abolitionists and American Slavery, rev. ed. (New York: Hill and Wang, 1997), 164–165.

87. Jo-Ann Morgan, *Uncle Tom's Cabin as Visual Culture* (Columbia: University of Missouri Press, 2007), 2–3, 24; Ann Douglass, "Introduction," in Harriet Beecher Stowe, *Uncle Tom's Cabin or, Life Among the Lowly* (New York: Penguin Books, 1982), 9.

88. Annie DeWolf Middleton to N. Russell Middleton, August 6, 1852, N. Russell Middleton Papers, #507, Southern Historical Collection, Wilson Library, University of North Carolina at Chapel Hill.

89. On the Middletons' continued slaveholding, see Alicia Hopton Middleton, *Life in Carolina and New England During the Nineteenth Century: As Illustrated by Reminiscences and Letters of the Middleton Family of Charleston South Carolina and of the De Wolf Family of Bristol Rhode Island* (Bristol, RI: privately printed, 1929).

90. Manisha Sinha, *The Counter-Revolution of Slavery: Politics and Ideology in Antebellum South Carolina* (Chapel Hill: University of North Carolina Press, 2000), 72–73.

91. In George Smith Cook's written records, one finds evidence that suggests he made other enslaved caretaker photographs. See his entry for June 12, 1851, "Missy Aiken + Nurse [sup?] ¼ 5.00," in Account Book 1851–1854, George Smith Cook Collection. Likewise, see Cook's entry from May 22, 1862: "Baby Seabrook + Nurse 4$ 1/6 4," Account Book March 1862–Jan 1863, George S. and Huestis P. Cook Papers.

92. On lynching photography, see Dora Apel and Shawn Michelle Smith, *Lynching Photographs* (Berkeley: University of California Press, 2007); Shawn Michelle Smith, *Photography on the Color Line: W. E. B. Du Bois, Race, and Visual Culture* (Durham: Duke University Press, 2004), ch. 4.

93. One could also find daguerreotypes as large as 15" by 17" and small enough to fit lockets or rings—though these were less common. Taft, *Photography and the American Scene*, 78.

94. Taft, *Photography and the American Scene*, 160–162.

95. David Henkin, *The Postal Age: The Emergence of Modern Communications in Nineteenth-Century America* (Chicago: University of Chicago Press, 2006), 59.

96. Edward J. Pringle to Mary Pringle, August 18, 1856, Box 28/630, Folder 28/630/08: Correspondence, 1855–1856, Alston-Pringle-Frost Papers, Manuscripts, South Carolina Historical Society. While Edward J. Pringle called the images "pictures" in his letter, the language he used to describe them clearly indicates that these images were photographs. Edward's recent history of correspondence with his mother adds further weight to the fact that these images were photographs. In 1854 Mary, Edward's mother, wrote about Edward in a letter to her daughter: "He has our Daguerreotypes hung around him; he never imagined, that the Boston group could ever have been so peculiarly valuable to him. He begs for a great family picture, with children and grandchildren." See Mary Pringle to daughter, June 13, 1854, Box 28/630, Folder 28/630/7: Correspondence 1854, Alston-Pringle-Frost Papers, Manuscripts, South Carolina Historical Society.

97. Edward J. Pringle, *Slavery in the Southern States, by a Carolinian* (Cambridge: John Bartlett, 1852).

98. Pringle, *Slavery in the Southern States*, 25.

99. Other male slaves were pictured in their servants' clothing, including Henry Page, a coachman owned by Mann Valentine. See Gregg D. Kimball, *American City, Southern Place: A Cultural History of Antebellum Richmond* (Athens: University of Georgia Press, 2000), 155.

100. Benjamin Drew, *A North-Side View of Slavery: The Refugee, Or the Narratives of Fugitive Slaves in Canada* (Boston: John P. Jewett, 1856; New York: Johnson Reprint, 1968), 29.

101. Drew Gilpin Faust, ed., *The Ideology of Slavery: Proslavery Thought in the Antebellum South, 1830–1860* (Baton Rouge: Louisiana State University Press, 1981); Larry E. Tise, *Proslavery: A History of the Defense of Slavery in America, 1701–1840* (Athens: University of Georgia Press, 1987); George M. Frederickson, *The Black Image in the White Mind: The Debate on Afro-American Character and Destiny, 1817–1914* (New York: Harper & Row, 1972); Eugene D. Genovese, *The Slaveholders' Dilemma: Freedom and Progress in Southern Conservative Thought, 1820–1860* (Columbia: University of South Carolina Press, 1992); Lacy K. Ford, *Deliver Us from Evil: The Slavery Question in the Old South* (New York: Oxford University Press, 2009); Abruzzo, *Polemical Pain*; Jeffrey Robert Young, *Domesticating Slavery: The Master Class in Georgia and South Carolina, 1670–1837* (Chapel Hill: University of North Carolina Press, 1999); Willie Lee Rose, "The Domestication of Slavery," in *Slavery and Freedom*, ed. William W. Freehling (New York: Oxford University Press, 1982).

102. James M. Clifton, ed., *Life and Labor on Argyle Island: Letters and Documents of a Savannah River Rice Plantation, 1833–1867* (Savannah, GA: Beehive Press, 1978), 134, 169, 183, 230.

103. Louis Manigault, attached note "Hector," Photograph Collection, Manigault Family, Charleston Museum.

104. H. Garbanati, "Now and Then," *American Journal of Photography*, October 15, 1858.

105. "Photography in Louisville, KY," *Photographic and Fine Art Journal*, September 1855.

106. For one potential exception, see "Daguerreotype of a Slave Woman, Clarke County, Georgia, 1853," Vanishing Georgia, Georgia Archives, Morrow, Georgia, http://dlg.galileo.usg.edu/vanga/id:clr210-92 (accessed June 15, 2017). This woman poses with a book, but there are no records indicating whether she was enslaved or not. Gail DeLoach, email to author, July 2011.

107. E. K. Hough, "Expressing Character in Photographic Pictures," *American Journal of Photography*, December 15, 1858, 211–215.

108. Shane White and Graham White, *Stylin': African American Expressive Culture, from Its Beginnings to the Zoot Suit* (Ithaca, NY: Cornell University Press, 1998), 58–59.

109. White and White, *Stylin'*, 59.

110. Quoted in White and White, *Stylin'*, 61.
111. See Maurie D. McInnis, *Slaves Waiting for Sale: Abolitionist Art and the American Slave Trade* (Chicago: University of Chicago Press, 2011).
112. On the hand-coloring of daguerreotypes, ambrotypes, and tintypes, see Sarah Kennel, Diane Waggoner, and Alice Carver-Kubik, *In the Darkroom: An Illustrated Guide to Photographic Processes Before the Digital Age* (New York: Thames and Hudson, 2009); and Jeff L. Rosenheim, *Photography and the American Civil War* (New York: Metropolitan Museum of Art, 2013), 17–23.
113. June 10, 1859, Diary of Margaret Ann Morris (Meta) Grimball, Margaret Ann Morris Grimball Family Papers, South Carolina Historical Society.
114. June 10, 1859, Diary of Margaret Ann Morris (Meta) Grimball.
115. Dion Boucicault, *The Octoroon, or, Life in Louisiana; A Play in Five Acts*, Project Gutenberg ebook, accessed June 29, 2015.
116. Robert E. May, "John Quitman and His Slaves: Reconciling Slave Resistance with the Proslavery Defense," *Journal of Southern History* 46, no. 4 (November 1980), 553, 567. My thanks to May for initially spotting this photographic exchange.
117. May, "John Quitman and His Slaves," 568.
118. John Quitman to Eliza, February 27, 1847, Quitman Family Papers, 1784–1978, UPA Microfilm, Records of Ante-Bellum Southern Plantations from the Revolution through the Civil War, University Publications of America, Series J, Selections from the Southern Historical Collection, Part 6, Reel 7, OCLC No. 12894903.
119. Louisa Quitman to John Quitman, April 27, 1847, Quitman Family Papers.
120. It is worth noting that the Quitmans' expressions hinged on the notion of a loyal slave. It is unclear how the Quitmans displayed this image in the years to come, but it might have contributed, to some extent, to their later shock when, during the Civil War, Harry "threatened to desert Monmouth and was dissuaded only by the granting of wages." See May, "John A. Quitman and His Slaves," 569.
121. Edward J. Pringle to Mary Pringle, August 18, 1856, Folder 28/630/08: Correspondence, 1855–1856, Alston-Pringle-Frost Papers, Manuscripts, South Carolina Historical Society.
122. G. W. F. Hegel, *The Phenomenology of Mind*, trans. J. B. Baillie (Mineola, NY: Dover Publications, 2003), 2–3.
123. June 10, 1859, Diary of Margaret Ann Morris (Meta) Grimball.
124. John Quitman to "My beloved Wife," February 20, 1847, Quitman Family Papers.
125. William Dusinberre, *Them Dark Days: Slavery in the American Rice Swamps* (New York: Oxford University Press, 1996). On slave patrols, see Sally E. Hadden, *Slave Patrols: Law and Violence in Virginia and the Carolinas* (Cambridge, MA: Harvard University Press, 2001).
126. William Capers Sr. to Louis Manigault, April 9 and April 13, 1863, Louis Manigault Papers.

127. "How to Catch Them," *New York Times*, January 19, 1860, 8. Though photo historians have linked the practices of photographic surveillance in the nineteenth century to state institutions, Manigault's advertisements suggest they included the far more local power of southern masters. John Tagg, *The Burden of Representation: Essays on Photographies and Histories* (Minneapolis: University of Minnesota Press, 1993).

128. Louis Manigault to Charles W. Henry, April 19, 1863, Box VI, Folder 131, Manigault Family Papers, South Caroliniana Library, University of South Carolina.

129. Stephanie McCurry, *Confederate Reckoning: Power and Politics in the Civil War South* (Cambridge, MA: Harvard University Press, 2012), 235.

130. The year after Dolly escaped, a field hand named July fled but was shot by a Confederate soldier and had his leg amputated in Savannah. Dusinberre, *Them Dark Days*, 144.

CHAPTER 2: ENDURING IMAGES

1. Harriet Beecher Stowe, *Uncle Tom's Cabin, or, Life Among the Lowly* (New York: Penguin Books, 1981), 68.

2. Prints of George Washington were some of the most commonly displayed images in early republican and antebellum America. See Wendy Wick Reaves and Sally Pierce, "Translations from the Plate: The Marketplace of Public Portraiture," in *Young America: The Daguerreotypes of Southworth & Hawes*, ed. Grant B. Romer and Brian Wallis (New York: Steidl, George Eastman House, and the International Center of Photography, 2005), 91.

3. This omission is not due to a lack of historical interest in the lives of antebellum enslaved people. In the 1970s, historians offered pathbreaking analyses of enslaved people's songs, stories, family ties, and religious practices. These studies include John Blassingame, *The Slave Community: Plantation Life in the Antebellum South*, rev. ed. (New York: Oxford University Press, 1979); Herbert Gutman, *The Black Family in Slavery and Freedom, 1750–1925* (New York: Pantheon, 1976); George Rawick, *From Sundown to Sunup: The Making of a Black Community* (Westport, CT: Greenwood, 1972); and Lawrence W. Levine, *Black Culture and Black Consciousness: Afro-American Folk Thought from Slavery to Freedom* (New York: Oxford University Press, 1977). Later works include Clarence Walker, *Deromanticizing Black History: Critical Essays and Reappraisals* (Knoxville: University of Tennessee Press, 1991); Nell Painter, "Soul Murder and Slavery: Toward a Fully Loaded Cost Accounting," in *U.S. History as Women's History: New Feminist Essays*, ed. Linda K. Kerber, Alice Kessler-Harris, and Kathryn Kish Sklar (Chapel Hill: University of North Carolina Press, 1995), 125–146; Deborah Gray White, *Ar'n't I a Woman? Female Slaves in the Plantation South* (New York: W. W. Norton, 1985); Charles Joyner, *Down by the Riverside: A South Carolina Slave Community* (Urbana: University of Illinois Press, 1984); Steven Hahn, *A Nation Under Our Feet: Black Political Struggles in the Rural*

South from Slavery to the Great Migration (Cambridge, MA: Belknap Press of Harvard University Press, 2003); Stephanie M. H. Camp, *Closer to Freedom: Enslaved Women and Everyday Resistance in the Plantation South* (Chapel Hill: University of North Carolina Press, 2004); Anthony E. Kaye, *Joining Places: Slave Neighborhoods in the Old South* (Chapel Hill: University of North Carolina Press, 2007); and Sylviane A. Diouf, *Slavery's Exiles: The Story of The American Maroons* (New York: New York University Press, 2014).

4. Walter Johnson, *Soul by Soul: Life Inside the Antebellum Slave Market* (Cambridge, MA: Harvard University Press, 1999), 7; and Lacy Ford, "Reconsidering the Internal Slave Trade: Paternalism, Markets, and the Character of the Old South," in *The Chattel Principle: Internal Slave Trades in the Americas*, ed. Walter Johnson (New Haven, CT: Yale University Press, 2004), 146. Other works on the internal slave trade include Michael Tadman, *Speculators and Slaves: Masters, Traders, and Slaves in the Old South* (Madison: University of Wisconsin Press, 1989); Robert H. Gudmestad, *A Troublesome Commerce: The Transformation of the Interstate Slave Trade* (Baton Rouge: Louisiana State University Press, 2003); Steven Deyle, *Carry Me Back: The Domestic Slave Trade in American Life* (New York: Oxford University Press, 2005); and Phillip D. Troutman, "Slave Trade and Sentiment in Antebellum Virginia," PhD diss., University of Virginia, 2000.

5. Calvin Schermerhorn, *Money over Mastery, Family over Freedom: Slavery in the Antebellum Upper South* (Baltimore: Johns Hopkins University Press, 2011), 3; Walter Johnson, "Introduction: The Future Store," in *The Chattel Principle: Internal Slave Trades in the Americas*, ed. Walter Johnson (New Haven, CT: Yale University Press, 2004), 12–13.

6. Scholars have only begun to illuminate how enslaved people responded to their commodification and the circumstances of domestic human trafficking, by exploring how enslaved people understood their appraisal and market values, examining the emotions elicited by the trade, and revealing the select number of literate slaves who maintained affective ties through letter writing. Daina Ramey Berry, *The Price for Their Pound of Flesh: The Value of the Enslaved, from Womb to Grave, in the Building of a Nation* (Boston: Beacon Press, 2017); Phillip Troutman, "Correspondences in Black and White: Sentiment and the Slave Market Revolution," in *New Studies in the History of American Slavery*, ed. Edward E. Baptist and Stephanie M. H. Camp (Athens: University of Georgia Press, 2006), 211–242. Heather Andrea Williams incorporates slaves' letters as evidence, and draws upon the methods of the history of emotions, in her exploration of enslaved people's feelings in relation to the trade. Heather Andrea Williams, *Help Me to Find My People: The African American Search for Family Lost in Slavery* (Chapel Hill: University of North Carolina Press, 2012). Calvin Schermerhorn has illuminated how slaves built social networks in response to the slave trade in *Money over Mastery*. This chapter does not intervene in the debate over whether slaves maintained and sought a

nuclear family, as Herbert Gutman argues, or whether they positioned a "malleable extended family" as their ideal, as Brenda Stevenson asserts. The evidence I have found reveals photographic exchanges within nuclear families, but this does little to disprove Stevenson's arguments. See Gutman, *The Black Family in Slavery and Freedom*, and Brenda E. Stevenson, *Life in Black and White: Family and Community in the Slave South* (New York: Oxford University Press, 1996).

7. Olaudah Equiano, *The Interesting Narrative of the Life of Olaudah Equiano, or Gustavus Vassa, the African, Written by Himself*, ed. Angelo Costanzo (Ontario: Broadview Press, 2004), 78.

8. Frederick Douglass, *Narrative of the Life of Frederick Douglass, an American Slave* (New York: Anchor Books, 1989), 31.

9. Daphne Williams, WPA Slave Narrative Project, Texas Narratives, vol. 16, part 4, 160, Federal Writers' Project, U.S. Work Projects Administration, Manuscript Division, Library of Congress.

10. In the letter that described this scene, John would also complain about a frequently sick slave, relating how he was "growing very tired of a property which occasions so much anxiety, and yields so little profit." To John, enslaved people were at once underperforming commodities and meaningful spectators. John Jones to Mary Jones, April 8, 1851, Charles Colcock Jones Papers, Louisiana Research Collection, Tulane University. For more on the Jones family and this incident, see Erskine Clarke, *Dwelling Place: A Plantation Epic* (New Haven, CT: Yale University Press, 2005), 245–246.

11. This incident likely occurred in the early 1820s. See Francis Fedric, *Slave Life in Virginia and Kentucky; or, Fifty Years of Slavery in the Southern States of America* (1863), Documenting the American South, University Library, University of North Carolina at Chapel Hill, http://docsouth.unc.edu/neh/fedric/menu.html.

12. Julia Blanks, WPA Slave Narrative Project, Texas Narratives, vol. 16, part 1, 4, Federal Writers' Project, U.S. States Work Projects Administration, Manuscript Division, Library of Congress.

13. Quoted in Clarke, *Dwelling Place*, 126–127.

14. This was likely a slave chapel built by the Episcopal Church in Rockville, an area on Wadmalaw Island. Albert Sidney Thomas, *A Historical Account of the Protestant Episcopal Church in South Carolina, 1820–1957* (Columbia, SC: R. L. Bryan, 1957), 339. On Osborn and Durbec, see Matthew Fox-Amato, "Plantation Tourism," in Mazie M. Harris, *Paper Promises: Early American Photography* (Los Angeles: J. Paul Getty Museum, 2018).

15. Ida Henry, WPA Slave Narrative Project, Oklahoma Narratives, vol. 13, Federal Writers' Project, U.S. Work Projects Administration, Manuscript Division, Library of Congress. On devotional and didactic images in nineteenth-century American Protestantism, see David Morgan, *Protestants and Pictures: Religion, Visual Culture, and the Age of American Mass Production* (New York: Oxford University Press, 1999).

16. On enslaved people's engagement with folk arts and crafts, see John Michael Vlach, *By the Work of Their Hands: Studies in Afro-American Folklife* (Ann Arbor: UMI Research Press, 1991). On doll-making in particular, see Robin Bernstein, *Racial Innocence: Performing American Childhood from Slavery to Civil Rights* (New York: New York University Press, 2011), ch. 2.
17. Edgar Allan Poe, "The Daguerreotype," in *Classic Essays on Photography*, ed. Alan Trachtenberg (New Haven, CT: Leete's Island Books, 1980), 38.
18. Geoffrey Batchen, "Vernacular Photographies," *History of Photography* 24, no. 3 (Autumn 2000): 263.
19. Eliza Ripley, *Social Life in Old New Orleans, Being Recollections of My Girlhood* (New York: D. Appleton, 1912), 125. On African American writers' responses to the emergence of photography, see Sarah Blackwood, "Fugitive Obscure: Runaway Slave Portraiture and Early Photographic Technology," *American Literature* 81, no. 1 (March 2009): 93–125.
20. James Presley Ball, *Ball's Splendid Mammoth Pictorial Tour of the United States: Comprising Views of the African Slave Trade, of Northern and Southern Cities, of Cotton and Sugar Plantations, of the Mississippi, Ohio and Susquehanna Rivers, Niagara Falls, &c.* (Cincinnati, OH: A. Pugh, 1855), 8.
21. See, for instance, the quarter-plate daguerreotype for "Master Leslie Nichols Col Boy" in January 1850. Entry for January 14, 1850, Account Books 1845–1861, George Smith Cook Collection, Manuscript Division, Library of Congress, Washington, DC. Even for this notation, though, it is difficult to know whether this slave came in with Leslie Nichols or whether he came in on his own. The same is true for a notation in which Mr. [Motte?] Pringle purchased a quarter-plate daguerreotype for $5.00 and was followed by "Negro 1/6 3.00." See entry for August 20, 1851, Account Books 1845–1861, George Smith Cook Collection.
22. Entries for November 10, 1849, and June 13, 1851, Account Books 1845–1861, George Smith Cook Collection.
23. Antebellum Charleston did boast a relatively large and successful free black community. Ira Berlin, *Slaves Without Masters: The Free Negro in the Antebellum South* (New York: New Press, 1974), 221, 236.
24. John W. Bear, *The Life and Travels of John W. Bear, "The Buckeye Blacksmith"* (Baltimore: D. Binswanger, 1873), 23–108.
25. Bear, *The Life and Travels of John W. Bear*, 138–146.
26. Bear, *The Life and Travels of John W. Bear*, 147–148.
27. Bear, *The Life and Travels of John W. Bear*, 148.
28. On naming, see Joyner, *Down by the Riverside*, 217–222.
29. Adam Rothman, *Slave Country: American Expansion and the Origins of the Deep South* (Cambridge, MA: Harvard University Press, 2005).
30. Johnson, *Soul by Soul*, 5–7.
31. John Quincy Adams, *Narrative of the Life of John Quincy Adams, When in Slavery, and Now as a Freeman* (1872), Documenting the American South. University Library, University of North Carolina at Chapel Hill, http://docsouth.unc.edu/neh/adams/menu.html.

32. Given the sizable scholarly literature on the internal economy, one might expect that past scholars would have uncovered the history of slaves using photographs. Yet this history has likely remained unanalyzed for two reasons. First, George Smith Cook's papers stand as the only archived records, as far as I have found, from a southern photographer. Second, the Southern Claims Commission, a key source base used by scholars such as Dylan Penningroth, would not have detailed photographs amongst slaves' property. As Penningroth notes, during the early 1870s the Southern Claims Commission sought to "hear claims from Unionist southerners who had lost 'stores or supplies…taken or furnished for the use of the [Union] army' during the Civil War." Almost five hundred former slaves filed claims. Yet the parameters of the claims—"movable property taken by Union troops for legitimate army use"—meant that slaves would not have sought compensation for photographs. See Dylan C. Penningroth, *The Claims of Kinfolk: African American Property and Community in the Nineteenth-Century South* (Chapel Hill: University of North Carolina Press, 2003), 5, 139. Other works that address the internal economy include Kathleen M. Hilliard, *Masters, Slaves, and Exchange: Power's Purchase in the Old South* (New York: Cambridge University Press, 2014); Roderick A. McDonald, *The Economy and Material Culture of Slaves: Goods and Chattels on the Sugar Plantations of Jamaica and Louisiana* (Baton Rouge: Louisiana State University Press, 1993); Philip D. Morgan, "The Ownership of Property by Slaves in the Mid-Nineteenth-Century Low Country," *Journal of Southern History* 49, no. 3 (August 1983): 399–420; David E. Paterson, "Slavery, Slaves, and Cash in a Georgia Village, 1825–1865," *Journal of Southern History* 75, no. 4 (November 2009): 879–930; Timothy J. Lockley, "Trading Encounters Between Non-Elite Whites and African Americans in Savannah, 1790–1860," *Journal of Southern History* 66, no. 1 (February 2000): 25–48; Jeff Forret, "Slaves, Poor Whites, and the Underground Economy of the Rural Carolinas," *Journal of Southern History* 70, no. 4 (November 2004): 783–824; Loren Schweninger, "Slave Independence and Enterprise in South Carolina, 1780–1865," *South Carolina Magazine* 93, no. 2 (April 1992): 101–125; Larry E. Hudson Jr., *To Have and to Hold: Slave Work and Family Life in Antebellum South Carolina* (Athens: University of Georgia Press, 1997).
33. McDonald, *The Economy and Material Culture of Slaves*, 81–85, 243–258.
34. Penningroth, *The Claims of Kinfolk*, 46–51, 77.
35. Penningroth, *The Claims of Kinfolk*, 78.
36. Slaves also sold crops on plantations to their owners. In Louisiana, for instance, slaves sold pumpkins in the mid-1840s for 2 cents apiece; they garnered 37.5 to 70 cents per barrel of corn from the 1830s to the 1850s. McDonald, *The Economy and Material Culture of Slaves*, 53–70.
37. Penningroth, *The Claims of Kinfolk*, 65.
38. Peter Kolchin, *American Slavery, 1619–1877*, rev. ed. (New York: Hill and Wang, 2003), 110.

39. Paterson, "Slavery, Slaves, and Cash in a Georgia Village," 892. By comparison, the average free laborer in 1856 earned $1.22 per day, and artisans earned $1.94 per day. See Penningroth, *The Claims of Kinfolk*, 78.

40. McDonald, *The Economy and Material Culture of Slaves*, 61.

41. Joan Severa, *Dressed for the Photographer: Ordinary Americans and Fashion, 1840–1900* (Kent, OH: Kent State University Press, 1995), 60–61.

42. Mary Telfair to William Neyle Habersham, October 8, 1841, Box 19, Folder 174, Telfair Family Papers, Georgia Historical Society, Archival materials on deposit from the Telfair Museum of Art, courtesy the Telfair Museum of Art, Savannah, GA. Telfair used the spelling "Juddy" in her letter. On Mary Telfair and her slaves, see Jeffrey Robert Young, "To 'Venerate the Spot' of 'Airy Visions': Slavery and the Romantic Conception of Place in Mary Telfair's Savannah," in *Slavery and Freedom in Savannah*, ed. Leslie M. Harris and Daina Ramey Berry (Athens: University of Georgia Press, 2014).

43. Charles Ball, *Slavery in the United States: A Narrative of the Life and Adventures of Charles Ball, a Black Man* (1837), Documenting the American South. University Library, University of North Carolina at Chapel Hill, http://docsouth.unc.edu/neh/ballslavery/menu.html.

44. William Kingsford, *Impressions of the West and South During a Six Weeks' Holiday* (Toronto: A. H. Armour, 1858), 48.

45. Martha Stuart interview, Box 4, Folder 8, Marcus Christian Collection, Louisiana and Special Collections Department, Earl K. Long Library, University of New Orleans.

46. Penningroth, *The Claims of Kinfolk*, 55.

47. McDonald, *The Economy and Material Culture of Slaves*, 80; Paterson, "Slavery, Slaves, and Cash in a Georgia Village," 918.

48. Dr. L. S. Thompson, *The Story of Mattie J. Jackson* (1866), Documenting the American South. University Library, University of North Carolina at Chapel Hill, http://docsouth.unc.edu/neh/jacksonm/menu.html.

49. Robert Taft, *Photography and the American Scene* (New York: Dover Publications, 1938), 98.

50. McDonald, *The Economy and Material Culture of Slaves*, 81, 84–85.

51. Taft, *Photography and the American Scene*, 81; Andrea L. Volpe, "Cheap Pictures: Cartes de Visite Portrait Photographs and Visual Culture in the United States, 1860–1877," PhD dissertation, Rutgers University, 1999, 44–45.

52. Paterson, "Slavery, Slaves, and Cash in a Georgia Village," 852.

53. On southern suspicions of the subversive nature of northern peddlers, see Joseph Thomas Rainer, "The Honorable Fraternity of Moving Merchants: Yankee Peddlers in the Old South, 1800–1860," PhD dissertation, College of William and Mary, 2000.

54. "Another Emissary," *Montgomery Weekly Mail*, November 9, 1860. My thanks to Norwood A. Kerr of the Alabama Department of Archives and History for finding this source. This "man by the name of Palmer" was

likely E. G. Palmer, who had been working in Opelika since at least
September 1860. It is unclear whether Palmer gave slaves bowie knives
when he photographed them, or whether he kept his business and his
subversive actions separate. From the language in the article, it appears
that Palmer's work as a daguerrean was incidental to his punishment.
Frances Robb, "Checklist of Photographers and Others Associated with
Photography in Alabama, 1839–1861," in *The Daguerreian Annual: Official
Yearbook of the Daguerreian Society*, ed. Mark S. Johnson (Pittsburgh:
Daguerreian Society, 2004), 239.

55. "Warning to Evil Doers," *Alabama Whig*, May 5, 1859.
56. Timothy J. Lockley emphasizes how whites' economic self-interests drove
commercial interactions with slaves. See Lockley, "Trading Encounters
Between Non-Elite Whites and African Americans in Savannah."
57. In 1860, Alabama had approximately 435,000 slaves compared to 2,690
free black people. Joseph C. G. Kennedy, *Population of the United States in
1860* (Washington, DC: Government Printing Office, 1864), 8.
58. McDonald, *The Economy and Material Culture of Slaves*, 68. As
Timothy J. Lockley shows, the issue of biracial trading on Sundays was
controversial in Savannah from at least the 1820s through the Civil War.
See Lockley, "Trading Encounters Between Non-Elite Whites and African
Americans in Savannah, 1790–1860," 40–48.
59. Forret, "Slaves, Poor Whites, and the Underground Economy of the Rural
Carolinas," 816.
60. Limited evidence suggests that enslaved people made wooden dolls,
though no evidence illuminates conditions of production or use. See
Wendy Lavitt, *American Folk Dolls* (New York: Alfred A. Knopf, 1982),
68–71; and Bernstein, *Racial Innocence*, ch. 2.
61. Stephanie Camp documents another instance in which a Mississippian
enslaved woman named California displayed abolitionist images in her
cabin. Camp, *Closer to Freedom*, 97–98.
62. As anthropologist Mark Auslander notes, this assemblage—consistent with
the *minkisi* medicinal compilations of the Kongo—"evidently functioned
as a portable extension of Rosa's persona, created to travel with Ashley
and produce around her a protective aura as she encountered travails
throughout her life." Mark Auslander, "Rose's Gift: Slavery, Kinship, and
the Fabric of Memory," *Present Pasts* 8, no. 1 (March 2017), DOI: http://doi
.org/10.5334/pp.78. On the fugitive, see William Still, *The Underground
Railroad* (Philadelphia: Porter & Coates, 1871).
63. Beyond material possessions, naming practices offered a significant
avenue for enslaved people to confirm and articulate individuality (as well
as social ties). John C. Inscoe, "Carolina Slave Names: An Index to
Acculturation," *Journal of Southern History* 49, no. 4 (November 1983):
527–554.
64. Ambrose Andrews, trans., "Theory of Portraiture," *Photographic Art
Journal*, February 1853, 104.

65. Rebecca K. Shrum, *In the Looking Glass: Mirrors and Identity in Early America* (Baltimore: Johns Hopkins University Press, 2017), ch. 3; Ann Smart Martin, *Buying into the World of Goods: Early Consumers in Backcountry Virginia* (Baltimore: Johns Hopkins University Press, 2008), ch. 6.
66. Bear, *The Life and Travels of John W. Bear*, 148.
67. Penningroth, *Claims of Kinfolk*, 101; Megan Kate Nelson, *Ruin Nation: Destruction and the American Civil War* (Athens: University of Georgia Press, 2012), 94.
68. On westward expansion and photographic exchanges, see David Henkin, *The Postal Age: The Emergence of Modern Communications in Nineteenth-Century America* (Chicago: University of Chicago Press, 2006).
69. Louisa Picquet and Hiram Mattison, *Louisa Picquet, the Octoroon, or Inside Views of Southern Domestic Life* (1861), Documenting the American South, University Library, University of North Carolina at Chapel Hill, http://docsouth.unc.edu/neh/picquet/menu.html.
70. Anika Blew to her mother, July 26, 1857, Austin-Twyman Papers, Special Collections Research Center, Swem Library, College of William and Mary.
71. Troutman, "Correspondences in Black and White," 229.
72. Oats's wife signed her name "Lucrethia" in a letter to Oats, while the owner spelled it "Lucretia." Ira Berlin and Leslie S. Rowland, eds., *Families and Freedom: A Documentary History of African-American Kinship in the Civil War Era* (New York: New Press, 1997), 160–163.
73. William Still, *The Underground Railroad* (Philadelphia: Porter & Coates, 1871).
74. Adams, *Narrative of the Life of John Quincy Adams*.
75. Troutman, "Correspondences in Black and White."
76. Janet Duitsman Cornelius, *"When I Can Read My Title Clear": Literacy, Slavery, and Religion in the Antebellum South* (Columbia: University of South Carolina Press, 1991), 12–32.
77. Troutman, "Correspondences in Black and White," 216.
78. *Louisa Picquet, the Octoroon*, 30–31.
79. *Louisa Picquet, the Octoroon*, 33–35.
80. "A New Mode of Catching Runaways," *Liberator*, September 21, 1849.
81. "A Touching Story: An Escaped Slave Redeems His Relatives from Bondage," *Liberator*, October 24, 1862, 172.
82. William Craft, *Running a Thousand Miles for Freedom; or, The Escape of William and Ellen Craft from Slavery* (1860), Documenting the American South, University Library, University of North Carolina at Chapel Hill, http://docsouth.unc.edu/neh/craft/craft.html.
83. Craft, *Running a Thousand Miles for Freedom*.
84. On fugitives' self-fashioning, see David Waldstreicher, "Reading the Runaways: Self-Fashioning, Print Culture, and Confidence in Slavery in the Eighteenth-Century Mid-Atlantic," *William and Mary Quarterly* 56, no. 2 (April 1999): 243–272.

85. Historians John Hope Franklin and Loren Schweninger argue that forging free papers happened a great deal in New Orleans. John Hope Franklin and Loren Schweninger, *Runaway Slaves: Rebels on the Plantation, 1790–1860* (New York: Oxford University Press, 1999), 133.

86. Jordon went on to relate the following series of events: the overseer, hunting for a different runaway, found the papers in Jordon's cabin; Jordon's master sold him to a new master, Mr. Valsin; Jordon attempted to run away to Union lines during the war and was caught and put in jail to be executed; Jordon was saved from execution when a new master from Texas, Mr. Maxwell, bought him; when the war ended, Jordon was freed, and he reunited with his mother and a wife he married while at Mr. Valsin's. See Octavia V. Rogers Albert, *The House of Bondage, or, Charlotte Brooks and Other Slaves, Original and Life Like, as They Appeared in Their Old Plantation and City Slave Life; Together with Pen-Pictures of the Peculiar Institution, with Sights and Insights into Their New Relations as Freedmen, Freemen, and Citizens* (1890), Documenting the American South, University Library, University of North Carolina at Chapel Hill, http://docsouth.unc.edu/neh/albert/menu.html.

87. On the Archers, see Carol D. Hammond, "Richard Thompson Archer and the Burdens of Proprietorship: The Life of a Natchez District Planter," PhD dissertation, University of North Texas, 2001.

88. Ann B. Archer to Richard T. Archer, January 4, 1856, Box 2E649, Richard Thompson Archer Family Papers, 1790–1919, Briscoe Center for American History, University of Texas at Austin.

89. Charles Alexander, *Battles and Victories of Allen Allensworth, A.M., Ph.D., Lieutenant-Colonel, Retired, U.S. Army* (1914), Documenting the American South, University Library, University of North Carolina at Chapel Hill, http://docsouth.unc.edu/neh/alexander/menu.html.

90. Alexander, *Battles and Victories of Allen Allensworth.*

91. Albert J. Raboteau, *Slave Religion: The "Invisible Institution" in the Antebellum South*, rev. ed. (New York: Oxford University Press, 2004), 82.

92. On spatial control in the nineteenth-century South, see Camp, *Closer to Freedom.*

93. Charles Ball, *Slavery in the United States: A Narrative of the Life and Adventures of Charles Ball, a Black Man, Who Lived Forty Years in Maryland, South Carolina and Georgia, as a Slave Under Various Masters, and Was One Year in the Navy with Commodore Barney, During the Late War* (1837), Documenting the American South, University Library, University of North Carolina at Chapel Hill, http://docsouth.unc.edu/neh/ballslavery/ball.html.

94. Camp, *Closer to Freedom*, 62.

95. Douglass, *Narrative of the Life of Frederick Douglass*, 63.

96. Solomon Northup, *Twelve Years a Slave* (New York: Penguin Books, 2012), 149. Nicholas Mirzoeff has noted the role of visual surveillance in plantation slavery in his *The Right to Look: A Counterhistory of Visuality* (Durham, NC: Duke University Press, 2011).

97. John Knight to William Beall, March 18, 1844, John Knight Papers, David M. Rubenstein Rare Book and Manuscript Library, Duke University.

98. Johnson, *Soul by Soul*, 138–149.

99. Lawrence T. Jones III, *Lens on the Texas Frontier* (College Station: Texas A&M University Press, 2014), 32; Lawrence T. Jones III, email to author, December 3, 2017.

100. Johnson, *Soul by Soul*, chs. 4–5.

101. Peter Bruner, *A Slave's Adventures Toward Freedom: Not Fiction, but the True Story of a Struggle* (1918), Documenting the American South, University Library, University of North Carolina at Chapel Hill, http://docsouth.unc.edu/neh/bruner/menu.html.

102. John Brown and Louis Alexis Chamerovzow, *Slave Life in Georgia: A Narrative of the Life, Sufferings, and Escape of John Brown, a Fugitive Slave, Now in England* (1855), Documenting the American South, University Library, University of North Carolina at Chapel Hill, http://docsouth.unc.edu/neh/jbrown/menu.html.

103. Douglass, *Narrative of the Life of Frederick Douglass*, 5.

104. Northup, *Twelve Years a Slave*, 170.

105. Ball, *Slavery in the United States*.

106. Ball, *Slavery in the United States*.

107. Douglass, *Narrative of the Life of Frederick Douglass*, 5.

108. Still, *The Underground Railroad*.

109. On self-objectification, see John Stauffer, "Creating an Image in Black: The Power of Abolition Pictures," in *Beyond Blackface: African Americans and the Creation of American Popular Culture, 1890–1930*, ed. W. Fitzhugh Brundage (Chapel Hill: University of North Carolina Press, 2011), and Shawn Michelle Smith, "'Pictures and Progress': Frederick Douglass on Photography," paper presented at "Artifacts as Evidence: The Material Record of Politics" colloquium, November 1, 2014, Washington University in St. Louis.

110. June 10, 1859, Diary of Margaret Ann Morris (Meta) Grimball, Margaret Ann Morris Grimball Family Papers, South Carolina Historical Society.

111. While Cook's logbooks from 1854 to 1862 have not survived, his logbooks from 1863 to 1864 are archived. In a six-month stretch from September 1863 to February 1864, Cook produced a number of images of African Americans. Cook's records in these years, like the early 1850s, switched between terms to designate African Americans. While he recorded photographs with the phrases "Col Girl" and "Black Girl," he also listed photographs for people labeled "Mrs of Color." On December 21, 1863, for instance, Cook recorded two 1/9 photographs, $6.00 each, for two women labeled as "Mrs of Color." On October 12, 1863, Cook also recorded a photograph for a "Mrs of Color." Yet he also made photographs for the following African Americans: "Col Girl" (September 7, 1863); "Col Girl" (September 10, 1863); "Black Girl" (October 19, 1863); "Black

Girl" (November 16, 1863); "Col^d Boy, Locket, $10–" (December 8, 1863); "Black man" (December 14, 1863); "Black Boy" (December 14, 1863); "Col^d Boy" (December 16, 1863); "Colored girl" (February 1, 1864); "black Girl" (February 14, 1864). Most of these photographs were not labeled, and may have been daguerreotypes; the two purchased by the "Black Man" and the "Black Boy" were both sixth-plate ambrotypes. The images ranged in price from $5 to $12, but most were between $5 and $8. Most images were sixth-plate photographs, the most common size in the mid-nineteenth century. George Smith Cook Account Books 1863–1864, George Smith Cook Collection.

112. "A Returned Fugitive Slave Again Free," *Liberator*, May 1, 1863, 71.
113. Troutman, "Correspondences in Black and White," 241.
114. William Benjamin Gould, *Diary of a Contraband: The Civil War Passage of a Black Sailor*, ed. William B. Gould IV (Stanford, CA: Stanford University Press, 2002), 167.
115. Gould, *Diary of a Contraband*, 184–185.
116. Gould, *Diary of a Contraband*, 33–37.
117. Gould, *Diary of a Contraband*, 149.
118. Adams, *Narrative of the Life of John Quincy Adams*.

CHAPTER 3: REALIZING ABOLITION

1. Robert Douglass to Abby Kelley Foster, May 12, 1846, Folder 22: Letters, 1846, May–November, Abby Kelley Foster Papers, Manuscripts, American Antiquarian Society. On Robert Douglass Jr., see Aston Gonzalez, "The Art of Racial Politics: The Work of Robert Douglass Jr., 1833–46," *Pennsylvania Magazine of History and Biography* 138, no. 1 (January 2014): 5–37.

2. On interracial friendships, see John Stauffer, *The Black Hearts of Men: Radical Abolitionists and the Transformation of Race* (Cambridge, MA: Harvard University Press, 2001). On abolitionism and religion, see Robert H. Abzug, *Cosmos Crumbling: American Reform and the Religious Imagination* (New York: Oxford University Press, 1994). On letter-writing, see Lawrence J. Friedman, *Gregarious Saints: Self and Community in American Abolitionism, 1830–1870* (Cambridge: Cambridge University Press, 1982), 51–54. More broadly, the best starting place on abolitionism is Manisha Sinha, *The Slave's Cause: A History of Abolition* (New Haven, CT: Yale University Press, 2016).

3. In this vein, scholars have focused on how photography helped Sojourner Truth and Frederick Douglass to forge their public identities. See Nell Irvin Painter, *Sojourner Truth: A Life, a Symbol* (New York: W. W. Norton, 1996); Augusta Rohrbach, "Profits of Protest: The Market Strategies of Sojourner Truth and Louisa May Alcott," in *Prophets of Protest: Reconsidering the History of American Abolitionism*, ed. Timothy McCarthy and John Stauffer (New York: New Press, 2006); Stauffer, *The Black Hearts of Men*; Teresa Zackodnik, "The 'Green-Backs of Civilization': Sojourner

Truth and Portrait Photography," *American Studies* 46, no. 2 (Summer 2005): 117–143; Darcy Grimaldo Grigsby, "Negative-Positive Truths," *Representations* 113, no. 1 (Winter 2011): 16–38; Darcy Grimaldo Grigsby, *Enduring Truths: Sojourner's Shadows and Substance* (Chicago: University of Chicago Press, 2015); John Stauffer, Zoe Trodd, and Celeste-Marie Bernier, eds., *Picturing Frederick Douglass: An Illustrated Biography of the Nineteenth Century's Most Photographed American* (New York: W. W. Norton, 2015); Marcy J. Dinius, "Seeing Ourselves as Others See Us: Frederick Douglass's Reflections on Daguerreotypy and Racial Difference," in *Photography and Its Origins*, ed. Tanya Sheehan and Andres Mario Zervigon (New York: Routledge, 2015), 118–128; and Maurice O. Wallace and Shawn Michelle Smith, eds., *Pictures and Progress: Early Photography and the Making of African American Identity* (Durham, NC: Duke University Press, 2012).

4. Phillip Lapsansky, "Graphic Discord: Abolitionist and Anti-abolitionist Images," in *The Abolitionist Sisterhood: Women's Political Culture in Antebellum America*, ed. Jean Fagin Yellin and John C. Van Horne (Ithaca, NY: Cornell University Press, 1994); Jean Fagan Yellin, *Women and Sisters: The Antislavery Feminists in American Culture* (New Haven, CT: Yale University Press, 1989); Jo-Ann Morgan, *Uncle Tom's Cabin as Visual Culture* (Columbia: University of Missouri Press, 2007); Maurie D. McInnis, *Slaves Waiting for Sale: Abolitionist Art and the American Slave Trade* (Chicago: University of Chicago Press, 2011); Marcus Wood, *Blind Memory: Visual Representations of Slavery in England and America, 1780–1865* (New York: Routledge, 2000); Marcus Wood, *The Horrible Gift of Freedom: Atlantic Slavery and the Representation of Emancipation* (Athens: University of Georgia, 2010); Marcus Wood, *Black Milk: Imagining Slavery in the Visual Cultures of Brazil and America* (Oxford: Oxford University Press, 2013); Mary Niall Mitchell, "'The Real Ida May: A Fugitive Tale in the Archives," *Massachusetts Historical Review* 15 (2013): 54–88; Bernard F. Reilly Jr., "The Art of the Antislavery Movement," in *Courage and Conscience: White and Black Abolitionists in Boston*, ed. Donald M. Jacobs (Bloomington: Indiana University Press, 1993). On popular representations of free black people, see Jasmine Nichole Cobb, *Picture Freedom: Remaking Black Visuality in the Early Nineteenth Century* (New York: New York University Press, 2015). On the role of moral suasion and public opinion in the abolitionist movement, see Aileen S. Kraditor, *Means and Ends in American Abolitionism: Garrison and His Critics on Strategy and Tactics, 1834–1850* (New York: Pantheon Books, 1967); James Brewer Stewart, "Peaceful Hopes and Violent Experiences: The Evolution of Reforming and Radical Abolitionism, 1831–1837," *Civil War History* 17, no. 4 (December 1971): 293–309; Carleton Mabee, *Black Freedom: The Nonviolent Abolitionists from 1830 to the Civil War* (New York: Macmillan, 1970); Timothy Patrick McCarthy and John Stauffer, eds., *Prophets of Protest: Reconsidering the History of American Abolitionism* (New York: New Press, 2006). Patrick Rael

discusses black leaders' interest in shaping public sentiment in his *Black Identity and Black Protest in the Antebellum North* (Chapel Hill: University of North Carolina Press, 2002).

5. Karen Halttunen, "Humanitarianism and the Pornography of Pain in Anglo-American Culture," *American Historical Review* 100, no. 2 (April 1995): 303–334; Elizabeth B. Clark, "'The Sacred Rights of the Weak': Pain, Sympathy, and the Culture of Individual Rights in Antebellum America," *Journal of American History* 82, no. 2 (September 1995): 463–493.

6. Paul Goodman, *Of One Blood: Abolitionism and the Origins of Racial Equality* (Berkeley: University of California Press, 1998); Stephen Kantrowitz, *More than Freedom: Fighting for Black Citizenship in a White Republic, 1829–1889* (New York: Penguin, 2012); Martha S. Jones, *All Bound Up Together: The Woman Question in African-American Public Culture, 1830–1900* (Chapel Hill: University of North Carolina Press, 2007); Ronald G. Walters, *The Antislavery Appeal: American Abolitionism After 1830* (New York: W. W. Norton, 1978), ch. 2.

7. The relation between photographs of pain, empathy, and political engagement continues to interest scholars of visual culture. Susan Sontag has inspired much of this work in her theoretical books about the capacity of photography to spur empathy and voyeurism, a process by which spectatorship has come to constitute a form of political engagement in the modern world. See Susan Sontag, *On Photography* (New York: Farrar, Straus and Giroux, 1973); Susan Sontag, *Regarding the Pain of Others* (New York: Picador, 2003); and Sharon Sliwinski, *Human Rights in Camera* (Chicago: University of Chicago Press, 2011).

8. Kantrowitz, *More than Freedom*, 51. On abolitionists of the early republic, and the transition to the 1830s, see Richard S. Newman, *Fighting Slavery in the Early Republic: The Transformation of American Abolitionism* (Chapel Hill: University of North Carolina Press, 2001).

9. Goodman, *Of One Blood*, 66.

10. On Garrison's shift, see Goodman, *Of One Blood*, ch. 4; Kantrowitz, *More than Freedom*, 52–53.

11. Invented in the 1790s in Europe, lithography grew influential in America in the late 1820s and 1830s, as various firms emerged, particularly in Boston (Pendleton), New York (Imbert, Mesier, and Currier), Philadelphia (Pendleton, Kearney, and Childs), Hartford (Kellogg), and Baltimore (Weber). Jay T. Last, *The Color Explosion: Nineteenth-Century American Lithography* (Santa Ana, CA: Hillcrest Press, 2005), 17.

12. Lapsansky, "Graphic Discord," 202.

13. On "imagined communities" forged through print culture, see Benedict Anderson, *Imagined Communities: Reflections on the Origin and Spread of Nationalism*, rev. ed. (Verso: London, 2006).

14. George W. Prescott to Bracket L. Prescott, December 10, 1835, Helen M. Blount Prescott Papers, #1509, Southern Historical Collection, Wilson Library, University of North Carolina at Chapel Hill.

15. Daniel Walker Howe, *What Hath God Wrought: The Transformation of America, 1815–1848* (New York: Oxford University Press, 2007), 427–430. On the postal campaign, see also Bertram Wyatt-Brown, "The Abolitionists' Postal Campaign of 1835," *Journal of Negro History* 50, no. 4 (October 1965): 227–238. On the industrialization of antebellum printing, see Ronald J. Zboray, "Antebellum Reading and the Ironies of Technological Innovation," *American Quarterly* 40, no. 1 (March 1988): 65–82.

16. The punishment for circulating images was up to ten years in prison. V. E. Howard and A. Hutchinson, comps., *The Statutes of the State of Mississippi* (New Orleans: E. Johns, 1840), 672, 720. For context on conflicts over image circulation in the 1830s, see Camp, *Closer to Freedom*, 99–104.

17. Angelina Emily Grimké, *Appeal to the Christian Women of the South* (New York: Arno Press, 1969), 32.

18. On this notion of "spectatorial sympathy," see Halttunen, "Humanitarianism and the Pornography of Pain in Anglo-American Culture."

19. On the iconography of the kneeling slave, see Savage, *Standing Soldiers, Kneeling Slaves*.

20. Grimké, *Appeal to the Christian Women of the South*, 23.

21. Theodore Dwight Weld to Angelina Grimké Weld, December 15, 1837, Box 4, Weld-Grimké Papers, William L. Clements Library, University of Michigan.

22. James Oakes, *Freedom National: The Destruction of Slavery in the United States, 1861–1865* (New York: W. W. Norton, 2013), 14.

23. L.M.C., "The Ladies' Fair," *Liberator*, January 2, 1837, 3.

24. Floyd Rinhart and Marion Rinhart, *The American Daguerreotype* (Athens: University of Georgia Press, 1981), 91.

25. Peter Bacon Hales, *Silver Cities: Photographing American Urbanization, 1839–1939*, rev. ed. (Albuquerque: University of New Mexico Press, 2005), 15–16.

26. For the frontispiece, see William Craft, *Running a Thousand Miles for Freedom; or, The Escape of William and Ellen Craft from Slavery* (1860), Documenting the American South, University Library, University of North Carolina at Chapel Hill, http://docsouth.unc.edu/neh/craft/craft.html.

27. Richard J. Powell, "Cinque: Antislavery Portraiture and Patronage in Jacksonian America," *American Art* 11, no. 3 (Autumn 1997): 71.

28. Frederick Douglass advertised the Goodridge brothers' business as early as 1848. *The North Star*, December 15, 1848. On the Goodridge brothers, see John Vincent Jezierski, *Enterprising Images: The Goodridge Brothers, African American Photographers 1847–1922* (Detroit, MI: Wayne State University Press, 2000).

29. The passage of the Fugitive Slave Act, however, led Washington to emigrate to Liberia in the early 1850s. Marcy Dinius, *The Camera and the*

Press: American Visual and Print Culture in the Age of the Daguerreotype (Philadelphia: University of Pennsylvania Press, 2012), ch. 5.

30. Deborah Willis, *Reflections in Black: A History of Black Photographers 1840 to the Present* (New York: W. W. Norton, 2000), 7; and Deborah Willis, *J. P. Ball: Daguerrean and Studio Photographer* (New York: Garland, 1993).

31. *Liberator*, February 4, 1848.

32. Harriet Beecher Stowe, *Uncle Tom's Cabin or, Life Among the Lowly* (New York: Penguin Books, 1982), 68.

33. Dr. John Theophilus Kramer, "The Slave Auction," *Liberator*, September 16, 1859.

34. Alan Trachtenberg, "Photography: The Emergence of a Keyword," in *Photography in Nineteenth-Century America*, ed. Martha A. Sandweiss (Fort Worth, TX: Amon Carter Museum, 1991), 17.

35. "Morals of Society in the 'Old Dominion,' " *Liberator*, January 7, 1853, 1.

36. *Frederick Douglass' Paper*, February 24, 1854, 3.

37. The most famous example is British artist Eyre Crowe and his images of the slave trade in 1850s Richmond. See McInnis, *Slaves Waiting for Sale*.

38. In Walker's narrative, he only briefly mentioned a discussion with a few of the fugitives before they departed. He "had an interview" with them and indicated he would "share the risk with them." Jonathan Walker, *Trial and Imprisonment of Jonathan Walker, at Pensacola, Florida, for Aiding Slaves to Escape from Bondage: With an Appendix Containing a Sketch of His Life* (Boston: Anti-Slavery Office, 1845), 10.

39. In lectures, Walker showed his actual hand and scars to the crowd. Martin A. Berger, "White Suffering and the Branded Hand," Mirror of Race, http://www.mirrorofrace.org/show_interp.php?photo_id=18, accessed December 13, 2017.

40. "The Twelfth National Anti-Slavery Bazaar," *Liberator*, January 23, 1846.

41. Berger, "White Suffering and the Branded Hand."

42. Berger, "White Suffering and the Branded Hand."

43. Philip Hone, *The Diary of Philip Hone, 1828–1851*, ed. Bayard Tuckerman (New York: Dodd, Mead, 1889), 1:391.

44. Samuel Morse, "The Daguerrotipe," *New York Observer*, April 20, 1839, 62.

45. Lois E. Horton, "Kidnapping and Resistance: Antislavery Direct Action in the 1850s," in *Passages to Freedom: The Underground Railroad in History and Memory*, ed. David W. Blight (Washington, DC: Smithsonian Books, 2004), 166–167.

46. William Wells Brown, *Narrative of William W. Brown, a Fugitive Slave* (1847), Documenting the American South, University Library, University of North Carolina at Chapel Hill, http://docsouth.unc.edu/neh/brown47/menu.html.

47. John Brown and Louis Alexis Chamerovzow, *Slave Life in Georgia: A Narrative of the Life, Sufferings, and Escape of John Brown, a Fugitive Slave, Now in England* (1855), Documenting the American South, University Library, University of North Carolina at Chapel Hill, http://docsouth.unc.edu/neh/jbrown/menu.html.

48. This speech was reported in Dublin's *Evening Packet and Correspondent*. Frederick Douglass, "Irish Christians and Non-Fellowship with Man-Stealers: An Address Delivered in Dublin, Ireland, on 1 October 1845," in *The Frederick Douglass Papers: Series One: Speeches, Debates, and Interviews*, vol. 1: *1841–1846*, ed. John Blassingame (New Haven, CT: Yale University Press, 1979), 36. See also Sinha, *The Slave's Cause*, 425.

49. Quoted in Timothy Patrick McCarthy, "A Culture of Dissent: American Abolitionism and the Ordeal of Equality," PhD dissertation, Columbia University, 2006, 263.

50. "The Twelfth National Anti-Slavery Bazaar," *Liberator*, January 23, 1846.

51. "The Branded Hand," *Chicago Daily Tribune*, August 2, 1878, 1.

52. Mazie M. Harris, *Paper Promises: Early American Photography* (Los Angeles: J. Paul Getty Museum, 2018); Jenkins, *Images and Enterprise*, 39–40.

53. For other prints based upon daguerreotypes, see the lithograph of Anthony Burns. John Andrews, engraver, *Anthony Burns*, one print on wove paper: wood engraving with letterpress, c. 1855, Library of Congress Prints and Photographs Online Catalog, http://www.loc.gov/pictures/item/2003689280.

54. Frederick Douglass, review of *A Tribute for the Negro*, *North Star*, April 7, 1849, 2.

55. Douglass, review of *A Tribute for the Negro*.

56. Rael, *Black Identity and Black Protest in the Antebellum North*, ch. 5.

57. Rael, *Black Identity and Black Protest in the Antebellum North*, 163; Lapsansky, "Graphic Discord," 217–220. On Clay, especially his 1839 series *Practical Amalgamation*, see also Elise Lemire, *"Miscegenation": Making Race in America* (Philadelphia: University of Pennsylvania Press, 2002), ch. 4.

58. Stauffer, Trodd, and Bernier, eds., *Picturing Frederick Douglass*.

59. On scientific racism, works include George W. Frederickson, *The Black Image in the White Mind: The Debate on Afro-American Character and Destiny, 1817–1914* (New York: Harper & Row, 1971), especially ch. 3; on visual culture and scientific racism in particular, see Charles Colbert, *A Measure of Perfection: Phrenology and the Fine Arts in America* (Chapel Hill: University of North Carolina Press, 1997), ch. 6.

60. Stauffer, Trodd, and Bernier, eds., *Picturing Frederick Douglass*, part I.

61. Douglass, review of *A Tribute for the Negro*.

62. Stauffer, Trodd, and Bernier, eds., *Picturing Frederick Douglass*, xxv–xxvi, 16.

63. Painter, *Sojourner Truth*, ch. 20.

64. Elmira was a key site in the broader patchwork of escape networks and was linked to networks of escape in Pennsylvania and the activities of Philadelphia activist William Still. For more on Jones's biography and Elmira, see Tendai Mutunhu, "John W. Jones: Underground Railroad Station-Master," *Negro History Bulletin*, March 1, 1978, 41, 2.

65. As Joan Severa notes, the "wideawake" was a popular 1850s style. Severa, *Dressed for the Photographer*, 121.

66. Brown, *Slave Life in Georgia.*
67. Brown, *Slave Life in Georgia.*
68. On free blacks in antebellum America, see Leon F. Litwack, *North of Slavery: The Negro in the Free States, 1790–1860* (Chicago: University of Chicago Press, 1961); and James Oliver Horton, *Free People of Color: Inside the African American Community* (Washington, DC: Smithsonian Institution Press, 1993).
69. There were, of course, exceptions. Mary Niall Mitchell offers a fascinating discussion of the photograph of Ida May, an image that led many northerners to feel they were looking at slavery. Mitchell, "The Real Ida May."
70. The daguerreotype is reproduced and described in the *Friends' Intelligencer and Journal* in an 1896 article. The article offered biographies of each of the members and noted that William Still presently held the original image. "An Anti-Slavery Group of 1850," *Friends' Intelligencer and Journal* LIII, no. 43, October 24, 1896, 732–735, Friends Historical Library of Swarthmore College, SW09-A0011499, http://triptych.brynmawr.edu/cdm/ref/collection/HC_QuakSlav/id/11520.
71. Ronald M. Gifford II, "George Thompson and Trans-Atlantic Antislavery, 1831–1865," PhD dissertation, Indiana University, 1999, 77.
72. Gonzalez, "The Art of Racial Politics," 12.
73. On the frontispieces of Equiano and Wheatley, see Wood, *Black Milk*, 109–116.
74. "A Priceless Picture," *Philadelphia Inquirer*, December 26, 1889.
75. Gifford, "George Thompson and Trans-Atlantic Antislavery," 284.
76. William Farmer, "Attacks of Frederick Douglass and John Scoble upon George Thompson, Esq., M.P.," *Liberator*, January 2, 1852, 4.
77. Stauffer, *Black Hearts of Men*, 62–65. Such photo albums were points of pride for many activists. Black Garrisonian William Cooper Nell took great satisfaction in his personal collection, remarking to white abolitionist Amy Kirby Post, "My sister Louisa is now again pleasantly situated as a house-keeper = I dined with her and the two on last Sunday = My handsome Book and all my collection of Daguerreotypes they consider an attraction on the Centre table and Mantel piece." *William Cooper Nell: Selected Writings 1832–1874*, ed. Dorothy Porter Wesley and Constance Porter Uzelac (Baltimore: Black Classic Press, 2002), 352.
78. "An Anti-Slavery Group of 1850."
79. Frederick Douglass, "Lecture on Pictures," 7, Frederick Douglass Papers, Manuscripts, Library of Congress.
80. Email from Mary Ellen Sweeney, Susan B. Anthony House, January 18, 2013.
81. James Brewer Stewart, *Holy Warriors: The Abolitionists and American Slavery* (New York: Hill and Wang, 1996), 72–73. On anti-abolitionism, see also Emma Jones Lapsansky, "'Since They Got Those Separate Churches': Afro-Americans and Racism in Jacksonian Philadelphia," *American Quarterly* 32 (1980); David Grimsted, "Rioting in Its Jacksonian Setting," *American Historical Review* 77, no. 2 (April 1972): 361–397.

82. "Convention of Fanatics at Cazenovia," *Buffalo Morning Express*, August 28, 1850, 4.

83. Hugh C. Humphreys, "Agitate! Agitate! Agitate! The Great Cazenovia Fugitive Slave Law Convention and its Rare Daguerreotype," *Madison County Heritage* 19 (1994): 36.

84. Lydia Maria Child to Francis Jackson, May 13, 1858, Special Collections, Loose Mss. Child, Massachusetts Historical Society.

85. Aaron M. Powell, *Personal Reminiscences of the Anti-Slavery and Other Reforms and Reformers* (New York: Caulon Press, 1899), 163.

86. On reform and language, see Walters, *The Antislavery Appeal*, 21.

87. The photographic archive shows how many social and political organizations defined themselves through early photography. See, for instance, the daguerreotype of a group of Christian socialists from Cambridge, MA, and an 1850 daguerreotype of Democratic and Free Soil Party members in Massachusetts. "The Christian Socialists," quarter-plate daguerreotype by unknown photographer, ca. 1860, Photo 1.309, Photo Archives, Massachusetts Historical Society; "Members of the Massachusetts Democratic and Free Soil Parties," whole plate daguerreotype by Josiah Johnson Hawes, 1852, Photo 1.358L, Photo Archives, Massachusetts Historical Society.

88. Stewart, *Holy Warriors*, 124.

89. Stanley W. Campbell, *The Slave Catchers: Enforcement of the Fugitive Slave Law, 1850–1860* (Chapel Hill: University of North Carolina Press, 1968), 51–52.

90. Frederick Douglass, "The Fugitive Slave Law," August 11, 1852, in *The Life and Writings of Frederick Douglass*, vol. II, *Pre-Civil War Decade, 1850–1860*, ed. Philip S. Foner (New York: International Publishers), 207.

91. Horton, "Kidnapping and Resistance," 166.

92. Horton, "Kidnapping and Resistance"; Jane H. Pease and William H. Pease, "Confrontation and Abolition in the 1850s," *Journal of American History* 58, no. 4 (March 1972): 923–937.

93. "Circular from the Chaplin Fund Committee," *North Star*, September 5, 1850. Concerning the Cazenovia daguerreotype, some of the material in this chapter was originally published as Matthew Fox-Amato, "An Abolitionist Daguerreotype, New York, 1850," in *Getting the Picture: The Visual Culture of the News*, ed. Jason Hill and Vanessa R. Schwartz (London: Bloomsbury, 2015).

94. "A Letter to the American Slaves from Those Who Have Fled from American Slavery," *North Star*, September 5, 1850, 3.

95. Stauffer, *Black Hearts of Men*, 164; "An Affray—The Arrest of William Chaplin," *National Era*, August 15, 1850; Humphreys, "Agitate!," 11. On Chaplin, see also Friedman, *Gregarious Saints*, 97–101.

96. "A Letter to the American Slaves from Those Who Have Fled from American Slavery."

97. "Convention of Slaves at Cazenovia," *North Star*, September 5, 1850.

98. *Liberator*, September 6, 1850.

99. Stauffer, *Black Hearts of Men*, 163–165.
100. Humphreys, "Agitate!," 18, 25.
101. Humphreys, "Agitate!," 26. Chaplin would not leave jail until December 1850. "Convention of Slaves at Cazenovia," *North Star*, September 5, 1850; "William L. Chaplin," *National Era*, December 26, 1850.
102. "Senator Sumner to Passmore Williamson," *Frederick Douglass' Paper*, August 31, 1855. For context on Williamson, see Pamela C. Powell, "The Case of Passmore Williamson," in *The Daguerreian Annual 2000* (Pittsburgh: Daguerreian Society, 2000).
103. Mary Grew to Passmore Williamson, September 13, 1855, Passmore Williamson Prison Visitors' Book, Chester County Historical Society Library, West Chester, PA.
104. James Oliver Horton, "A Crusade for Freedom: William Still and the Real Underground Railroad," in *Passages to Freedom: The Underground Railroad in History and Memory*, ed. David W. Blight (Washington, DC: Smithsonian Books, 2004), 186–187; Powell, "The Case of Passmore Williamson," 131–133.
105. Horton, "Kidnapping and Resistance," 171. See also Sinha, *The Slave's Cause*, 523–527.
106. John Doy, *The Narrative of John Doy of Lawrence, Kansas: "A Plain Unvarnished Tale"* (New York, 1860), Gale, Cengage Learning. University of Southern California Libraries.
107. *National Era* republished reports from the St. Louis *Democrat*. See "Rescue of Dr. Doy—Particulars," *National Era*, August 4, 1859. DaLee, originally from New York State, had received photography instruction in San Francisco during the mid-1850s before returning east and starting a daguerreotype gallery in Lawrence, Kansas, in 1858. Little is known about the photographer's politics, though the very fact that he took the image of Doy suggests at the very least a measure of sympathy for antislavery proponents. On DaLee, see Peter E. Palmquist and Thomas R. Kailbourn, *Pioneer Photographers of the Far West: A Biographical Dictionary, 1840–1865* (Stanford, CA: Stanford University Press, 2000), 192–193.
108. "A Letter to the American Slaves from Those Who Have Fled from American Slavery."
109. "Fourth Anniversary of the Jerry Rescue," *Frederick Douglass' Paper*, August 24, 1855.
110. Hazel Catherine Wolf, *On Freedom's Altar: The Martyr Complex in the Abolition Movement* (Madison: University of Wisconsin Press, 1952), 62.
111. Lewis Tappan to Passmore Williamson, November 5, 1855, Passmore Williamson Prison Visitors' Book, Chester County Historical Society Library, West Chester, PA.
112. Emil Luders, *Passmore Williamson, in Moyamensing Prison for Alleged Contempt of Court*, lithograph on watercolor, c. 1855, Library of Congress Prints and Photographs Online Catalog, http://www.loc.gov/pictures/item/2003689277.

113. "The Wellington Rescuers," *Frank Leslie's Illustrated Newspaper*, May 7, 1859.
114. Doy, *The Narrative of John Doy of Lawrence, Kansas*.
115. Joshua Brown, *Beyond the Lines: Pictorial Reporting, Everyday Life, and the Crisis of Gilded Age America* (Berkeley: University of California Press, 2002), 46–58.
116. "Portrait of John Brown," *Liberator*, December 9, 1859.
117. For Hyatt's biography, see the finding aid to the Thaddeus Hyatt Papers, 1843–1898, http://www.kshs.org/p/thaddeus-hyatt-papers-1843 -1898/14047.
118. "Aid for the Family of John Brown," *Liberator*, November 25, 1859.
119. *Liberator*, November 25, 1859. By the summer of 1860, Hyatt had profited $2,600. See "Distribution of John Brown Fund," *Douglass' Monthly*, October 1860.
120. For coverage of John Brown, see *Frank Leslie's Illustrated Newspaper*, October 29, November 5, 12, 19, 26, and December 10, 17, 1859. John Stauffer, "The 'Terrible Reality' of the First Living-Room Wars," in *War/Photography: Images of Armed Conflict and Its Aftermath*, ed. Anne Wilkes Tucker, Will Michels, and Natalie Zelt (New Haven, CT: Yale University Press, 2012), 84.
121. R. Blakeslee Gilpin, *John Brown Still Lives! America's Long Reckoning with Violence, Equality, and Change* (Chapel Hill: University of North Carolina Press, 2011), 14, 43.
122. "Tribute of Respect, Commemorative of the Worth and Service of John Brown, of Osawatomie," *Liberator*, January 27, 1860, 2.
123. Lydia Maria Child to Thaddeus Hyatt, November 17, 1859, *The Collected Correspondence of Lydia Maria Child*, 1817–1880, microfiche series, ed. Patricia G. Holland and Milton Meltzer.
124. *Frank Leslie's Illustrated Newspaper*, December 10, December 17, November 19, 1859.
125. Stewart, *Holy Warriors*, 72–73.
126. *The Pro-Slavery Riot on November 7, 1837. Death of Rev. E. P. Lovejoy*, wood engraving, Missouri History Museum.
127. For a discussion of the publicity that surrounded abolitionist martyrs, see Gara, *The Liberty Line*, 134–150.
128. On images of poverty—including the 1890s New York tenement scenes of Jacob Riis and the 1930s rural photographs of the Farm Securities Administration artists and Walker Evans—see, for starters, Bonnie Yochelson and Daniel Czitrom, *Rediscovering Jacob Riis: Exposure Journalism and Photography in Turn-of-the-Century New York* (New York: New Press, 2007), and William Stott, *Documentary Expression and Thirties America* (Chicago: University of Chicago Press, 1986). On images of atrocity, see Jay Prosser, Geoffrey Batchen, Mick Gidley, and Nancy K. Miller, eds., *Picturing Atrocity: Photography in Crisis* (London: Reaktion Books, 2012).

129. David W. Blight, ed., *Passages to Freedom: The Underground Railroad in History and Memory* (Washington: Smithsonian Books, 2004), 3.

130. For scholarship on the Underground Railroad, see Blight, ed., *Passages to Freedom*; Catherine Clinton, *Harriet Tubman: The Road to Freedom* (New York: Back Bay Books, 2004); Keith P. Griffler, *Front Line of Freedom: African Americans and the Forging of the Underground Railroad in the Ohio Valley* (Lexington: University Press of Kentucky, 2004); Gara, *The Liberty Line*; Scott Hancock, "Crossing Freedom's Fault Line: The Underground Railroad and Recentering African Americans in Civil War Causation," *Civil War History* 59, no. 2 (June 2013): 169–205; Graham Russell Gao Hodges, *David Ruggles: A Radical Black Abolitionist and the Underground Railroad in New York City* (Chapel Hill: University of North Carolina Press, 2010); Nikki M. Taylor, *Frontiers of Freedom: Cincinnati's Black Community, 1802–1868* (Athens: Ohio University Press, 2005), ch. 7; R. J. M. Blackett, *Making Freedom: The Underground Railroad and the Politics of Slavery* (Chapel Hill: University of North Carolina Press, 2013); and Eric Foner, *Gateway to Freedom: The Hidden History of the Underground Railroad* (New York: W. W. Norton, 2015).

131. Clinton, *Harriet Tubman*, 64.

132. J. H. Tibbets to Elizabeth Nicholson, 1884, Box 2, Folder 2, Theodore L. Steele Papers, M0263, Indiana Historical Society, Indianapolis.

133. For more on Still and the new Vigilance Committee's use of newspapers and lectures to publicize their work, see Elizabeth Varon, "'Beautiful Providences': William Still, the Vigilance Committee, and Abolitionists in the Age of Sectionalism," in *Antislavery and Abolition in Philadelphia: Emancipation and the Long Struggle for Racial Justice in the City of Brotherly Love*, ed. Richard Newman and James Mueller (Baton Rouge: Louisiana State University Press, 2011).

134. William Still, *The Underground Railroad* (Philadelphia: Porter & Coates, 1871).

135. Still, *The Underground Railroad*.

136. The Philadelphia Vigilance Committee does not appear to have publicized these photographs in the antebellum era; in his postbellum book, William Still published illustrations of Galloway and Green, perhaps based upon their antebellum images.

137. Clinton, *Harriet Tubman*, 64.

138. Ben had escaped, a fact the paper attributed to Ben's experience in the courts, where he "must have heard many declarations of the principles; of abstract human rights, even in a Georgia court; and as he probably never read, the Dred Scott decision, he seems to have applied these principles to his own case." "A Judge in a Fix," *Douglass' Monthly*, August 1860.

139. The Fugitive Slave Law was not struck down until June 28, 1864. Campbell, *The Slave Catchers*, 194.

140. Levi Coffin, *Reminiscences of Levi Coffin, the Reputed President of the Underground Railroad; Being a Brief History of the Labors of a Lifetime in Be Half of the Slave, with the Stories of Numerous Fugitives, Who Gained Their Freedom Through His Instrumentality, and Many Other Incidents* (London [1876]), 606–608.

141. Taft, *Photography and the American Scene*, 23, 98–99, 164–165.

142. Rinhart and Rinhart, *The American Daguerreotype*, 104, 263–267.

143. Katherine C. Grier, *Cultures and Comfort: People, Parlors, and Upholstery, 1850–1930* (Rochester: Strong Museum, 1988), ch. 1.

144. J. B. Rogers, *War Pictures: Experiences and Observations of a Chaplain in the U.S. Army in the War of the Southern Rebellion* (Chicago: Church & Goodman, 1863), 129.

145. "Anniversary of West India Emancipation," *Liberator*, August 5, 1859.

146. "Anniversary of West India Emancipation."

147. On lantern slide lectures, see James R. Ryan, "On Visual Instruction," in *The Nineteenth-Century Visual Culture Reader*, ed. Vanessa R. Schwartz and Jeannene M. Przyblyski (New York: Routledge, 2004).

148. Sunday, July 5, 1857, in Charlotte Forten Grimké, *The Journals of Charlotte Forten Grimké*, ed. Brenda Stevenson (New York: Oxford University Press, 1988), 235.

149. Photography was a distinctly emotional form of social movement glue. As Ronald G. Walters wrote decades ago, "To conceive of antislavery factions as ideologically defined is also to miss the nonrational elements in abolitionism, including its intense emotional hold. It had a power, an urgency that has never been satisfactorily explained and cannot be in terms of ideas alone." Ronald G. Walters, "The Boundaries of Abolitionism," in *Antislavery Reconsidered: New Perspectives on the Abolitionists*, ed. Lewis Perry and Michael Fellman (Baton Rouge: Louisiana State University Press, 1979), 16.

150. "Charge of Theft and Abetting Slaves to Runaway," *Louisville Courier*, August 17, 1858, 1. My thanks to Tom Calarco for pointing me toward this citation.

151. "The Underground Railroad," *New York Daily Times*, January 28, 1856, 6; Still, *The Underground Railroad*.

152. Clinton, *Harriet Tubman*, 76–77.

153. Still, *The Underground Railroad*.

154. David S. Cecelski, *The Fire of Freedom: Abraham Galloway and the Slaves' Civil War* (Chapel Hill: University of North Carolina Press, 2012), 22–24.

155. William Wells Brown, *The Rising Sun; Or, the Antecedents and Advancement of the Colored Race* (Boston: A. G. Brown, 1874; reprint, Miami: Mnemosyne, 1969), 537.

156. "A Kidnapper and a Runaway Arrested," *Louisville Daily Journal*, May 9, 1860, 3. My thanks to Richard Blackett for pointing out this citation. Blackett writes about the incident in his *Making Freedom*, 74–75.

157. I take the term "guerrilla tactic" from Keith P. Griffler, who uses it in his *Front Line of Freedom*.

158. Clinton, *Harriet Tubman*, 74.
159. Sinha, *The Slave's Cause*, 439.
160. "Harriet Tubman," *Commonwealth*, July 17, 1863, 1. Though the author called Tubman's images daguerreotypes, it is likely that Tubman was traveling with tintypes or cartes de visite by 1863, as these lighter-weight formats would have been easier to transport.
161. Photo historians have argued that photographic identification bolstered state-sponsored surveillance in the nineteenth century, but Tubman shows how this application of the technology could just as easily aid the efforts of those who subverted southern masters and national laws. John Tagg, *The Burden of Representation: Essays on Photographies and Histories* (Minneapolis: University of Minnesota Press, 1993).

CHAPTER 4: DOMESTICATING FREEDOM

1. Henry Grimes Marshall to Hattie, Suffolk, Virginia, April 6, 1863 (assn M: 1222), William L. Clements Library, University of Michigan. For more on Marshall's biography, see Finding Aid for Henry Grimes Marshall Papers, 1861–1865, William L. Clements Library, University of Michigan, https:// quod.lib.umich.edu/c/clementsmss/umich-wcl-M-1222mar?rgn=Entire+F inding+Aid;view=text;q1=henry+grimes+marshall.
2. Walter Dinmore to Cook, January 11, 1861, George Smith Cook Collection, Manuscript Division, Library of Congress; Edwin Mayall for Thomas Faris to Cook, January 28, 1861, George S. and Huestis P. Cook Papers, The Valentine.
3. James McPherson, *Battle Cry of Freedom: The Civil War Era* (New York: Oxford University Press, 1988), 264–265.
4. McPherson, *Battle Cry of Freedom*, 254.
5. Webster and Brothers to Cook, March 18, 1861, George S. and Huestis P. Cook Papers. M. Harvey of Philadelphia also asked for a portrait from Cook in late February 1861. See M. Harvey to Cook, February 22, 1861, George S. and Huestis P. Cook Papers.
6. Bob Zeller, *The Blue and Gray in Black and White: A History of Civil War Photography* (London: Praeger, 2005), 31–35.
7. Quoted in Zeller, *The Blue and Gray in Black and White*, 33.
8. Zeller, *The Blue and Gray in Black and White*, 44.
9. "Interior of Fort Sumter," *Charleston Mercury*, April 16, 1861, 2.
10. *Charleston Mercury*, May 6, 1861.
11. McPherson, *Battle Cry of Freedom*, 279–282.
12. *Charleston Daily Courier*, April 16, 1861, 1.
13. On ruins and the Civil War, see Megan Kate Nelson, *Ruin Nation: Destruction and the American Civil War* (Athens: University of Georgia Press, 2012). On how photography shaped the geographical imagination in the nineteenth century, see Joan M. Schwartz and James R. Ryan, eds., *Picturing Place: Photography and the Geographical Imagination* (London: I. B. Tauris, 2003).

14. Alexander H. Stephens, "Cornerstone Address," in *Southern Pamphlets on Secession, November 1860–April 1861*, ed. Jon L. Wakelyn (Chapel Hill: University of North Carolina Press, 1996), 406, 403.

15. *Macon Daily Telegraph*, May 20 1861, 3.

16. For a similar visual composition, see the carte de visite of a Confederate captain and a young black boy, made by Macon, Georgia, photographer A. J. Riddle, in Zeller, *The Blue and Gray in Black and White*, 38.

17. John Wallace Comer, November 16, 1864, Comer Family Papers #167-z, Southern Historical Collection, Wilson Library, University of North Carolina at Chapel Hill.

18. John Wallace Comer to "My Dear Mother + Relatives," June 14, 1864. In another letter, likely to Comer's mother, Comer requested to be sent "my Pipe + Tobacco Pouch on Tuesday. Give them to Burrell." See John Wallace Comer, November 16, 1864, Comer Family Papers.

19. John Wallace Comer to "My Dear Mother + Relatives," June 14, 1864, Comer Family Papers.

20. Kate Stone, *Brokenburn: The Journal of Kate Stone, 1861–1865*, ed. John Q. Anderson (Baton Rouge: Louisiana State University Press, 1955), 175.

21. Stone, *Brokenburn*, 193.

22. Pompey and Dan were slaves of Joe and Willy Carson's family; Kate Stone and her family were close friends of the Carson family, originally from Louisiana, which also took refuge in Texas during the war. Stone, *Brokenburn*, 287.

23. McPherson, *Battle Cry of Freedom*, 274.

24. McPherson, *Battle Cry of Freedom*, 313–314.

25. Receipt from January 19, 1861, from Garrigues & Magee, George Smith Cook Collection.

26. See Account Book, August 1860–December 1861, George S. and Huestis P. Cook Papers.

27. Joseph T. Zealy to George Smith Cook, April 20, 1861, George Smith Cook Collection.

28. Harvey Teal, *Partners with the Sun: South Carolina Photographers, 1840–1940* (Columbia: University of South Carolina Press, 2001), 85, 120.

29. Editorial, *American Journal of Photography*, September 16, 1863.

30. "Editorial Miscellany," *American Journal of Photography*, October 15, 1861, 240.

31. "Day Breaking," *Humphrey's Journal*, February 15, 1862, 320.

32. Editorial, *American Journal of Photography*, April 15, 1865, 479.

33. Editorial, *American Journal of Photography*, September 16, 1863.

34. "Our Art in Rebeldom—The Latest News from Dixie," *American Journal of Photography*, May 1, 1864, 507.

35. "Photography in Charleston," *Charleston Mercury*, October 31, 1860.

36. *Charleston Mercury*, May 6, 1861.

37. For more on this incident, see Matthew Fox-Amato, "Plantation Tourism," in Mazie M. Harris, *Paper Promises: Early American Photography* (Los Angeles: J. Paul Getty Museum, 2018).

38. On Douglass's lectures about photography, see John Stauffer, Zoe Trodd, and Celeste-Marie Bernier, eds., *Picturing Frederick Douglass: An Illustrated Biography of the Nineteenth Century's Most Photographed American* (New York: W. W. Norton, 2015), part IV; Laura Wexler, "'A More Perfect Likeness': Frederick Douglass and the Image of the Nation" and Ginger Hill, "'Rightly Viewed': Theorizations of Self in Frederick Douglass's Lectures on Pictures," in *Pictures and Progress: Early Photography and the Making of African American Identity*, ed. Maurice O. Wallace and Shawn Michelle Smith (Durham, NC: Duke University Press, 2012).

39. Frederick Douglass, "Lecture on Pictures," December 3, 1861, in *Picturing Frederick Douglass*, ed. Stauffer, Trodd, and Bernier, 127, 132.

40. "The Cruelties of Slavery," *National Anti-Slavery Standard*, July 4, 1863, 2.

41. "A Typical Negro," *Harper's Weekly*, July 4, 1863.

42. An article in the *New-York Daily Tribune* testified to this version of the story. See "The Realities of Slavery: 'Poor Peter,'" *New-York Daily Tribune*, December 3, 1864, 4. David Silkenat has done important work in raising questions about the story in *Harper's Weekly*. He suggests that in the *Harper's Weekly* triptych published on July 4, the subject in the left image was Gordon, the subject in the middle image was Peter, and the image on the right-hand side was fabricated. David Silkenat, "'A Typical Negro': Gordon, Peter, Vincent Colyer, and the Story Behind Slavery's Most Famous Photograph," *American Nineteenth Century History* 15, no. 2 (2014): 169–186.

43. The *Harper's Weekly* story detailed how McPherson and Oliver, two southern photographers who began catering to Union troops after the fall of New Orleans, took the photographs. David Silkenat, however, suggests that we might reconsider this claim, highlighting how the *Scourged Back* cartes de visite lacked the photographers' insignia, which was a common practice at the time. Silkenat, "'A Typical Negro,'" 171.

44. On medical photography, see Alan Trachtenberg, *Reading American Photographs: Images as History, Mathew Brady to Walker Evans* (New York: Hill and Wang, 1989), 116–118.

45. "The Dumb Witness," *Liberator*, June 12, 1863. Another surgeon stressed how he had "found a large number of four hundred contrabands examined by me to be as badly lacerated as the specimen presented in the enclosed photograph." Quoted in Louis P. Masur, "'Pictures Have Now Become a Necessity': The Use of Images in American History Textbooks," *Journal of American History* 84, no. 4 (March 1998): 1418. Photo historian Kathleen Collins cites a third surgeon, S. K. Towle, of the 30th Regiment, Massachusetts Volunteers. See Kathleen Collins, "The Scourged Back," *History of Photography* 9, no. 1 (1985): 43–45.

46. David Silkenat has shown that the fugitive sat for at least three different images of similar composition. The version published in this book easily became the most widely circulated carte de visite. Silkenat as well as Bruce Laurie argue that the man posed on at least two different occasions to create the three images. See Silkenat, "'A Typical Negro,'" 172, and

Bruce Laurie, "'Chaotic Freedom' in Civil War Louisiana: The Origins of an Iconic Image," *Massachusetts Review* 2, no. 1 (November 2016).

47. "The Scourged Back," *New York Independent*, May 28, 1863.

48. "The Dumb Witness," *Liberator*, June 12, 1863.

49. Margaret Abruzzo, *Polemical Pain: Slavery, Cruelty, and the Rise of Humanitarianism* (Baltimore: Johns Hopkins University Press, 2011).

50. As the *Liberator* maintained, months after "the martyrdom was undergone, and the wounds here healed, but as long as the flesh lasts will this fearful impress remain." "The Dumb Witness," *Liberator*, June 12, 1863.

51. "The Scourged Back," *New York Independent*, May 28, 1863, 4.

52. "The Scourged Back," *New York Independent*, May 28, 1863, 4.

53. On photographic icons, see Robert Hariman and John Louis Lucaites, *No Caption Needed: Iconic Photographs, Public Culture, and Liberal Democracy* (Chicago: University of Chicago Press, 2007).

54. "The 'Peculiar Institution' Illustrated," *The National Anti-Slavery Standard*, June 20, 1863, 3. Notably, southerners contested the narratives, but not the photograph's authenticity. In late July 1863, an article in the *Southern Illustrated News* leveled its attack on the *Harper's* account. It quoted the narrative attached to the *Harper's* triptych, which described slave torture—floggings, burnings, burying slaves and dropping ashes on them—on the estate of Mrs. Gillespie on the Black River. As the paper noted, "A more palpable falsehood was never published in any Yankee paper." Southerners would allow the photograph but protest its representativeness. "A Typical Negro," *Southern Illustrated News*, July 25, 1863. Thank you to Joshua Brown for alerting me to this source.

55. "The Dumb Witness," *The Liberator*, June 12, 1863.

56. "The Scourged Back," *New York Independent*, May 28, 1863, 4.

57. "The Scourged Back," *New York Independent*, May 28, 1863, 4.

58. "The Scourged Back," *New York Independent*, May 28, 1863, 4.

59. "The Scourged Back," *New York Independent*, May 28, 1863, 4.

60. "The Realities of Slavery: 'Poor Peter,'" *New-York Daily Tribune*, December 3, 1864, 4.

61. Abolitionists and Republicans began to push for a national amendment to abolish slavery—the Thirteenth Amendment, which failed the first time, in April 1864. Many abolitionists supported Lincoln's presidential campaign in the fall of 1864, tying his victory to emancipation. Eric Foner, *The Fiery Trial: Abraham Lincoln and American Slavery* (New York: W.W. Norton, 2010), 294, 300.

62. Foner, *Fiery Trial*, 241–242.

63. "The New England Anti-Slavery Convention," *National Anti-Slavery Standard*, June 13, 1863, 2.

64. Nell Irvin Painter, *Sojourner Truth: A Life, a Symbol* (New York: W. W. Norton, 1996), 187.

65. He also revealed how he used it as propaganda to stem British support of the Confederacy. According to the *Liberator*, Thompson told one American

lecture audience that, in Britain, "immense placards were displayed in the principal towns and cities calling public attention to the meetings held on American affairs, and comprehensively unfolding the successive deceits of the secessionists." *The Liberator*, February 19, 1864.

66. For discussions of the cartes de visite of the white-looking children, see Mary Niall Mitchell, *Raising Freedom's Child: Black Children and Visions of the Future After Slavery* (New York: New York University Press, 2008), and Kathleen Collins, "Portraits of Slave Children," *History of Photography* 9, no. 3 (1985): 187–210.

67. "The Dumb Witness," *Liberator*, June 12, 1863.

68. "The 'Peculiar Institution' Illustrated," *National Anti-Slavery Standard*, June 20, 1863, 3.

69. "The Scarred Back," *New York Independent*, August 13, 1863, 4.

70. "The 'Scarred Back' Photograph," *National Antislavery Standard*, July 25, 1863, 3.

71. "White and Colored Slaves," *Harper's Weekly*, January 30, 1864.

72. "Mostly About a Slave's Back," *National Antislavery Standard*, August 22, 1863, 4.

73. On the consecration of images, see David Freedberg, *The Power of Images: Studies in the History and Theory of Response* (Chicago: University of Chicago Press, 1989), 89.

74. Cornelia Hancock, *Letters of a Civil War Nurse, Cornelia Hancock, 1863–1865*, ed. Henrietta Stratton Jaquette (Lincoln: University of Nebraska Press, 1998), 32.

75. Another reason these images might not have been seriously studied is because of a long-standing scholarly emphasis on postwar photo books such as Gardner's 1866 *Sketch Book*. Anthony Lee and Elizabeth Young discuss Gardner's *Sketch Book* images of African Americans, but not the broader photographic landscape. See Anthony W. Lee and Elizabeth Young, *On Alexander Gardner's* Photographic Sketch Book of the Civil War (Berkeley: University of California Press, 2007).

76. See, for instance, the experience of George E. Stephens, who was a free black man from the North who served as a Union cook. Eric Foner, *Forever Free: The Story of Emancipation and Reconstruction* (New York: Alfred A. Knopf, 2005), 43.

77. Trachtenberg, *Reading American Photographs*, ch. 2; Keith F. Davis, "'A Terrible Distinctness': Photography of the Civil War Era," in *Photography in Nineteenth-Century America*, ed. Martha A. Sandweiss (Fort Worth, TX: Amon Carter Museum, 1991); William A. Frassanito, *Antietam: The Photographic Legacy of America's Bloodiest Day* (New York: Charles Scribner's Sons, 1978); Mary Panzer, *Mathew Brady and the Image of History* (Washington, DC: Smithsonian Books, 1997); Lee and Young, *On Alexander Gardner's* Photographic Sketch Book of the Civil War; Zeller, *The Blue and Gray in Black and White*; Keith F. Davis, *George N. Barnard: Photographer of Sherman's Campaign* (Kansas City, MO: Hallmark Cards,

1990); Keith Davis, *The Origins of American Photography: From Daguerreotype to Dry-Plate, 1839–1865* (Kansas City, MO: Hall Family Foundation and Nelson-Atkins Museum of Art, 2007); J. Matthew Gallman and Gary W. Gallagher, eds., *Lens of War: Exploring Iconic Photographs of the Civil War* (Athens: University of Georgia Press, 2015); Jeff L. Rosenheim, *Photography and the American Civil War* (New York: Metropolitan Museum of Art, 2013); John Stauffer, "The 'Terrible Reality' of the First Living-Room Wars," in *War/Photography: Images of Armed Conflict and Its Aftermath*, ed. Anne Wilkes Tucker, Will Michels, and Natalie Zelt (New Haven, CT: Yale University Press, 2012); Mark Dunkleman and Michael Winey, "Precious Shadows: The Importance of Photographs to Civil War Soldiers," *Military Images* 16, no. 1 (July–August 1994): 6–13. On the visual culture of the Civil War more broadly, see Steven Conn, "Narrative Trauma and Civil War History Painting, or Why Are These Pictures So Terrible?" *History and Theory* 41, no. 4 (December 2002): 17–42; William F. Thompson, *The Image of War: The Pictorial Reporting of the American Civil War* (Baton Rouge: Louisiana State University Press, 1994); Joshua Brown, *Beyond the Lines: Pictorial Reporting, Everyday Life, and the Crisis of Gilded Age America* (Berkeley: University of California Press, 2002), 46–57; and Alice Fahs, *The Imagined Civil War: Popular Literature of the North and South, 1861–1865* (Chapel Hill: University of North Carolina Press, 2001).

78. On the total number of photographers, see Davis, *The Origins of American Photography*, 173. On statistics for the Army of the Potomac, see Davis, "'A Terrible Distinctness,'" 144.

79. Davis, "'A Terrible Distinctness,'" 133.

80. Frassanito, *Antietam*, 17.

81. Dunkleman and Winey, "Precious Shadows," 6–13.

82. John P. Reynolds Journal, 43, James S. Schoff Civil War Collection, William L. Clements Library, University of Michigan.

83. Because of its close proximity to the heavy concentration of northern photographers in the Northeast and mid-Atlantic, the eastern seaboard—particularly Maryland, Virginia, and Union-controlled areas of South Carolina and Georgia—received more visual coverage than the Upper South and the Mississippi Valley, at least when it came to mass-produced views sold by major photographic firms. It was relatively easy for artists stationed in Washington, D.C., the home of Alexander Gardner's firm, to travel to Virginia, or for artists from the Northeast to take a steamer to South Carolina. But geography had little influence on the availability of portraits, as local artists in all regions catered to the two armies.

84. Quoted in W. Jeffrey Bolster and Hilary Anderson, *Soldiers, Sailors, Slaves, and Ships: The Civil War Photographs of Henry P. Moore* (Concord: New Hampshire Historical Society, 1999), 15.

85. Henry Rogers Smith to parents and sister, January 17, 1862, and Henry Rogers Smith to "Dear Sister," February 2, 1862, Henry Rogers Smith Papers, Folders 1–2, Manuscripts, American Antiquarian Society.

86. Henry Rogers Smith to "Father Mother Sister and all," February 16, 1862, Folder 2, Henry Rogers Smith Papers.

87. Martha A. Sandweiss, *Print the Legend: Photography and the American West* (New Haven, CT: Yale University Press, 2002), 224–225.

88. William F. Thompson, *The Image of War: The Pictorial Reporting of the American Civil War* (Baton Rouge: Louisiana State University Press, 1989), 30.

89. *John P. Reynolds Civil War Reminiscences, ca. 1897*, 2:17, Manuscripts, Massachusetts Historical Society.

90. Steven Hahn, "But What Did the Slaves Think of Lincoln?" in *Lincoln's Proclamation: Emancipation Reconsidered*, ed. William A. Blair and Karen Fisher Younger (Chapel Hill: University of North Carolina Press, 2009). Other works that deal with slaves' wartime experiences include Steven Hahn, *A Nation Under Our Feet: Black Political Struggles in the Rural South from Slavery to the Great Migration* (Cambridge, MA: Belknap Press of Harvard University Press, 2003); Armstead L. Robinson, *Bitter Fruits of Bondage: The Demise of Slavery and the Collapse of the Confederacy, 1861–1865* (Charlottesville: University of Virginia Press, 2005); Thavolia Glymph, "Rose's War and the Gendered Politics of a Slave Insurgency in the Civil War," *Journal of the Civil War Era* 3, no. 4 (December 2013): 501–532; Stephanie McCurry, *Confederate Reckoning: Power and Politics in the Civil War South* (Cambridge, MA: Harvard University Press, 2010); Bruce Levine, *The Fall of the House of Dixie: The Civil War and the Social Revolution That Transformed the South* (New York: Random House, 2013); James Oakes, *Freedom National: The Destruction of Slavery in the United States, 1861–1865* (New York: W. W. Norton, 2013); Ira Berlin, Barbara J. Fields, Steven F. Miller, Joseph P. Reidy, and Leslie S. Rowland, *Slaves No More: Three Essays on Emancipation and the Civil War* (Cambridge: Cambridge University Press, 1992); Leslie A. Schwalm, *A Hard Fight for We: Women's Transition from Slavery to Freedom in South Carolina* (Urbana: University of Illinois Press, 1997); Jim Downs, *Sick from Freedom: African American Illness and Suffering During the Civil War and Reconstruction* (New York: Oxford University Press, 2012); Cam Walker, "Corinth: The Story of a Contraband Camp," *Civil War History* 20, no. 1 (March 1974): 5–22; Susan Eva O'Donovan, *Becoming Free in the Cotton South* (Cambridge, MA: Harvard University Press, 2007); Louis S. Gerteis, *From Contraband to Freedman: Federal Policy Toward Southern Blacks, 1861–1865* (Westport, CT: Greenwood Press, Inc., 1973); Chandra Manning, "Working for Citizenship in Civil War Contraband Camps," *Journal of the Civil War Era* 4, no. 2 (June 2014): 172–204; Chandra Manning, *Troubled Refuge: Struggling for Freedom in the Civil War* (New York: Alfred A. Knopf, 2016).

91. Foner, *The Fiery Trial*, 167.

92. Oakes, *Freedom National*, 89.

93. Henry Rogers Smith to "Father Mother Sister and all," February 16, 1862, Folder 2, Henry Rogers Smith Papers.

94. McCurry, *Confederate Reckoning*, 8.

95. *Harper's Weekly*, August 17, 1861.

96. Foner, *Fiery Trial*, 175.

97. Foner, *Fiery Trial*, 215.

98. Chandra Manning, *What This Cruel War Was Over: Soldiers, Slavery, and the Civil War* (New York: Vintage Books, 2007), 49.

99. Entry for February 10, 1863, in Cyrus F. Boyd, *The Civil War Diary of Cyrus F. Boyd, Fifteenth Iowa Infantry, 1861–1863*, ed. Mildred Throne (Millwood, NY: Kraus Reprint, 1977), 121.

100. Entry for June 17, 1862, in Rufus Kinsley, *Diary of a Christian Soldier: Rufus Kinsley and the Civil War*, ed. David C. Rankin (Cambridge: Cambridge University Press, 2004), 98.

101. Quoted in Manning, *What This Cruel War Was Over*, 45.

102. Ira Berlin, Joseph P. Reidy, and Leslie S. Rowland, *Freedom's Soldiers: The Black Military Experience in the Civil War* (Cambridge: Cambridge University Press, 1998), 87; Leon Litwack, *Been in the Storm So Long: The Aftermath of Slavery* (New York: Vintage Books, 1979), 97–98.

103. Kate Masur, "'A Rare Phenomenon of Philological Vegetation': The Word 'Contraband' and the Meanings of Emancipation in the United States," *Journal of American History* 93, no. 4 (March 2007): 1056, 1059–1060.

104. William Cullen Bryant II, "A Yankee Soldier Looks at the Negro," *Civil War History* 7, no. 2 (June 1961): 147.

105. Masur, "'A Rare Phenomenon of Philological Vegetation,'" 1064–1065; Litwack, *Been in the Storm So Long*, 133; Manning, *Troubled Refuge*, chs. 1–2.

106. *Facts Concerning the Freedmen: Their Capacity and Their Destiny* (Boston, 1863), 9, Gale, Cengage Learning, Washington University, http://galenet.galegroup.com.libproxy.wustl.edu/servlet/Sabin?af=RN&ae=CY1079251 35&srchtp=a&ste=14.

107. Manning, *What This Cruel War Was Over*, 92.

108. Manning, *What This Cruel War Was Over*, 92–93.

109. Downs, *Sick from Freedom*, 36.

110. Historian Chandra Manning has done important work in scouring the private letters and diaries of soldiers to illuminate their perceptions of slavery and emancipation. Studying the photographs of soldiers extends this attention to non-elites during wartime. See Manning, *What This Cruel War Was Over*.

111. Letter from Joseph Emery Fiske, January, 1863, *War Letters of Capt. Joseph E. Fiske, Harvard '61: Written to His Parents During the War of Rebellion from Andover Theological Seminary and Encampments in North Carolina and from Southern Prison* (Wellesley, MA: Maugus Press, 1900), 22.

112. Finding Aid, Charles F. Tew Papers, William L. Clements Library, University of Michigan.

113. Charles F. Tew to "My Dear Wife + Children," March 27, 1862, Charles F. Tew Papers, William L. Clements Library, University of Michigan.

114. Charles F. Tew to "My Dear Wife and family," June 15, 1862, Charles F. Tew Papers.

115. Lawrence N. Powell, *New Masters: Northern Planters During the Civil War and Reconstruction* (New Haven, CT: Yale University Press, 1980), 24–30.

116. Charles F. Tew to wife and family, August 5, 1864, Charles F. Tew Papers.

117. Charles F. Tew to wife and family, August 15, 1864, Charles F. Tew Papers.

118. Lt. Henry Crydenwise, 73rd U.S. Colored Troops, to Parents and all, December 22, 1863, Bayou Boeuf, LA, Henry Crydenwise Papers, Stuart A. Rose Manuscript, Archives, and Rare Books Library, Woodruff Library, Emory University.

119. William King, *Diary of William King* (1864), Documenting the American South, University Library, University of North Carolina at Chapel Hill, http://docsouth.unc.edu/imls/kingwilliam/king.html.

120. Frank Pettit to Parents, Brothers & Sisters, Newport News, Virginia, Thursday, March 12, 1863, Letters of Frederick Pettit, 1862–1864, Civil War Times Illustrated Collection, U.S. Army Heritage and Education Center, Carlisle, PA.

121. Charles Cooper Nott, *The Coming Contraband: A Reason Against the Emancipation Proclamation, Not Given by Mr. Justice Curtis, to Whom It Is Addressed, by an Officer in the Field* (New York: G. P. Putnam, 1862), 2.

122. Senex, "Contraband," *Christian Recorder*, August 9, 1862, 126.

123. "The Great Speech: Frederick Douglass on the War," *Christian Recorder*, January 18, 1862, 10–11.

124. "A Night with the New Jersey Cavalry," *Harper's Weekly*, May 9, 1863.

125. Henry Rogers Smith to brother, February 7, 1862, Henry Rogers Smith Papers.

126. Letter from Joseph Emery Fiske, December 8, 1862, *War Letters of Capt. Joseph E. Fiske, Harvard '61: Written to His Parents During the War of Rebellion from Andover Theological Seminary and Encampments in North Carolina and from Southern Prison* (Wellesley, MA: Maugus Press, 1900), 18.

127. Powell, *New Masters*, 24–30.

128. Nelson, *Ruin Nation*, 121–135.

129. Tew to wife, July 25, 1863, Charles F. Tew Papers.

130. Entry for January 8, 1864, *Passages from the Life of Henry Warren Howe: Consisting of Diary and Letters Written During the Civil War, 1861–1865* (Lowell, MA: Courier-Citizen, 1899), 59.

131. Eric Lott, *Love and Theft: Blackface Minstrelsy and the American Working Class* (New York: Oxford University Press, 1993).

132. Bryant, "A Yankee Soldier Looks at the Negro," 136.

133. *Passages from the Life of Henry Warren Howe*, 93. See also Litwack, *Been in the Storm So Long*, 128.

134. Henry Bibb, *Narrative of the Life and Adventures of Henry Bibb, an American Slave, Written by Himself* (1849), Documenting the American South, University Library, University of North Carolina at Chapel Hill, http://docsouth.unc.edu/neh/bibb/bibb.html.

135. Alexander Gardner likely sold *Beaufort, South Carolina*. "Our Mess," titled as *Our Mess at Beaufort, S.C.*, as a stereograph and carte de visite.

Alexander Gardner, *Catalogue of Photographic Incidents of the War from the Gallery of Alexander Gardner* (Washington, DC: H. Polkinhorn, 1863), 11.

136. John Eaton Jr. to Levi Coffin, July 5, 1864, in Joseph Warren, *Extracts from Reports of Superintendents of Freedmen*, 2nd ser. (Vicksburg, MS: Freedmen Press Print, 1864), 52.

137. Rufus Saxton et al., "The Freedmen of Georgia," *Freedmen's Record*, February 1865, 26.

138. Gardner, *Catalogue of Photographic Incidents of the War*.

139. Alexander Gardner, *Gardner's Photographic Sketch Book of the Civil War* (New York: Dover Publications, 1959).

140. Lee and Young, *On Alexander Gardner's* Photographic Sketch Book of the Civil War, 80.

141. Gardner, *Catalogue of Photographic Incidents of the War*.

142. Quoted in Litwack, *Been in the Storm So Long*, 131.

143. Charles F. Tew to "My Wife and Children," December 14, 1863, Charles F. Tew Papers.

144. Berlin et al., *Slaves No More*, 46.

145. Gardner, *Catalogue of Photographic Incidents of the War*.

146. "Contrabands Coming In," *Harper's Weekly*, January 31, 1863.

147. Fahs, *The Imagined Civil War*, 163–165; *Heroes in Ebony—The Captors of the Rebel Steamer Planter, Robert Small, W. Morrison, A. Gradine and John Small*, one print: wood engraving, 1862, Library of Congress Prints and Photographs Online Catalog, http://www.loc.gov/pictures/item/99403228; *Robert Smalls, Captain of the Gun-boat "Planter"*; *The Gun-boat "Planter," Run out of Charleston, S.C., by Robert Smalls, May 1862*, two prints: wood engraving, 1862, Library of Congress Prints and Photographs Online Catalog, http://www.loc.gov/pictures/item/97512451.

148. Fahs, *The Imagined Civil War*, 163–169.

149. On this transition, see Fahs, *The Imagined Civil War*, ch. 5.

150. Deborah Willis and Barbara Krauthamer, *Envisioning Emancipation: Black Americans and the End of Slavery* (Philadelphia: Temple University Press, 2013), 59–127.

151. *Colored Army Teamsters, Cobb Hill, Virginia*, one photographic print, 1864, Library of Congress Prints and Photographs Online Catalog, Gladstone Collection of African American Photographs, http://www.loc.gov/pictures/item/2010651606; Willis and Krauthamer, *Envisioning Emancipation*, 100.

152. *Petersburg, Virginia. Gen. Edward Ferrero and Staff*, one negative: glass, wet collodion, September 1864, Library of Congress Prints and Photographs Online Catalog, http://www.loc.gov/pictures/item/cwp2003006269/PP.

153. James Gibson, *Contrabands on Mr. Foller's Farm, Cumberland, May 14, 1862*, one photographic print on stereo card: albumen, hand colored, Library of Congress Prints and Photographs Online Catalog, http://www.loc.gov/pictures/item/2011646155.

154. Ronald S. Coddington, *African American Faces of the Civil War: An Album* (Baltimore: Johns Hopkins University Press, 2012), 50, 44, 72, 144, 198.

On photographic portraits of United States Colored Troops, see J. Matthew Gallman, "Snapshots: Images of Men in the United States Colored Troops," in *American Nineteenth Century History* 13, no. 2 (June 2012): 127–151.

155. Coddington, *African American Faces of the Civil War*, 31–34.
156. Crydenwise to Parents and all, December 22, 1863.
157. Bartlett Yancey Malone, *The Diary of Bartlett Yancey Malone* (1919), Documenting the American South, University Library, University of North Carolina at Chapel Hill, http://docsouth.unc.edu/fpn/malone/malone.html.
158. Davis, *George N. Barnard*, 48; *Weekly Vincennes Gazette*, December 24, 1864.
159. Davis, "'A Terrible Distinctness': Photography of the Civil War Era," 137.
160. Laura Schiavo, "'A Collection of Endless Extent and Beauty': Stereographs, Vision, Taste and the American Middle Class, 1850–1880," PhD dissertation, George Washington University, 2003, 157–159; David Jaffee, "Anthony's *Broadway on a Rainy Day*," *Common-Place* 10, no. 4 (2010).
161. Oliver Wendell Holmes, "The Stereoscope and the Stereograph," *Atlantic*, June 1859.
162. This image was likely taken in 1861, as Geary's letters reveal that he was stationed only miles away from Harpers Ferry (in Sandy Hook, Maryland, and Point of Rocks, Maryland) from the summer to winter of 1861. John White Geary, *A Politician Goes to War: The Civil War Letters of John White Geary*, ed. William Alan Blair (University Park: Pennsylvania State University Press, 1995), 1–33, 85, 150, 187, 221.
163. Charles F. Tew to wife and family, August 15, 1864, Charles F. Tew Papers.

EPILOGUE: THE PHOTOGRAPHIC LEGACY OF
AMERICAN SLAVERY

1. On ruins, see Megan Kate Nelson, *Ruin Nation: Destruction and the American Civil War* (Athens: University of Georgia Press, 2012).
2. For biographical information on John Oliver, see James Brewer Stewart, *Wendell Phillips: Liberty's Hero* (Baton Rouge: Louisiana State University Press, 1986), 274.
3. Oliver noted it was the unnamed wife of Henry Abrams. John Oliver to Wendell Phillips, July 6, 1866, Series II, Wendell Phillips Papers, 1555–1882 (MS Am 1953), Houghton Library, Harvard University. In his autobiography, former slave Peter Randolph described a similar incident in which the back of a former slave was photographed after a former master had whipped and burned her. See Peter Randolph, *From Slave Cabin to the Pulpit: The Autobiography of Rev. Peter Randolph: The Southern Question Illustrated and Sketches of Slave Life* (1893), Documenting the American South, University Library, University of North Carolina at Chapel Hill, http://docsouth.unc.edu/neh/randolph/randolph.html.

4. "A Cruel Punishment," *Harper's Weekly*, July 28, 1866.
5. Francis Jackson Garrison, "A Catalogue of Portraits of American Abolitionists and of Their Allies and Opponents in the United States and in Great Britain and Ireland, 1831–1865," Box 1, "Portraits of American Abolitionists, 1850-1890," Photo Coll. 81, Massachusetts Historical Society.
6. Garrison, "A Catalogue of Portraits of American Abolitionists."
7. Steven J. Ross, *Working Class Hollywood: Silent Film and the Shaping of Class in America* (Princeton, NJ: Princeton University Press, 1998); Cara Caddoo, *Envisioning Freedom: Cinema and the Building of Modern Black Life* (Cambridge, MA: Harvard University Press, 2014).
8. Leigh Raiford, *Imprisoned in a Luminous Glare: Photography and the African American Freedom Struggle* (Chapel Hill: University of North Carolina Press, 2011).
9. On the memory of the Civil War and slavery, see, for starters, David Blight, *Race and Reunion: The Civil War in American Memory* (Cambridge, MA: Belknap Press of Harvard University Press, 2001).
10. For statistics on Gowrie, see William Dusinberre, *Them Dark Days: Slavery in the American Rice Swamps* (New York: Oxford University Press, 1996), 50–52, 76.
11. Louis Manigault Family Record Book, Vol. II, Louis Manigault Papers, 177.01.01.02, South Carolina Historical Society.
12. Stephanie McCurry, *Confederate Reckoning: Power and Politics in the Civil War South* (Cambridge, MA: Harvard University Press, 2010), 233–238.
13. Mrs. Irby Morgan, *How It Was: Four Years Among the Rebels* (1892), Documenting the American South, University Library, University of North Carolina at Chapel Hill, http://docsouth.unc.edu/fpn/morgan/morgan.html.
14. Harriet Pindar married twice—first to Joseph Mooney of Ringgold, Georgia, on December 6, 1855, in Savannah, then to Dr. William Woods in Savannah on January 20, 1864. It is unclear whether she received the enslaved people for her first or second marriage. Harriet's mother, Ann Margaret Tebeau Pinder, died on May 23, 1864, four months after Harriet married a second time. Harriet Pindar's name also sometimes appears as Pinder in the documentary record. For genealogical information on Harriet Pindar and Ann Margaret Tebeau Pinder, see F. Claiborne Johnston Jr., *The Pinder/Ellett Families of Virginia and Georgia and Allied Families (Pinder, Tebeau, Treutlen, Ellett, Spears, Womack, Sublett, Cheatham, Smith, Trabue) with Some Accounts of the Pinder/Pindar Family Trail in the Bahama Islands, Bermuda and Barbados* (Richmond: F. C. Johnston, 1988), Main Collection, Georgia Historical Society. I am grateful to the Georgia Historical Society for confirming the lack of a definitive spelling for Pinder/Pindar. Georgia Historical Society Research Center Staff, email to author, August 23, 2017.
15. Walter Johnson, *River of Dark Dreams: Slavery and Empire in the Cotton Kingdom* (Cambridge, MA: Belknap Press of Harvard University Press, 2013), 192.

16. One finds similar evidence in the descriptions attached to other cased photographs. For instance, the photograph of Rosetta in Chapter 1 has the following note attached in the Gibbes Museum collections: "Rosetta or 'Mama' as she was called—Belonged to Mrs. Paul FitzSimons, then to her daughter Mrs. J. Motte Alston, my Grandmother—From Jennie C. Calvert my cousin—To be given to the Carolina Art Association—Charleston, SC." Caption to *Rosetta*, Unknown Artist, n.d.; Ambrotype; 2 ½ × 2 inches (image), 3 11/16 × 3 3/16 inches (case); XX1978.002; image courtesy of the Gibbes Museum of Art/Carolina Art Association.

17. Mary Pringle, for instance, described a family picture taken in 1868 that included Cretia, a former slave. Mary Pringle to Susan Pringle, May 6, 1868, Box 28, Alston-Pringle-Frost Papers, Manuscripts, South Carolina Historical Society; see also the postwar nursemaid photograph in Mr. and Mrs. L. P. Ray, *Twice Sold, Twice Ransomed: Autobiography of Mr. and Mrs. L. P. Ray* (1926), Documenting the American South, University Library, University of North Carolina at Chapel Hill, http://docsouth.unc.edu/neh/rayemma/rayemma.html; Sadai Burge Gray, *Little Sadai: Journal of Miss Sadai C. Burge, 1874* (Atlanta: Keelin Press, 1952), 55; Laura Wexler, *Tender Violence: Domestic Visions in an Age of U.S. Imperialism* (Chapel Hill: University of North Carolina Press, 2000), ch. 2.

18. *Life of Maumer Juno of Charleston, S.C.: A Sketch of Juno (Waller) Seymour* (Atlanta: Foote & Davies, 1892), 8.

19. *Life of Maumer Juno*, 15.

20. Quoted in James Allen, Hilton Als, John Lewis, and Leon F. Litwack, *Without Sanctuary: Lynching Photography in America* (Santa Fe, NM: Twin Palms, 2000), 11.

21. Shawn Michelle Smith, *Photography on the Color Line: W. E. B. Du Bois, Race, and Visual Culture* (Durham, NC: Duke University Press, 2004), 121.

22. Smith, *Photography on the Color Line*, 127.

23. It should be noted that Jerome Dowd, the researcher, saw art as what he called a "civilizing influence" for African Americans, whom he clearly viewed as racially inferior. As he wrote, "If they had more opportunities to gratify their love for art they would drink less liquor, commit less crime, and in many ways become better citizens." See Jerome Dowd, "Art in Negro Homes," *Southern Workman* 30, no. 1 (January 1901): 90–95.

24. Heather Andrea Williams, *Help Me to Find My People: The African American Search for Family Lost in Slavery* (Chapel Hill: University of North Carolina Press, 2012), 155.

25. Before ex-slave John Roy Lynch became a Mississippi congressman, he worked from 1866 to 1869 in Natchez, Mississippi, photography studios. Meanwhile, former slave James C. Farley began working in a chemical department in Richmond before becoming an operator for G. W. Davis in 1875; Farley's photographs were shown at the 1884 Colored Industrial Fair in Richmond and at the 1885 World Exposition in New Orleans. On Lynch, see John Stauffer, "Interspatialism in the Nineteenth-Century

South: The Natchez of Henry Norman," *Slavery and Abolition* 29, no. 2 (June 2008): 258; and John Roy Lynch, *Reminiscences of an Active Life: The Autobiography of John Roy Lynch*, ed. John Hope Franklin (Chicago: University of Chicago Press, 1970; reprint, University Press of Mississippi, 2008), 40–41. On Farley, see Rev. William J. Simmons, *Men of Mark: Eminent, Progressive and Rising* (1887), Documenting the American South, University Library, University of North Carolina at Chapel Hill, http:// docsouth.unc.edu/neh/simmons/simmons.html.

26. Print Box 1, African Americans, Miscellaneous Subjects Image Collection (P0003), North Carolina Collection Photographic Archives, Wilson Library, University of North Carolina at Chapel Hill; Mary Everhard Collection, Amon Carter Museum of American Art, www.cartermuseum.org/imu/acm/ #browse=enarratives.4433.

27. Ronald S. Coddington, *African American Faces of the Civil War: An Album* (Baltimore: Johns Hopkins University Press, 2012), 198.

28. Elizabeth Merwin Wickham, *A Lost Family Found: An Authentic Narrative of Cyrus Branch and His Family, Alias John White* (1869), Documenting the American South, University Library, University of North Carolina at Chapel Hill, http://docsouth.unc.edu/neh/wickham/wickham.html.

29. *Life of Maumer Juno*, 20.

30. Crowe (Milburn J.), Photograph Album PI/2005.0015, Courtesy of the Mississippi Department of Archives and History.

31. Ida B. Wells, "A Red Record," in *Southern Horrors and Other Writings: The Anti-Lynching Campaign of Ida B. Wells, 1892–1900*, ed. Jacqueline Jones Royster (Boston: Bedford Books, 1997), 104, 118.

32. Michael Bieze, *Booker T. Washington and the Art of Self-Representation* (New York: Peter Lang, 2008).

33. Smith, *Photography on the Color Line*.

BIBLIOGRAPHY

MANUSCRIPT COLLECTIONS
American Antiquarian Society
Abby Kelley Foster Papers
Henry Rogers Smith Papers

Baker Library, Harvard Business School
R. G. Dun & Co. Credit Report Volumes
Scovill Manufacturing Company Records

Briscoe Center for American History, University of Texas at Austin
Richard Thompson Archer Family Papers, 1790–1919

Chester County Historical Society Library, West Chester, PA
Passmore Williamson Prison Visitors' Book

David M. Rubenstein Rare Book and Manuscript Library, Duke University
John Knight Papers
Louis Manigault Papers

Georgia Historical Society
Telfair Family Papers

Houghton Library, Harvard University
Wendell Phillips Papers

Indiana Historical Society
Theodore L. Steele Papers

Library of Congress Manuscript Collections
Frederick Douglass Papers
George Smith Cook Collection
WPA Slave Narrative Project, Federal Writers' Project, U.S. Work Projects
    Administration

Louisiana Research Collection, Tulane University
Charles Colcock Jones Papers

*Louisiana and Special Collections Department, Earl K. Long Library, University of
New Orleans*
Marcus Christian Collection

Manuscript, Archives, and Rare Book Library, Emory University
Burge Family Papers

Henry Crydenwise Papers
Pindar Family Papers, 1800–1979

Maryland Historical Society
Douglass Hamilton Thomas Manuscript Collection

Massachusetts Historical Society
Special Collections, Loose Mss., Child

South Carolina Historical Society
Alston-Pringle-Frost Papers
Louis Manigault Papers
Margaret Ann Morris Grimball Family Papers

South Caroliniana Library, University of South Carolina
Charles Izard Manigault Papers
Manigault Family Papers
Zelotus Lee Holmes Papers

Southern Historical Collection, Wilson Library, University of North Carolina at Chapel Hill
Comer Family Papers
Helen M. Blount Prescott Papers
N. Russell Middleton Papers

Special Collections Research Center, Swem Library, College of William and Mary
Austin-Twyman Papers

University of Virginia Library, University of Virginia
Ellis Family Daguerreotypes
Isaac Jefferson Memoirs and Daguerreotype, Tracy M. McGregor Library
Minor Family Papers, 1838–1944
Papers of Various Lynchburg, VA Families

The Valentine, Richmond, VA
George S. and Huestis P. Cook Papers

Virginia Historical Society
Cogbill Family Papers, 1852–1889
Cogbill Family Bible Records, 1812–1977

William L. Clements Library, University of Michigan
Charles F. Tew Papers
Hancock Papers
Handy Family Papers
Henry Grimes Marshall Papers
Weld-Grimké Papers

W. S. Hoole Special Collections Library, University of Alabama
Thomas Hubbard Hobbs Diaries
William P. Abrams Diaries

NEWSPAPERS
The Alabama Whig
American Journal of Photography
Baltimore American
Buffalo Morning Express
The Charleston Daily Courier
The Charleston Mercury
Chicago Daily Tribune
The Commonwealth
The Corsair
The Christian Recorder
The Daily Picayune
Douglass' Monthly
Frank Leslie's Illustrated Newspaper
The Freedmen's Record
Frederick Douglass' Paper
Harper's Weekly
Humphrey's Journal
The Liberator
Louisville Courier
Louisville Daily Journal
The Macon Daily Telegraph
Montgomery Weekly Mail
National Anti-Slavery Standard
The National Era
New York Daily Times
New-York Daily Tribune
New York Independent
New York Observer
The North Star
The Philadelphia Inquirer
The Photographic and Fine Art Journal
Southern Illustrated News
Southern Literary Messenger
The Sun

PRIMARY WRITTEN MATERIALS
Adams, John Quincy. *Narrative of the Life of John Quincy Adams, When in Slavery, and Now as a Freeman*. 1872. Documenting the American South. University Library, University of North Carolina at Chapel Hill. http://docsouth.unc. edu/neh/adams/menu.html.
Albert, Octavia V. Rogers. *The House of Bondage, or, Charlotte Brooks and Other Slaves, Original and Life Like, as They Appeared in Their Old Plantation and City Slave Life; Together with Pen-Pictures of the Peculiar Institution, with Sights and Insights into Their New Relations as Freedmen, Freemen, and Citizens.*

1890. Documenting the American South. University Library, University of North Carolina at Chapel Hill. http://docsouth.unc.edu/neh/albert/menu.html.

Alexander, Charles. *Battles and Victories of Allen Allensworth, A.M., Ph.D., Lieutenant-Colonel, Retired, U.S. Army*. 1914. Documenting the American South. University Library, University of North Carolina at Chapel Hill. http://docsouth.unc.edu/neh/alexander/menu.html.

Alston, J. Motte. *Rice Planter and Sportsman: The Recollections of J. Motte Alston, 1821–1909*. Columbia: University of South Carolina Press, 1953.

Ball, Charles. *Slavery in the United States: A Narrative of the Life and Adventures of Charles Ball, a Black Man*. 1837. Documenting the American South. University Library, University of North Carolina at Chapel Hill. http://docsouth.unc.edu/neh/ballslavery/menu.html.

Ball, James Presley. *Ball's Splendid Mammoth Pictorial Tour of the United States: Comprising Views of the African Slave Trade, of Northern and Southern Cities, of Cotton and Sugar Plantations, of the Mississippi, Ohio and Susquehanna Rivers, Niagara Falls, &c*. Cincinnati: A. Pugh, 1855.

Bear, John W. *The Life and Travels of John W. Bear, "The Buckeye Blacksmith." Written by Himself*. Baltimore: D. Binswanger, 1873.

Bibb, Henry. *Narrative of the Life and Adventures of Henry Bibb, An American Slave, Written by Himself*. 1849. Documenting the American South. University Library, University of North Carolina at Chapel Hill. http://docsouth.unc.edu/neh/bibb/bibb.html.

Boucicault, Dion. *The Octoroon, or, Life in Louisiana: A Play in Five Acts*. n.d. Project Gutenberg ebook.

Boyd, Cyrus F. *The Civil War Diary of Cyrus F. Boyd, Fifteenth Iowa Infantry, 1861–1863*. Edited by Mildred Throne. Millwood, NY: Kraus Reprint Co., 1977.

Brown, John, and Louis Alexis Chamerovzow. *Slave Life in Georgia: A Narrative of the Life, Sufferings, and Escape of John Brown, a Fugitive Slave, Now in England*. 1855. Documenting the American South. University Library, University of North Carolina at Chapel Hill. http://docsouth.unc.edu/neh/jbrown/menu.html.

Brown, William Wells. *Narrative of William W. Brown, a Fugitive Slave*. 1847. Documenting the American South. University Library, University of North Carolina at Chapel Hill. http://docsouth.unc.edu/neh/brown47/menu.html.

Brown, William Wells. *The Rising Sun: or, The Antecedents and Advancement of the Colored Race*. Boston: A. G. Brown, 1874; reprint, Miami: Mnemosyne Publishing, 1969.

Bruner, Peter. *A Slave's Adventures Toward Freedom: Not Fiction, but the True Story of a Struggle*. 1918. Documenting the American South. University Library, University of North Carolina at Chapel Hill. http://docsouth.unc.edu/neh/bruner/menu.html.

Bryant, William Cullen II. "A Yankee Soldier Looks at the Negro." *Civil War History* 7, no. 2 (June 1961): 133–148.

Burge, Dolly Lunt. *The Diary of Dolly Lunt Burge, 1848–1879*. Edited by Christine Jacobson Carter. Athens: University of Georgia Press, 1997.

Child, Lydia Maria. *The Collected Correspondence of Lydia Maria Child, 1817–1880*. Microfiche series. Edited by Patricia G. Holland and Milton Meltzer. 1979.

Clifton, James M., ed. *Life and Labor on Argyle Island: Letters and Documents of a Savannah River Rice Plantation, 1833–1867*. Savannah, GA: Beehive Press, 1978.

Coffin, Levi. *Reminiscences of Levi Coffin, the Reputed President of the Underground Railroad; Being a Brief History of the Labors of a Lifetime in Be Half of the Slave, with the Stories of Numerous Fugitives, Who Gained Their Freedom Through His Instrumentality, and Many Other Incidents.* London: [1876].

Craft, William. *Running a Thousand Miles for Freedom; or, The Escape of William and Ellen Craft from Slavery.* 1860. Documenting the American South. University Library, University of North Carolina at Chapel Hill, 2001, http://docsouth.unc.edu/neh/craft/craft.html.

Douglass, Frederick. *The Frederick Douglass Papers*, series one, *Speeches, Debates, and Interviews*, volume 1, *1841–1846*. Edited by John Blassingame. New Haven, CT: Yale University Press, 1979.

Douglass, Frederick. *The Life and Writings of Frederick Douglass*, volume II, *Pre-Civil War Decade, 1850–1860*. Edited by Philip S. Foner. New York: International Publishers, 1950.

Douglass, Frederick. *Narrative of the Life of Frederick Douglass, and American Slave*. New York: Anchor Books, 1989.

Dowd, Jerome. "Art in Negro Homes." *Southern Workman* 30, no. 1 (January 1901): 90–95.

Doy, John. *The Narrative of John Doy of Lawrence, Kansas: "A Plain Unvarnished Tale."* New York, 1860. Gale, Cengage Learning. University of Southern California Libraries.

Drew, Benjamin. *A North-Side View of Slavery: The Refugee, Or the Narratives of Fugitive Slaves in Canada.* Boston: John P. Jewett, 1856; New York: Johnson Reprint Corporation, 1968.

Emerson, Ralph Waldo. *Emerson in His Journals*. Edited by Joel Porte. Cambridge, MA: Belknap Press of Harvard University Press, 1982.

Equiano, Olaudah. *The Interesting Narrative of The Life of Olaudah Equiano, or Gustavus Vassa, the African, Written by Himself.* Edited by Angelo Costanzo. Ontario: Broadview Press, 2004.

Facts Concerning the Freedmen: Their Capacity and Their Destiny. Boston, 1863. Gale, Cengage Learning. Washington University. http://galenet.galegroup.com.libproxy.wustl.edu/servlet/Sabin?af=RN&ae=CY107925135&srchtp=a&ste=14.

Fedric, Francis. *Slave Life in Virginia and Kentucky; or, Fifty Years of Slavery in the Southern States of America*. 1863. Documenting the American South. University Library, University of North Carolina at Chapel Hill. http://docsouth.unc.edu/neh/fedric/menu.html.

Fiske, Joseph E. *War Letters of Capt. Joseph E. Fiske, Harvard '61: Written to his Parents During the War of Rebellion from Andover Theological Seminary and Encampments in North Carolina and from Southern Prison.* Wellesley, MA: Maugus Press, 1900.

Gardner, Alexander. *Catalogue of Photographic Incidents of the War from the Gallery of Alexander Gardner.* Washington, DC: H. Polkinhorn, 1863.

Gardner, Alexander. *Gardner's Photographic Sketch Book of the Civil War.* New York: Dover Publications, 1959.

Geary, John White. *A Politician Goes to War: The Civil War Letters of John White Geary.* Edited by William Alan Blair. University Park, PA: Pennsylvania State University Press, 1995.

Gould, William B. *Diary of a Contraband: The Civil War Passage of a Black Soldier.* Edited by William B. Gould IV. Stanford: Stanford University Press, 2002.

Gray, Sadai Burge. *Little Sadai: Journal of Miss Sadai C. Burge, 1874.* Atlanta: Keelin Press, 1952.

Grimké, Angelina Emily. *Appeal to the Christian Women of the South.* Reprint ed. New York: Arno Press, 1969.

Grimké, Charlotte Forten. *The Journals of Charlotte Forten Grimké.* Edited by Brenda Stevenson. New York: Oxford University Press, 1988.

Hammond, James Henry. *Remarks of Mr. Hammond, of South Carolina, on the Question of Receiving Petitions for the Abolition of Slavery in the District of Columbia, Delivered in the House of Representatives, February 1, 1836.* Washington, DC: Duff Green, 1836.

Hancock, Cornelia. *Letters of a Civil War Nurse, Cornelia Hancock, 1863–1865.* Edited by Henrietta Stratton Jaquette. Lincoln: University of Nebraska Press, 1998.

Hegel, G. W. F. *The Phenomenology of Mind.* Translated by J.B. Baillie. Mineola, NY: Dover Publications, 2003.

Holmes, Oliver Wendell. "The Stereoscope and the Stereograph." *Atlantic,* June 1859.

Hone, Philip. *The Diary of Philip Hone, 1828–1851,* volume 1. Edited by Bayard Tuckerman. New York: Dodd, Mead, 1889.

Howard, V. E., and A. Hutchinson, comps. *The Statutes of the State of Mississippi.* New Orleans: E. Johns, 1840.

Johnston, F. Claiborne Jr. *The Pinder/Ellett Families of Virginia and Georgia and Allied Families (Pinder, Tebeau, Treutlen, Ellett, Spears, Womack, Sublett, Cheatham, Smith, Trabue) With Some Accounts of the Pinder/Pindar Family Trail in the Bahama Islands, Bermuda and Barbados.* Richmond, VA: F. C. Johnston, 1988.

King, William. *Diary of William King.* 1864. Documenting the American South. University Library, University of North Carolina at Chapel Hill. http://docsouth.unc.edu/imls/kingwilliam/king.html.

Kingsford, William. *Impressions of the West and South During a Six Weeks' Holiday.* Toronto: A. H. Armour, 1858.

Kinsley, Rufus. *Diary of a Christian Soldier: Rufus Kinsley and the Civil War.* Edited by David C. Rankin. Cambridge: Cambridge University Press, 2004.

Life of Maumer Juno of Charleston, S.C.: A Sketch of Juno (Waller) Seymour. Atlanta: Foote & Davies, 1892.

Malone, Bartlett Yancey. *The Diary of Bartlett Yancey Malone.* 1919. Documenting the American South. University Library, University of North Carolina at Chapel Hill. http://docsouth.unc.edu/fpn/malone/malone.html.

Middleton, Alicia Hopton. *Life in Carolina and New England During the Nineteenth Century: As Illustrated by Reminiscences and Letters of the Middleton Family of Charleston South Carolina and of the De Wolf Family of Bristol Rhode Island.* Bristol, RI: privately printed, 1929.

Morgan, Mrs. Irby. *How It Was: Four Years Among the Rebels.* Documenting the American South. University Library, University of North Carolina at Chapel Hill. http://docsouth.unc.edu/fpn/morgan/morgan.html.

Nell, William Cooper. *William Cooper Nell: Selected Writings, 1832–1874.* Edited by Dorothy Porter Wesley and Constance Porter Uzelac. Baltimore: Black Classic Press, 2002.

Noble, Louis Legrand. *The Life and Works of Thomas Cole.* Edited by Elliot S. Vesell. Cambridge, MA: Belknap Press of Harvard University Press, 1964.

Northup, Solomon. *Twelve Years a Slave.* New York: Penguin Books, 2012.

Nott, Charles Cooper. *The Coming Contraband: A Reason Against the Emancipation Proclamation, Not Given by Mr. Justice Curtis, to Whom It Is Addressed, by an Officer in the Field.* New York: G. P. Putnam, 1862.

Passages from the Life of Henry Warren Howe: Consisting of Diary and Letters Written During the Civil War, 1861–1865. Lowell, MA: Courier-Citizen, 1899.

Pennington, James W. C. *The Fugitive Blacksmith; or, Events in the History of James W. C. Pennington, Pastor of a Presbyterian Church, New York, Formerly a Slave in the State of Maryland, United States.* 1848. Documenting the American South. University Library, University of North Carolina at Chapel Hill. http://docsouth.unc.edu/neh/penning49/penning49.html.

Picquet, Louisa, and Hiram Mattison. *Louisa Picquet, the Octoroon, or Inside Views of Southern Domestic Life.* 1861. Documenting the American South. University Library, University of North Carolina at Chapel Hill. http://docsouth.unc.edu/neh/picquet/menu.html.

Poe, Edgar Allan. "The Daguerreotype." In *Classic Essays on Photography*, edited by Alan Trachtenberg. New Haven, CT: Leete's Island Books, 1980.

Powell, Aaron M. *Personal Reminiscences of the Anti-Slavery and Other Reforms and Reformers.* New York: Caulon Press, 1899.

Pringle, Edward J. *Slavery in the Southern States, by a Carolinian.* Cambridge: John Bartlett, 1852.

Quitman Family Papers, 1784–1978. UPA Microfilm, Records of Ante-Bellum Southern Plantations from the Revolution Through the Civil War. University Publications of America, Series J, Selections from the Southern Historical Collection, Part 6, Reel 7, OCLC No. 12894903.

Randolph, Peter. *From Slave Cabin to the Pulpit: The Autobiography of Rev. Peter Randolph: The Southern Question Illustrated and Sketches of Slave Life*. 1893. Documenting the American South. University Library, University of North Carolina at Chapel Hill. http://docsouth.unc.edu/neh/randolph/randolph.html.

Ray, Mr. and Mrs. L. P. *Twice Sold, Twice Ransomed: Autobiography of Mr. and Mrs. L.P. Ray*. 1926. Documenting the American South. University Library, University of North Carolina at Chapel Hill. http://docsouth.unc.edu/neh/rayemma/rayemma.html.

Ripley, Eliza. *Social Life in Old New Orleans, Being Recollections of My Girlhood*. New York: D. Appleton, 1912.

Rogers, J. B. *War Pictures: Experiences and Observations of a Chaplain in the U.S. Army in the War of the Southern Rebellion*. Chicago: Church & Goodman, 1863.

Root, Marcus A. *The Camera and the Pencil*. Philadelphia: M. A. Root, J. B. Lippincott, and D. Appleton, 1864.

Ryder, James F. *Voigtländer and I: In Pursuit of Shadow Catching*. Cleveland: Cleveland Printing and Publishing Company, 1902; reprint, New York: Arno Press, 1973.

Simmons, Rev. William J. *Men of Mark: Eminent, Progressive and Rising*. 1887. Documenting the American South. University Library, University of North Carolina at Chapel Hill, 2000. http://docsouth.unc.edu/neh/simmons/simmons.html.

Stephens, Alexander H. "Cornerstone Address." In *Southern Pamphlets on Secession, November 1860—April 1861*, edited by Jon L. Wakelyn. Chapel Hill: University of North Carolina Press, 1996.

Still, William. *The Underground Railroad*. Philadelphia: Porter & Coates, 1871.

Stone, Kate. *Brokenburn: The Journal of Kate Stone, 1861–1865*. Edited by John Q. Anderson. Baton Rouge: Louisiana State University Press, 1955.

Stowe, Harriet Beecher. *Uncle Tom's Cabin, or, Life Among the Lowly*. New York: Penguin Books, 1981.

Thompson, Dr. L. S. *The Story of Mattie J. Jackson*. 1866. Documenting the American South. University Library, University of North Carolina at Chapel Hill, 1999. http://docsouth.unc.edu/neh/jacksonm/menu.html.

Walker, Jonathan. *Trial and Imprisonment of Jonathan Walker, at Pensacola, Florida, for aiding slaves to escape from bondage: With an Appendix Containing a Sketch of His Life*. Boston: Anti-Slavery Office, 1845.

Warren, Rev. Joseph. *Extracts from Reports of Superintendents of Freedmen*, second series. Vicksburg, MS: Freedmen Press Print, 1864.

Wells, Ida B. "A Red Record." In *Southern Horrors and Other Writings: The Anti-Lynching Campaign of Ida B. Wells, 1892–1900*, edited by Jacqueline Jones Royster. Boston: Bedford Books, 1997.

Werge, John. *The Evolution of Photography*. London: Piper & Carter, 1890.

Wickham, Elizabeth Merwin. *A Lost Family Found: An Authentic Narrative of Cyrus Branch and His Family, Alias John White*. 1869. Documenting the American South. University Library, University of North Carolina at Chapel Hill. http://docsouth.unc.edu/neh/wickham/wickham.html.

SECONDARY SOURCES

Abruzzo, Margaret. *Polemical Pain: Slavery, Cruelty, and the Rise of Humanitarianism.* Baltimore: Johns Hopkins University Press, 2011.

Abzug, Robert H. *Cosmos Crumbling: American Reform and the Religious Imagination.* New York: Oxford University Press, 1994.

Allen, James, Hilton Als, John Lewis, and Leon F. Litwack. *Without Sanctuary: Lynching Photography in America.* Santa Fe, NM: Twin Palms, 2000.

Anderson, Benedict. *Imagined Communities: Reflections on the Origin and Spread of Nationalism.* Rev. ed. Verso: London, 2006.

Anishanslin, Zara. *Portrait of a Woman in Silk: Hidden Histories of the British Atlantic World.* New Haven, CT: Yale University Press, 2016.

Apel, Dora, and Shawn Michelle Smith. *Lynching Photographs.* Berkeley: University of California Press, 2007.

Auslander, Mark. "Rose's Gift: Slavery, Kinship, and the Fabric of Memory." *Present Pasts* 8, no. 1 (March 2017). DOI: http://doi.org/10.5334/pp.78.

Ayers, Edward L. *What Caused the Civil War? Reflections on the South and Southern History.* New York: W. W. Norton, 2005.

Baptist, Edward E. *The Half Has Never Been Told: Slavery and the Making of American Capitalism.* New York: Basic Books, 2014.

Barnes, L. Diane, Brian Schoen, and Frank Towers, eds. *The Old South's Modern Worlds: Slavery, Region, and Nation in the Age of Progress.* Oxford: Oxford University Press, 2011.

Batchen, Geoffrey. "Snapshots: Art History and the Ethnographic Turn." *Photographies* 1, no. 2 (September 2008): 121–142.

Batchen, Geoffrey. "Vernacular Photographies." *History of Photography* 24, no. 3 (Autumn 2000): 262–271.

Bay, Mia. *The White Image in the Black Mind: African-American Ideas about White People, 1830–1925.* New York: Oxford University Press, 2000.

Beckert, Sven. *Empire of Cotton: A Global History.* New York: Knopf, 2014.

Beckert, Sven, and Seth Rockman, eds. *Slavery's Capitalism: A New History of American Economic Development.* Philadelphia: University of Pennsylvania Press, 2016.

Berger, John. *About Looking.* New York: Vintage International, 1991.

Berger, Martin A. "White Suffering and the Branded Hand." n.d. Mirror of Race. http://www.mirrorofrace.org/show_interp.php?photo_id=18.

Berlin, Ira. *Slaves Without Masters: The Free Negro in the Antebellum South.* New York: New Press, 1974.

Berlin, Ira, and Leslie S. Rowland, eds. *Families and Freedom: A Documentary History of African-American Kinship in the Civil War Era.* New York: New Press, 1997.

Berlin, Ira, Joseph P. Reidy, and Leslie S. Rowland. *Freedom's Soldiers: The Black Military Experience in the Civil War.* Cambridge: Cambridge University Press, 1998.

Berlin, Ira, Barbara J. Fields, Steven F. Miller, Joseph P. Reidy, and
Leslie S. Rowland. *Slaves No More: Three Essays on Emancipation and the
Civil War*. Cambridge: Cambridge University Press, 1992.

Bernier, Celeste-Marie, and Zoe Trodd, eds. "Slavery and Memory in Black
Visual Culture." *Slavery and Abolition* 34, no. 2 (May 2013).

Bernstein, Robin. *Racial Innocence: Performing American Childhood from Slavery
to Civil Rights*. New York: New York University Press, 2011.

Berry, Daina Ramey. *The Price for Their Pound of Flesh: The Value of the Enslaved,
from Womb to Grave, in the Building of a Nation*. Boston: Beacon Press, 2017.

Bieze, Michael. *Booker T. Washington and the Art of Self-Representation*.
New York: Peter Lang, 2008.

Bindman, David, and Henry Louis Gates Jr., eds. *The Image of the Black in
Western Art, IV, Part 1*. Cambridge, MA: Belknap Press of Harvard
University Press, 2012.

Bindman, David, and Henry Louis Gates Jr., eds. *The Image of the Black in
Western Art, IV, Part 2*. Cambridge, MA: Belknap Press of Harvard
University Press, 2012.

Blackett, R. J. M. *Making Freedom: The Underground Railroad and the Politics of
Slavery*. Chapel Hill: University of North Carolina Press, 2013.

Blackwood, Sarah. "Fugitive Obscure: Runaway Slave Portraiture and Early
Photographic Technology." *American Literature* 81, no. 1 (March 2009):
93–125.

Blassingame, John W. *The Slave Community: Plantation Life in the Antebellum
South*. Rev. ed. New York: Oxford University Press, 1979.

Blight, David. *Race and Reunion: The Civil War in American Memory*. Cambridge,
MA: Belknap Press of Harvard University Press, 2001.

Blight, David W., ed. *Passages to Freedom: The Underground Railroad in History
and Memory*. Washington, DC: Smithsonian Books, 2004.

Boime, Albert. *The Art of Exclusion: Representing Blacks in the Nineteenth Century*.
Washington, DC: Smithsonian Institution Press, 1990.

Bolster, W. Jeffrey, and Hilary Anderson. *Soldiers, Sailors, Slaves, and Ships:
The Civil War Photographs of Henry P. Moore*. Concord: New Hampshire
Historical Society, 1999.

Brown, Elspeth H., and Thy Phu, eds. *Feeling Photography*. Durham, NC: Duke
University Press, 2014.

Brown, Joshua. *Beyond the Lines: Pictorial Reporting, Everyday Life, and the Crisis
of Gilded Age America*. Berkeley: University of California Press, 2002.

Brown, Joshua. "Historians and Photography." *American Art* 21, no. 3 (2007): 9–13.

Burke, Peter. *Eyewitnessing: The Use of Images as Historical Evidence*. Ithaca, NY:
Cornell University Press, 2001.

Caddoo, Cara. *Envisioning Freedom: Cinema and the Building of Modern Black
Life*. Cambridge, MA: Harvard University Press, 2014.

Camp, Stephanie M. H., and Edward E. Baptist. "Introduction: A History of
the History of Slavery in the Americas." In *New Studies in the History of
American Slavery*, edited by Edward E. Baptist and Stephanie M. H. Camp.
Athens: University of Georgia Press, 2006.

Camp, Stephanie M. H. *Closer* to *Freedom: Enslaved Women and Everyday Resistance in the Plantation South.* Chapel Hill: University of North Carolina Press, 2004.

Campbell, Stanley W. *The Slave Catchers: Enforcement of the Fugitive Slave Law, 1850–1860.* Chapel Hill: University of North Carolina Press, 1968.

Campt, Tina M. *Image Matters: Archive, Photography, and the African Diaspora in Europe.* Durham, NC: Duke University Press, 2012.

Carlebach, Michael L. *The Origins of Photojournalism in America.* Washington, DC: Smithsonian Institution Press, 1992.

Carlson, Hannah. "Vulgar Things." *Common-Place* 7, no. 2 (January 2007). http://common-place.org/book/vulgar-things.

Cecelski, David S. *The Fire of Freedom: Abraham Galloway and the Slaves' Civil War.* Chapel Hill: University of North Carolina Press, 2012.

Clark, Elizabeth B. "'The Sacred Rights of the Weak': Pain, Sympathy, and the Culture of Individual Rights in Antebellum America." *Journal of American History* 82, no. 2 (1995): 463–493.

Clarke, Erskine. *Dwelling Place: A Plantation Epic.* New Haven, CT: Yale University Press, 2005.

Clinton, Catherine. *Harriet Tubman: The Road to Freedom.* New York: Back Bay Books, 2004.

Clinton, Catherine. *The Plantation Mistress: Woman's World in the Old South.* New York: Pantheon Books, 1982.

Cobb, Jasmine Nichole. *Picture Freedom: Remaking Black Visuality in the Early Nineteenth Century.* New York: New York University Press, 2015.

Coddington, Ronald S. *African American Faces of the Civil War: An Album.* Baltimore: Johns Hopkins University Press, 2012.

Colbert, Charles. *A Measure of Perfection: Phrenology and the Fine Arts in America.* Chapel Hill: University of North Carolina Press, 1997.

Collins, Kathleen. "Portraits of Slave Children." *History of Photography* 9, no. 3 (July–September 1985).

Collins, Kathleen. "The Scourged Back." *History of Photography* 9, no. 1 (January–March 1985).

Conkey, Margaret W. "Images Without Words: The Construction of Prehistoric Imaginaries for Definitions of 'Us.'" *Journal of Visual Culture* 9, no. 3 (December 2010): 272–283.

Conn, Steven. "Narrative Trauma and Civil War History Painting, or Why Are These Pictures so Terrible?" *History and Theory* 41, no. 4 (December 2002): 17–42.

Copeland, Huey, Krista Thompson, and Darcy Grimaldo Grigsby, eds. "New World Slavery and the Matter of the Visual." *Representations* 113, no. 1 (Winter 2011): 1–163.

Cornelius, Janet Duitsman. *"When I Can Read My Title Clear": Literacy, Slavery, and Religion in the Antebellum South.* Columbia: University of South Carolina Press, 1991.

Dain, Bruce. *A Hideous Monster of the Mind: American Race Theory in the Early Republic.* Cambridge, MA: Harvard University Press, 2002.

Davis, David Brion. *The Problem of Slavery in Western Culture*. Ithaca, NY: Cornell University Press, 1966.

Davis, Keith F. *George N. Barnard: Photographer of Sherman's Campaign*. Kansas City, MO: Hallmark Cards, 1990.

Davis, Keith F. "'A Terrible Distinctness': Photography of the Civil War Era." In *Photography in Nineteenth-Century America*, edited by Martha A. Sandweiss. Fort Worth, TX: Amon Carter Museum, 1991.

Davis, Keith F. *The Origins of American Photography: From Daguerreotype to Dry-Plate, 1839–1865*. Kansas City, MO: Hall Family Foundation and Nelson-Atkins Museum of Art, 2007.

Dennett, Daniel. "Conditions of Personhood." In *The Identities of Persons*, ed. Amelie Oksenberg Rorty. Berkeley: University of California Press, 1976.

Deyle, Steven. *Carry Me Back: The Domestic Slave Trade in American Life*. Oxford: Oxford University Press, 2005.

Dinius, Marcy J. *The Camera and the Press: American Visual and Print Culture in the Age of the Daguerreotype*. Philadelphia: University of Pennsylvania Press, 2012.

Dinius, Marcy J. "Seeing Ourselves as Others See Us: Frederick Douglass's Reflections on Daguerreotypy and Racial Difference." In *Photography and Its Origins*, ed. Tanya Sheehan and Andres Mario Zervigon, 118–128. New York: Routledge, 2015.

Diouf, Sylviane A. *Slavery's Exiles: The Story of the American Maroons*. New York: New York University Press, 2014.

Douglass, Ann. "Introduction." In Harriet Beecher Stowe, *Uncle Tom's Cabin or, Life Among the Lowly*, 7–34. New York: Penguin Books, 1982.

Downs, Jim. *Sick from Freedom: African-American Illness and Suffering During the Civil War and Reconstruction*. Oxford: Oxford University Press, 2012.

Dunkleman, Mark, and Michael Winey. "Precious Shadows: The Importance of Photographs to Civil War Soldiers." *Military Images* 16, no. 1 (July–August 1994): 6–13.

Dusinberre, William. *Them Dark Days: Slavery in the American Rice Swamps*. New York: Oxford University Press, 1996.

Edwards, Elizabeth. "Thinking Photography Beyond the Visual?" In *Photography: Theoretical Snapshots*, edited by J. J. Long, Andrea Noble, and Edward Welch. London: Routledge, 2009.

Edwards, Elizabeth, and Janice Hart. "Introduction: Photographs as Objects." In *Photographs Objects Histories: On the Materiality of Images*, edited by Elizabeth Edwards and Janice Hart. London: Routledge, 2004.

Eustace, Nicole, Eugenia Lean, Julie Livingston, Jan Plamper, William M. Reddy, and Barbara H. Rosenwein. "*AHR* Conversation: The Historical Study of Emotions." *American Historical Review* 117, no. 5 (December 2012): 1487–1531.

Evans, Jennifer V. "Seeing Subjectivity: Erotic Photography and the Optics of Desire." *American Historical Review* 118, no. 2 (April 2013): 430–462.

Fahs, Alice. *The Imagined Civil War: Popular Literature of the North and South, 1861–1865*. Chapel Hill: University of North Carolina Press, 2001.

Faust, Drew Gilpin, ed. *The Ideology of Slavery: Proslavery Thought in the Antebellum South, 1830–1860*. Baton Rouge: Louisiana State University Press, 1981.

Faust, Drew Gilpin. *James Henry Hammond and the Old South: A Design for Mastery*. Baton Rouge: Louisiana State University Press, 1982.

Fehrenbach, Heide, and Davide Rodogno, eds. *Humanitarian Photography: A History*. Cambridge: Cambridge University Press, 2015.

Foner, Eric. *The Fiery Trial: Abraham Lincoln and American Slavery*. New York: W. W. Norton, 2010.

Foner, Eric. *Forever Free: The Story of Emancipation and Reconstruction*. New York: Alfred A. Knopf, 2005.

Foner, Eric. *Gateway to Freedom: The Hidden History of the Underground Railroad*. New York: W. W. Norton, 2015.

Ford, Lacy K. *Deliver Us from Evil: The Slavery Question in the Old South*. Oxford: Oxford University Press, 2009.

Ford, Lacy. "Reconsidering the Internal Slave Trade: Paternalism, Markets, and the Character of the Old South." In *The Chattel Principle: Internal Slave Trades in the Americas*, edited by Walter Johnson. New Haven, CT: Yale University Press, 2004.

Foresta, Merry A., and John Wood. *Secrets of the Dark Chamber: The Art of the American Daguerreotype*. Washington, DC: Smithsonian Institution Press, 1995.

Forret, Jeff. "Slaves, Poor Whites, and the Underground Economy of the Rural Carolinas." *Journal of Southern History* 70, no. 4 (2004): 783–824.

Fox-Amato, Matthew. "Plantation Tourism." In Mazie Harris, *Paper Promises: Early American Photography*. Los Angeles: J. Paul Getty Museum, 2018.

Fox-Genovese, Elizabeth. *Within the Plantation Household: Black and White Women of the Old South*. Chapel Hill: University of North Carolina Press, 1988.

Frank, Robin Jaffee. *Love and Loss: American Portrait and Mourning Miniatures*. New Haven, CT: Yale University Press, 2000.

Franklin, John Hope, ed. *Reminiscences of an Active Life: The Autobiography of John Roy Lynch*. Chicago: University of Chicago Press, 1970; reprint, University Press of Mississippi, 2008.

Franklin, John Hope, and Loren Schweninger. *Runaway Slaves: Rebels on the Plantation, 1790–1860*. New York: Oxford University Press, 1999.

Frassanito, William A. *Antietam: The Photographic Legacy of America's Bloodiest Day*. New York: Charles Scribner's Sons, 1978.

Frederickson, George M. *The Black Image in the White Mind: The Debate on Afro-American Character and Destiny, 1817–1914*. New York: Harper & Row, 1972.

Freedberg, David. *The Power of Images: Studies in the History and Theory of Response*. Chicago: University of Chicago Press, 1989.

Friedman, Lawrence J. *Gregarious Saints: Self and Community in American Abolitionism, 1830–1870*. Cambridge: Cambridge University Press, 1982.

Fusco, Coco, and Brian Wallis, eds. *Only Skin Deep: Changing Visions of the American Self.* New York: Harry N. Abrams, 2003.

Gallman, J. Matthew. "Snapshots: Images of Men in the United States Colored Troops." *American Nineteenth Century History* 13, no. 2 (June 2012): 127–151.

Gallman, Matthew, and Gary W. Gallagher, eds. *Lens of War: Exploring Iconic Photographs of the Civil War.* Athens: University of Georgia Press, 2015.

Gara, Larry. *The Liberty Line: The Legend of the Underground Railroad.* Lexington: University of Kentucky Press, 1961.

Genovese, Eugene D. *Roll, Jordan, Roll: The World the Slaves Made.* New York: Vintage Books, 1972.

Genovese, Eugene D. *The Slaveholders' Dilemma: Freedom and Progress in Southern Conservative Thought, 1820–1860.* Columbia: University of South Carolina Press, 1992.

Gerteis, Louis S. *From Contraband to Freedman: Federal Policy Toward Southern Blacks, 1861–1865.* Westport, CT: Greenwood Press, 1973.

Gifford, Ronald M. II. "George Thompson and Trans-Atlantic Antislavery, 1831–1865." PhD dissertation, Indiana University, 1999.

Gillespie, Sarah Kate. *The Early American Daguerreotype: Cross-Currents in Art and Technology.* Washington, DC: The Smithsonian Institution, 2016.

Gilpin, R. Blakeslee. *John Brown Still Lives! America's Long Reckoning with Violence, Equality, and Change.* Chapel Hill: University of North Carolina Press, 2011.

Glymph, Thavolia. *Out of the House of Bondage: The Transformation of the Plantation Household.* Cambridge: Cambridge University Press, 2008.

Glymph, Thavolia. "Rose's War and the Gendered Politics of a Slave Insurgency in the Civil War." *Journal of the Civil War Era* 3, no. 4 (December 2013): 501–532.

Goldsby, Jacqueline. *A Spectacular Secret: Lynching in American Life and Literature.* Chicago: University of Chicago Press, 2006.

Gonzalez, Aston. "The Art of Racial Politics: The Work of Robert Douglass Jr., 1833–46." *Pennsylvania Magazine of History and Biography* 138, no. 1 (January 2014): 5–37.

Goodman, Paul. *Of One Blood: Abolitionism and the Origins of Racial Equality.* Berkeley: University of California Press, 1998.

Gordon-Reed, Annette. *The Hemingses of Monticello: An American Family.* New York: W. W. Norton, 2008.

Greenberg, Kenneth. *Honor and Slavery.* Princeton, NJ: Princeton University Press, 1996.

Grier, Katherine C. *Cultures and Comfort: People, Parlors, and Upholstery, 1850–1930.* Rochester, NY: Strong Museum, 1988.

Griffler, Keith P. *Front Line of Freedom: African Americans and the Forging of the Underground Railroad in the Ohio Valley.* Lexington: University Press of Kentucky, 2004.

Grigsby, Darcy Grimaldo. "Negative-Positive Truths." *Representations* 113, no. 1 (2011): 16–38.

Grigsby, Darcy Grimaldo. *Enduring Truths: Sojourner's Shadows and Substance.* Chicago: University of Chicago Press, 2015.

Grimsted, David. "Rioting in Its Jacksonian Setting." *American Historical Review* 77, no. 2 (April 1972): 361–397.

Gross, Ariela J. *Double Character: Slavery and Mastery in the Antebellum Southern Courtroom.* Princeton, NJ: Princeton University Press, 2000.

Gudmestad, Robert H. *Steamboats and the Rise of the Cotton Kingdom.* Baton Rouge: Louisiana State University Press, 2011.

Gudmestad, Robert H. *A Troublesome Commerce: The Transformation of the Interstate Slave Trade.* Baton Rouge: Louisiana State University Press, 2003.

Gutman, Herbert. *The Black Family in Slavery and Freedom, 1750–1925.* New York: Pantheon, 1976.

Hadden, Sally E. *Slave Patrols: Law and Violence in Virginia and the Carolinas.* Cambridge, MA: Harvard University Press, 2001.

Hahn, Steven. "But What Did the Slaves Think of Lincoln?" In *Lincoln's Proclamation: Emancipation Reconsidered*, edited by William A. Blair and Karen Fisher Younger. Chapel Hill: University of North Carolina Press, 2009.

Hahn, Steven. *A Nation Under Our Feet: Black Political Struggles in the Rural South from Slavery to the Great Migration.* Cambridge, MA: Belknap Press of Harvard University Press, 2003.

Hales, Peter B. *Silver Cities: The Photography of American Urbanization, 1839–1915.* Philadelphia: Temple University Press, 1984.

Halttunen, Karen. "Humanitarianism and the Pornography of Pain in Anglo-American Culture." *American Historical Review*, 100, no. 2 (1995): 303–334.

Hammond, Carol D. "Richard Thompson Archer and the Burdens of Proprietorship: The Life of a Natchez District Planter." PhD dissertation, University of North Texas, 2001.

Hancock, Scott. "Crossing Freedom's Fault Line: The Underground Railroad and Recentering African Americans in Civil War Causation." *Civil War History* 59, no. 2 (June 2013): 169–205.

Hariman, Robert, and John Louis Lucaites. *No Caption Needed: Iconic Photographs, Public Culture, and Liberal Democracy.* Chicago: University of Chicago Press, 2007.

Harris, Mazie M. *Paper Promises: Early American Photography.* Los Angeles: J. Paul Getty Museum, 2018.

Harris, Michael D. *Colored Pictures: Race and Visual Representation.* Chapel Hill: University of North Carolina Press, 2003.

Harris, Neil. *Humbug: The Art of P. T. Barnum.* Chicago: University of Chicago Press, 1973.

Hartman, Saidiya V. *Scenes of Subjection: Terror, Slavery, and Self-Making in Nineteenth-Century America.* New York: Oxford University Press, 1997.

Haynes, David. *Catching Shadows: A Directory of Nineteenth-Century Texas Photographers.* Austin: Texas State Historical Association, 1993.

Henkin, David. *City Reading: Written Words and Public Spaces in Antebellum New York.* New York: Columbia University Press, 1998.

Henkin, David. *The Postal Age: The Emergence of Modern Communications in Nineteenth-Century America*. Chicago: University of Chicago Press, 2006.

Hill, Ginger. "'Rightly Viewed': Theorizations of Self in Frederick Douglass's Lectures on Pictures." In *Pictures and Progress: Early Photography and the Making of African American Identity*, edited by Maurice O. Wallace and Shawn Michelle Smith. Durham, NC: Duke University Press, 2012.

Hilliard, Kathleen M. *Masters, Slaves, and Exchange: Power's Purchase in the Old South*. New York: Cambridge University Press, 2014.

Hodges, Graham Russell Gao. *David Ruggles: A Radical Black Abolitionist and the Underground Railroad in New York City*. Chapel Hill: University of North Carolina Press, 2010.

Horton, James Oliver. "A Crusade for Freedom: William Still and the Real Underground Railroad." In *Passages to Freedom: The Underground Railroad in History and Memory*, edited by David W. Blight. Washington, DC: Smithsonian Books, 2004.

Horton, James Oliver. *Free People of Color: Inside the African American Community*. Washington, DC: Smithsonian Institution Press, 1993.

Horton, Lois E. "Kidnapping and Resistance: Antislavery Direct Action in the 1850s." In *Passages to Freedom: The Underground Railroad in History and Memory*, edited by David W. Blight. Washington, DC: Smithsonian Books, 2004.

Howe, Daniel Walker. *What Hath God Wrought: The Transformation of America, 1815–1848*. Oxford: Oxford University Press, 2007.

Hudson, Larry E. Jr. *To Have and to Hold: Slave Work and Family Life in Antebellum South Carolina*. Athens: University of Georgia Press, 1997.

Humphreys, Hugh C. "Agitate! Agitate! Agitate! The Great Cazenovia Fugitive Slave Law Convention and Its Rare Daguerreotype." *Madison County Heritage* 19 (1994).

Hunt, Lynn, ed. *The New Cultural History*. Berkeley: University of California Press, 1989.

Inscoe, John C. "Carolina Slave Names: An Index to Acculturation." *Journal of Southern History* 49, no. 4 (November 1983): 527–554.

Inscoe, John C., and Paul Finkleman, eds. *Macmillan Encyclopedia of World Slavery*, volume 2. New York: Macmillan Reference, 1998.

Jaffee, David. *A New Nation of Goods: The Material Culture of Early America*. Philadelphia: University of Pennsylvania Press, 2010.

Jaffee, David. "Anthony's *Broadway on a Rainy Day*." *Common-Place* 10, no. 4 (2010).

Jaffee, David. "One of the Primitive Sort: Portrait Makers of the Rural North, 1760–1860." In *The Countryside in the Age of Capitalist Transformation: Essays in the Social History of Rural America*, edited by Steven Hahn and Jonathan Prude. Chapel Hill: University of North Carolina Press, 1985.

Jaffee, David. "Peddlers of Progress and the Transformation of the Rural North, 1760–1860." *Journal of American History* 78, no. 2 (1991): 511–535.

Jenkins, Reese V. *Images and Enterprise: Technology and the American Photographic Industry, 1839–1925*. Baltimore: Johns Hopkins University Press, 1975, 1987.

Jezierski, John Vincent. *Enterprising Images: The Goodridge Brothers, African American Photographers 1847–1922*. Detroit: Wayne State University Press, 2000.

Johnson, Walter, ed. *The Chattel Principle: Internal Slave Trades in the Americas*. New Haven, CT: Yale University Press, 2004.

Johnson, Walter. "On Agency." *Journal of Social History* 37, no. 1 (Fall 2003): 113–124.

Johnson, Walter. *River of Dark Dreams: Slavery and Empire in the Cotton Kingdom*. Cambridge, MA: Belknap Press of Harvard University Press, 2013.

Johnson, Walter. *Soul by Soul: Life Inside the Antebellum Slave Market*. Cambridge, MA: Harvard University Press, 1999.

Jones, Lawrence T. III. *Lens on the Texas Frontier*. College Station: Texas A&M University Press, 2014.

Jones, Martha S. *All Bound Up Together: The Woman Question in African-American Public Culture, 1830–1900*. Chapel Hill: University of North Carolina Press, 2007.

Jordan, Winthrop D. *White over Black: American Attitudes Toward the Negro, 1550–1812*. Chapel Hill: University of North Carolina Press, 1968.

Joyner, Charles. *Down by the Riverside: A South Carolina Slave Community*. Urbana: University of Illinois Press, 1984.

Kantrowitz, Stephen. *More Than Freedom: Fighting for Black Citizenship in a White Republic, 1829–1889*. New York: Penguin Press, 2012.

Kasher, Steven. *America and the Tintype*. New York: International Center of Photography, 2008.

Kaye, Anthony E. *Joining Places: Slave Neighborhoods in the Old South*. Chapel Hill: University of North Carolina Press, 2007.

Kaye, Anthony E. "The Second Slavery: Modernity in the Nineteenth-Century South and the Atlantic World." *Journal of Southern History* 75, no. 3 (August 2009): 627–650.

Kelly, Catherine E. *Republic of Taste: Art, Politics, and Everyday Life in Early America*. Philadelphia: University of Pennsylvania Press, 2016.

Kennel, Sarah, Diane Waggoner, and Alice Carver-Kubik. *In the Darkroom: An Illustrated Guide to Photographic Processes Before the Digital Age*. New York: Thames and Hudson, 2009.

Kimball, Gregg D. *American City, Southern Place: A Cultural History of Antebellum Richmond*. Athens: University of Georgia Press, 2000.

Kolchin, Peter. *American Slavery, 1619–1877*. Rev. ed. New York: Hill and Wang, 2003.

Kraditor, Aileen S. *Means and Ends in American Abolitionism: Garrison and His Critics on Strategy and Tactics, 1834–1850*. New York: Pantheon Books, 1967.

Kriz, Kay Dian, and Geoff Quilley, eds. *An Economy of Colour: Visual Culture and the Atlantic World, 1660–1830*. Manchester: Manchester University Press, 2003.

Kuebler-Wolf, Elizabeth. "The Perfect Shadow of His Master: Proslavery Ideology in American Visual Culture, 1700–1920." PhD dissertation, Indiana University, 2005.

Lapsansky, Emma Jones. "'Since They Got Those Separate Churches': Afro-Americans and Racism in Jacksonian Philadelphia." *American Quarterly* 32 (1980).

Lapsansky, Phillip. "Graphic Discord: Abolitionist and Anti-abolitionist Images." In *The Abolitionist Sisterhood: Women's Political Culture in Antebellum America*, edited by Jean Fagin Yellin and John C. Van Horne. Ithaca, NY: Cornell University Press, 1994.

Last, Jay T. *The Color Explosion: Nineteenth-Century American Lithography*. Santa Ana, CA: Hillcrest Press, 2005.

Laurie, Bruce. "'Chaotic Freedom' in Civil War Louisiana: The Origins of an Iconic Image." *Massachusetts Review* 2, no. 1 (November 2016).

Lavitt, Wendy. *American Folk Dolls*. New York: Alfred A. Knopf, 1982.

Lee, Anthony W., and Elizabeth Young. *On Alexander Gardner's Photographic Sketch Book of the Civil War*. Berkeley: University of California Press, 2007.

Lemire, Elise. *"Miscegenation": Making Race in America*. Philadelphia: University of Pennsylvania Press, 2002.

Levine, Bruce. *The Fall of the House of Dixie: The Civil War and the Social Revolution That Transformed the South*. New York: Random House, 2013.

Levine, Lawrence W. *Black Culture and Black Consciousness: Afro-American Folk Thought from Slavery to Freedom*. Oxford: Oxford University Press, 1977.

Linfield, Susie. *The Cruel Radiance: Photography and Political Violence*. Chicago: University of Chicago Press, 2010.

Lippert, Amy K. DeFalco. *Consuming Identities: Visual Culture in Nineteenth-Century San Francisco*. New York: Oxford University Press, 2018.

Litwack, Leon F. *Been in the Storm So Long: The Aftermath of Slavery*. New York: Alfred A. Knopf, 1979.

Litwack, Leon F. *North of Slavery: The Negro in the Free States, 1790–1860*. Chicago: University of Chicago Press, 1961.

Lockley, Timothy J. "Trading Encounters Between Non-Elite Whites and African Americans in Savannah, 1790–1860." *Journal of Southern History* 66, no. 1 (2000): 25–48.

Lott, Eric. *Love and Theft: Blackface Minstrelsy and the American Working Class*. New York: Oxford University Press, 1993.

Lugo-Ortiz, Agnes, and Angela Rosenthal, eds. *Slave Portraiture in the Atlantic World*. New York: Cambridge University Press, 2013.

Mabee, Carleton. *Black Freedom: The Nonviolent Abolitionists from 1830 to the Civil War*. New York: MacMillan, 1970.

Manning, Chandra. *Troubled Refuge: Struggling for Freedom in the Civil War*. New York: Alfred A. Knopf, 2016.

Manning, Chandra. *What This Cruel War Was Over: Soldiers, Slavery, and the Civil War*. New York: Vintage Books, 2007.

Manning, Chandra. "Working for Citizenship in Civil War Contraband Camps." *Journal of the Civil War Era* 4, no. 2 (June 2014): 172–204.

Marrs, Aaron W. *Railroads in the Old South: Pursuing Progress in a Slave Society.* Baltimore: Johns Hopkins University Press, 2009.

Martin, Ann Smart. *Buying into the World of Goods: Early Consumers in Backcountry Virginia.* Baltimore: Johns Hopkins University Press, 2008.

Masur, Kate. "'A Rare Phenomenon of Philological Vegetation': The Word 'Contraband' and the Meanings of Emancipation in the United States." *Journal of American History* 93, no. 4 (March 2007).

Masur, Louis P. "'Pictures Have Now Become a Necessity': The Use of Images in American History Textbooks." *Journal of American History* 84, no. 4 (1998): 1409–1424.

May, Robert E. "John Quitman and His Slaves: Reconciling Slave Resistance with the Proslavery Defense." *Journal of Southern History* 46, no. 4 (1980): 551–570.

McCandless, Barbara. "The Portrait Studio and the Celebrity: Promoting the Art." In *Photography in Nineteenth-Century America*, edited by Martha A. Sandweiss. Fort Worth, TX: Amon Carter Museum, 1991.

McCarthy, Timothy Patrick. "A Culture of Dissent: American Abolitionism and the Ordeal of Equality." PhD dissertation, Columbia University, 2006.

McCarthy, Timothy Patrick, and John Stauffer, eds. *Prophets of Protest: Reconsidering the History of American Abolitionism.* New York: New Press, 2006.

McCurry, Stephanie. *Confederate Reckoning: Power and Politics in the Civil War South.* Cambridge, MA: Harvard University Press, 2010.

McCurry, Stephanie. *Masters of Small Worlds: Yeoman Households, Gender Relations, and the Political Culture of the Antebellum South Carolina Low Country.* New York: Oxford University Press, 1995.

McDonald, Roderick A. *The Economy and Material Culture of Slaves: Goods and Chattels on the Sugar Plantations of Jamaica and Louisiana.* Baton Rouge: Louisiana State University Press, 1993.

McInnis, Maurie D. *Slaves Waiting for Sale: Abolitionist Art and the American Slave Trade.* Chicago: University of Chicago Press, 2011.

McPherson, James. *Battle Cry of Freedom: The Civil War Era.* Oxford: Oxford University Press, 1988.

Merish, Lori. *Sentimental Materialism: Gender, Commodity Culture, and Nineteenth-Century American Literature.* Durham, NC: Duke University Press, 2000.

Mirzoeff, Nicholas. *The Right to Look: A Counterhistory of Visuality.* Durham, NC: Duke University Press, 2011.

Mitchell, Mary Niall. *Raising Freedom's Child: Black Children and Visions of the Future After Slavery.* New York: New York University Press, 2008.

Mitchell, Mary Niall. "The Real Ida May: A Fugitive Tale in the Archives." *Massachusetts Historical Review* 15 (2013): 54–88.

Moeller, Susan. *Compassion Fatigue: How the Media Sell Disease, Famine, War, and Death.* New York: Routledge, 1999.

Molineux, Catherine. *Faces of Perfect Ebony: Encountering Atlantic Slavery in Imperial Britain.* Cambridge, MA: Harvard University Press, 2012.

Morgan, David. *Protestants and Pictures: Religion, Visual Culture, and the Age of Mass Production.* New York: Oxford University Press, 1999.

Morgan, Jo-Ann. *Uncle Tom's Cabin as Visual Culture.* Columbia: University of Missouri Press, 2007.

Morgan, Philip D. "The Ownership of Property by Slaves in the Mid-Nineteenth-Century Low Country." *Journal of Southern History* 49, no. 3 (1983): 399–420.

Morris, Christopher. "The Articulation of Two Worlds: The Master-Slave Relationship Reconsidered." *Journal of American History* 85, no. 3 (December 1998): 982–1007.

Mutunhu, Tendai. "John W. Jones: Underground Railroad Station-Master." *Negro History Bulletin*, March 1, 1978.

Nelson, Megan Kate. *Ruin Nation: Destruction and the American Civil War.* Athens: University of Georgia Press, 2012.

Newhall, Beaumont. *The History of Photography from 1839 to the Present.* Rev. ed. New York: Museum of Modern Art, 1982.

Newman, Richard S. *Fighting Slavery in the Early Republic: The Transformation of American Abolitionism.* Chapel Hill: University of North Carolina Press, 2001.

Oakes, James. *Freedom National: The Destruction of Slavery in the United States, 1861–1865.* New York: W. W. Norton, 2013.

O'Donovan, Susan Eva. *Becoming Free in the Cotton South.* Cambridge, MA: Harvard University Press, 2007.

Painter, Nell Irvin. *Sojourner Truth: A Life, A Symbol.* New York: W. W. Norton, 1996.

Painter, Nell Irvin. "Soul Murder and Slavery: Toward a Fully Loaded Cost Accounting." In *U.S. History as Women's History: New Feminist Essays*, edited by Linda K. Kerber, Alice Kessler-Harris, and Kathryn Kish Sklar, 125–146. Chapel Hill: University of North Carolina Press, 1995.

Palmquist, Peter E., and Thomas R. Kailbourn. *Pioneer Photographers from the Mississippi to the Continental Divide: A Biographical Dictionary, 1839 to 1865.* Stanford, CA: Stanford University Press, 2005.

Palmquist, Peter E., and Thomas R. Kailbourn. *Pioneer Photographers of the Far West: A Biographical Dictionary, 1840–1865.* Stanford, CA: Stanford University Press, 2000.

Panzer, Mary. *Mathew Brady and the Image of History.* Washington, DC: Smithsonian Books, 1997.

Panzer, Mary. *Things As They Are: Photojournalism in Context Since 1965.* New York: Aperture Foundation, 2005.

Paoletti, Jo B. *Pink and Blue: Telling the Boys from the Girls in America.* Bloomington: Indiana University Press, 2012.

Parfait, Claire. *The Publishing History of* Uncle Tom's Cabin, *1852–2002.* Padstow: Ashgate, 2007.

Paterson, David E. "Slavery, Slaves, and Cash in a Georgia Village, 1825–1865." *Journal of Southern History* 75, no. 4 (2009): 879–930.

Pease, Jane H., and William H. Pease. "Confrontation and Abolition in the 1850s." *Journal of American History* 58, no. 4 (1972): 923–937.

Penningroth, Dylan C. *The Claims of Kinfolk: African American Property and Community in the Nineteenth-Century South*. Chapel Hill: University of North Carolina Press, 2003.

Powell, Lawrence N. *New Masters: Northern Planters During the Civil War and Reconstruction*. New Haven, CT: Yale University Press, 1980.

Powell, Pamela C. "The Case of Passmore Williamson." In *The Daguerreian Annual 2000*. Pittsburgh: Daguerreian Society, 2000.

Powell, Richard J. "Cinque: Antislavery Portraiture and Patronage in Jacksonian America." *American Art* 11, no. 3 (1997): 48–73.

Prosser, Jay, Geoffrey Batchen, Mick Gidley, and Nancy K. Miller, eds. *Picturing Atrocity: Photography in Crisis*. London: Reaktion Books Ltd., 2012.

Raboteau, Albert J. *Slave Religion: The "Invisible Institution" in the Antebellum South*. Rev. ed. Oxford: Oxford University Press, 2004.

Raeburn, John. *A Staggering Revolution: A Cultural History of Thirties Photography*. Urbana: University of Illinois Press, 2006.

Rael, Patrick. *Black Identity and Black Protest in the Antebellum North*. Chapel Hill: University of North Carolina Press, 2002.

Raiford, Leigh. *Imprisoned in a Luminous Glare: Photography and the African American Freedom Struggle*. Chapel Hill: University of North Carolina Press, 2011.

Rainer, Joseph Thomas. "The Honorable Fraternity of Moving Merchants: Yankee Peddlers in the Old South, 1800–1860." PhD dissertation, College of William and Mary, 2000.

Ramsay, Jack C. Jr. *Photographer—Under Fire: The Story of George S. Cook (1819–1902)*. Green Bay, WI: Historical Resources Press, 1994.

Rawick, George. *From Sundown to Sunup: The Making of a Black Community*. Westport, CT: Greenwood, 1972.

Reaves, Wendy Wick, and Sally Pierce. "Translations from the Plate: The Marketplace of Public Portraiture." In *Young America: The Daguerreotypes of Southworth & Hawes*, edited by Grant B. Romer and Brian Wallis. New York: Steidl, George Eastman House, and the International Center of Photography, 2005.

Reilly, Bernard F. Jr. "The Art of the Antislavery Movement." In *Courage and Conscience: White and Black Abolitionists in Boston*, edited by Donald M. Jacobs. Bloomington: Indiana University Press, 1993.

Rinhart, Floyd, and Marion Rinhart. *The American Daguerreotype*. Athens: University of Georgia Press, 1981.

Robb, Frances. "Checklist of Photographers and Others Associated with Photography in Alabama, 1839–1861." In *The Daguerreian Annual: Official Yearbook of the Daguerreian Society*, edited by Mark S. Johnson. Pittsburgh: The Daguerreian Society, 2004.

Robb, Frances. "Shot in Alabama: Daguerreotypy in a Deep South State."
In *The Daguerreian Annual: Official Yearbook of the Daguerreian Society*, edited
by Mark S. Johnson. Pittsburgh: The Daguerreian Society, 2004.

Robinson, Armstead L. *Bitter Fruits of Bondage: The Demise of Slavery and the
Collapse of the Confederacy, 1861–1865*. Charlottesville: University of Virginia
Press, 2005.

Rockman, Seth. "Slavery and Capitalism." *Journal of the Civil War Era* 2, no. 1
(March 2012).

Rogers, Molly. *Delia's Tears: Race, Science, and Photography in Nineteenth-Century
America*. New Haven, CT: Yale University Press, 2010.

Rohrbach, Augusta. "Profits of Protest: The Market Strategies of Sojourner
Truth and Louisa May Alcott." In *Prophets of Protest: Reconsidering the
History of American Abolitionism*, edited by Timothy McCarthy and John
Stauffer. New York: New Press, 2006.

Romer, Grant B., and Brian Wallis, eds. *Young America: The Daguerreotypes of
Southworth & Hawes*. New York: Steidl, George Eastman House, and the
International Center of Photography, 2005.

Rose, Willie Lee. "The Domestication of Slavery." In *Slavery and Freedom*,
edited by William W. Freehling. New York: Oxford University Press, 1982.

Rosenheim, Jeff L. *Photography and the American Civil War*. New York:
Metropolitan Museum of Art, 2013.

Ross, Steven J. *Working Class Hollywood: Silent Film and the Shaping of Class in
America*. Princeton, NJ: Princeton University Press, 1998.

Rothman, Adam. *Slave Country: American Expansion and the Origins of the Deep
South*. Cambridge, MA: Harvard University Press, 2005.

Rudisill, Richard. *Mirror Image: The Influence of the Daguerreotype on American
Society*. Albuquerque: University of New Mexico Press, 1971.

Ryan, James R. "On Visual Instruction." In *The Nineteenth-Century Visual Culture
Reader*, edited by Vanessa R. Schwartz and Jeannene M. Przyblyski.
New York: Routledge, 2004.

Sandweiss, Martha A., ed. *Photography in Nineteenth-Century America*. Fort
Worth, TX: Amon Carter Museum, 1991.

Sandweiss, Martha A. *Print the Legend: Photography and the American West*. New
Haven, CT: Yale University Press, 2002.

Savage, Kirk. *Standing Soldiers, Kneeling Slaves: Race, War, and Monument in
Nineteenth-Century America*. Princeton, NJ: Princeton University Press, 1997.

Schermerhorn, Calvin. *Money over Mastery, Family over Freedom: Slavery in the
Antebellum Upper South*. Baltimore: Johns Hopkins University Press, 2011.

Schermerhorn, Calvin. *The Business of Slavery and the Rise of American
Capitalism, 1815–1860*. New Haven, CT: Yale University Press, 2015.

Schiavo, Laura. "'A Collection of Endless Extent and Beauty': Stereographs,
Vision, Taste and the American Middle Class, 1850–1880." PhD
dissertation, George Washington University, 2003.

Schwalm, Leslie A. *A Hard Fight for We: Women's Transition from Slavery to
Freedom in South Carolina*. Urbana: University of Illinois Press, 1997.

Schwartz, Joan M., and James R. Ryan, eds. *Picturing Place: Photography and the Geographical Imagination*. London: I. B. Tauris, 2003.

Schweninger, Loren. "Slave Independence and Enterprise in South Carolina, 1780–1865." *South Carolina Magazine* 93, no. 2 (1992): 101–125.

Sekula, Allen. "The Body and the Archive." In *The Contest of Meaning: Critical Histories of Photography*, edited by Richard Bolton. Cambridge, MA: MIT Press, 1989.

Severa, Joan. *Dressed for the Photographer: Ordinary Americans and Fashion, 1840–1900*. Kent, OH: Kent State University Press, 1995.

Shaw, Gwendolyn DuBois. *Portraits of a People: Picturing African Americans in the Nineteenth Century*. Andover, MA: Addison Gallery of American Art, 2006.

Sheehan, Tanya, and Andres Mario Zervigon, eds. *Photography and Its Origins*. New York: Routledge, 2015.

Shrum, Rebecca K. *In the Looking Glass: Mirrors and Identity in Early America*. Baltimore: Johns Hopkins University Press, 2017.

Silkenat, David. "'A Typical Negro': Gordon, Peter, Vincent Colyer, and the Story Behind Slavery's Most Famous Photograph." *American Nineteenth Century History* 15, no. 2 (2014): 169–186.

Sinha, Manisha. *The Counter-Revolution of Slavery: Politics and Ideology in Antebellum South Carolina*. Chapel Hill: University of North Carolina Press, 2000.

Sinha, Manisha. *The Slave's Cause: A History of Abolition*. New Haven, CT: Yale University Press, 2016.

Sliwinski, Sharon. *Human Rights in Camera*. Chicago: University of Chicago Press, 2011.

Sloat, Caroline F., ed. *Meet Your Neighbors: New England Portraits, Painters, and Society, 1790–1850*. Amherst: University of Massachusetts Press, 1992.

Sontag, Susan. *On Photography*. New York: Farrar, Straus and Giroux, 1973.

Sontag, Susan. *Regarding the Pain of Others*. New York: Picador, 2003.

Smith, Mark M. *Debating Slavery: Economy and Society in the Antebellum American South*. Cambridge: Cambridge University Press, 1998.

Smith, Shawn Michelle. *American Archives: Gender, Race, and Class in Visual Culture*. Princeton, NJ: Princeton University Press, 1999.

Smith, Shawn Michelle. *Photography on the Color Line: W. E. B. Du Bois, Race, and Visual Culture*. Durham, NC: Duke University Press, 2004.

Spicer, Joaneath. *Revealing the African Presence in Renaissance Europe*. Baltimore: Walters Art Museum, 2012.

Stampp, Kenneth. *The Peculiar Institution: Slavery in the Ante-Bellum South*. New York: Vintage Books, 1956.

Stanley, Amy Dru. "Slave Breeding and Free Love: An Antebellum Argument over Slavery, Capitalism, and Personhood." In *Capitalism Takes Command: The Social Transformation of Nineteenth-Century America*, edited by Michael Zakim and Gary J. Kornblith, 119–144. Chicago: University of Chicago Press, 2012.

Stauffer, John. *The Black Hearts of Men: Radical Abolitionists and the Transformation of Race*. Cambridge, MA: Harvard University Press, 2001.

Stauffer, John. "Creating an Image in Black: The Power of Abolition Pictures." In *Beyond Blackface: African Americans and the Creation of American Popular Culture, 1890–1930*, edited by W. Fitzhugh Brundage. Chapel Hill: University of North Carolina Press, 2011.

Stauffer, John. "Interspatialism in the Nineteenth-Century South: The Natchez of Henry Norman." *Slavery and Abolition* 29, no. 2 (June 2008): 247–263.

Stauffer, John. "The 'Terrible Reality' of the First Living-Room Wars." In *War/Photography: Images of Armed Conflict and Its Aftermath*, edited by Anne Wilkes Tucker, Will Michels, and Natalie Zelt. New Haven, CT: Yale University Press, 2012.

Stauffer, John, Zoe Trodd, and Celeste-Marie Bernier, eds. *Picturing Frederick Douglass: An Illustrated Biography of the Nineteenth Century's Most Photographed American*. New York: W. W. Norton, 2015.

Stemmler, Joan K. "The Physiognomical Portraits of Johann Caspar Lavater." *Art Bulletin* 75, no. 1 (March 1993): 151–168.

Stevenson, Brenda E. *Life in Black and White: Family and Community in the Slave South*. New York: Oxford University Press, 1996.

Stewart, James Brewer. *Holy Warriors: The Abolitionists and American Slavery*. Rev. ed. New York: Hill and Wang, 1997.

Stewart, James Brewer. "Peaceful Hopes and Violent Experiences: The Evolution of Reforming and Radical Abolitionism, 1831–1837." *Civil War History* 17, no. 4 (December 1971): 293–309.

Stewart, James Brewer. *Wendell Phillips: Liberty's Hero*. Baton Rouge: Louisiana State University Press, 1986.

Stott, William. *Documentary Expression and Thirties America*. Chicago: University of Chicago Press, 1986.

Tadman, Michael. *Speculators and Slaves: Masters, Traders, and Slaves in the Old South*. Madison: University of Wisconsin Press, 1989.

Taft, Robert. *Photography and the American Scene: A Social History, 1839–1889*. New York: Dover Publications, 1938.

Tagg, John. *The Burden of Representation: Essays on Photographies and Histories*. Minneapolis: University of Minnesota Press, 1993.

Taylor, Nikki M. *Frontiers of Freedom: Cincinnati's Black Community, 1802–1868*. Athens: Ohio University Press, 2005.

Teal, Harvey. *Partners with the Sun: South Carolina Photographers, 1840–1940*. Columbia: University of South Carolina Press, 2001.

Thomas, Albert Sidney. *A Historical Account of the Protestant Episcopal Church in South Carolina, 1820–1957*. Columbia, SC: R. L. Bryan, 1957.

Thompson, William F. *The Image of War: The Pictorial Reporting of the American Civil War*. Baton Rouge: Louisiana State University Press, 1994.

Tickner, Lisa. *The Spectacle of Women: Imagery of the Suffrage Campaign, 1907–14*. Chicago: University of Chicago Press, 1988.

Tise, Larry E. *Proslavery: A History of the Defense of Slavery in America, 1701–1840*. Athens: University of Georgia Press, 1987.

Towers, Frank. "Partisans, New History, and Modernization: The Historiography of the Civil War's Causes, 1861–2011." *Journal of the Civil War Era* 1, no. 2 (2011): 237–264.

Trachtenberg, Alan. "Photography: The Emergence of a Keyword." In *Photography in Nineteenth-Century America*, edited by Martha A. Sandweiss. Fort Worth: Amon Carter Museum, 1991.

Trachtenberg, Alan. *Reading American Photographs: Images as History, Mathew Brady to Walker Evans*. New York: Hill and Wang, 1989.

Troutman, Phillip. "Correspondences in Black and White: Sentiment and the Slave Market Revolution." In *New Studies in the History of American Slavery*, edited by Edward E. Baptist and Stephanie M. H. Camp, 211–242. Athens: University of Georgia Press, 2006.

Troutman, Phillip D. "Slave Trade and Sentiment in Antebellum Virginia." PhD dissertation, University of Virginia, 2000.

Tucker, Anne Wilkes, Will Michels, and Natalie Zelt, eds. *War/Photography: Images of Armed Conflict and Its Aftermath*. New Haven, CT: Yale University Press, 2012.

Tucker, Jennifer. *Nature Exposed: Photography as Eyewitness in Victorian Science*. Baltimore: Johns Hopkins University Press, 2005.

Varon, Elizabeth. "'Beautiful Providences': William Still, the Vigilance Committee, and Abolitionists in the Age of Sectionalism." In *Antislavery and Abolition in Philadelphia: Emancipation and the Long Struggle for Racial Justice in the City of Brotherly Love*, edited by Richard Newman and James Mueller. Baton Rouge: Louisiana State University Press, 2011.

Varon, Elizabeth R. *Disunion! The Coming of the American Civil War, 1789–1859*. Chapel Hill: University of North Carolina Press, 2008.

Vlach, John Michael. *By the Work of Their Hands: Studies in Afro-American Folklife*. Ann Arbor: UMI Research Press, 1991.

Vlach, John Michael. "Perpetuating the Past: Plantation Landscape Paintings Then and Now." In *Landscape of Slavery: The Plantation in American Art*, edited by Angela D. Mack and Stephen G. Hoffius. Columbia: University of South Carolina Press, 2008.

Vlach, John Michael. *The Planter's Prospect: Privilege and Slavery in Plantation Paintings*. Chapel Hill: University of North Carolina Press, 2002.

Volpe, Andrea L. "Cheap Pictures: Cartes de Visite Portrait Photographs and Visual Culture in the United States, 1860–1877." PhD. dissertation, Rutgers University, 1999.

Waldstreicher, David. "Reading the Runaways: Self-Fashioning, Print Culture, and Confidence in Slavery in the Eighteenth-Century Mid-Atlantic." *William and Mary Quarterly* 56, no. 2 (April 1999): 243–272.

Walker, Clarence. *Deromanticizing Black History: Critical Essays and Reappraisals*. Knoxville: University of Tennessee Press, 1991.

Walker, Cam. "Corinth: The Story of a Contraband Camp." *Civil War History* 20, no. 1 (March 1974): 5–22.

Wallace, Maurice O., and Shawn Michelle Smith, eds. *Pictures and Progress: Early Photography and the Making of African American Identity*. Durham, NC: Duke University Press, 2012.

Wallace-Sanders, Kimberly. *Mammy: A Century of Race, Gender, and Southern Memory*. Ann Arbor: University of Michigan Press, 2008.

Wallis, Brian. "Black Bodies, White Science: Louis Agassiz's Slave Daguerreotypes." *American Art* 9, no. 2 (1995): 38–61.

Walters, Ronald G. *The Antislavery Appeal: American Abolitionism After 1830*. New York: W. W. Norton, 1978.

Walters, Ronald G. "The Boundaries of Abolitionism." In *Antislavery Reconsidered: New Perspectives on the Abolitionists*, edited by Lewis Perry and Michael Fellman. Baton Rouge: Louisiana State University Press, 1979.

Welke, Barbara Young. *Law and the Borders of Belonging in the Long Nineteenth Century*. New York: Cambridge University Press, 2010.

Wexler, Laura. "'A More Perfect Likeness': Frederick Douglass and the Image of the Nation." In *Pictures and Progress: Early Photography and the Making of African American Identity*, edited by Maurice O. Wallace and Shawn Michelle Smith. Durham, NC: Duke University Press, 2012.

Wexler, Laura. *Tender Violence: Domestic Visions in an Age of U.S. Imperialism*. Chapel Hill: University of North Carolina Press, 2000.

White, Deborah Gray. *Ar'n't I a Woman? Female Slaves in the Plantation South*. New York: W. W. Norton, 1985.

White, Shane, and Graham White. *Stylin': African American Expressive Culture, from Its Beginnings to the Zoot Suit*. Ithaca: Cornell University Press, 1998.

Williams, Heather Andrea. *Help Me to Find My People: The African American Search for Family Lost in Slavery*. Chapel Hill: University of North Carolina Press, 2012.

Willis, Deborah. *J. P. Ball: Daguerrean and Studio Photographer*. New York: Garland, 1993.

Willis, Deborah. *Reflections in Black: A History of Black Photographers 1840 to the Present*. New York: W. W. Norton, 2000.

Willis, Deborah, and Barbara Krauthamer. *Envisioning Emancipation: Black Americans and the End of Slavery*. Philadelphia: Temple University Press, 2013.

Willis, Deborah, and Carla Williams. *The Black Female Body: A Photographic History*. Philadelphia: Temple University Press, 2002.

Wilson, Jackie Napolean. *Hidden Witness: African American Images from the Dawn of Photography to the Civil War*. New York: St. Martin's Press, 1999.

Wilson, Michael L. "Visual Culture: A Useful Category of Historical Analysis?" In *The Nineteenth-Century Visual Culture Reader*, edited by Vanessa R. Schwartz and Jeannene M. Przyblyski. New York: Routledge, 2004.

Wolf, Hazel Catherine. *On Freedom's Altar: The Martyr Complex in the Abolition Movement*. Madison: University of Wisconsin Press, 1952.

Wood, Marcus. *Black Milk: Imagining Slavery in the Visual Cultures of Brazil and America*. Oxford: Oxford University Press, 2013.

Wood, Marcus. *Blind Memory: Visual Representations of Slavery in England and America, 1780–1865*. New York: Routledge, 2000.

Wood, Marcus. *The Horrible Gift of Freedom: Atlantic Slavery and the Representation of Emancipation*. Athens: University of Georgia Press, 2010.

Wood, Peter H. *Near Andersonville: Winslow Homer's Civil War*. Cambridge, MA: Harvard University Press, 2010.

Woods, Michael E. *Emotional and Sectional Conflict in the Antebellum Era*. New York: Cambridge University Press, 2014.

Wyatt-Brown, Bertram. "The Abolitionists' Postal Campaign of 1835." *Journal of Negro History* 50, no. 4 (October 1965): 227–238.

Yellin, Jean Fagan. *Women and Sisters: The Antislavery Feminists in American Culture*. New Haven, CT: Yale University Press, 1989.

Yochelson, Bonnie, and Daniel Czitrom. *Rediscovering Jacob Riis: Exposure Journalism and Photography in Turn-of-the-Century New York*. New York: New Press, 2007.

Young, Jeffrey Robert. *Domesticating Slavery: The Master Class in Georgia and South Carolina, 1670–1837*. Chapel Hill: University of North Carolina Press, 1999.

Young, Jeffrey Robert. "To 'Venerate the Spot' of 'Airy Visions': Slavery and the Romantic Conception of Place in Mary Telfair's Savannah." In *Slavery and Freedom in Savannah*, edited by Leslie M. Harris and Daina Ramey Berry. Athens: University of Georgia Press, 2014.

Young, William Russell III. "H. B. Hillyer: Life and Career of a Nineteenth Century Texas Photographer." MA thesis, University of Texas at Austin, 1985.

Zackodnik, Teresa. "The 'Green-Backs of Civilization': Sojourner Truth and Portrait Photography." *American Studies* 46, no. 2 (2005): 117–143.

Zboray, Ronald J. "Antebellum Reading and the Ironies of Technological Innovation." *American Quarterly* 40, no. 1 (March 1988): 65–82.

Zeller, Bob. *The Blue and Gray in Black and White: A History of Civil War Photography*. London: Praeger, 2005.

INDEX